Gorbachev and Yeltsin as Leaders

How did Gorbachev and Yeltsin get away with transforming and replacing the Soviet system and its foreign relations? Why did they act as they did in pushing for such radical changes? And how will history evaluate their accomplishments? In this unique and original study, George W. Breslauer compares and evaluates the leadership strategies adopted by Gorbachev and Yeltsin at each stage of their administrations: political rise, political ascendancy, and political decline. He demonstrates how these men used the power of ideas to mobilize support for their policies, to seize the initiative from political rivals, and to mold their images as effective problem solvers, indispensable politicians, and symbols of national unity and élan. *Gorbachev and Yeltsin as Leaders* also compares these men with Khrushchev and Brezhnev, yielding new insight into the nature of Soviet and post-Soviet politics and into the dynamics of "transformational" leadership more generally. The book is an important contribution to the analysis and evaluation of political leadership. It is exceptionally well written and accessible to the nonspecialist.

Professor George W. Breslauer is Dean of Social Sciences and Chancellor's Professor of Political Science at the University of California, Berkeley. He is an author or editor of twelve books on Soviet and Russian politics and is Editor-in-Chief of the journal *Post-Soviet Affairs*. He is a member of the Council on Foreign Relations and in 1997 won the distinguished teaching award of the social science division of UC Berkeley.

Gorbachev and Yeltsin as Leaders

GEORGE W. BRESLAUER

University of California at Berkeley

CAMBRIDGE
UNIVERSITY PRESS

PUBLISHED BY THE PRESS SYNDICATE OF THE UNIVERSITY OF CAMBRIDGE
The Pitt Building, Trumpington Street, Cambridge, United Kingdom

CAMBRIDGE UNIVERSITY PRESS
The Edinburgh Building, Cambridge CB2 2RU, UK
40 West 20th Street, New York, NY 10011-4211, USA
477 Williamstown Road, Port Melbourne, VIC 3207, Australia
Ruiz de Alarcón 13, 28014 Madrid, Spain
Dock House, The Waterfront, Cape Town 8001, South Africa

http://www.cambridge.org

First published 2002

Printed in the United States of America

Typeface Sabon 10/13 pt.   *System* AMS-TEX   [FH]

A catalog record for this book is available from the British Library.

Library of Congress Cataloging in Publication Data
Breslauer, George W.
Gorbachev and Yeltsin as leaders / George W. Breslauer.
p.   cm.
Includes bibliographical references and index.
ISBN 0-521-81486-3 – ISBN 0-521-89244-9 (pbk.)
1. Soviet Union – Politics and government – 1985–1991.   2. Russia (Federation) – Politics
and government – 1991– .   3. Gorbachev, Mikhail Sergeevich, 1931– .   4. Yeltsin, Boris
Nikolaevich, 1931– .   I. Title.

DK288.B74   2002
947.085′4 – dc21   2001052443

ISBN 0 521 81486 3 hardback
ISBN 0 521 89244 9 paperback

I dedicate this book to my wife, Yvette Assia Breslauer, my daughter, Michelle, my son, David, my mother, Marianne Schaeffer Breslauer, and the memory of my father, Henry Edward Breslauer.

Contents

Preface

This book is about two men – Mikhail Gorbachev and Boris Yeltsin – who presided from 1985–1999 over the tumultuous transition from Soviet to post-Soviet politics. The speed of change during the first half of that period was remarkable. In 1985, the Soviet Union appeared to be an entrenched entity, capable of defending itself against all challenges to the Communist Party's right to rule at home and in Eastern Europe, and determinedly pursuing a policy of great-power competition abroad. By the end of 1987, *glasnost'* had broken out, the public media were increasingly challenging old doctrines, and the Soviet leadership was starting to make one-sided concessions to the United States on fundamental issues of national security. By the end of 1989, relatively free elections had taken place, Party officials were being voted out of office, communism had collapsed in Eastern Europe, the Soviet Army had retreated in defeat from Afghanistan, and the Cold War was coming to an end. By the end of 1991, an oppositional figure had been elected president of Russia, both communism and the Soviet Union had collapsed, and independent Russia had emerged as a seemingly helpless supplicant of the West. By the end of 1993, independent Russia had experienced two wrenching years of political and economic turmoil at home and was coming to realize the limits of Western willingness to assist its transition from communism. If one had gone to sleep in Moscow in 1985–1986 and woken up in 1992–1993, the change would have been unfathomable.

Without presupposing that Gorbachev and Yeltsin made all these things happen, it is fair to say that things would have happened quite differently had different individuals been in charge. Their acts of leadership were crucial. Both men will surely go down in history as having left a major mark on their country's condition as it approached the twenty-first century. The questions

I address in this book are: Why did these men act as they did? (Chapters 1, 2, 11) How did they get away with it – that is, how did they build support for their programs? (Chapters 3–10) And how might we evaluate their successes and failures as leaders? (Chapters 12–14)

My main concern is to document each man's leadership strategy. My theoretical approach emphasizes the dilemmas faced by leaders in building and maintaining their political authority (their credibility as problem solvers and politicians), the reasons they chose their political strategies and policy programs, and the consequences (intended and unintended) of those choices.

To tap into their authority-building strategies, I conduct a detailed analysis of their public rhetoric, backed up by analysis of the voluminous memoir literature – including memoirs by the two protagonists, Gorbachev and Yeltsin. From these texts and from related actions and signals, I reconstruct the given leader's program. I show how he used the diagnoses and prescriptions embedded in his public utterances to reach out to targeted audiences and constituencies whose support and involvement were essential to his purposes at each stage of his administration. I depict Gorbachev and Yeltsin as leaders of an ongoing and shifting political dialogue with friends and foes at home and abroad, a dialogue that helped to structure a fluid political scene. The immediate purpose of the dialogue was political communication; the larger purpose was to convince people that the speaker had a vision, ideas, and ideals worth supporting and that he also had the political skill, determination, and will to get his way. These were not "just words." They were words that shaped his reputation and credibility – and thereby mightily influenced his capacity to govern. As Richard Neustadt wrote about the American president: "He makes his personal impact by the things he says and does. Accordingly, his choices of what he should say and do, and how and when, are his means to conserve and tap the sources of his power."[1]

Given my purposes, the principal sources for such a study are the public statements of these leaders: their formal speeches at home and abroad, their press conferences, their press releases, and their unrehearsed comments in public forums. The memoirs of their political associates and advisors, in turn, give us insight into the relationship between the leaders' public and private utterances. The memoirs of Gorbachev and Yeltsin provide insight into their personal histories, their self-images, and the ways in which they wished to be remembered. Supplementary interviews with political actors – some by

---

[1] Richard E. Neustadt, *Presidential Power: The Politics of Leadership* (New York: Wiley, 1960), p. 179.

me, most by other scholars who have published on these leaders – allow me to check on the accuracy of published sources.

The public statements and memoirs of politicians must be interpreted with great care. They contain large doses of manipulative rhetoric and, presumably, factual falsehoods. But used judiciously, and with an eye to themes that are repeated in front of multiple audiences, they are an invaluable source of insight into what the leader was trying to accomplish during each stage of his administration. Similarly, memoirs of people who worked with these leaders must be approached with caution about the authors' private agendas. Some were written by people who bore grudges; others by people who idolized their former boss. Some strain to appear balanced in their judgments; others drip with contempt or glow with adoration. As with all historical documents, we must analyze them with a healthy dose of skepticism about their possible biases. But we may have confidence in our depictions to the extent that multiple sources – public and private communications, hostile and adulatory memoirs, published materials and interviews – converge in their testimony about each man's orientations and actions at given moments in time.

A word is in order about the provenance of these leaders' speeches and memoirs. Gorbachev and Yeltsin occasionally wrote their own speeches or statements; they also improvised during press conferences and impromptu encounters. But their major speeches were usually written by teams of speechwriters. This does not mean that such speeches may not be taken as indicators of their political strategies and policy preferences. On the contrary. Both men usually attended closely to the contents of the speeches they did not write,[2] and their speechwriters were very much aware of how the leader wished to represent himself in public. Both men frequently edited successive versions of speeches that were being written for them.

Yeltsin's three major memoirs appeared, respectively, in 1990 (before he became president of Russia); in 1994 (in the middle of his presidency); and in 2000 (after his resignation).[3] They provide valuable sources of insight into the man's personality, beliefs, and political strategy. All three books were ghost-written by Valentin Yumashev, an erstwhile journalist who became one of Yeltsin's closest aides, advisors, and confidantes. Yeltsin was intimately involved in shaping and editing the contents of the first memoir, somewhat less

---

[2] This may have been true of Yeltsin less often after his health took major turns for the worse in 1996–1997.

[3] Boris Yeltsin, *Against the Grain: An Autobiography,* trans. by Michael Glenny (New York: Summit, 1990); Boris Yeltsin, *The Struggle for Russia,* trans. by Catherine A. Fitzpatrick (New York: Random House, 1994); Boris Yeltsin, *Midnight Diaries* (New York: Public Affairs, 2000).

involved in shaping (but probably closely involved in editing) the second, and largely detached from the process of producing the third memoir. Nonetheless, Yumashev was so close to Yeltsin for so many years that we can take for granted that he came to know his boss's preferences and perspectives very well. He could have finished his sentences. And that is what he did, at a minimum, in writing the third memoir. For that very reason, we can take the third memoir, like the first two, as expressions of how Yeltsin wanted the public to remember him and his leadership. Factual details must still be treated with the usual skepticism, but that does not distinguish Yeltsin's memoirs from those of any other leader.

Gorbachev produced several books during and after his leadership of the USSR. From all accounts, he attended very closely to their contents. His book, *Perestroika,* which was not a memoir but a statement of Gorbachev's philosophy, appeared in 1987[4] and was written by a collective with which Gorbachev worked closely. His massive, two-volume memoirs[5] were written after his retirement from public office; he was deeply involved in their production as well. According to a personal communication to me from Professor Archie Brown (St. Antony's College, Oxford University), who received the information from aides of Gorbachev, Gorbachev talked about particular themes with his close associates. Those sessions were recorded and transcribed. He then read everything through and heavily annotated the transcript. Sometimes he resisted attempts by others to make him appear more far-sighted or "advanced" in his thinking at a given time than he believed himself to have been. Most of the words are his own – delivered orally and then confirmed and amended by him in typescript.

The difference in political context between 1985–1989 and 1991–1996 may explain why the memoirs of Gorbachev's colleagues tend to be political memoirs while those of Yeltsin's colleagues tend to be more personal memoirs. Gorbachev's colleagues worked or struggled with him on the resolution of fundamental policy issues. Some of them were fellow members of the Politburo; some were close aides. But both memoir-producing *aides* (such as Boldin, Chernyaev, Shakhnazarov, and Grachev) and memoir-producing *associates* (such as Politburo members Ligachev, Medvedev, Ryzhkov, Kriuchkov, Yakovlev, and Shevardnadze) observed him as he attempted to manipulate the Politburo and Central Committee – or, later, the Congress of People's

4 Mikhail Gorbachev, *Perestroika: New Thinking for Our Country and the World* (New York: Perennial, 1987).
5 Mikhail Gorbachev, *Zhizn' i reformy,* 2 vols. (Moscow: Novosti, 1996).

Deputies – to support him on the issues. Their memoirs expose us to Gorbachev the decisionmaker and coalition builder.

Most of the memoirs about Yeltsin, by contrast, were written by aides (Gaidar, Filatov, Korzhakov, Kostikov, Baturin, Satarov, Pikhoia), men and women who were not co-members of an authoritative decisionmaking body of which Yeltsin was chairman. They rarely observed him deliberating policy with authoritative politicians and reaching decisions based on consensus or majority rule. Yeltsin, unlike Gorbachev, was not accountable to a formal collective leadership. Hence, most of Yeltsin's key decisions as president were made by Yeltsin himself in closed counsel. The memoirs about his years in power, therefore, tend to stress his personality traits and the way he treated subordinates or antagonists. They are more revealing about Yeltsin the man than Yeltsin the decisionmaker and coalition builder.

For these reasons, when we use the memoir literature to explore Gorbachev's political personality, we must anticipate that those memoirs will tell us more about Gorbachev's political behavior in formal contexts than about his private, informal interactions and inclinations. Nonetheless, we can relate this evidence to other sources of information about Gorbachev, including many observers' interviews with people who knew him earlier in life, to paint a broad portrait of the man's private personality. Similarly, when we explore Yeltsin's decisionmaking processes, we must anticipate that his aides' memoirs will provide limited access. Even so, by analyzing Yeltsin's political rhetoric in varieties of forums at successive points in time – and by relating this to the self-image projected in his memoirs and the observations of associates about his shifting moods – we can reconstruct his rationales for the many important decisions he had to make.

From these varied texts, I specify each leader's domestic and foreign-policy programs and how these evolved over time. Through frequent comparison and contrast with analogous patterns of rhetoric and behavior by Khrushchev and Brezhnev, which I analyzed in an earlier study,[6] I attempt to deepen our understanding of continuity and change over the past fifty years of Soviet and Russian politics.

Passages and portions of selected chapters, now much revised, appeared previously in published form. Portions of Chapter 4 and passages within Chapter 5 appeared in "How Do You Sell a Concessionary Foreign Policy?" *Post-Soviet Affairs*, vol. 10, no. 3 (July–September 1994), pp. 277–90.

---

[6] George W. Breslauer, *Khrushchev and Brezhnev as Leaders: Building Authority in Soviet Politics* (London: Allen & Unwin, 1982).

Portions of Chapter 7 appeared in "Boris Yeltsin and the 'Invention' of a Russian Nation-State" (co-authored with Catherine Dale), *Post-Soviet Affairs,* vol. 13, no. 4 (October–December 1997), pp. 303–32. Portions of Chapter 8 appeared in "Boris Yel'tsin as Patriarch," *Post-Soviet Affairs,* vol. 15, no. 2 (April–June 1999), pp. 186–200. Portions of Chapter 9 appeared in earlier form in "Yeltsin's Political Leadership: Why Invade Chechnya?" in George Breslauer et al., *Russia: Political and Economic Development* (Claremont, CA: The Keck Center, 1995), pp. 1–24. Much of Chapter 13 appeared in earlier form in "Evaluating Gorbachev as Leader," *Soviet Economy,* vol. 5, no. 4 (October–December 1989), pp. 299–340. Portions of Chapter 14 appeared in "Personalism and Proceduralism: Boris Yeltsin and the Institutional Fragility of the Russian System," in Victoria Bonnell and George W. Breslauer (Eds.), *Russia in the New Century: Stability or Disorder?* (Boulder, CO: Westview, 2000), pp. 35–58. Portions of Chapter 12, as well as passages within Chapters 13 and 14, appeared in "Evaluating Gorbachev and Yeltsin as Leaders," in Archie Brown and Lilia Shevtsova (Eds.), *Political Leadership in the Russian Transition* (Washington, DC & Moscow: Carnegie Endowment for International Peace, 2001), pp. 45–66.

Many institutions have supported my research on this book during the past decade. I am grateful to the University of California at Berkeley, the Carnegie Corporation of New York, and The National Council for Eurasian and East European Research for research and travel grants. The Center for Slavic and East European Studies at UC Berkeley and its successor – The Institute for Slavic, East European, and Eurasian Studies – have unfailingly provided me with the ideal organizational and collegial contexts for sharing the ideas and generating the excitement on which all ambitious projects depend. Certainly, I could not have produced this book without the support of all these institutions. I hope I have justified their trust.

Many individuals assisted me with critiques of earlier drafts of the entire manuscript. It is a great pleasure to acknowledge and thank them here: Richard D. Anderson, Archie Brown, Valerie Bunce, Timothy Colton, Keith Darden, M. Steven Fish, James Goldgeier, Stephen Hanson, Jeffrey Kopstein, David Laitin, James Richter, Richard Samuels, Ilya Vinkovetsky, Edward W. Walker, Lucan Way, and Stephen White. I remain fully responsible for the end product.

I wish also to acknowledge the role of many graduate students at the University of California, Berkeley, whose research assistance helped me to gather materials over the years. Four graduate students did much more than gather materials; they assisted materially in analyzing them. My thanks to Catherine Dale, with whom I co-authored an article that became the basis for portions of Chapter 7. My thanks also to Matthew J. von Bencke, Leonid Kil, and Ilya Vinkovetsky. Ilya, in particular, deserves credit for both the huge numbers of hours he put in and the exceptional analytic subtlety he brought to our examination of speeches and memoirs.

Finally, I am indebted to my family for their patience, support, good cheer, and genuine enthusiasm over a long period. My children, Michelle and David, have grown up with "Gorby" and "Boris." My 25 years of marriage to Yvette have been distracted by four "best men" who stood constantly in the wings, begging for attention: Nikita, Leonid, Mikhail, and Boris. Throughout, the balance of life has been a good one. Soviet and Russian politics gave me objects of interest and stimulation as I pursued my intellectual curiosities. Yvette, Michelle, and David made every day a sweet one by giving me three best friends to come home to.

Leadership Strategies in Soviet and Post-Soviet Politics

In order to accomplish what they did, Gorbachev and Yeltsin had to overcome many obstacles to change. Doing so required them to exercise leadership, which I define as a process of stretching social constraints in the pursuit of social goals.[1] Those constraints are of several kinds: (1) organizations, institutions, and processes that structure politics and administration; (2) the material interests of individuals and groups; and (3) the identities, ideologies, and cultures of individuals and groups. Typically, in an established or entrenched system, these constraints reinforce each other. Ideologies and cultures come to justify the institutions and processes that structure both political life and the distribution of tangible rewards across the population. Those institutions and processes ensure the continuation of policies that cater to prevailing identities and that reproduce existing patterns of social and political inequality.

The Stalinist system came to be such an entrenched system, but certain features of that system did not survive for long after the death of its founder. Stalin's successors rejected a continuation of mass terror and economic austerity, rule by a despot, and perpetual confrontation with the capitalist world. Beyond that, they grappled with the challenge of reforming (Khrushchev, 1953–1964), adapting (Brezhnev, 1964–1982), or transforming (Gorbachev, 1985–1991) the Soviet system of monopolistic rule by the Communist Party–State and "anti-imperialist struggle" abroad, whereas Yeltsin (1989–1999) sought to destroy the system completely and to replace it with a workable alternative.

---

[1] For the definition of leadership as a process of "stretching constraints," see Warren Ilchman and Norman Uphoff, *The Political Economy of Growth* (Berkeley, CA: University of California Press, 1969).

In an earlier book, I examined the strategies deployed by Khrushchev and Brezhnev for reforming and adapting the Soviet system.[2] In the present volume, I switch the focus to their successors. Both volumes concentrate on the exercise of leadership, but this volume focuses on that most difficult and far-reaching variant called "transformational leadership."

Generalizations about transformational leadership can be found in the substantial literature on leadership in private corporations,[3] public bureaucracies,[4] and states.[5] The concept is defined in a variety of ways, but typically it involves a process of fundamental change in the culture and ordering principles of a unit. Bringing this about is a daunting challenge. To effect such change, the leader must do several things:

- Highlight publicly the incompatibility between emerging environmental demands, on the one hand, and current ordering principles and cultural assumptions, on the other.

---

[2] George W. Breslauer, *Khrushchev and Brezhnev as Leaders: Building Authority in Soviet Politics* (London: Allen & Unwin, 1982); see also James Richter, *Khrushchev's Double Bind* (Baltimore: Johns Hopkins University Press, 1994), and Richard D. Anderson, *Public Politics in an Authoritarian State: Making Foreign Policy during the Brezhnev Era* (Ithaca, NY: Cornell University Press, 1993). The studies by Richter and Anderson applied my framework to foreign policy under Khrushchev and Brezhnev and found that the patterns I had highlighted in domestic policy are equally observable in foreign policy. Moreover, Anderson elaborated and enriched the framework by synthesizing decisionmaking theory in a novel way, thereby reinforcing our findings through deductive logic. William J. Tompson published a political biography of Khrushchev using archival sources made available thanks to *glasnost'* (*Khrushchev: A Political Life* [New York: St. Martin's, 1995]). Tompson's book did not seek to test any theory, or even much to relate patterns and findings to existing Western literature on Khrushchev. Nonetheless, his periodization of Khrushchev's years in power tracks well with my findings, as does his depiction of Khrushchev's policy advocacy. Sergei Khrushchev's massive study–memoir (*Nikita Khrushchev and the Creation of a Superpower,* trans. by Shirley Benson [University Park: Pennsylvania State University Press, 2000]) concentrates on foreign policy and is a valuable source of information about Nikita Khrushchev's foreign policy values, world view, and emotions. But it does not provide much insight into the content and evolution of Khrushchev's political strategies and perceptions, perhaps because, as the author noted in an earlier volume, father did not often confide in his family about Kremlin politics (Sergei Khrushchev, *Khrushchev on Khrushchev: An Inside Account of the Man and His Era / by his son,* ed. & trans. by William Taubman [Boston, MA: Little, Brown, 1990], pp. 186–7).

[3] For example, Philip Selznick, *Leadership in Administration* (New York: Harper & Row, 1957); Noel M. Tichy and Mary Anne Devanna, *The Transformational Leader* (New York: Wiley, 1986).

[4] Jameson W. Doig and Erwin C. Hargrove, *Leadership and Innovation* (Baltimore: Johns Hopkins University Press, 1967).

[5] James MacGregor Burns, *Leadership* (New York: Harper & Row, 1978); Howard Gardner, *Leading Minds* (New York: Basic Books, 1995).

- Outline an alternative vision of political organization and culture that will restore a harmonious relationship between the transformed unit and its environment.
- Mobilize constituencies in support of that vision.
- Prevent defenders of the existing order from sabotaging transformation.
- Put specific programs in place that will result in the replacement of the existing order with one that is better suited to the environmental demands of tomorrow.

But leaders – be they adaptive, reformist, or transformational – must do more than just devise and sell a vision for a better tomorrow. They must also convince audiences that they, and they alone, possess the skills required to guide the country toward realizing that vision. Hence, their goals are both programmatic and personal. They attempt simultaneously to persuade large numbers of people that their program for change is desirable and realizable *and* that their occupancy of the highest office is necessary to bring about that change. These two emphases, the programmatic and the personal, are mutually reinforcing. The more a leader inspires people to believe in his program, the more those people will be inclined to believe in his competence as a leader. The more they believe in his competence, the more latitude he has to enact and implement his program. And the more effectively he implements his program, the more enthusiastically will people believe in both his vision and his leadership skills. I refer to this interactive process of persuasion, inspiration, and mutual identification as "building authority."

Building authority is not the same as consolidating power, though leaders in competitive political orders attempt to do both. As I use the term, "authority" is legitimized, credible power.[6] Building authority is the process by which leaders seek to legitimize their policy programs and demonstrate their competence or indispensability as problem solvers and politicians. A concern with building authority assumes that intimidation and bribery may not always be effective in mobilizing political support if the leader is broadly perceived to be incompetent or dispensable. A leader may consolidate his grip on power through intimidation and bribery. Such methods may be sufficient to retain that grip in such despotic and nonideological regimes as prevailed, say, in Cuba under Batista or Nicaragua under the Somozas. But intimidation and bribery, while features of the policy process in most systems, are usually

---

[6] This is not the standard Weberian definition of "authority"; instead, it follows Amitai Etzioni, *The Active Society* (New York: Free Press, 1968, p. 360), where authority is defined as "legitimate power."

insufficient to get one's way in nondespotic, ideological regimes, as in the Soviet Union after Stalin. Such regimes tolerate legitimate political competition (whether within an oligarchic elite or within an inclusive liberal democracy) and justify themselves in ideological terms. In such contexts, a leader's capacity to effect change cannot be increased beyond a certain point on the basis of bribery and intimidation alone. He must also build his authority by demonstrating a capacity to effect changes that will appeal to the beliefs, identities, and cultural orientations of targeted constituents.

In order to elaborate further on the process of building authority, to generate hypotheses to consider when examining Gorbachev's and Yeltsin's leadership, and to set the backdrop for understanding the constraints that Gorbachev faced when he came to power, I will begin by reviewing Khrushchev's and Brezhnev's leadership strategies. Although neither of these men was a transformational leader, their exercise of leadership illustrates two distinct strategies of authority building in a Soviet-type system. And the limitations they shared provided object lessons for both Gorbachev and Yeltsin in the 1980s.

AUTHORITY BUILDING AFTER STALIN

If it was to move beyond Stalinism, the Soviet system required a leader who was committed to significant change. Whatever Stalin's political successors might have thought about the desirability and necessity of "high Stalinism," most of them did not think it feasible to maintain following his death. They viewed as unsustainable the level of tension within society as a result of the police terror, the Gulag camps that were bulging with political prisoners, the exhausting pace of life, and the extreme material austerity. Most of them viewed as undesirable a situation in which the secret police – a state within a state – might be used against them by a new Stalin. Most of them feared that perpetual confrontation with the capitalist world could lead to nuclear war.

The result of these intense, shared fears was a series of quick decisions to reduce the level of tension at home and abroad: arrest and execution of the head of the secret police and his top associates; proclamation of a new deal for the Soviet consumer; and a series of conciliatory offerings to the United States and its allies. This was a watershed that reflected a rapidly emerging and growing sentiment within the leadership. It comprised something I have called the "post-Stalin consensus."[7] That consensus remained in force right through the collapse of the USSR. As far as we know, at no time in the subsequent 38 years was serious consideration given in Politburo deliberations to

---

[7] Breslauer, *Khrushchev and Brezhnev*, p. 18.

the option of returning to the extremes of Stalinism. The new deal was political and economic, domestic and international; it gave reassurance both to the population at large and to the ruling elite.

The post-Stalin consensus, however, was largely a negative one. True, it promised the population a new era of physical and material security. It also partially based the legitimacy of the regime on improvements in the standard of living of the population. But it did not specify much more than that. It left plenty of room for fundamental disagreement among Soviet leaders about the vision to be pursued, the price to be paid by varied domestic interests in pursuit of that vision, and the sacrifices in traditional values to be suffered for the attainment of new goals. It also left unclear how competing politicians would justify the break with Stalinism and their programs for moving beyond Stalinism.

For this was a regime in which ideas mattered greatly. The Communist Party of the Soviet Union (CPSU) for decades had depicted all of Soviet history as the implementation of a grand design for building a utopian society at home and abroad.[8] The Party had legitimized its political monopoly by claiming exclusive insight into how to achieve that utopian goal. Hence, if there was to be a break with Stalinism, it would be necessary to explain why, at this point in time, a change of course was required. It might not have been necessary to blacken the historical image of Stalin in order to undermine the entrenched Stalinist interests and identities that impeded changing course. But it certainly was necessary to explain the change in ideological terms, and to spell out the reasons that the Stalinist legacy had become a brake on forward movement toward the good society. This tension between the perceived requirements of forward movement and allegiance to traditional values would be a focus of political conflict for decades thereafter.[9]

---

[8] For good demonstrations of this, see Mikhail Heller and Aleksandr Nekrich, *Utopia in Power: The History of the Soviet Union from 1917 to the Present* (New York: Summit, 1986), and Martin Malia, *The Soviet Tragedy: A History of Socialism in Russia, 1917–1991* (New York: Free Press, 1994).

[9] The extraordinary importance of doctrinal justifications in communist regimes is the key reason we focus so carefully on leaders' public statements in studying politics in those regimes. Because of Stalin's canonization of Lenin's thoughts and words, the leaders' words in these societies became central as acts of political communication and coordination. All officials and most citizens knew this; officials in particular therefore read the words of leaders very carefully for small variations in meaning and text. They parsed small nuances of phrase for deeper meaning. When Western Kremlinologists used the same technique to document changes in policy and politics, they were often ridiculed in the West. Those critics mistakenly assumed that one could read leaders' speeches in communist regimes essentially as one reads leaders' speeches in liberal democracies. In fact, Kremlinologists were treating those speeches much as communist officials did. It is striking how many memoirs published during the past decade refer to speeches and newspaper articles as key moments in Soviet politics.

As the leadership made its break with the extremes of Stalinism, deeper issues about the Leninist legacy came to the fore. How to prevent criticism of Stalinism from evolving into criticism of that system's origins in Leninism? How to prevent expanded political participation from challenging the leading role of the Party and its monopoly of political, economic, and social life? How to rein in the secret police, and to narrow the definition of political crime, without justifying the substitution of a system based on rule of law? How to improve the economy without a genuine decentralization of economic power that might challenge the sanctity of central planning and the right of Party officials to intervene, at will, in administrative affairs? How to strike deals with the "imperialists," in order to manage the nuclear balance of power, without forsaking one's commitments to leadership of the "anti-imperialist struggle" and the world communist movement?

These tensions between the goals of the post-Stalin era and the deeper legacy of Leninism were not immediately obvious to Soviet leaders. But as liberalization of speech and publication expanded under Khrushchev and Brezhnev, more members of the critical intelligentsia could be heard raising questions about the compatibility of certain features of Soviet Leninism with the attainment of the new goals. Hence, political conflict under Khrushchev and Brezhnev rarely concerned whether or not to pursue those new goals. Rather, it centered on the costs to be borne – in terms of traditional values – when pursuing them. As a result, in building his authority, the Party leader rarely chose between traditional values and new goals; he instead sought to synthesize the two, or to put together packages that borrowed from each. Both Khrushchev and Brezhnev sought to demonstrate their political skills and programmatic vision by forging policies that would allegedly attain post-Stalin goals without undercutting the legitimacy and stability of the monopolistic, Party-led system.

It was not difficult to justify such amalgams. The Soviet political tradition was multifaceted and contradictory, containing both "reformist" and "conservative" strands.[10] Yet there were limits to the degree of diversity easily legitimized by that tradition. Marxism–Leninism could not justify a social system based on political freedom, the dominance of market coordination and private property in the economy, or a permanent accommodation with imperialism on the global stage. Hence, Stalin's successors faced the challenge of devising innovative policies that would move beyond Stalinism without embracing classical liberal approaches to the domestic organization and foreign relations of the country. Only after 33 years of experimentation with efforts to

---

[10] See Stephen F. Cohen, "The friends and foes of change: Reformism and conservatism in the Soviet Union," *Slavic Review,* vol. 38, no. 2 (June 1979), pp. 187–202.

reform and adapt the system within these limits did leaders emerge within the Politburo who were willing to press for something more far-reaching – something that challenged the Party's monopoly at home and its anti-imperialist mission abroad. That was the point at which reform evolved into transformation of the system and, eventually, its replacement with an alternative. It was also the point at which the system itself started to come apart.

STRATEGIES FOR SQUARING THE CIRCLE

Khrushchev sought initially to demonstrate that increased consumer satisfaction could be realized without massive reallocation of funds out of the military and heavy-industrial sectors. He also sought to prove that a reduction of bureaucratic centralism could be achieved without a loss of administrative control, and that expanded criticism of officialdom could be reconciled with the maintenance of tight political control and strict censorship. The key to synthesizing these conflicting priorities, in his eyes, was to combine partial political liberalization with a reduction in the socioeconomic privileges of Party officials, expansion of the role of Party activists at the expense of full-time Party officials, and the generation of nationwide fervor through ambitious campaigns for social transformation and economic growth. However, restructuring political relationships within the system required a confrontation with powerful political interests, which was one reason that Khrushchev pressed his campaigns against Joseph Stalin and his legacy. By the time Khrushchev was overthrown in 1964, the Soviet Union had broken decisively with the extremes of Stalinism. But Khrushchev had much less to show for his efforts to provide the Soviet people with material abundance, social equality, and a sense of authentic political participation.

Brezhnev based his authority within the political establishment on a program that replaced Khrushchev's political and social reforms with patriotic appeals ("Soviet patriotism") and budgetary redistributions. Rather than restructure authority relations, Brezhnev proposed to accelerate economic growth by pouring enormous resources into agriculture, wages, Siberian development, and imports of foreign goods. He sought to reconcile political control with "socialist legality" by squelching the anti-Stalin campaign and cracking down on dissidents while simultaneously creating a more predictable and less pressured environment for politically conformist experts. Brezhnev defined his role as an intra-establishment consensus builder who would not confront (or radically deprive) the major institutional interests in the system.

Whatever their differences, Khrushchev and Brezhnev were both "Party men." Neither of them believed in, or advocated, democratic pluralism or an end to the "leading role of the Party." Both men forged programs that relied heavily on Party activism and political intervention in economic and social affairs for their realization. Both men sought to create a sense of nationwide fervor on behalf of their programs. The turn away from utopian values after Khrushchev did not mean abandoning efforts to generate mobilizational fervor per se. (Recall that, under Brezhnev, construction of the Baikal–Amur railroad was dubbed "The Project of the Century.") The difference was that Khrushchev sought to redefine the character of Party mobilization in an anti-elitist direction, thereby challenging the prerogatives of the Party *apparatchiki*. He advocated new methods of mobilization with active Party members and specialists taking the lead. In contrast, Brezhnev advocated methods of mobilization that would further the achievement of post-Stalin goals without challenging the prerogatives and privileges of full-time officials of the Party–State.

The two leaders differed less in their foreign policies than in their domestic policies. They both pursued strategies of "offensive détente."[11] They both opted to build their authority by demonstrating that they could compete globally with "imperialism" and simultaneously strike deals with the United States that would manage the nuclear relationship. They both promised to do so from a position of strength and to secure Washington's recognition of the USSR as a co-equal and global superpower. In sum, they both promised to deliver peace through strength. Khrushchev, however, promised far more than he could deliver in the near term and sought to compensate for the shortfall through bluff: for example, public exaggeration of Soviet missile capability that was meant to intimidate Western leaders into making concessions. When his bluff was called by Western governments, he was thrown onto the political defensive, both at home and abroad, and sought new ways to recoup his credibility. During 1963–1964, frightened by the close brush with nuclear war during the Cuban Missile Crisis and desperate for a success that would bolster his credibility within the Central Committee, Khrushchev pursued a foreign policy that came close to abandoning the Soviet commitment to allies in the world communist movement. He was so desperate for "peace" that he was willing to abandon "strength."[12]

This policy was dropped by Khrushchev's successors, partly out of national pride and partly because the U.S. military escalation in Vietnam strengthened hardliners within the leadership.[13] Brezhnev abandoned bluff and sought deliberately to build the military strength required to play the role of a co-equal

---

[11] The term was coined by Jack Snyder in "The Gorbachev revolution: A waning of Soviet expansionism?" *International Security*, vol. 12, no. 3 (Winter 1987/88), pp. 93–131, at p. 103.

[12] See Richter, *Khrushchev's Double Bind*, ch. 7.

[13] Ibid., ch. 8.

superpower and interventionist global power. Only then did he reenter into a détente relationship with the United States. Brezhnev also recommitted the Soviet Union to its communist allies and promised to build a détente with the imperialist camp that would actually advance the goals of the world communist movement.

Khrushchev was ousted from office in October 1964, criticized for both his policies and his leadership style; Brezhnev died in office, but only after a lengthy period that would subsequently be dubbed "stagnation" at home and abroad. Thus, neither of them succeeded in squaring the circle: how to combine the Communist Party's monopoly on power with policies that could revitalize an entrenched, overbureaucratized system at home and keep pace with the United States abroad. Their policy programs – and the fallback positions they adopted after their initial programs were discredited – proved incapable of improving all-round economic performance, public élan, or Soviet standing abroad.

TACTICS FOR GETTING ONE'S WAY

Khrushchev, the reformer, embraced a leadership style that was anti-establishment and confrontational – what might be called "Leninist populism." He mobilized the masses against the "bureaucrats." Brezhnev, the conservative, adopted a leadership style that was establishmentarian and consensual. These were distinct approaches to leadership within a post-Stalinist, Leninist system.

Khrushchev's strategy was to exploit the atmosphere of crisis after Stalin to make common cause with the masses against intransigent forces within the establishment. He played upon elite fears of social unrest by intentionally raising popular expectations, or prematurely publicizing policy proposals, and then arguing within the political elite that growing popular disaffection made the acceptance of these proposals a necessity. He leaked Politburo deliberations to selected, interested audiences in order to intimidate other actors in the policymaking process. He invited members of the intelligentsia to join him in criticizing the inherited order. He invited nonmembers to be present, or to give speeches, at meetings of the Party's Central Committee in order to bias the discussions in a particular direction and to intimidate skeptics. When his policies started to falter, and when he could no longer deliver on his inflated promises, Khrushchev intensified the anti-Stalin campaign, blamed officials of the Party and state for the shortfalls, purged many of them, and launched an assault on Party organs at all levels of the hierarchy.

Brezhnev's rejection of political populism, as well as his greater emphasis on throwing money at problems, were consistent with his posture as a consensus builder and political broker among interests within the establishment.

His goals were conservative and his leadership strategy was tailored to them. He eschewed appealing to the masses over the heads of his colleagues, avoided playing upon elite fears of the masses, and shunned raising consumer expectations for personal political gain. Instead, Brezhnev presented himself as the leader best qualified to build coalitions that would induce the most powerful institutional interests to reorient their operations and to make the system, as structured, work more effectively. And he promised to do all this without political purges.

AUTHORITY BUILDING AND PUBLIC POLITICS

The contrast in authority-building strategies between these two men highlights a feature of the Soviet system that becomes crucial to understanding the dilemmas and opportunities facing Gorbachev and Yeltsin. The Soviet political order was based on a heavily defended system of *private politics*. Important deliberations and decisionmaking took place within the upper reaches of the Party–State hierarchy, in arenas that were dominated by the trustees of a privileged class of full-time officials of the Communist Party, the economic bureaucracy, the military, and the security services. Secrecy and a façade of unanimity were the prevailing norms. A leader like Brezhnev, who was comfortable with brokering relations among these elite interests, could easily respect the prevailing norms. But a leader like Khrushchev, who wanted to reform the system and challenge some of its fundamentals, would have to defy the norms of secrecy and unanimity. He would have to mobilize new social forces to challenge the prerogatives of entrenched interests. He would have to propose doctrinal revisions and challenge some of the sacred cows of Stalinist doctrine. This was not a matter of choice. If he wanted to reform the system (which *was* a matter of choice), his authority-building strategy would have to challenge the notion that politics is entirely a private affair. Otherwise, he would remain too much a captive of the interests that dominated the Soviet political establishment.

Leaders who sought to go beyond reform and to *transform* the system would have to embrace even more far-reaching strategies for building political leverage. They would have to defy the norms of private politics to an even greater extent than Khrushchev had. Indeed, one of the central dramas of the Gorbachev and Yeltsin eras was the creation of an autonomous public realm: the transformation of politics from a private affair into a public affair. Gorbachev eventually viewed freer speech (*glasnost'*), greater freedom of association, a freer press, and competitive elections as necessary to revitalize the system, awaken society, and neutralize entrenched interests that might obstruct the transformation of the Soviet system into some sort of "socialist democracy." For Yeltsin, that public arena became his ticket to political resurrection in 1989 and the avenue through which he later became president of Russia. Gorbachev's authority-building dilemma was how to open a public arena without destroying the system he was seeking peaceably to transform. Yeltsin's authority-building *opportunity* in the 1980s lay in his exploitation of that public arena, to Gorbachev's political disadvantage. But Yeltsin's authority-building dilemma after the collapse of the Soviet Union became: how to build a new system in a context of intense, public political competition?

Expansion of the arenas of political conflict may be a necessary condition for both reform and transformation of the system, but such expansion is far from a sufficient condition; indeed, it can be used as easily for reactionary purposes. Mao Zedong, for example, mobilized Red Guards during the Cultural Revolution as a way of smashing bureaucratic conservatism and repressing nonconformist thought. Only when expansion is combined with liberalization of political expression is it capable of serving the cause of progressive reform or transformation of the system. Only when some degree of autonomy is granted to public arenas can political conflict within those arenas advance the progressive transformation of the system. Under such conditions, dissident or "revisionist" ideas come to play a causal role in making change possible and in shaping the direction of that change.

Leaders who wish to seize the political initiative in order to reform or transform the system need allies outside the political establishment. They need to mobilize new social forces in order to use them as a wedge against entrenched conservative forces. For those regimes in which ideas are important, activation of such social forces must be legitimized while channels are created through which their voices can be heard. Hence, Soviet leaders who sought to reform or transform politics since Stalin had to transform both the *language* and the *arenas* of contestation.

For example, Khrushchev's anti-Stalin campaign, beginning in 1956 and extending through the end of his reign, sought to break through the "bureaucratism" that he claimed to be a fundamental constraint on progress. His campaign emboldened journalists and members of the cultural intelligentsia to disseminate public critiques of the existing state of affairs. Many of these works bordered on critiques of the system of rule – the ordering principles of the polity – as opposed to the traditional tendency to blame all problems on the individual deficiencies of specific officials. Under Khrushchev, then, the permissible explanation for failure was allowed to ascend to a much higher level of abstraction. His doctrinal innovations at Party Congresses in 1956,

1959, and 1961 provided intellectual space for members of the newly reborn "critical intelligentsia" to push still further their critiques of the system. Eventually, they went further than Khrushchev could abide, both personally and politically. Periodically, Khrushchev cracked down and tried to rein in the scope of permissible criticism – only to expand it again when pushing his reformist agenda.

Brezhnev's purposes as a consolidator of the system did not require him to expand either the arenas of politics or the level of generalization of criticism. To the contrary, Brezhnev made top-level policymaking less transparent and permeable than it had been under Khrushchev and worked faithfully within established arenas. He also put an end to the anti-Stalin campaign, rescinded earlier doctrinal changes, and reduced the scope of permissible criticism to within-system levels. This approach to the structure and language of politics was tailored to conservative and consolidative purposes.

Gorbachev, in turn, sought to transform the system more fully than even Khrushchev. His campaign for *glasnost'* therefore allowed the scope of permissible criticism to rise to unprecedented levels. While Gorbachev, as we shall see, feared that excessive criticism of the Stalinist past might undermine him politically, he nonetheless encouraged the critical intelligentsia to run with his doctrinal innovations and to develop an increasingly systemic critique of current problems. Expanded public criticism, he hoped, would stimulate the initiative of educated youth, expose bureaucratic obstruction, and build legitimacy for an emerging political order. That criticism would also build a constituency to support Gorbachev politically and to which he could point in order to intimidate advocates of a political backlash.

Boris Yeltsin exploited the new arenas and publics called forth by Gorbachev and helped to radicalize them far beyond what Gorbachev desired. Moreover, he founded new arenas himself, such as the Russian presidency, and helped turn criticism of the old regime into rejection of the entire communist system. In the process, he outflanked Gorbachev politically and, intentionally or not, helped to bring down Gorbachev, the Soviet system, and the USSR.

Both reformist and transformational leadership in a monopolistic, Leninist system require a leader to propagate heretical new ideas, create new public arenas, and mobilize previously intimidated social forces into politics. Such leadership requires strategically focused public criticism to undermine the enemies of change, and it requires new constituencies to provide a new political base for a new political order. All this is counterintuitive in several respects. It is extremely risky to subject your *own* system to criticism and to bring new, unpredictable social forces and radical ideas into politics. No leader can easily predict or control the consequences. For a leader concerned with nothing more than retaining power, there are other (and much safer) ways of conducting politics. But at a certain point, when a political system is mired in stagnation, standing pat may fail as an authority-building strategy despite the very same possibilities for intimidation, patronage allocation, and coalition building around material interests that allowed previous leaders to resist change. When that point is reached, the winning political strategy is to propagate an "idea whose time has come."

In sum, reforming or transforming the Soviet political order required changes in policy, political organization, and the language of politics; changing just one by itself would be insufficient. In established systems, reigning ideologies and structures tend to be mutually reinforcing. Leaders who wish to overcome constraints on change therefore must operate at two levels: (1) they must build coalitions of material interests to support needed changes in policy and organization; and (2) they must propagate new ideas that both delegitimize the old way of doing things and create legitimacy for new ways of doing things. The core of the challenge is how to change the system, or build a new one, without sacrificing your authority and power in the process.

STAGES OF ADMINISTRATION

I have noted similarities and differences between Khrushchev and Brezhnev in their approaches to problem solving and politics. I have only alluded to the fact that both of their administrations passed through at least three distinct stages. Each stage reflected the authority-building challenges facing the leader at that point during his tenure in office, and each stage was marked by a distinct approach to problem solving and political self-justification by the leader. The three-stage rhythms of change within each administration are suggestive of shifting political incentives and opportunities as politicians exercise leadership. This will become relevant as we analyze the dilemmas that Gorbachev and Yeltsin encountered at analogous stages of their administrations.

When we look back on the Khrushchev and Brezhnev years, we find in each administration that a stage of political succession struggle and power consolidation was followed by a period of ascendancy of the Party leader, which in turn was followed by the frustration of his programmatic goals and a decline in his authority. Each stage posed a distinct authority-building challenge to the leader. In the first stage – before he had consolidated his power, outflanked his rivals, or expanded his role to become chief architect of domestic and foreign policy – the Party leader concentrated on putting together a coalition that was biased in the direction of traditional interests. Thus, in this initial stage, both Khrushchev and Brezhnev most strongly advocated the development of heavy industry and defense. Both men pointed to threats from the "imperialists" and emphasized the protection of traditional values more than the adoption of new approaches. Both leaders also introduced policy innovations to clean up some of the mess inherited from their predecessors. In particular, both came forth with large-scale programs for agricultural development that were justified as necessary to ensure reliable supplies of food for the urban population. At the same time, both men tried to seize the initiative by pinning the "extremist" label on their political rivals, suggesting that those rivals were either too conservative or too radical to protect traditional values and simultaneously move the country forward.

Yet after consolidating their power and purging (Khrushchev) or outflanking (Brezhnev) their rivals, both men expanded their roles and selectively incorporated into their programs elements of the policies associated with the more reformist of their defeated rivals. Each of them presented a comprehensive program for forward-looking changes in both domestic and foreign policies that constituted a more balanced synthesis of traditional values and new approaches than they had advocated earlier. Both leaders now claimed to speak for "all the people."

In both cases, however, the synthesis proved overly optimistic and unworkable. Brezhnev's synthesis was arguably less ambitious and optimistic than Khrushchev's, a fact that reflected Brezhnev's conservatism, his political dependence on a self-protective political establishment, and lessons learned from the Khrushchev experience. But Brezhnev's program remained highly optimistic nonetheless, promising to expand production in both heavy and light industry and simultaneously to deliver both détente with the imperialists and intensified competition in the Third World.

Because of the gap that resulted between promises and achievements, the credibility of both Khrushchev's and Brezhnev's claims came to be doubted. Each man then tried to reestablish his credibility, reshuffle his support coalition, and redefine his program. Each leader went through several bouts of such changes during his remaining years in office.[14]

---

[14] Some people argue (in passing and without elaboration or documentation) that Khrushchev did not perceive himself to be on the political defensive in 1960–1964 and that the changes he introduced in that period were efforts to salvage his *program,* not his political authority (Richard Ned Lebow and Janice Gross Stein, *We All Lost the Cold War* [Princeton, NJ: Princeton University Press, 1994], pp. 403–4, fn. 57). I have also received personal communications from a reader to this effect. And it is at the basis of all literature that treats the Soviet general secretary as politically unassailable (as in, for example, Dmitrii Volkogonov, *Autopsy for an Empire: The Seven Leaders Who Built the Soviet Regime* [New York: Free Press, 1998]). This objection cuts to the heart of my approach to the study of politics and is worth rebutting. The interpretation does not explain why Khrushchev was so devoted to his program (pure idealism?). And it assumes implausibly that he had sufficient power to be oblivious to the prospect that his mistakes and shortfalls could immediately be held against

Gorbachev's and Yeltsin's years in power can be divided into three analogous stages. Indeed, that is the basis for the organization of this book. Each of these leaders went through a stage of succession and consolidation, followed by a stage of ascendancy, which gave way to a stage of decline. Even so, with the emergence of an autonomous public arena in the 1980s and 1990s and with the collapse of the Soviet system, the political incentives facing Gorbachev and Yeltsin differed dramatically from those facing Khrushchev and Brezhnev. Hence, we will find some novel twists on the conclusions of my earlier study – twists that reflect the difference between the task of reforming or adapting the Soviet system, on the one hand, and the task of transforming or replacing it, on the other.

AUTHORITY-BUILDING STRATEGIES:
AUDIENCES, SOURCES, AND RESONANCE

Authority building is a process of establishing and maintaining one's credibility among constituencies that have the power to make or break one's hold over either policymaking or office. It is a process that is universal to contexts marked by competitive politics. And it is all the more important in the context of *ideological* politics, in which the struggle over ideas bears on the very identity of the political community. But where do authority-building strategies come from? What are the audiences for one's authority-building strategies? What determines whether one's ideas resonate with those audiences? Let us address these issues in the established Soviet context under Khrushchev and Brezhnev before exploring how things changed under Gorbachev and Yeltsin.

---

him by others in the leadership – an especially implausible assumption in a regime in which political struggle had been so intense and so costly to the losers. By contrast, I treat leaders in politically competitive regimes as actors who view both power preservation and authority maintenance as prerequisites for the realization of their programs, and I view them as living with constant uncertainty about the state of their power, authority, and credibility. They may or may not be faced with crystallized factional opposition: I am persuaded by the evidence that Khrushchev and Brezhnev did not face such overt, sustained opposition. But they had to be constantly attentive to the possible reactions of associates who could undermine their political security. Hence, even if they did not proclaim publicly, "I am on the political defensive!" (which would not be smart politics), defensive rhetoric and counteroffensive behavior when their programs are faltering is a good indicator of leaders' efforts to re-seize the political initiative when the ambitious programs they sponsored have been discredited. They enjoyed a great deal of power to define policy, even during the third stage of their administrations. But their perceived level of political insecurity rose as the credibility of their programs and promises declined. Ultimately, my claims may have to be treated as an assumption of this study, rather than a fully documented demonstration, since the private perceptions and fears of leaders – whatever they might have said openly in a recorded Politburo meeting now in the archives – are things they would have experienced but kept to themselves.

We are trying to understand the factors that entered into the calculations of Soviet politicians as they competed for the highest office in the land.
Clearly, the first consideration on their minds was: What strategy is most
likely to work? How can I mobilize powerful supporters in greater quan-
tity, and more effectively, than my competitors? In thinking about this, a
politician in any competitive system will focus on what is important to the
(s)electorate: its interests and identities. He will think about the coalitions
that might be built among existing interest groups, the promises that could
be made to induce them to support him, and the more diffuse ideas and symbols he could invoke that would resonate with his (s)electors' notions of social
progress.

In scanning the array of interests in the political establishment at a given
moment in time, our hypothetical competitor would certainly want to avoid
alienating the most powerful, entrenched interests in the system. Nonetheless, he could not afford to be identified with a "stand-pat" position, as he
would also sense a yearning among the elite for ways of getting the country
out of the mess bequeathed by his predecessor. This is the point at which we
reach the limits of a structural approach to the prediction of leadership behavior. The leading roles of the Communist Party, the military–industrial
complex, the economic planners, and the security organs were constants
throughout the post-Stalin era. But leadership strategies for combining interests across institutions, for selectively defying the interests of some of those
institutions, and for constructing diffuse appeals to broader identity considerations varied greatly.

That variation was more a product of the personal ideas and strategies
of competing politicians than of institutional structures: ideas about how to
combine the old and the new; political strategies formulated under conditions
of immense uncertainty about what was likely to work; ideas and strategies
propagated with the intention of defining a political niche for oneself and
denying that niche to one's competitors. The value of an authority-building
approach is that, without denying the constraining impact of structures, it
highlights the tendency of leaders to forge and justify programs that cannot
be predicted from knowing solely the structure of political organization and
the content of dominant interests in the polity.[15] And the structural approach
is particularly ill-suited to predicting the effectiveness of leadership strategies
once the system is in crisis – as was the case after Gorbachev began his efforts to transform the system. At that point, the interaction among leadership

---

[15] As Keynes once wrote: "I am sure that the power of vested interests is vastly exaggerated compared with the gradual encroachment of ideas" (John Maynard Keynes, *The General Theory*
[New York: Harcourt Brace, 1936], p. 383).

strategies, crumbling structures, and newly mobilized social forces was much more open-ended.

Another ideational factor that cannot be predicted simply from knowing the structures and interests of the regime is the *climate of opinion within the political establishment* at the point of political succession. That climate influences the strategies adopted by political competitors. After Stalin, a widespread (though far from unanimous) yearning existed within the political establishment and intelligentsia for restoring to the people and the elite a sense of physical security; this sentiment coexisted with a yearning within many quarters of the political establishment for restoring a sense of dynamism, for "getting the country moving again." The coexistence of these palpable sentiments meant both that "movement" should not be in the direction of a continuation of Stalinism and that promising physical security to cadres should not be equated with stagnation in policy. Khrushchev sensed these yearnings, shared them, played upon them, and worked to shape their policy expression. By contrast, after Khrushchev, officials of the Party and state yearned primarily for a period of tranquility and predictability that would regularize and guarantee their material privileges, their job security, and their autonomy from both unregulated mass criticism and arbitrary leaders. At the same time, they hoped for leadership that would clean up the economic and administrative disarray of Khrushchev's last years in office. Brezhnev sensed, shared, and responded to these yearnings.

Political competitors also appeal to ideas, not just interests, when they attempt to build clientele networks based on a sense of shared identity. The symbols leaders invoke in packaging their programs are chosen to resonate with the identities of audiences within the political elite. Leaders attempt to plug into traditional notions of national glory, need, or international standing, into notions of societal progress, solidarity, and élan, and into core ideas of the ideological tradition. Even in a regime like Brezhnev's, where the conservative and consolidative thrust of policy seemed to pander only to material and status interests, the leader framed his policy choices in ways that played to audiences' concern for national élan: Brezhnev's large-scale agricultural programs of 1965–1966; his programs for development of the Non-Black-Earth Zone and Siberia; accelerated construction of the Baikal–Amur railway and territorial–industrial complexes; and his "Peace Program" of 1971. All these projects were presented as glorious means of moving the country toward transcendant domestic and international goals.[16]

---

[16] On Marxist–Leninist elites as believers in the capacity of their systems to transcend historical constraints, see Stephen Hanson, *Time and Revolution* (Chapel Hill: University of North Carolina Press, 1997).

But they had to do so credibly. Targeted individuals will calculate whether the appeals being sent their way are likely to yield the promised results and likely to prevail in any subsequent power struggle. To the extent that proposals are not credible, they can be dismissed as empty promises, wishful thinking, or the desperate rhetoric of a political loser. The winning strategy is for a politician to craft a set of appeals that link the past to the future in ways that are plausible and in ways that allow him to seize the policy initiative, throw his rivals onto the political defensive, and thereby induce potential clients to support the man who is likely to win (a bandwagoning effect). Brezhnev and Khrushchev were able to fashion programs that credibly (to Party–State officials) combined selected traditional values with new solutions to problems and that, they claimed, would move the country forward, aggrandize the material interests of certain constituencies, and do so skillfully under the leadership of patrons likely to prevail in the power struggle. Thus, authority building in Soviet politics involved making a credible claim to possessing scarce problem-solving and political skills.

The initial reliance of Khrushchev and Brezhnev on hardline constituencies appears to validate a structural explanation for their behavior as political competitors. It may, in fact, validate the notion that the autonomous role of personal ideas is diminished when the stakes involved are of the highest order: political survival or demise.[17] Both men initially appealed more to the material interests of key constituencies, and to traditional features of the reigning ideology, than they would after they had won the power struggle. But why did these leaders expand their coalitions and programs once they had achieved ascendancy in the leadership? Why did they not simply stick with the coalition with which they had won the power struggle – a coalition that, in both cases, allied them with the two most powerful interests in the system: the Party apparatus and the military–industrial complex?

One answer is cognitive: a stand-pat strategy was not credible to those who believed in the post-Stalin consensus; elite audiences came to perceive the contradictions within the system as urgently in need of being addressed, however gingerly (Brezhnev) or boldly (Khrushchev). Another answer is ideological and emotional: the regime's optimistic ideological tradition encouraged an expansive vision of the system's capacity to build a society of abundance for all the people. A third answer is political: this was still a Leninist system, and the leader was accorded no fixed term of office. Hence, post-Stalin leaders

---

[17] "[T]he lower the cost of expressing one's convictions the more important the convictions will be as a determinant of choice" (Douglass C. North, *Institutions, Institutional Change and Economic Performance* [Cambridge University Press, 1990], p. 43).

experienced a felt need for *political overinsurance,* even after they had consolidated their power. The political uncertainty about procedures and term of office gave the leader an incentive to build outsized (rather than minimal) winning coalitions, which in turn led him eventually to sponsor programs that appealed to constituencies located across a wide band of the political spectrum.[18] Having won the power struggle by appealing to concentrated interests that had exceptionally intense preferences, he acquired the power to become more inclusive as well as the incentive to insure himself politically by drawing previously excluded interests and identities into his coalition. Whether his personal goal was to hedge against risk through insurance or to increase his political independence by reducing his reliance on a small coalition, the behavioral result was the same: an expanded coalition.

Whatever the reasons for promulgating so ambitious a program, the leader found himself on the political defensive after the shortcomings of that program became manifest. This is a point at which personality became an especially important determinant of the leader's behavior. His response to frustration was far less dictated by a clear perception of what the political traffic would bear. Khrushchev became extraordinarily erratic during his last four years in office. In both domestic and foreign affairs, he searched frantically for panaceas that would help him regain lost authority, and he confronted the most powerful and entrenched interests in the system. Brezhnev instead adopted a deliberate strategy of returning to the coalition on which he had ridden to the top in the 1960s and of using whatever resources he could marshal to try to salvage as much of his comprehensive program as possible.

AUTHORITY BUILDING AND POST-SOVIET POLITICS

Comparison of Khrushchev's and Brezhnev's authority-building strategies allowed me to generalize about the nature of Soviet politics. But is the framework applicable to a system that is crumbling or being replaced, as was the case from 1988 through 1999? In this book, I intend to demonstrate that it is in fact relevant to the new context. In good measure, that relevance stems from the framework's initial derivation from the study of democratic regimes. The idea of leadership as a process of stretching social constraints – and of authority building as a necessary precondition for acquiring the leverage to do so

---

[18] This point was made in Richter, *Khrushchev's Double Bind*. Lack of a fixed term of office is also a feature of parliamentary regimes. However, in Leninist regimes, the felt need for political overinsurance is reinforced mightily by the unattractiveness of political retirement and the lack of autonomous arenas in society in which to build alternative careers or to launch a political comeback.

successfully – is a universal of politics in competitive regimes, whether these are competitive oligarchies or pluralist democracies. Indeed, I first developed the idea when reading Neustadt's classic study of the American presidency, in which he argued that "Presidential power is the power to persuade."[19] The Soviet regime in the post-Stalin era, it seemed to me, had become a competitive oligarchy within which political competition was expressed publicly as a contest of ideas. While coercion and patronage remained key bases for political compliance in Soviet politics, ideas had grown in importance as the price to be paid for political failure had declined.[20] I concluded that something useful could be learned about Soviet politics by looking at policy advocacy as more than just a game of power maximization and by looking at political leverage as more than just the power to command and coerce. It follows logically that the basic framework is eminently applicable to successor regimes that embrace public and democratic modes of political contestation, for that framework derived originally from the study of a democratic regime.

There are still other reasons to apply the framework to post-Soviet Russia. First, seizing the initiative and thus throwing one's competitors onto the political defensive is a widely used strategy among competing politicians in competitive oligarchies as well as in public, democratic politics. Second, the division of administrations into stages reflects something more general, though such stages will vary in length and character in different systems. The stages of struggle for succession (the electoral campaign in liberal democracies) followed by "honeymoon" or ascendancy periods followed by declining authority form a familiar pattern. It is striking, for example, how many British prime ministers (even the "great" ones) ended their careers in office on a note of failure or repudiation.[21] Finally, there is a commonality in the tendency of politicians to promise more than they can deliver and then to struggle with a loss of credibility when their inability to deliver becomes obvious. This phenomenon is hardly restricted to Soviet politics, though huge gaps between aspirations and capacity are certainly characteristic of communist regimes. For all these reasons, we shall see that an authority-building framework helps

---

[19] Richard Neustadt, *Presidential Power: The Politics of Leadership* (New York: Wiley, 1960), p. 10.

[20] Put differently, politicians were more likely to speak their minds in private and political venues once they no longer had to fear being shot for being on the wrong side of an argument or political struggle.

[21] See Richard Rose, *The Prime Minister in a Shrinking World* (Cambridge, U.K.: Polity Press, 2001); on governing cycles in communist and democratic systems, see Valerie Bunce, *Do New Leaders Make a Difference?: Executive Succession and Public Policy under Capitalism and Socialism* (Princeton, NJ: Princeton University Press, 1981).

to illuminate the evolution of Boris Yeltsin's presidency, even though his leadership was no longer being exercised within a Marxist–Leninist Party–State.

Thus far, I have been discussing the context within which political choice takes place; I have said less about the personalities and personal beliefs of the leaders in question. Such was also the case with my book on Khrushchev and Brezhnev, in which I was more interested in highlighting features of the system that led to a number of similarities across their administrations. The personal factor, however, must loom larger – much larger – in a book about Gorbachev and Yeltsin. Khrushchev's reformism and Brezhnev's conservatism had long pedigrees within Soviet history, as did Gorbachev's initial strategy of reformism during 1985–1987. But Gorbachev's subsequent decision to push for transformation of the system, and Yeltsin's decision to try to destroy and replace the Leninist system, were unprecedented acts by political leaders of the system itself. One cannot explain these choices without reference to these leaders' personalities and beliefs before they came to power, which is the focus of the next chapter.

2

Gorbachev and Yeltsin: Personalities and Beliefs

Most of the time they were in power, both Gorbachev and Yeltsin were less constrained by formal political structures than Khrushchev and Brezhnev had been. We must therefore understand the personalities and beliefs of Gorbachev and Yeltsin if we hope to specify the determinants of many of their policy choices.

GORBACHEV AS A POLITICAL PERSONALITY

There is nothing in Gorbachev's biography to suggest the personality of a rebel. Rather, Gorbachev comes across as an organization man, one who joined the Communist Party at a younger age than did Yeltsin and who found his greatest honors and satisfactions in life within that organization.[1] Gorbachev came to Moscow as a young man from the provinces who was eager to "make it" in the capital and to rise within the political hierarchy. One of the first things he did after matriculation at Moscow State University was to become a Young Communist League (Komsomol) activist. He applied for candidate membership of the CPSU at the youngest age allowable. Gorbachev's career took him through the law faculty at Moscow State University, during which time he became head of his class's Komsomol, followed by a conventional career climbing the ladder of the political hierarchy – first in the Young Communist League, then in the Party apparatus. Once in the Party apparatus, he never left it. Whereas some analysts treat this career path as predicting the mentality of a "conservative" *apparatchik,* it is more accurate to

---

[1] This distinction first appeared in Dmitry Mikheyev, *Russia Transformed* (Indianapolis, IN: Hudson Institute, 1996), pp. 49ff.

treat it as predicting faith in the "leading role of the Party" within Soviet "socialist" society, and belief in proper organization and Party-led mobilization as the guarantor of progress toward "realizing the full potential of socialism." Gorbachev's attraction to Party work derived from the possibility of doing *political* work as a leader of people. He was repelled by the deskwork of bureaucrats and rejected a career in the procuracy when it was offered to him.

Like Gorbachev, Yeltsin was repelled by formal, bureaucratic deskwork and preferred to work directly with people involved in solving concrete problems. Both men prided themselves on their motivational skills. But Yeltsin, unlike Gorbachev, was drawn to complex, *technical* tasks of construction engineering and prided himself on the mastery of technical skills that would allow him to reach new heights in grandiose acts of construction. He worked in economic administration for many years before being recruited into the Party apparatus. During his rise within the Party–State apparatus, Yeltsin was evaluated in terms of the construction projects put up under his leadership. Gorbachev, as the Komsomol leader in Stavropol, was evaluated by his superiors according to more abstract, subjective, and political criteria.

Gorbachev's personality as a well-adjusted organization man within a political bureaucracy mirrored the well-adjusted relationship he enjoyed with his family. Gorbachev had a friendly, affectionate relationship with his father. The father and son worked together around the clock to bring in the harvest when Mikhail was a teen-ager; they discussed news and confided in each other. The father treated the son like an equal. In the summer of 1948, as they worked side by side, Mikhail earned a medal, *Orden' Trudovogo Krasnogo Znameni* (The Order of the Red Banner of Labor), and his father received the more prestigious *Orden' Lenina* (The Order of Lenin). Gorbachev took pride in this accomplishment for the rest of his life; in his memoirs, written in the 1990s, he still described this as his greatest honor.[2] Throughout most of his political life within the *nomenklatura* hierarchy, Gorbachev seems to have believed in the system and to have been committed to improving its functioning.

Gorbachev knew how to get ahead by getting along. In one-on-one conversation, he was the type of man who could "read" the orientations and preferences of his interlocutors, shift his own posture to accord with theirs, and get them to believe that he was sympathetic to their position – even when his goal was to change their mind.[3] This trait served him well as he rose

---

[2] Mikhail Gorbachev, *Zhizn' i reformy*, vol. 1 (Moscow: Novosti, 1996), p. 56.

[3] These were impressions an American journalist reached from interviewing people who knew Gorbachev as a young man (Hedrick Smith, *The New Russians* [New York: Random House, 1990], pp. 41, 49). Archie Brown (*The Gorbachev Factor* [Oxford & New York: Oxford

within the hierarchy. He greeted many Politburo members who visited and vacationed in Stavropol in the 1970s, socializing with them in informal settings.[4] He managed to impress them both as politically reliable and as an intelligent, dynamic regional leader with interesting new ideas about how to make the system perform better. As D'Agostino pithily summarizes it, "Gorbachev's various patrons might often have been at odds with each other, but Gorbachev seems somehow not to have accumulated enemies, not even the enemies of his friends."[5] There is no evidence either of the seething resentment toward superiors in Moscow or of the severe impatience that Yeltsin appears to have suppressed, at times imperfectly, during the early 1980s.

Once co-opted into the Brezhnev Politburo, Gorbachev seated himself as far from Brezhnev as possible and avoided showing his disgust when Brezhnev made a gaffe.[6] He notes in his memoirs that, in Brezhnev's Moscow, the most important thing was to "know one's place": never to overstep the boundaries of one's position and rank.[7] Once in power, Gorbachev's tactical caution remained a defining characteristic of his political personality, even as he was attempting to change the system. Fyodor Burlatskii, on the basis of interviews with many of Gorbachev's aides and associates, argues that Gorbachev was "prone to compromise" and preferred to play "the sure hand," which "irritated the direct and passionate Yeltsin," who was more inclined to take risks.[8]

Colleagues describe Gorbachev as a man of immense energy, passion, intelligence, and eagerness to solve problems.[9] One aide describes Gorbachev's

University Press, 1996], p. 37) makes the more limited claim that Gorbachev possessed "an ability to get along with people of different views and dispositions." Reportedly, psychologists who worked for the U.S. Central Intelligence Agency, and who were observing Gorbachev during his years in power, concluded that "he is keenly intuitive; he senses the situation and reads people on the spot, managing his inner reactions so that he can shift from charming to tough to malleable to menacing in the space of moments" (reported in Gail Sheehy, *The Man Who Changed the World* [New York: HarperCollins, 1990], p. 10).

4   V. I. Boldin, *Krushenie p'edestala: Shtrikhi k portretu M.S. Gorbacheva* (Moscow: Respublika, 1995), p. 127; see also Brown, *The Gorbachev Factor*, pp. 49–51.

5   Anthony D'Agostino, *Gorbachev's Revolution* (New York: NYU Press, 1998), p. 58.

6   Gorbachev, *Zhizn'*, vol. 1, pp. 182–3.

7   Ibid, p. 182.

8   Fyodor Burlatskii, *Glotok svobody*, vol. 2 (Moscow: RIK Kul'tura, 1997), pp. 122, 129–30. Admittedly, this is tricky terminology. One could also argue that Gorbachev, while in power, was "risk-acceptant" in seeking to transform the system and that Yeltsin, in 1985–1989, was "reckless." The distinction among terms like "caution," "risk-acceptance," and "recklessness" often hinges on the observer's values or on his perception of the magnitude of constraints on change.

9   Anatolii Chernyaev, *Shest' let s Gorbachevym* (Moscow: Progress, 1993) pp. 8–9; Pavel Palazchenko, *My Years with Gorbachev and Shevardnadze: The Memoir of a Soviet Interpreter* (University Park: Pennsylvania State University Press, 1997), p. 107. Both Boldin and Ligachev,

ability to become genuinely fascinated by new things, a trait that hardly characterized older members of the Brezhnev Politburo in the 1970s.[10] Another aide, Anatolii Chernyaev, accompanied Gorbachev to Western Europe in 1972 and was mightily impressed by how effectively Gorbachev briefed Belgian communists on the "battle for bread" that was then being conducted in the USSR, as well as by his enthusiasm and liveliness: "he clearly stood out in comparison to other regional Party leaders with his extraordinariness (*nye-ordinarnost'*) and his passion."[11] When he returned to Moscow, Chernyaev told his boss, Boris Ponomarev (head of the International Department of the Central Committee), that Gorbachev was just the right kind of Party official "to uphold the 'image' of the CPSU among fraternal parties," adding that he had never before met anyone as good as Gorbachev at impressing foreigners.[12]

Gorbachev's passion and enthusiasm were not just for show. Chernyaev also reports that, while driving through the Belgian and Dutch countryside in 1972, Gorbachev "almost did not look outside.... [Instead], he grabbed me by the elbows and 'proved,' 'proved,' 'proved' how important it was to do this or that in Stavropol."[13] Gorbachev would "prove" that something needed to be done – or could be done – and would thereby convince his audiences that it *had* to be done. Here we see a preview of the general secretary whose leadership style was based on convincing people that *perestroika* was desirable, necessary, and feasible: "there is no other way." Indeed, Gorbachev was a self-confident debater, a man who took pride in his capacity for logical argumentation and impressive self-presentation. In his memoirs he claims that, by his junior year as a law student, he could debate as well as the very best of his classmates. He prided himself on not being afraid to show weakness by asking questions; this honed his skills as a debater.[14]

Many political leaders are self-confident and have strong egos; indeed, that may be a prerequisite for achieving "greatness." But Gorbachev's self-confidence was joined to a genuinely *optimistic* mind-set. Many observers

---

antagonists of Gorbachev when they wrote their memoirs, recall Gorbachev's workaholic tendencies (Yegor Ligachev, *Inside Gorbachev's Kremlin* [New York: Pantheon, 1993], p. 148; Boldin, *Krushenie*, p. 34); see also the sources used in Brown, *The Gorbachev Factor*, pp. 31–43, and Smith, *The New Russians*, pp. 41, 44ff., 59ff. Sheehy (*The Man*, p. 136) quotes the Soviet Ambassador to the United States, after his first meeting with Gorbachev, as calling him "an insatiable hurricane of a person."

[10] Palazchenko, *My Years*, p. 107; for testimony to this effect by people who knew him during his days at Moscow State University, see Smith, *The New Russians*, pp. 46–7.

[11] Chernyaev, *Shest' let*, p. 8.

[12] Ibid.

[13] Ibid.

[14] Gorbachev, *Zhizn'*, vol. 1, p. 61.

recall the young Gorbachev as an optimist, which is all the more remarkable considering the apocalyptic circumstances of his youth (collectivization, the Great Terror, and World War II). His official translator reports that General Secretary Gorbachev was intensely optimistic about the realizability of the reforms he had begun.[15] Others witnessed this trait but did not share the optimism. As one close advisor is reported to have said in the late-1980s: "I know we can't succeed. But when I get in front of that warm and charming man who wants so much to do something for the country, I have no heart to tell him that we can't succeed."[16] Whether at the level of local campaigns in Stavropol or with respect to reform of the Soviet system as a whole, Gorbachev was clearly an idealist whose beliefs and actions were sustained by a passionate and optimistic, yet carefully controlled, personality.

Optimism, passion, intensity, curiosity, egocentrism, insatiable energy, and self-confidence – combined with risk control, prudence, and calculating other-directedness – are personality traits that Gorbachev brought to the table as he chose his political strategy for reforming the system, once he had the power to do so. But such traits do not reveal the *content* of a person's beliefs: just what are they optimistic, passionate, and energetic about, and toward what ends do they exercise prudence and risk control? For these questions, we must explore Gorbachev's political beliefs.

GORBACHEV'S POLITICAL BELIEFS

Gorbachev's political rise was likely facilitated by his combination of demonstrated political reliability and personal dynamism, both in "selling" the system to external audiences and in experimenting with the system to make it work better. Indeed, these traits lent credibility to his claims, once appointed general secretary, that he would make the system realize its full potential. But what did he believe in? And why did he become a *reformist* general secretary?

There is considerable disagreement in the scholarly literature about Gorbachev's ideological commitments. Most of the debate, however, concerns how far Gorbachev's beliefs and attitudes evolved during his years as general secretary of the Central Committee of the CPSU. One view has it that, through a combination of domestic and international influences, he evolved by 1989–1990 into a social democrat and an anti-Leninist – akin, in these respects, to

---

[15] Palazchenko, *My Years*, p. 123.
[16] Dusko Doder and Louise Branson, *Gorbachev: Heretic in the Kremlin* (New York: Viking, 1990), p. 304.

the leadership of the Socialist Party of Spain.[17] A contrary view argues that he evolved into a "socialist democrat" akin to the Mensheviks of 1917, as opposed to having become a Bernsteinian socialist or a social democrat.[18] Still others view Gorbachev as either confused, bungling, or consistently despotic.[19]

There is less disagreement about Gorbachev's political and ideological commitments before he came to power in 1985. Gorbachev shared the sense of patriotic fervor that many members of his generation experienced in the wake of World War II and the period of reconstruction that followed. Thereafter, as he built his career, his views on policy were heavily influenced by Khrushchev's de-Stalinization campaign and by the widespread corruption and socioeconomic stagnation of the late-Brezhnev era.[20] Moreover, his travels in Eastern and Western Europe during the late 1960s exposed him to the relative opulence of the West – all the more so when compared to conditions in Stavropol[21] – while the invasion of Czechoslovakia in 1968 left him ambivalent about the wisdom and justice of suppressing the "Prague Spring."[22] These points of attraction and repulsion combined to make him susceptible to new ideas about how to reform the system – or how to assist the system to realize its potential – once he had a chance to make a difference in the late 1970s.[23]

According to associates and aides, by the early 1980s Gorbachev was already an anti-Stalinist and a reform communist who was convinced that the

---

[17] See Brown, *The Gorbachev Factor,* and Robert D. English, *Russia and the Idea of the West: Gorbachev, Intellectuals and the End of the Cold War* (New York: Columbia University Press, 2000).

[18] Ken Jowitt, *New World Disorder: The Leninist Extinction* (Berkeley: University of California Press, 1992), ch. 6; Stephen E. Hanson, *Time and Revolution: Marxism and the Design of Soviet Institutions* (Chapel Hill: University of North Carolina Press, 1997), ch. 6; D'Agostino, *Gorbachev's Revolution.*

[19] On Gorbachev as a despotic bungler who sought to strengthen the socialist system, not fundamentally transform it, see Donald Murray, *A Democracy of Despots* (Boulder, CO: Westview, 1995); on Gorbachev as a confused Leninist who sought to democratize socialism but had little idea how to do so, see Jerry F. Hough, *Democratization and Revolution in the USSR, 1985–1991* (Washington, DC: Brookings Institution, 1997).

[20] On this score, Hanson and Brown are in agreement (Hanson, *Time and Revolution,* p. 183; Brown, *The Gorbachev Factor,* pp. 39–41 and ch. 3). There are also incidents from Gorbachev's earlier years that reveal a streak of resentment against those who enjoyed undeserved privilege; see the incidents reported in D'Agostino, *Gorbachev's Revolution,* p. 53, and Sheehy, *The Man,* pp. 74–5.

[21] Dmitry Mikheyev, *The Rise and Fall of Gorbachev* (Indianapolis, IN: Hudson Institute, 1992), p. 32; Brown, *The Gorbachev Factor,* pp. 41–3.

[22] Brown, *The Gorbachev Factor,* p. 41; English, *Russia and the Idea,* pp. 181–2.

[23] Brown (*The Gorbachev Factor,* pp. 40–1) documents the ambivalence-enhancing impact of these revelations on Gorbachev's thinking. Moreover, in Stavropol Gorbachev participated in the resettlement of populations that had been deported by Stalin but were allowed by Khrushchev to return to their native lands (D'Agostino, *Gorbachev's Revolution,* p. 53).

Soviet system needed to change ("we cannot go on living in this way"[24]) but who imagined such change to be much more modest than the transformations he would eventually sponsor in the late 1980s.[25] Consistent with his upbringing within the Party apparatus, Gorbachev came to power believing that the root of most problems lay in corrupted cadres and that a necessary (though not sufficient) condition for solving most problems was the recruitment of uncorrupted cadres. He thought that reform would succeed and the system would realize its potential only if the right personnel were recruited into key positions in the Party apparatus.[26] According to his closest aide, Gorbachev's initial goal was to replace personnel and then to build "businesslike, comradely, and honest" relations within the Communist Party.[27] This vision required him to purge the corrupted cadres and mobilize the uncorrupted cadres by persuading them to join him in building a reformed Leninist political order. It called for restructuring authority relationships, though it did not anticipate the extent of restructuring that would be required to restore the legitimacy and effectiveness of the political order.

With respect to international relations, Gorbachev also shed some fundamental beliefs and predispositions of the Brezhnev era. Before he came to power, Gorbachev had already concluded that an end to the Cold War was a necessary condition for restoring the Soviet Union's health at home and prestige abroad, that Soviet foreign policy had to be demilitarized (including withdrawal from Afghanistan), that Soviet domination of Eastern Europe by military means had to end, and that the Soviet Union had to develop close ties with West European governments.[28] Moreover, he articulated a commitment to nonviolence as a principle of political order ("*nye streliat'*": "no more shooting"[29]) that would eventually have portentous consequences for his control of processes of change within Eastern Europe and the Soviet Union as well. It is doubtful that he was a committed pacifist, but he clearly much preferred that the renewal of socialism be based on persuasion and not on violence. Thus, rather than viewing Gorbachev as an "uncommitted thinker,"[30] it is more fruitful to think of him as starting his general secretaryship as an

---

[24] Cited in Brown, *The Gorbachev Factor*, p. 81.

[25] Ibid., ch. 3; Smith, *The New Russians*, pp. 68–72.

[26] Chernyaev, *Shest' let*, p. 123; Gorbachev, *Zhizn'*, vol. 1, pp. 286–92 (chapter entitled: "Cadres decide everything"); Boldin, *Krushenie*, pp. 45–7.

[27] Chernyaev, *Shest' let*, p. 23.

[28] For documentation, see English, *Russia and the Idea*, pp. 183–4, 194, 199–200.

[29] Andrei Grachev, *Kremlevskaia khronika* (Moscow: EKSMO, 1994), p. 113.

[30] Janice Gross Stein, "Political learning by doing: Gorbachev as uncommitted thinker and motivated learner," *International Organization*, vol. 48, no. 2 (Spring 1994), pp. 155–83.

anti-Stalinist, a "reform communist," and an anti-militarist who was already committed to creating a less militarized international order and a reformed socialist political order at home. Beyond that, the evidence suggests that Gorbachev was actively searching and feeling his way and was indeed a highly "motivated learner."[31]

Such beliefs were not incompatible with being an organization man who enjoyed good relations with his superiors. Many journalists, academics, and officials were "within-system" dissidents who had come to view Brezhnevism as an embarrassment and were searching for a reformist alternative. Khrushchev's de-Stalinization had been a formative experience for them, just as it was for Gorbachev. Moreover, the Marxist–Leninist tradition held out the vision of a one-party socialist democracy, which allowed these people to rationalize that (a) the alternative to Stalinism was not capitalism but rather reform Leninism and (b) "socialism" could be made consistent with procedural democracy.[32]

Gorbachev viewed the achievement of such a goal as requiring more than just organizational measures. It also required painstaking doctrinal justification. He placed great stock in the power of ideas, both oral and written, as a means of mobilizing support and demobilizing potential opponents. This reflected his education and belief in Marxism–Leninism, his training in legal studies, and his self-confidence as a debater. While a regional Party leader, he placed great stock in logical argumentation as a means of justifying policy choices. Colleagues in Stavropol recall his knowledge of Party history, the works of Lenin, and Marxism–Leninism.[33] In the first years of *perestroika*, Gorbachev again immersed himself in Lenin's works, which he re-read; he had a complete set of Lenin's works in his office and often read passages aloud to his chief of staff, V. Boldin. According to Boldin, Gorbachev believed that publications made possible the spreading of the word, which was crucial to progress: "he considered his words to be the main thing, one of the most important instruments of accomplishment (*metodov raboty*)."[34] But to Gorbachev this was more than just political justification; his attention to "the word" was also part of an active, intellectual search within the record of Lenin's last years for relevant truths about how to reform Soviet socialism.

---

[31] Ibid.

[32] For a book-length exposition of this thesis by one such within-system dissident, see Roy Medvedev, *On Socialist Democracy* (Nottingham, U.K.: Spokesman, 1977); a good source of insight into the reformist mentality in the Politburo after Gorbachev came to power is Chernyaev, *Shest' let*, passim.

[33] Brown, *The Gorbachev Factor*, pp. 31–2.

[34] Boldin, *Krushenie*, p. 12; also see pp. 132, 133, 293, 378.

As general secretary, Gorbachev edited and re-edited texts of articles and speeches with great passion. He devoted his vacation of August 1987 to completion of his book, *Perestroika: New Thinking for our Country and the World*.[35] As late as 1988, Gorbachev read transcripts of the first Party congresses after 1917 in connection with his desire to reorganize the apparatus.[36] Thus, Gorbachev sought political rhetoric that would provide compelling slogans, extended theoretical justification of policy changes, and a guide to programmatic development.

Gorbachev was not an impulsive or extemporaneous debater. He liked to mull issues; he developed his thoughts through contemplation, discussion, and writing. He searched constantly for evidence of success or failure in public policy and simultaneously searched for new theoretical formulations or generalizations to reconcile empirical reality with socialist theory. He was, then, a contemplative man who, by Leninist standards, kept an open mind and was eager to learn. He liked to go for long walks in the woods with his wife or his colleagues to talk about issues and develop his ideas.[37] When he visited Canada in 1983, during Andropov's time in power, Gorbachev abandoned the official program and spent hours talking with then-Ambassador Aleksandr Yakovlev about the future of Russia.[38] In both Stavropol and Moscow, Gorbachev sought out informed, cultured people – including foreigners – for extended discussions, during which he worked out his own ideas.[39] It was during a long stroll with Eduard Shevardnadze in 1984 that the two men came to agreement that "everything has gone rotten."[40]

Given his combination of idealism, optimism, energy, intelligence, demonstrated political reliability, and cautious, manipulative political tactics, Gorbachev was perhaps ideally suited to the task he set for himself: to break the Soviet Union out of the Brezhnevite mold at home and abroad before would-be opponents could mobilize to prevent him from doing so. It is more difficult to conceive of Boris Yeltsin successfully doing the same had he been general secretary in 1985–1987.

---

[35] New York: Harper & Row, 1988.

[36] Chernyaev, *Shest' let*, p. 223.

[37] In his memoirs, he credits nature with "forming" him and his views (Gorbachev, *Zhizn'*, vol. 1, p. 173; see also p. 172).

[38] Grachev, *Kremlevskaia*, p. 140; see also the documentation and discussion in English, *Russia and the Idea*, p. 184.

[39] Grachev, *Kremlevskaia*, pp. 177–8; English, *Russia and the Idea*, pp. 180–6.

[40] Brown, *The Gorbachev Factor*, p. 81; Carolyn McGiffert Ekedahl and Melvin A. Goodman, *The Wars of Eduard Shevardnadze* (University Park: Pennsylvania State University Press, 1997), p. 30.

YELTSIN'S POLITICAL PERSONALITY AND BELIEFS

In 1985, after he had been in power only a few months, Gorbachev brought to Moscow to work in the Central Committee apparatus a provincial Party leader, Boris Yeltsin, who had headed the Sverdlovsk Party organization, one of the largest in the country, for almost a decade. As we now know, neither Gorbachev nor most other members of the Politburo anticipated the trouble they were buying.[41]

Within the ranks of regional Party first secretaries in the late-Brezhnev era, several types of leaders could be found. The distinction was not generational. All of them, for reasons of either identity or material interests, shared a common commitment to the "leading role of the Party" in the political system. But beyond that, their political personalities diverged. Some, such as Grishin (Moscow) and Romanov (Leningrad), were the aristocrats of Brezhnevite infamy; they reflected and reinforced the personal corruption of the era and stood for continuity in policy. Others, such as Ligachev (Tomsk), were the puritans who found corruption to be shameful and who honed their skills on trying to crack down on corruption within their province. Still others, such as Bogomiakov (Tyumen), were technocratic in their orientation and sought to integrate rational, scientific expertise and orderly procedure into problem solving within their domains. And a few others, such as Shevardnadze of Georgia, were gutsy reformists who sought ways to decentralize aspects of the command system in order to devise a Party-led system that would be more efficient and more legitimate. The puritans, technocrats, and reformists would eventually part ways, but they all initially thought of themselves as opponents of corrupt Brezhnevism and as believers in *perestroika*.

Yeltsin had been first secretary of the Sverdlovsk Party organization since 1976. Before that, most of his professional life had been spent as a construction engineer and supervisor of construction projects. His love of construction comes through in his first autobiography and was clearly a passion of his during early adulthood.[42] There is no evidence that Yeltsin was corrupt

---

[41] Gorbachev's prime minister, Nikolai Ryzhkov, claims in his memoirs that he warned Gorbachev and Ligachev against appointing Yeltsin as first secretary of the Moscow city Party committee. According to Ryzhkov, he advised them about Yeltsin that "even though he is a builder, by his nature he is a destroyer" (Nikolai Ryzhkov, *Desiat' let velikikh potriasenii* [Moscow, 1995], p. 139). Ryzhkov had worked with Yeltsin for many years in Sverdlovsk.

[42] Boris Yeltsin, *Against the Grain: An Autobiography*, trans. by Michael Glenny (New York: Summit, 1990), pp. 43–56, 78–9, 108; for details of Yeltsin's work in construction, see Leon Aron, *Boris Yeltsin: A Revolutionary Life* (London: HarperCollins, 2000), ch. 2.

as Party leader in Sverdlovsk; like Ligachev, whose recommendation was the trigger for drawing him into the central Party apparatus, Yeltsin lived a relatively austere personal life and fought against political corruption. He used his powers as Party leader in Sverdlovsk to prosecute campaigns against corrupt members of the *nomenklatura* and some of the socioeconomic privileges they enjoyed. He thus combined the technical skills of a technocrat with the personal and political orientation so valued by the puritans.[43]

As for his accomplishments as local Party leader, the central Party leadership had every reason to expect that he would fulfill their hopes. His record during almost nine years as head of the Sverdlovsk *obkom* (provincial Party committee) indicated that he was a tough, effective taskmaster. Yeltsin himself referred to his leadership as analogous to that of a tsar, in total control of his province.[44] In dealing with officials, "[w]hether I was chairing a meeting, running my office, or delivering a report to a plenum – everything that one did was expressed in terms of pressure, threats, and coercion."[45]

Had this been all, Yeltsin might have satisfied Brezhnev but not Gorbachev and Ligachev. But there was more. He is said to have been relatively popular among the population of this large, important province. He is said to have improved the economic situation and the standard of living in Sverdlovsk province, pushing his subordinates hard but never asking them to work any harder than he – a workaholic's workaholic – was himself prepared to work. He was personally involved in supervising construction projects in the province, not defining his role as that of a paper-pusher. He lobbied the authorities in Moscow for large sums of money to fund major new projects in the province. He pressed for greater regional autonomy in industrial administration, so that campaigns for restructuring of enterprises could yield results.[46]

This was the CPSU's ideal of a leader: someone capable of effectively leading campaigns of *shturmovshchina* (storming) while gaining some popularity among the bulk of the population. Yeltsin apparently believed in the system

[43] See Aron, *Boris Yeltsin,* pp. 45–6, 86, 88, 104–5; Mikheyev, *Russia Transformed,* pp. 52–7; John Morrison, *Boris Yeltsin: From Bolshevik to Democrat* (New York: Dutton, 1991), pp. 31–42; Yeltsin, *Against the Grain,* pp. 43–70, 88–9. Yeltsin was also very fond of alcohol, which distinguished him from Ligachev. And Gorbachev cursed frequently during private discussions with aides, in contrast to Yeltsin. (Neither Gorbachev nor Yeltsin nor Ligachev was a smoker.) "Puritanism," as here used, merely means uncorrupted.

[44] Yeltsin, *Against the Grain,* p. 70; Boris Yeltsin, *The Struggle for Russia,* trans. by Catherine A. Fitzpatrick (New York: Random House, 1994), p. 179.

[45] Quoted in Morrison, *Boris Yeltsin,* p. 40.

[46] For documentation of the claims in this paragraph, see Aron, *Boris Yeltsin,* ch. 3.

and was skilled at making it work. In sum, he found ways of selectively over-coming "stagnation" without challenging the leading role of the Party.[47] This was the traditional ideal of the Party leader who was tough, bright, informed, relentless, and respected – except among the corrupt officials whom Yeltsin tried to purge. But presumably that was fine with Gorbachev and Ligachev, who shared this goal and who brought Yeltsin to Moscow and, eight months later, put him in charge of cleaning up corruption in the huge Moscow city Party organization.

Yeltsin also appeared to be politically reliable. His speeches as regional Party leader were often critical of central planning organs for paying insuf-ficient attention to regional needs.[48] But such was the case, more generally, with speeches by the most dynamic and influential regional first secretaries, including Gorbachev before he came to Moscow in 1978.[49] On politically sensitive issues, Yeltsin apparently toed the line – and then some. When an anthrax epidemic broke out in the province in April 1979, Yeltsin did an excel-lent job of preventing the outside world from learning of it.[50] When, in 1978, the Politburo ordered the bulldozing of the house in which the Tsar Nicholas and his family had been executed by the Bolsheviks in 1918, Yeltsin carried out the orders immediately, fully, and efficiently.[51] When the cultural intelli-gentsia pushed too far to circumvent the censors, Yeltsin cracked down.[52] In sum, there was no reason for the authorities in Moscow to believe that Yeltsin was a maverick or a loose cannon, much less a liberal.

Yeltsin's leadership style in Sverdlovsk was idiosyncratic for the region, and this could have caught the eye of the Central Committee apparatus. Re-searchers have found that, in contrast to his predecessors, he had an open style

---

[47] Studies of Yeltsin's earlier career that reach conclusions roughly equivalent to those in this paragraph include Aron, *Boris Yeltsin,* chs. 1–3, and Mikheyev, *Russia Transformed,* ch. 3. For a more critical view, see Pilar Bonet, "Lord of the manor: Boris Yeltsin in Sverdlovsk *oblast',"* Occasional Paper no. 260 (Washington, DC: Kennan Institute, 1995), p. 1, and Pilar Bonet, "Nevozmozhnaia Rossiia. Boris Yeltsin, provintsial v Kremlye," translated from the Spanish by G. Luk'ianova in *Ural* (Yekaterinburg), no. 4 (April 1994), pp. 24, 141.

[48] See Aron, *Boris Yeltsin,* pp. 60–78.

[49] For a content analysis of the speeches of regional Party leaders in the late 1970s, see George W. Breslauer, "Is there a generation gap in the Soviet political elite?" *Soviet Studies,* vol. 36, no. 1 (January 1984), pp. 1–25.

[50] Aron, *Boris Yeltsin,* pp. 52–3.

[51] Ibid., pp. 111–13.

[52] Ibid., pp. 118–25; for other examples of Yeltsin's political conformism in those days, see Yu. M. Baturin, A. L. Il'in, V. F. Kadatskii, V. V. Kostikov, M. A. Krasnov, A. Ya. Livshits, K. F. Nikiforov, L. G. Pikhoia, and G. A. Satarov, *Epokha Yel'tsina: Ocherki politicheskoi istorii* (Moscow: Vagrius, 2001), pp. 38, 40.

of leadership: he met regularly with groups and held lengthy, candid question-and-answer sessions with them. He addressed the public regularly on local television. During the Andropov era, he led "raids" on local retail stores to force them to expose hoarded goods and release them for public purchase. He often came to work by public transportation, not always using the limousines available to regional Party first secretaries.[53] None of this, however, would necessarily have alarmed members of the Politburo who were considering him for promotion. As long as Yeltsin remained in firm control of his region, maintained social stability, and fulfilled the economic Plan, then an open, accessible style of leadership was a plus, for it demonstrated that Party leadership could simultaneously be exacting, effective, and, if not popular, at least respected. Yeltsin's use of public transportation both reinforced his anti-corruption campaign and muted popular resentment of Party privileges. Indeed, Gorbachev himself, when head of the Stavropol Party organization, frequently walked to work.[54]

Some questions might have been raised by a glance at Yeltsin's résumé. He had never served as a second-in-command. In Mikheyev's opinion, Yeltsin's meteoric rise within the Party organization "allowed him to skip a critically important part of the process of integration into the Party's organizational culture: he was never forced to adopt the humiliating posture of total submissiveness and the denigrating requirement to please one's superiors by all possible means."[55] This, according to Mikheyev, allowed him to retain both some independence of mind and some self-confidence and identity,[56] which may have been one of the roots of Yeltsin's maverick qualities in Gorbachev's Politburo. But assuming it was noticed by those considering his promotion in 1984–1985, it would not necessarily have raised eyebrows. For the new Soviet leaders were looking for uncorrupted and talented officials who could improve and selectively reform the system without challenging its essential features. They were not looking for Brezhnevite aristocrats, whose independence of mind and initiative (if they ever possessed them) had been fully ground down

---

[53] Mikheyev, *Russia Transformed,* p. 56; Vladimir Solovyov and Elena Klepikova, *Boris Yeltsin: A Political Biography* (New York: Putnam, 1992), pp. 152–4; Aron, *Yeltsin,* pp. 79–92. Yeltsin's chief of staff during 1993–1995 reports in his memoir that he saw a television program about Yeltsin during his years as Party leader in Sverdlovsk province in which Yeltsin came across as a loyal Party functionary, but even then he "exhibited a kind of openness, energy, and good knowledge of the subject about which he spoke freely" (Sergei Filatov, *Sovershenno nesekretno* [Moscow: Vagrius, 2000], pp. 421–2).

[54] Donald Morrison (Ed.), *Mikhail S. Gorbachev: An Intimate Biography* (New York: Time, 1988), p. 98.

[55] Mikheyev, *Russia Transformed,* p. 57.

[56] Ibid., p. 58.

by the Party's personnel mechanisms. The fact that Yeltsin had a background that prevented him from becoming complacent and corrupt would have been viewed as an asset; it was not necessarily a sign that he would become a disruptive force within the Politburo.

What the central Party leaders probably did not know was that Yeltsin had other personality traits that, when combined with his lack of submissiveness, would indeed make him a loose cannon. Yeltsin was impulsive, temperamental, easy to offend, and very sensitive to slights. He did not imagine himself just a construction engineer who had become a Party boss; he thought of himself as a turnaround artist, capable of undertaking wholesale cleanup operations that would break most men. When momentous results were not forthcoming, Yeltsin became frustrated and angry.[57]

Moreover, and more seriously, Yeltsin chafed in positions of subordination and was upset, as Sverdlovsk Party leader, that his peers (Gorbachev and Ligachev) had risen farther and faster within the Party apparatus than he had. He admitted as much in his first autobiography, written and published in 1990.[58] Central Party leaders would not have known, in 1984, just how resentful he was on this score. Nor would they have known that when Central Committee secretary Ligachev had earlier come to visit Sverdlovsk for an inspection tour, Yeltsin had to exit the car in which they were riding together in order to contain his rage at Ligachev's demeaning questions about why things allegedly were not done in Sverdlovsk the way Ligachev had done them in Tomsk. Yeltsin summoned his deputy in the car behind them to take his place in the car with Ligachev, lest Yeltsin say or do something impulsive.[59] None of this boded well for Yeltsin's containing his emotions in Moscow and being a team player.[60]

In addition to being impulsive and impatient, Yeltsin had been a risk-taker – indeed, a risk-seeker – all his life. It may not be an exaggeration to say that he was genetically programmed for risk, and developmentally he became addicted to it. His brother Mikhail wrote that Boris always "lived on the edge

---

[57] On Yeltsin's self-image, see Yeltsin, *Against the Grain*, pp. 76–80, 108–10, 114, 118–25, 231.

[58] Ibid., pp. 72–3.

[59] Bonet, "Nevozmozhnaia Rossiia," pp. 105–6; presumably Ligachev did not learn of this, because John Morrison reports that Ligachev was extremely enthusiastic about Yeltsin when he returned to Moscow (Morrison, *Boris Yeltsin*, p. 42). Aron (*Yeltsin*, pp. 116–17) reports on something like this incident but does not have Yeltsin exiting the car – just grinding his teeth.

[60] A source that cannot be cited also told me that, when Yeltsin was in Texas in 1989, he became so angry at something said by his American host that he ordered the chauffeur to stop the car, exited it in the middle of the ride, and began running down the street to contain his anger. An analogous example is found in Yeltsin's walking out of a televised interview with Leslie Stahl in Moscow in June 1992 (Associated Press, June, 1992).

of possibilities."[61] Yeltsin's first two autobiographies are littered with examples, from early childhood through 1993, of his inclination to live on the edge. His risk-seeking did not find expression in the technological realm: as a construction engineer, he engaged in careful study before tackling complex tasks. Rather, it found expression in his personal and political life. Yeltsin reports several instances of his talking back to hierarchical superiors during the Stalin era and getting away with it.[62] As a child of only 11 years, he claims to have used the primary school graduation ceremony to denounce publicly a teacher who, he felt, was treating the students unfairly.[63]

Yeltsin's adventuresome spirit often led him into close brushes with death and, in a few cases, with political ruin. As a child, he insisted on trying to defuse a hand grenade that he and his friends had stolen from an ammunition depot. As his friends stood back at his insistence, he handled the grenade; it exploded and blew off two of his fingers.[64] I count nineteen such incidents in the two autobiographies, not all of them quite as dramatic but several of them equally so.[65] Even if some of the stories are apocryphal, no literature on Yeltsin has attempted to refute the general pattern. Someone who has led this kind of life and always survived close brushes develops an enormous confidence in his survival capacities, if he did not have it to begin with. That confidence, in turn, further fuels the inclination to succumb to impulse and to continue taking risks. In the case of Yeltsin, it even led him to believe in his own predestination: "It always seems as if someone is rescuing me. I've even begun to believe that I'm under some mysterious protection."[66]

Many of Yeltsin's traits were not unique to him among post-Stalinist leaders. Indeed, they bore some striking resemblances to Nikita Khrushchev. Khrushchev was also a risk-taker (though not a self-destructive one). Khrushchev also had an impulsive streak and was hugely impatient to see results. He too was temperamental and very sensitive to slights. Indeed, more than many

---

[61] Mikheyev, *Russia Transformed,* p. 66.

[62] Yeltsin, *Against the Grain,* pp. 27, 50, 53.

[63] Ibid., p. 27.

[64] Ibid., p. 29.

[65] Ibid., pp. 22, 29, 36, 45, 46, 47, 258–9; Yeltsin, *The Struggle for Russia,* pp. 30, 46–7, 61, 93, 117–19, 191–2, 194, 195–6, 239.

[66] Yeltsin, *The Struggle for Russia,* p. 197 (see also pp. 84, 120, 142, 193, 205, 211); Yeltsin, *Against the Grain,* pp. 19, 154, 162. In his most recent memoir, published nine months after he resigned from the presidency, Yeltsin writes that, in a golf cart, "I like to zoom downhill and aim for a tree, then turn at the last moment. That's how I relax" (Boris Yeltsin, *Midnight Diaries* [New York: Public Affairs, 2000], p. 311). It is doubtful that, in his present physical condition, Yeltsin engages in this practice; his use of the present tense in this passage more than strains credulity.

others in the late-Stalinist Politburo, Khrushchev chafed under the humiliation of Stalin's rule, though he was astute enough not to risk his life by challenging the despot. And Khrushchev, too, proved to be a loose cannon in the post-Stalin leadership, first in launching his anti-Stalin campaign and later in reacting to the frustration of his program. Eventually, his capriciousness cost him his job. The difference was that, in the 1950s and early 1960s, Khrushchev was on top, while in the 1980s, Yeltsin was a junior member of Gorbachev's Politburo.[67]

Ironically, Gorbachev, who was on top in the 1980s, was haunted by the prospect that, if he moved too fast with his reforms, he might suffer Khrushchev's fate and be forced out of office. It appears not to have occurred to him that a man with some of Khrushchev's personality traits and perspectives would join the leadership team and complicate his own political life – precisely because Gorbachev's caution, embraced to avoid Khrushchev's fate, so frustrated the neo-Khrushchevian, Yeltsin!

In addition to being of almost identical age, Yeltsin shared with Gorbachev a number of personality traits: enormous energy, passion, intensity, self-confidence, egocentrism, workaholic tendencies, and a highly retentive memory. He also shared Gorbachev's disillusionment with Brezhnevism and his urge to improve the socialist system, initially by purging corrupt cadres. Both men were provincials of peasant background, men whose families had suffered greatly during collectivization and the Great Terror and who were offended by corruption and unearned privilege. Both came from austere backgrounds – Yeltsin more so than Gorbachev – but made their careers by dint of extraordinarily hard work.[68] As regional Party leaders, both men were

---

[67] Reading in Aron's book about Yeltsin's style of leadership in Sverdlovsk, I am struck by other parallels with Khrushchev: (1) Yeltsin's leadership of construction projects (Aron, *Yeltsin*, p. 31) is reminiscent of Khrushchev's hands-on, no-nonsense, workaholic style in supervising construction of the Moscow subway in the 1930s (see William J. Tompson, *Khrushchev: A Political Life* [London: St. Martin's, 1995], ch. 2); (2) both men abhorred leadership "from the desk," wanting to get personally involved in the construction (Aron, p. 38; Tompson, p. 45); (3) both men sought to strengthen the disciplinary responsibility of the work collective and the effect of collective material rewards (Aron, p. 67; George W. Breslauer, *Khrushchev and Brezhnev as Leaders* [London: Allen & Unwin, 1982], chs. 2, 4); (4) Yeltsin put forth a proposal for the regional deconcentration of industry during the Brezhnev era that was strikingly similar to Khrushchev's *sovnarkhoz* scheme of 1957 (Aron, p. 76 – Aron remarks on this parallel with Khrushchev); and (5) both men were quick to blame local officials for setbacks and to call immediately for their dismissal (Aron, p. 83; Breslauer, *Khrushchev and Brezhnev*, chs. 3, 6).

[68] Indeed, they both wore (and wore out) only one suit throughout their college years, which in both cases ended with graduation in 1955. But Gorbachev grew up in better material conditions than Yeltsin. The Stavropol *krai* is part of the productive Black Earth (*chernozem*)

ambitious, hard-working, relatively uncorrupted, and innovative in devising local experiments that might improve the operations of the local economy and that might also (they claimed) fruitfully be generalized to the national economy.[69] Both men devised a more populist, consultative style of leadership of their provinces than was standard under Brezhnev. And, of course, both men had to temper their dissatisfactions by engaging in the dissimulation and doublespeak that were requisites for political survival.

But beyond all this, the two men diverged. One type of divergence was in their educational and career paths. Gorbachev had been on a "political" track during his college years, whereas Yeltsin was on an engineering track. Gorbachev studied ideology in great depth and with seeming belief in the genius of the Marxist–Leninist tradition. Yeltsin focused his learning on the concrete engineering tasks of the construction trades, studying Marxism–Leninism only insofar as required by the curriculum or by his later application for Party membership.[70] Both men came to be skeptical of received wisdoms that did not accord with the realities they witnessed around them; Gorbachev was fond of quoting to his classmates the Hegelian notion that "truth is concrete." But Gorbachev's mind was geared toward melding empirical observations with the discovery of abstract theoretical generalizations about the system as a whole, whereas Yeltsin's was geared toward the discovery of everyday, scientific, and administrative practices that would solve concrete problems.

Gorbachev sought out Komsomol and Communist Party membership at the earliest moments of eligibility, whereas Yeltsin had to be approached by the Party when he reached the limit of upward mobility within his trade beyond which advancement required that one be a member of the Party. Hence, though he was born in the same year as Gorbachev, Yeltsin joined the Party nine years later than had Gorbachev (1961 versus 1952). Yeltsin worked in construction for thirteen years after university before being recruited into the

---

region. The Urals, where Yeltsin grew up, are significantly poorer. In addition, by virtue of being in the village – and having a grandfather who was the collective farm chairman – Gorbachev's family had better access to food than Yeltsin's. It may or may not be indicative, but if one looks at Yeltsin's photographs as a teen-ager and college student at Ural Polytechnic, he is tall but thin as a stick. In contrast, Gorbachev in photographs from his college years begins to acquire a pudgy round face; note the contrast between the earlier pictures and his engagement photograph with Raisa in Sheehy's *The Man*. For Yeltsin's photographs, see the Russian version of Yeltsin's last autobiography, *Prezidentskii marafon* (Moscow: AST, 2000). I am grateful to Ilya Vinkovetsky for drawing my attention to this contrast.

[69] Compare Brown, *The Gorbachev Factor* (pp. 45–6) with Aron, *Boris Yeltsin* (pp. 64–9, 75–6).

[70] Yeltsin's former advisors and associates write: "A builder by profession, he sought out projects that could yield tangible and possibly quick results. He was little interested in theory or abstract discussions on general themes" (Baturin et al., *Epokha*, p. 803).

Party apparatus; even then, he spent his first eight years within the apparatus supervising construction in the province. He did not assume a nonspecialist rank within the Party apparatus until 1976, when he was catapulted into the position of first secretary of the regional Party organization. Gorbachev, by contrast, joined the Komsomol and then the Communist Party apparatus almost immediately after graduating from the university, and he worked his way up each hierarchy almost entirely in political generalist (rather than economic specialist) positions.

One of the most striking differences between the biographies of Gorbachev and Yeltsin lies in the timing of their exposure to international, cosmopolitan influences. One might refer to this as the timing of their "deprovincialization." Gorbachev came to Moscow in 1950, at the age of 19, and spent the next five years exposed to the culture of the capital and to students from Eastern Europe. Yeltsin did not leave the provinces for any extended period of residence until 1985, when he was 54 years of age!

Whether for reasons of nurture or nature, the two men's personalities and mentalities also differed considerably in ways that would influence the choices they made as leaders in Moscow. Yeltsin's impatience, impulsiveness, envy, and sensitivity to slight made him an unpredictable force within the Gorbachev Politburo. Nobody who has studied Gorbachev attributes such traits to him. Whereas Yeltsin was a demanding and at times brutish "boss" by temperament, Gorbachev was more comfortable accepting criticism from his subordinates and associates. Whereas Yeltsin was a provincial who was eager to learn new technical skills, Gorbachev was a would-be cosmopolitan who was eager to expand his understanding of the world beyond the borders of the USSR.[71] Yeltsin was by temperament a risk-seeker; Gorbachev, though not averse to risk, was more cautious. It is hard to imagine Yeltsin fashioning for himself the cautious political strategies that Gorbachev devised as general secretary had Yeltsin, not Gorbachev, become Party leader in 1985. Yeltsin's personality and mentality were better suited to the role of angry and utterly determined revolutionary hero, which he adopted in 1988–1989 and pursued until he had helped to bring down both Gorbachev and the system that Gorbachev was trying to construct.

CONCLUSION

I began this book by noting that its central focus is the authority-building and authority-maintenance strategies of Gorbachev and Yeltsin as they sought

---

[71] See English, *Russia and the Idea*, p. 330, fns. 112–13.

variously to reform, transform, destroy, and replace the Soviet system. Strategies are the means by which leaders seek to stretch the social constraints in their environment, both to realize their visions of social progress and to secure their credibility as effective problem solvers and politicians. The choices that leaders make are, in part, a function of how they define their visions and how they calculate the malleability of constraints on the realization of those visions. But those choices are also products of their attitudes toward conflict, risk, and compromise.

The choice of a political strategy is not a one-time thing; strategies vary over the course of a leader's administration. During the stage of political succession, political conflict is intense and rivals jockey for position. This constrains a competitor's choices to those that seem most likely to win the power struggle – to the extent that he is able to predict which strategy will be a winning one. During a leader's stage of ascendancy, he tends to have greater room for political maneuver and greater latitude to allow his personal preferences and predispositions to reshape his program. During the stage of decline, the leader is embattled but approaches this struggle from a position of ascendancy and relative strength when compared to his political leverage during the earlier stage of struggle for succession. Personal factors loom large in determining the choices a leader makes for how to combat the decline in his authority.

Though both Gorbachev and Yeltsin grew up within the Soviet system and though both believed in the "leading role of the Party" until at least 1987, their personalities and political mentalities differed in significant ways. In Chapter 11, I will address how these idiosyncratic factors influenced the ways in which each man exercised power and leadership.

3

The Rise of Gorbachev

The formal context of Soviet politics had not changed significantly by the time Gorbachev came to power in March 1985. He was chosen general secretary by a secret vote of the Politburo with consultative input from some of the most influential regional Party leaders in the Central Committee.[1] The reigning ideology remained Marxism–Leninism, and the audiences for authority-building strategies remained the elite representatives of the institutional pillars of the system. The short-term material interests and political identities of patrons and clients within those institutions remained essentially as they had been for decades. For these reasons, quite a few observers – while intrigued by the prospect of a young and articulate general secretary – did not harbor very high hopes that he would be inclined or able to transform the system. He was, after all, a product of that system and a man who had been chosen for advancement by the aged guardians of the Leninist system. If Suslov, Brezhnev, and Andropov could all endorse his meteoric rise into the highest reaches of power, how much of a free thinker could he possibly be?

What *had* changed, however, was the climate of opinion within the Soviet political establishment. That climate was quite different from the one that prevailed at the time of Khrushchev's ouster and was, in many ways, analogous to the one that had prevailed at the time of Stalin's death. Both 1953 and 1985 were marked by a widespread sense within the Politburo and Central Committee that something had to give, that things could not continue in the old way. Each period was marked by a collective loss of self-confidence about

[1] Archie Brown, *The Gorbachev Factor* (New York: Oxford University Press, 1996), pp. 82–8; Jerry F. Hough, *Democratization and Revolution in the USSR, 1985–1991* (Washington, DC: Brookings Institution, 1997), pp. 76–9.

the elite's ability to sustain enforcement of its formula for domination.[2] In both eras, there was a widespread sense that the main trajectory of both foreign and domestic policy was leading the country into a cul-de-sac or worse. Many officials in both periods feared domestic unrest if the situation were allowed to fester. In the 1950s and also in the 1980s, the Politburo and Central Committee were gripped by a sense of imminent threat from abroad. In both periods, many officials experienced not just a sense of fear but also a sense of bewilderment or embarrassment at the stagnation – both economic and ideological – into which the country had lapsed. In sum, in both periods a *negative consensus* prevailed within the political establishment: a widespread view that things could not continue as they had, that new approaches to solving problems were needed. Even though there was no positive consensus in either period as to the preferability of any set of alternative policies (other than a consensus in 1953 that the regime needed to deliver a higher standard of living to the populace), there was a growing sense of urgency about the need to "get the country moving again." In 1982 (after the death of Brezhnev) and again in 1984 (after the death of Andropov), the Old Guard held off this sentiment. By 1985, enough of them had departed the scene that the sentiment could prevail.[3]

Of course, more than thirty years separated the two successions; we would expect many things to have changed in the interim. There was no "Stalin question" in 1985, no need to demystify the exalted authority of the previous leader as a precondition for breaking with his policies. Likewise, there was no collective yearning to rein in the Party leader in order to avoid repetition of a murderous regime. In 1985 there was rather a sense of the need for vigorous leadership to push the country in new directions. Another difference

---

[2] I first advanced this proposition regarding 1985 in George W. Breslauer, "How do you sell a concessionary foreign policy?" *Post-Soviet Affairs*, vol. 10, no. 3 (July–September 1994), p. 280; it is also argued in Hough, *Democratization and Revolution*, p. 15. See also Paul Hollander, *Political Will and Personal Belief: The Decline and Fall of Soviet Communism* (New Haven, CT: Yale University Press, 2000).

[3] For good examples of these sentiments among men who would be leading members of Gorbachev's Politburo or leading aides to the general secretary, see Anatolii Chernyaev, *Shest' let s Gorbachevym* (Moscow: Progress, 1993), pp. 10–13, 27–9, 31–2, 55–6, 62–3; Nikolai Ryzhkov, *Perestroika: Istoriia predatel'stv* (Moscow: Novosti, 1992), p. 42; Nikolai Ryzhkov, *Desiat' let velikikh potriasenii* (Moscow: Assotsiatsiia "Kniga. Prosviashchenie. Miloserdie," 1995), pp. 42–6; Yegor Ligachev, *Inside Gorbachev's Kremlin: The Memoirs of Yegor Ligachev* (New York: Pantheon, 1993), pp. 15–16, 35. These men display a common alienation from the Brezhnev legacy, though specific points of alienation differed among them, as did their emotional reactions. Chernyaev, for example, emphasizes the shame and humiliation he experienced. Ryzhkov emphasizes his disgust with the Brezhnev administration's blocking of economic reform; Ligachev emphasizes his disgust with corruption among cadres.

was cognitive, as three decades of experimentation in domestic and foreign policies had led to a good deal of individual and collective learning about the feasibility of policies and programs. To solve the dilemmas in domestic and foreign relations, programs that had "sold" in the 1950s could not credibly be sold to the bulk of the political elite in the 1980s – just as programs successfully sold in the 1980s could not have been sold in the 1950s. A leader who tried to build his authority in 1985 by promising to achieve grandiose visions of rapid progress toward the "full and final victory of communism" at home and abroad would probably have been met by skepticism at best and by derisive laughter at worst.

By the mid-1980s, Stalin's successors had already attempted many variants of "minor reform" of the Soviet command economy, but to little effect. They had tried varied methods of improving the agricultural situation, except for genuine decentralization of authority – again to little effect. The pace of economic growth had slowed to a crawl, and in some sectors had reached zero- or negative-growth levels. Soviet leaders had achieved several "détentes" with the United States, but all had unraveled. They had built a huge military establishment but still were not being treated as an equal by the United States in global affairs. They had achieved nuclear parity but now were threatened by Ronald Reagan's Strategic Defense Initiative ("Star Wars"). Their alliance system had expanded to many corners of the globe, but it was embattled and very costly. After the Vietnam War, it appeared that the United States had lost the initiative in world affairs, only to manage a resurgence under Reagan. The vaunted Soviet Army was mired in Afghanistan, taking heavy losses.

Loss of self-confidence is a mood. A sense that things cannot continue in the old way, and that old visions of progress have been discredited as unworkable, are negative lessons. Moods and negative lessons do not lead logically to specific solutions for malaise. Indeed, given the diversity of material interests within the Soviet political establishment, we would expect no easy consensus to form on how to overcome the crisis. Most officials had few concrete ideas about what was likely to make the system as a whole deliver the goods more reliably. As is so often the case in such circumstances of collective insecurity and uncertainty, they were looking for leadership. Gorbachev promised to provide it.

Behind the scenes during Brezhnev's years in power, much searching for viable alternatives to both Khrushchevian utopianism and Brezhnevite conservatism – some of it published underground owing to censorship – took place among reformist intellectuals in the academic and journalistic worlds. Reformist experiments in domestic and foreign policy that had taken place sporadically under Khrushchev, that had been advocated unsuccessfully by

Brezhnev's prime minister (Aleksei Kosygin), and that had improved the Hungarian economy in the 1970s helped to keep alive and legitimize the vision of a "renewed socialism" and a workable East–West accommodation.[4] Gorbachev heard of these discussions and sought to tap into them privately when he was promoted to the position of Central Committee secretary in late 1978. His mentality was open-minded and empirically oriented, seeking to absorb experiences that might work better than had Brezhnev's policies (see Chapter 2). He had been attentive and receptive to events in Eastern Europe and to the lessons of Eurocommunism. His learning was steadily advanced by consultations with reformist specialists as he rose within the leadership between 1978 and 1982. Once exposed to data about the real state of the economy in the early 1980s, he agreed with Eduard Shevardnadze in 1984 that "[e]verything has gone rotten."[5] He told his wife on the eve of assuming the general secretaryship that "we cannot go on living in this way."[6]

But Gorbachev was more than just an amateur scientist seeking solutions to societal problems. He was also a politician on the rise. The two roles merged with urgency after Brezhnev died in 1982 and a series of political successions raised the stakes associated with expressing new ideas. As he aspired to become general secretary, he would have to think about solutions that he could sell politically and that would build his authority – his legitimacy and credibility – as a leader.

A democratic socialist vision at home, combined with an accommodationist strategy abroad, was only one of several approaches that had not yet been tried and discredited in the USSR. One alternative to radical reformism treated the main problem as a moral one: the extensive corruption of Soviet officialdom during the Brezhnev years. The solution appeared to be a policy of replacing corrupt personnel with a new cohort of uncorrupted cadres. Doing so would require a certain measure of *glasnost'* in order to train the public spotlight on the problem and enlist the public in campaigns to expose corrupt bureaucrats. The traditional Party "aristocracy" of the Brezhnev years would

---

[4] For analyses of the published discussions of alternatives, see Elizabeth Valkenier, *The Soviet Union and the Third World: An Economic Bind* (New York: Praeger, 1983); Jerry F. Hough, *The Struggle for the Third World: Soviet Debates and American Options* (Washington, DC: Brookings Institution, 1986); Franklyn Griffiths, "The sources of American conduct: Soviet perspectives and their policy implications," *International Security,* vol. 9, no. 1 (Fall 1984), pp. 30–50; Matthew Evangelista, *Unarmed Warriors: The Transnational Movement to End the Cold War* (Ithaca, NY: Cornell University Press, 1999).

[5] Brown, *The Gorbachev Factor,* p. 81; Carolyn McGiffert Ekedahl and Melvin A. Goodman, *The Wars of Eduard Shevardnadze* (University Park: Pennsylvania State University Press, 1997), p. 30.

[6] Brown, *The Gorbachev Factor,* p. 81.

be replaced by Cromwellian puritans who would no longer use public office for private material gain. The traditional Red Directors, or at least those corrupted by the Brezhnevite experience, would be replaced by honest and efficient technocrats whose rise to positions of authority had been partially frustrated in the 1970s. Under this alliance of puritans (such as Party secretary Yegor Ligachev) and technocrats (such as Prime Minister Nikolai Ryzhkov), more decisionmaking responsibility could be devolved to lower levels of the administrative hierarchy without fear that it would be abused. As a result, the economy would be managed more effectively and more productively, authentic social and work discipline would be enhanced, and hence the authority of the CPSU would rise. This was the approach that had been championed by Yuri Andropov during his short time as general secretary. It is the approach (and the man) lauded by both Ryzhkov and Ligachev in their memoirs.[7]

In foreign relations, one alternative to an East–West accommodation was the exploitation of Soviet nuclear capability to convince the West of the need to "do business" with the USSR on equal terms. This would have been a confrontational variant of the strategy of "offensive détente" that had informed Brezhnev's strategy in East–West relations. But to those who concluded that Brezhnev's approach had proven unworkable, there remained an alternative to confrontation: retrenchment from Soviet positions of overextension abroad. This was a feasible alternative to continuing in the old way. It required finding a way to get out of Afghanistan, even if the goals of the invasion had not been achieved. It required a reduction of commitments to Third World allies, and to some allies within the world communist movement, in order to bring Soviet global policy more into line with a newfound appreciation of the limits of Soviet capability. It entailed exploitation of the potential of the peace movement in Western Europe and North America, in the hope that these societies would force their leaders unilaterally to stop building and deploying new missiles and space-based weapons systems. In fact, these were the policies followed by Yuri Andropov during his fifteen months at the helm (November 1982–February 1984).[8]

Nor would this approach necessarily be vulnerable to the charge that it was antithetical to the Soviet tradition. Throughout Soviet history, there had been periods when the leadership had opted for a "breathing spell" in its global offensive in order to consolidate gains and attend to domestic problems.

---

[7] Ryzhkov, *Desiat' let,* pp. 43, 186, 188; Ligachev, *Inside Gorbachev's Kremlin,* pp. 16–17, 27–30, 51–2. Hough, *Democratization and Revolution,* also invokes the concepts of "puritans" and "technocrats," albeit in passing.

[8] Ryzhkov (*Desiat' let,* p. 50) also praises some of these features of Andropov's foreign policies.

Likewise, the strategy of playing upon contradictions within the imperialist camp (and among forces within capitalist countries) had a long pedigree in Soviet history.

Thus, while acknowledging that both Khrushchev and Brezhnev had promised far more than they could deliver, the anti-accommodationist and anti-liberal forces within the Soviet Politburo and Central Committee could credibly claim to possess alternative visions that had not yet been discredited. Those who had least credibility within this context were the "stand-patters": traditional Brezhnevites (such as Party secretaries Grigorii Romanov, Viktor Grishin, and Vladimir Shcherbitsky) who protected their material interests and pretended that things could indeed continue in the old way. The strength of those material interests and Leninist identities within the Central Committee and Politburo was such that Gorbachev would be chosen general secretary only after two other successors to Brezhnev (Yuri Andropov and Konstantin Chernenko) had died in office. Obviously, during the early 1980s, radical reform was not perceived to be the only alternative to Brezhnevism.

IN ANTICIPATION OF POLITICAL SUCCESSION

When Gorbachev was chosen general secretary in March 1985, Foreign Minister Andrei Gromyko, in his nomination speech, is said to have described him as a man with "a nice smile but iron teeth."[9] The implication was that Gorbachev was a new, more flexible, kind of leader – but no fool. He could hold his own with the best of them, at home and abroad. He would be able to get the country moving again without sacrificing core interests or values of the system. Little did Gromyko know that ultimately Gorbachev would falsify that prediction. At the time, however, Gorbachev may not have known it, either.

During the first year and a half that Gorbachev was in power, he presented himself as much the kind of leader that Gromyko had suggested. He did not conceal the fact that he stood for breaking with the old way of doing things. But he did so gingerly as he built his power base and forced the retirement of more leaders among the Brezhnevite stand-patters.

Domestic Policy and Politics

Members of the Politburo, as well as leading members of the Central Committee, knew that Gorbachev had been consulting and consorting with radical

---

[9] Dusko Doder in *The Washington Post* (March 17, 1985). Hough claims that this remark attributed to Gromyko may have been the product of a mere rumor (Hough, *Democratization and Revolution*, p. 77).

reformist academics and journalists during his years in Moscow.[10] They also knew that, in his years as head of the Stavropol province Party organization, he had sponsored some innovative measures for reorganizing economic production at the provincial level.[11] But they had little reason to suspect at the time that he would eventually sponsor a complete overhaul of the system. For Gorbachev was also correctly perceived as someone who had played by the Leninist rules of the game for decades. His speeches during 1976–1981 had been unexceptional by contemporary standards.[12] In rising from a provincial position to one in Moscow, Gorbachev had been sponsored – and thereby vouched for – by the likes of Suslov and Andropov, who were among the most influential members of the Old Guard. His speeches as a Politburo member from 1980 until late 1984 had not gone much beyond the policy consensus prevalent at the time, which was consistent with an Andropovite experimental approach to improving the performance of the economy and replacing corrupt cadres.[13] Moreover, he had reinforced the image of being a team player by properly biding his time after the death of Andropov and not contesting the choice of a stand-patter, Konstantin Chernenko, as general secretary.[14] Puritans and technocrats in the Central Committee also knew him

---

[10] Robert D. English, *Russia and the Idea of the West* (New York: Columbia University Press, 2000), p. 183.

[11] Brown, *The Gorbachev Factor*, pp. 45–7.

[12] A content analysis of speeches and published articles by provincial Party leaders in the RSFSR during 1976–1981 showed the post-Stalin generation of officials to be divided between those who made very few demands for change (less so even than their counterparts in the older generation of such leaders) and those who were very much more demanding and impatient in their rhetoric than all others. On this scale, Gorbachev (like Yeltsin) was in the latter group but had one of the lower scores within that group; notably, his rhetoric was demanding in content but not impatient in style. He did not stand out in any way. See George W. Breslauer, "Is there a generation gap in the Soviet political establishment: Demand articulation by RSFSR provincial Party first secretaries," *Soviet Studies*, vol. 36, no. 1 (January 1984), pp. 1–25. On other indicators, such as innovations introduced in Stavropol province or his muted advocacy of the decentralized link (*zvenevaia*) system in Soviet agriculture in the late 1970s (Brown, *The Gorbachev Factor*, pp. 45–6), Gorbachev comes across as experimental but not iconoclastic, much less strident, which is consistent with his placement in my content analysis of speeches. On Yeltsin's published demands of the center while Party leader in Sverdlovsk, see Leon Aron, *Boris Yeltsin: A Revolutionary Life* (London: HarperCollins, 2000), ch. 3.

[13] Hough (*Democratization and Revolution*, pp. 73–4) argues that Gorbachev's ceremonial speech of April 22, 1983, on the anniversary of Lenin's birth, was iconoclastic in presenting "an unmistakable endorsement of Lenin's New Economic Policy (NEP) and was followed by his ideas about taking objective economic laws more firmly into account … [and about] a skillful use of money–goods relations." Yet at that time Andropov was general secretary and the speech was quite consistent with suggestions found in the general secretary's published addresses. It would certainly have been compatible with laying the groundwork for a program modeled on Chinese or Hungarian reforms, which Andropov is said to have been considering at the time (Hough, *Democratization and Revolution*, p. 96–7).

[14] Brown, *The Gorbachev Factor*, p. 69.

to be both uncorrupted by Brezhnevite standards and a competent adminis-
trator, hence someone who fit their mold. In sum, Gorbachev projected the
image (whether manipulatively or not) of someone who could lead without
being overly threatening to core interests and identities within the political
establishment. He could advance new goals without threatening cherished
traditional values.[15]

But the question of the day was: Which traditional values were the most
cherished? The basic Leninist heritage, with its emphasis on the leading role
of the Party? Or the more recent opportunities for the *nomenklatura* to en-
rich itself? Gorbachev made clear where he stood on this issue even before
the death of Chernenko. As Chernenko's health started to fade in late 1984,
Gorbachev moved quickly to seize the initiative from the stand-patters and
to occupy a distinct ideological niche in the succession struggle. The time
had passed for being deferential and self-denying in the face of aspirations
of other, more senior members of the leadership. Gorbachev was ready for a
campaign speech. He defined himself publicly as someone who would revive
the best features of the Leninist heritage by pursuing political and economic
reforms at home and accommodation abroad.

He chose the occasion of a closed Party conference on ideology in December 1984 to make his move. His was the most radical single speech by a leading member of the Politburo since Khrushchev.[16] It was analogous in content
(though not in its timing) to Khrushchev's "secret speech" denouncing Stalin
in 1956, for Khrushchev had used that speech as a way of breaking through political deadlock and seizing the political initiative by defining radical change
in doctrine and policy as a moral and practical necessity. In December 1984,
Gorbachev, though not yet Party leader, signaled that he was prepared to
transform Soviet doctrine – the language of Soviet politics – in order formally
to delegitimize the Brezhnevite way of doing things. He did not yet challenge
the traditional arenas of politics. His speech was given in a private arena and
did not call for the creation of new public arenas; that would come later.
Still, Gorbachev's rivals among the Brezhnevite stand-patters understood the
implications of Gorbachev's words and felt threatened by them. Chernenko
himself tried to prevent Gorbachev from delivering the speech, but Gorbachev stood firm. Chernenko and his allies succeeded only in preventing the
speech from appearing in full in *Pravda*.[17]

[15] Ryzhkov (*Desiat' let,* p. 200) writes that only in 1987 did he realize just how different were his
     and Gorbachev's views on economic issues.
[16] The speech was reprinted in Mikhail S. Gorbachev, *Izbrannye rechi i stat'i,* vol. 2 (Moscow:
     Izdatel'stvo politicheskoi literatury, 1987), pp. 75–108; citations are from this source.
[17] See Hough, *Democratization and Revolution,* p. 73; Brown, *The Gorbachev Factor,* p. 82.

The address was phrased in abstract terms – as doctrinal speeches typically are – and did not elaborate on the specific policies that would follow from the doctrines endorsed. But it contained most of the code-words that would later become the hallmarks of Gorbachev's transformations: *perestroika, glasnost', reforma, demokratizatsiia,* the "human factor," and the need for cadres to "trust" people and to "respect their intellect." Like Khrushchev's speeches at the 20th Party Congress in February 1956, it was notable for the remarkable number of criticisms that bordered on "systemic" as well as for the rhetoric of impatience and urgency that filled the text.[18] Indeed, when Gorbachev spoke of production relations in the USSR having come into conflict with the mode of production, he was repeating the traditional Marxist definition of a pre-revolutionary situation.

This speech was an unmistakable assault on Brezhnevite "stand-pattism." Beyond that, it was an endorsement of not just one alternative to the policies prevailing under Chernenko. Rather, it created an umbrella of concepts and ideas under which representatives of all three alternatives to Brezhnevism could huddle: puritans (anti-corruption fighters), technocrats (rationalizers of the planned economy), and political reformists. Puritans and technocrats in the Central Committee could draw the conclusion that Gorbachev was advocating a policy of widespread replacement of corrupt and incompetent cadres, a policy with which they agreed. They could conclude that Gorbachev's rhetoric – which extolled the communist system, Marxist–Leninist ideals, and social discipline – simply implied a determination to purge the apparatus of corrupt cadres, to staff it with uncorruptible people such as themselves, and thereby to release the untapped potential of the socialist system. This would not necessarily have been threatening to them; nor would it presage any loss of political control over society. Indeed, Gorbachev's emphasis on the growing "contradictions" in Soviet society echoed Andropov's justification for his disciplinarian policies and anti-corruption campaign.[19] Similarly, Gorbachev's critique of Soviet methods of rule could have implied varied policy prescriptions. Khrushchev had pressed for similar goals without abandoning political centralization, the leading role of the Party, or Leninist anti-liberalism.

Puritans and technocrats could have viewed Gorbachev as simply saying that the situation had become too urgent to ignore – not an especially

[18] Khrushchev had not only criticized Stalin in his secret speech; in his published speech to the 20th Party Congress, he had criticized the "bureaucratism" of Soviet society and had called for a frontal assault to overcome it (*Pravda,* February 15, 1956).

[19] On the Andropov model in this regard, see Ernst Kux, "Contradictions in Soviet socialism," *Problems of Communism,* vol. 33, no. 6 (November–December 1984), pp. 1–27.

outrageous claim in light of the revolutionary workers' movement ("Solidarity") in fraternal Poland, which had almost brought down communism in that country in 1981. But compared with Gorbachev's prior caution in public speeches, and given his introduction of so many concepts associated with Khrushchev's anti-Stalin campaign of 1956, the Kosygin reforms of 1965, and the Prague Spring of 1968, this speech was also intended to appeal to, and activate, reformists within the Party and the critical intelligentsia. In the vision expressed to this heterogeneous audience, the puritans were promised a return to revolutionary rectitude, the technocrats were promised modernization and efficiency, and the critical intelligentsia were promised more opportunities to express themselves. All of them were promised a more efficient and productive economic system, a stronger Soviet Union, and a more consensual polity.

The ideas expressed by Gorbachev served as an umbrella for a wide range of groups whose interests often did not overlap. This is a crucial function performed by leaders who propagate new ideas. Gorbachev was not simply playing the role of a "political entrepreneur" who identifies the common "contract space" between established interests and defines a program that secures their support.[20] Rather, Gorbachev was creating a new set of political symbols that were ambiguous enough that puritans, technocrats, and radical political reformists could all assign their favored interpretation to those symbols. This ambiguity allowed Gorbachev to exercise the authority to make changes that in some ways would not have met with the approval of these groups.[21]

---

[20] For this view of leadership, see Oran R. Young, "Political leadership and regime formation: On the development of institutions in international society," *International Organization*, vol. 45, no. 3 (Summer 1991), pp. 281–308, esp. p. 288; see also James MacGregor Burns, *Leadership* (New York: Harper & Row, 1978), on "transactional leadership."

[21] It is noteworthy that two analyses of Gorbachev's politics that treat him as more power-hungry than principled entirely ignore this speech: Dmitry Mikheyev, *The Rise and Fall of Gorbachev* (Indianapolis, IN: Hudson Institute, 1992); and Anthony D'Agostino, *Gorbachev's Revolution* (New York University Press, 1998). By contrast, three analyses that treat Gorbachev as a committed radical reformer already in 1984 attach importance to this speech as an indicator or harbinger of Gorbachev's beliefs (Brown, *The Gorbachev Factor*, pp. 78ff.; Hough, *Democratization and Revolution*, p. 74; Robert D. English, *Russia and the Idea of the West: Gorbachev, Intellectuals and the End of the Cold War* [New York: Columbia University Press, 2000], p. 199). I treat this speech as an indicator of Gorbachev's authority-building strategy, whatever might have been his inner convictions at the time. The authority-building approach treats public statements as exercises in political impression management and political communication, though it also presumes that leaders come to be hostage to the political identities they define publicly for themselves.

Foreign Relations

Gorbachev's public statements on East–West relations at the time also suggested that he was capturing a broad ideological niche in the struggle to succeed Chernenko while simultaneously presenting himself as the man who could lead the country responsibly in new directions. He combined a vigorous defense of Soviet status in world affairs with an endorsement of flexibility and accommodation. He suggested that Chernenko's policies were leading the country into a dead end and that new ideas and postures were needed to avoid that fate. In his speech to the ideological conference of December 10, 1984, he had little to say about foreign affairs, but what he did say combined ritualistic rhetoric with a criticism that the USSR had allowed its opponents to steal from it the initiative on the global scene. Re-seizing the initiative would lead not to an escalation of the Cold War but rather to "constructive dialogue and practical measures leading to the lessening of international tension." [22]

Only eight days later, in a speech before the British parliament on December 18, 1984, that was reprinted in full in *Pravda*, Gorbachev elaborated on the meaning of flexibility. [23] There he foreshadowed many of the concepts that would later come to mark his accommodationist foreign policy. He called for a "healing" (*ozdorovlenie*) of international relations. He mentioned the need for "new thinking in the nuclear age" and the need for accommodations based on "a balance of interests" between East and West. He referred to *both* sides' interests as "legitimate" (*zakonnye*) and called for "sensible compromises" and trust based on "compatible (*sovpadaiushchie*) interests." He referred to Europe as "our common home." And he abandoned the traditional aversion to showing weakness by repeating several times that the USSR needed peace in order to pursue its domestic goals. Gorbachev did criticize the United States and tried to draw a distinction between the United States and Europe, but he did not dwell on it.

Similarly, Gorbachev's visit to Great Britain in December 1984 combined conciliatory rhetoric, a relaxed style, and a flexible way of thinking with tough-mindedness and a blunt, self-confident, articulate defense of Soviet pride and interests when challenged directly by members of parliament. Margaret Thatcher, at least, had seen beyond the latter and appreciated the potential implicit in the former, proclaiming: "I like Gorbachev. We can do business

---

[22] Gorbachev, *Izbrannye,* vol. 2, p. 103.
[23] Ibid., pp. 109–16.

together."[24] By contrast, Andrei Gromyko, in his nomination speech on behalf of Gorbachev less than three months later, may have viewed Gorbachev's performance in England as the harbinger of a more effective pursuit of "offensive détente."[25]

In sum, even before he became general secretary, Gorbachev signaled his intention to lead the Soviet Union out of what he defined as a cul-de-sac. He offered his own vigorous leadership to defuse East–West tensions and to overcome the crisis at home. While he made clear that he was entertaining reformist proposals for domestic change and that he was endorsing a greater measure of Soviet flexibility and conciliation in East–West relations, it was by no means clear how far he would push each of these tendencies. More specifically, his public statements left unclear the price in traditional values he would be willing to pay in order to advance these goals. Whereas his general posture as a new kind of leader was clear, his concrete policy positions were sufficiently ambiguous that they could have received explicit or tacit endorsement from a wide range of political types within the Politburo and Central Committee. This was a clever formula for seizing the initiative in a political competition. Only the stand-patters would be alienated. But their loss of self-confidence and dwindling numbers (with the passing of older members of the Politburo) made them increasingly ineffectual as a blocking coalition.

GORBACHEV IN POWER

Once he became general secretary in March 1985, Gorbachev's level of caution, traditionalism, and ambiguity suddenly increased. The one exception was cadres policy, in which Gorbachev moved rapidly, consolidating his power perhaps faster than any Party leader in Soviet history. Steadily and quickly, he enlarged his political machine and consolidated his power base by firing members of the Politburo, as well as stand-pat officials of the central and regional Party apparatuses, and replacing them with people he knew, respected, or trusted. But regarding actual policy changes, he moved slowly and cautiously; his rhetoric, though still novel, was less far-reaching than in his

---

[24] *The New York Times* (December 23, 1984).
[25] Gorbachev reiterated several of these themes in a more restrained speech before a domestic audience on February 20, 1985 (Gorbachev, *Izbrannye*, vol. 2, pp. 117–28, esp. pp. 125–6). This speech before his nominal electorate for the Supreme Soviet endorsed a perspective on international affairs that contrasted markedly with that endorsed by Gorbachev's Brezhnevite rival, Grigorii Romanov, in his own electoral speech (see *Leningradskaia pravda*, February 15, 1985).

December 1984 speech to the ideology conference. This led some observers at the time to assume that Gorbachev was little different in orientation from the Brezhnev generation. But that assumption ignored the impact on Gorbachev's behavior of politics, power consolidation, and authority-building imperatives. Gorbachev was building a political machine and temporarily deferring in policy to the more conservative forces within the Politburo and Central Committee.

Gorbachev's domestic policies from March 1985 to the fall of 1986 were noteworthy more for their traditionalism than for their reformism; they were more reminiscent of Andropov's policies than of Khrushchev's. As such, they must have appealed greatly to such puritans as Yegor Ligachev, whom Gorbachev was both promoting to the Politburo and drawing into the inner circle of the leadership. The economic policy of acceleration (*uskorenie*), for example, called for budgetary redistributions to the benefit of the machine-building sector, increased pressure on managers to economize on materials, and campaigns against lack of discipline among workers and managers alike. Administrative reorganizations that took place at the time did not challenge the principles of the command economy, much less introduce elements of a market economy. Instead, they intensified pressure on economic administrators. Anti-corruption campaigns were launched or expanded, increasing the opportunity for Gorbachev to build his political machine. Similarly, the anti-alcoholism campaign launched in May 1985 resembled traditional Soviet campaigns; in fact, we now know that it was supervised by Ligachev, though there is disagreement as to whether he was a driving force in adopting the policy.[26]

It remains unclear to what extent Gorbachev believed at the time that these policies would suffice to reenergize the economy – or to what extent his deferral to the puritans was driven by political calculation.[27] What is clear,

---

[26] According to Yegor Ligachev (*Inside Gorbachev's Kremlin*, pp. 335–9), he supported the campaign as a member of the Politburo and became "actively involved with the cause" (p. 336), but he was not its initiator. Yeltsin (Boris Yeltsin, *Against the Grain: An Autobiography*, trans. by Michael Glenny [New York: Summit, 1990], p. 127) presents a picture of a fanatical Ligachev running the campaign. Politburo member Nikolai Ryzhkov (*Perestroika*, pp. 93–5) depicts Ligachev and Solomentsev as the driving forces behind the campaign, a depiction that is supported by the memoirs of Gorbachev (*Zhizn' i reformy*, vol. I [Moscow: Novosti, 1995], p. 341).

[27] Gorbachev (*Zhizn' i reformy*, vol. I, p. 336) claims that he believed in 1985 that these policies, along with replacement of cadres, would indeed suffice. I find this hard to accept at face value, given the degree of radicalism of his speech to the Ideology Conference in December 1984 and the speed with which he jettisoned "acceleration" in 1986 and replaced it with radical

however, is that he used this time to prepare the ground for the possibility of more radical policies. For though his speeches during 1985 and through early 1986 were, on balance, less radical than those delivered during December 1984–February 1985, they included phrases and formulations that were associated with political and economic reform. On the one hand, we find themes such as "acceleration," discipline, the need for both workers and cadres to learn to think differently, and the need for greater "socialist democracy" (a favorite theme of Chernenko's). These themes were traditionalist in thrust, or at least could have been interpreted in traditional terms, and they tended to predominate quantitatively in his speeches of March 1985 through mid-1986. Yet, at the same time, Gorbachev continued to talk about the need for economic reform – a theme that was especially important to technocrats.[28] Gorbachev took back nothing he had said in December 1984. His speeches continued to note the need for *glasnost', perestroika,* and democratization, themes that were especially important to radical reformists.[29] Thus, at the 27th Party Congress (February 1986), Gorbachev spoke of the need for "radical reform," his first such reference.[30] In July 1986, he equated *perestroika* with a "real revolution."[31] As before, though, he remained vague about the specific policies that would flow from these principles, and their encasement in more traditionalist rhetoric allowed puritans and technocrats to feel less threatened by the radical phrases than they might otherwise have been.

For example, at the 27th Party Congress, Gorbachev proclaimed that "[a]ny restructuring of the economic mechanism ... begins with the restructuring of consciousness, the giving up of formed stereotypes of thinking and practice, [and a] clear understanding of new challenges."[32] Puritans could have understood this to mean that purging corrupt cadres and intensified

---

changes that assumed the causes of dysfunctions to be systemic. Moreover, closer inspection of this passage in his memoirs reveals the following. He writes that in 1985 his team ("we," never "I") really did initially hope to overcome stagnation through "acceleration." However, he also says that, having engaged in substantial analytical work in 1982–1984, he and his team were even then cognizant of the fact that a more substantial economic reform would "eventually" be necessary. Thus, acceleration was a needed jolt, to be followed by something more radical.

[28] See Ryzhkov, *Desiat' let* (pp. 44–5, 69, 83, 120, 255) for examples of the prime minister's urge for reforms that would diminish the Party's intervention in the operation of the economy. He even had a good word for Bukharin at the expense of Lenin (p. 255).

[29] Examples include Gorbachev, *Izbrannye,* vol. 2, pp. 130–1, 142–3, 150, 158, 433; vol. 3, pp. 235–43; vol. 4, pp. 37–8, 48, 50.

[30] Gorbachev, *Izbrannye,* vol. 3, p. 212.

[31] Ibid., vol. 4, p. 37.

[32] Gorbachev, *Izbrannye,* vol. 3, p. 217.

Party educational work among the workers were preconditions for changes in institutional structure. Gorbachev's "revolution," then, could have been interpreted as a cultural revolution, not a political revolution against the prerogatives of the Party apparatus. Similarly, in his speeches of March–April 1985, Gorbachev frequently cited the Party's paternalistic role as an educator (*vospitatel'*) of the Soviet people. In his speech upon being elected general secretary, for example, he argued that

[t]he deepening of socialist democracy is inextricably tied to the heightening of social consciousness.... We must continue to expand *glasnost'* in the work of Party, Soviet, state and social organizations. V. I. Lenin said that the state is rich because of the consciousness of the masses. Our practice has completely corroborated this conclusion. The better informed are the people, and the more consciously they act, the more actively they support the Party, its plans and programmatic aims.[33]

This was a decidedly elitist statement that could easily be interpreted by audiences within the Central Committee as assurance that, although changes were needed, they would not challenge the leading role of the Party.

Reassurance notwithstanding, the persistent inclusion of reformist phrases in speeches by the general secretary had potentially far-reaching implications in an ideocratic regime.[34] Those phrases amounted to a tacit repudiation of the self-congratulatory doctrinal formulations that had previously justified standing pat (or what Gorbachev would call "stagnation"). They thereby opened up intellectual and political space for reformist members of the journalistic community, academia, and the cultural intelligentsia to become publicly involved in the debate about alternatives to Brezhnevism. They allowed would-be political activists to point to statements by the general secretary as political cover for risky efforts to stretch the boundaries of legitimate public discourse and association. At this early stage in his administration, Gorbachev gingerly opened the space (and provided the cover) by combining traditionalist with reformist rhetoric while pursuing largely traditionalist policies. He was challenging the formal doctrines of Brezhnevism, but without yet challenging the primacy of private arenas of power and without alerting puritans and technocrats within the leadership to the potentially threatening implications of what was to come.

---

[33] Gorbachev, *Izbrannye*, vol. 2, pp. 130–1.

[34] An "ideocratic" regime is one in which the status and privileges of the ruling elite are justified with reference to a sacred ideological heritage of which the elite is the current trustee and embodiment.

To take another example, at this early stage Gorbachev did not yet treat *glasnost'* as an end in itself. Rather, he defined it as a necessary instrument for exposing bureaucrats who were hiding their malfeasance or incompetence. *Glasnost'* was a necessary searchlight and the beam now needed to be intensified. He also described it as a mechanism by which the Party would heighten its credibility with the masses and thereby induce them to contribute to realization of the Party's goals. But he had not yet crossed the divide between elitism and populism; the central authorities still needed to control the scope and focus of "openness." This was implicit in his coupling of *glasnost'* with traditional, elitist concepts.[35] Indeed, in June 1986, at a private meeting with leaders of the USSR Writers' Union, Gorbachev urged writers not to make the Stalin issue the centerpiece of their definitions of *glasnost'*. Why dissipate all our energies on arguments about the past, he asked, when we need to concentrate our attention and energies on the present and the future![36] Here too, Gorbachev's emphasis was on caution and on presenting himself as a leader who could balance and mediate conflicting intellectual agendas, political orientations, classes, and generations.

Words are important in a regime that seeks to legitimize itself with reference to a sacred ideological heritage. The populace may not believe in the tenets of the ideology, but the regime's constant defense of those tenets is meant to signal officialdom's collective unassailability. When a leader wants to change things significantly, he can mobilize new sources of support for his efforts by changing the doctrine and thereby signaling that representatives of the established order – and perhaps the order itself – are no longer unassailable. This is what Khrushchev's anti-Stalin campaign signaled. This also explains why it was so important for the conservative Brezhnev regime to put an end to the anti-Stalin campaign and to introduce new doctrinal formulations in order to re-defend the established order. Gorbachev was following Khrushchev's (not Brezhnev's) lead, though in a less confrontational way at this point. But in the 1980s, as in the 1950s, journalists, academics, and the critical intelligentsia took up the cause.

A similar pattern is observable in foreign relations. During the initial period of his administration, Gorbachev prepared the ground intellectually

---

[35] At the 27th Party Congress, he defined *glasnost'* as a vehicle for facilitating "political creativity of the masses" (*Izbrannye*, vol. 3, p. 241); in April 1986, he bundled *glasnost'* with "criticism and self-criticism" as prerequisites for forward movement (ibid., p. 352). *Glasnost'* only becomes an end in itself in Gorbachev's speeches beginning in January 1987 (*Izbrannye*, vol. 4, p. 358).

[36] See the account of this meeting in "Gorbachev meets Soviet writers: A Samizdat account," *Radio Liberty Research Report*, no. 399/86 (October 23, 1986).

for later foreign policy initiatives. We have seen that, from December 1984 through February 1985, Gorbachev had already signaled his identification with "new thinking" and other concepts that were harbingers of a more flexible posture in international affairs. This did not change during his first year in office, though his policies remained cautious and his rhetoric could be read both ways. At the 27th Party Congress in February 1986, for example, he referred to the war in Afghanistan as a "running sore," thus providing the first critical appraisal of that war in public by a Soviet general secretary.[37] Yet his comments on East–West relations at the same Congress combined a strongly accommodationist thrust with an equally strong denunciation of "U.S. imperialism."[38]

Similarly, in relations with the communist governments of Eastern Europe, Gorbachev proceeded with caution and ambiguity. One month after his election as general secretary, he reaffirmed the basic principles of the "Brezhnev Doctrine" (sanctioning Soviet use of force to prevent the overthrow of socialism) in a published speech on the renewal of the Warsaw Pact Treaty.[39] In the same month, however, he reportedly told some East European leaders privately that the USSR would not rescue them should their populations repudiate them.[40] During 1985–1986, Gorbachev addressed the issue of Eastern Europe very infrequently, concentrating on other matters. But in his speech to the 27th Party Congress, he did not endorse the Brezhnev Doctrine or its associated concepts and instead enunciated a more cooperative vision of Soviet relations with Eastern Europe.[41] Likewise, in a private speech to staff of

---

[37] *Izbrannye*, vol. 3, p. 251. Gorbachev was the fourth general secretary to preside over the war in Afghanistan. Andropov had called for an in-house, private policy review of the war but had not criticized the military effort in public.

[38] See Gorbachev's address to the Congress in *Pravda*, February 26, 1986, section I ("The Present-Day World: Basic Tendencies and Contradictions") and section IV ("The Basic Goals and Directions of the Party's Foreign-Policy Strategy"); see also the discussions of this speech in English, *Russia and the Idea*, pp. 209–10, and Brown, *The Gorbachev Factor*, pp. 221–2. The speech was marked by a tense and inconsistent coexistence of accommodative offerings and essentialist depictions of "U.S. imperialism," which traditionally implied the inability to ease tensions with that country. Thus: "Imperialism is impelled by its mainsprings and its very social and economic essence to translate the competition of the two systems into the language of military confrontation. Because of its social nature, imperialism continually generates aggressive, adventuristic policies.... This is especially typical of U.S. imperialism" (as translated in *Current Soviet Policies: The 27th Congress of the CPSU* [Columbus, OH: Current Digest of the Soviet Press, 1986], p. 13).

[39] *Pravda*, April 28, 1985.

[40] Brown, *The Gorbachev Factor*, p. 249, citing testimony by Chernyaev, Medvedev, and Gorbachev.

[41] *Pravda*, February 26, 1986; see also the discussion in Karen Dawisha, *Eastern Europe, Gorbachev, and Reform: The Great Challenge*, 2nd ed. (Cambridge University Press, 1990), p. 207.

the Ministry of Foreign Affairs in May 1986, Gorbachev insisted on the need for a more respectful Soviet attitude in dealing with Eastern Europe.[42]

The concepts that Gorbachev endorsed in both the Congress and the Ministry speeches were far less radical than those he would articulate later. They resembled innovations introduced by Khrushchev at the analogous stage of his administration when he, too, was trying to overcome a legacy of coercive domination and alienation in Soviet–East European relations, hoping to place those relations on a more cooperative and consensual basis but without encouraging anti-communist tendencies. Indeed, Khrushchev and Gorbachev, in the first stages of their administrations, may have shared the optimistic belief that an intermediate, stable equilibrium could be reached in Soviet relations with Eastern Europe – one that entailed neither coercive Soviet domination nor forced Soviet abdication.[43]

It is also noteworthy that Gorbachev did little at this stage to reduce the rate of growth of the Soviet military budget. He even increased Soviet military assistance to some clients in the Third World and briefly escalated the Soviet military offensive in Afghanistan, if only to improve the Soviet bargaining position in withdrawal negotiations.[44] He did not depart from his predecessors' strategy of offering incremental Soviet concessions in arms-control negotiations and of demanding equivalent, reciprocal concessions from the United States. Yet he did meet with President Reagan in Geneva (October 1985) and Reykjavik (October 1986), thus breaking the Soviet government's announced determination to avoid such meetings until the United States had abandoned its Strategic Defense Initiative. Although nothing concrete resulted from those two summits, Gorbachev and Reagan impressed each other and Gorbachev felt free thereafter to endorse the notion of total abolition of nuclear weapons as well as the principle of on-site inspection. Thus, in foreign as well as domestic policy, Gorbachev was both embracing traditional approaches and preparing the ground – intellectually and politically, but less so in policy – for more radical initiatives later on.

---

[42] Brown, *The Gorbachev Factor*, p. 242.

[43] Lévesque, in a comprehensive study, refers to these early years as a period of "Soviet immobilisme" in East European policy, which contrasted with the evolution of foreign policy concepts in other realms (Jacques Lévesque, *The Enigma of 1989: The USSR and the Liberation of Eastern Europe* [Berkeley: University of California Press, 1997], ch. 3).

[44] Raymond Garthoff, *The Great Transition: American–Soviet Relations and the End of the Cold War* (Washington, DC: Brookings Institution, 1994), p. 727.

4

Gorbachev Ascendant

The radicalization of Gorbachev's program and political strategy began in late 1986, with a signal going out that an expanded definition of *glasnost'* was now the "Party line." This indicated to editors of journals that censorship was to be relaxed and that they would be much freer to criticize. This was also the point at which Gorbachev started to extol the virtues of voluntary associations ("informals"). To dramatize, both at home and abroad, this expansion of the right of social forces to mobilize themselves autonomously, in December 1986 Gorbachev personally saw to the release from house arrest of the heroic symbol of dissidence, Andrei Sakharov. The following month he introduced to a plenary session of the Central Committee a wide-ranging program of "democratization," which included proposals for multicandidate, secret elections of Party, soviet, and managerial officials. In the same month, he announced that the Soviet Union would open up to the world economy by allowing joint ventures with foreign enterprises on Soviet soil.

In short order there followed new laws on cooperatives and "individual labor activity," which presaged new opportunities for legal entrepreneurial activity, and, in June 1987, a "Law on the State Enterprise" that signaled a push to dismantle the command economy. Almost all these initiatives in domestic policy were only first steps, a "foot in the door" approach, steps that delegitimized old values and justified in principle entirely new approaches to economic organization and the world economy. Almost all of them would be radicalized still further in the course of 1987–1988. Most dramatically, an extraordinary Party Conference in June 1988, which was televised nationally, laid plans for internal democratization of the CPSU, for the transfer of major decisionmaking authority from Party organs to the legislative councils (soviets) at all levels, and for the creation of a popularly elected legislature –

the Congress of People's Deputies – for which competitive, public elections would be held in March 1989. Indeed, one scholarly observer treats June 1988 as the point at which Gorbachev made the transition from being a reformer to being a transformer of the Soviet system.[1]

Unveiled within a few short months, these fresh initiatives vastly expanded Gorbachev's earlier programs. He was now establishing his political identity: a reformist (not a puritan or technocratic) vision of the future.

Gorbachev radicalized foreign policy as well. Building upon policy changes announced in 1986, Gorbachev made a series of stunning unilateral concessions that abandoned almost all Soviet negotiating positions in order to make possible completion of the INF ("Euromissile") Treaty in Washington, D.C., in December 1987. He announced in January 1988 that the Soviet Union would withdraw its troops from Afghanistan by May 1989 regardless of the consequences. He forced a breakthrough on the reduction of conventional forces in Europe by announcing at the United Nations, in December 1988, a large, unilateral reduction of Soviet forces. He assured his audiences that this would take place even if the United States and NATO failed to reciprocate in kind. He pledged in the same speech that the Soviet Union would not intervene militarily again in Eastern Europe. And, also in 1988, he began to urge conservative East European elites to accommodate liberalizing forces within their societies and to implement their own *perestroika* before it was too late.[2]

In sum, further radicalization of *glasnost'*, *perestroika,* democratization, and "new thinking" became the basis of Gorbachev's authority-building strategy during his stage of ascendancy. They marked his comprehensive program and the vision of the future he propounded. He was engaged in a relentless process of public desacralization and partial destruction of the Brezhnevite political-economic and sociopolitical orders. By desacralizing the established order, he was in effect stripping the *apparat* and the official classes of immunity from public, systemic criticism and thereby also emboldening the intelligentsia and the masses to believe that such forceful criticism could now be safely advanced in public. Televising the debates among Party officials at the June 1988 Party Conference was a means of simultaneously demystifying politics, subverting the notion that the "monolithic" Party had unique insight

---

[1] Archie Brown, *The Gorbachev Factor* (Oxford & New York: Oxford University Press, 1996), ch. 6.

[2] On the last point, see Karen Dawisha, *Eastern Europe, Gorbachev, and Reform: The Great Challenge,* 2nd ed. (Cambridge University Press, 1990), pp. 219–20, and Jacques Lévesque, *The Enigma of 1989: The USSR and the Liberation of Eastern Europe* (Berkeley: University of California Press, 1997), ch. 4 (entitled "The Second Half of 1988: The Turning Point").

into the "correct line," educating the population about alternative ways of thinking, and allowing people to believe that political initiative and involvement might be rewarding.

Such public criticism also assisted Gorbachev in his efforts to maintain the initiative against neo-Brezhnevite and newly conservative forces within the Central Committee and Politburo. Puritans such as Ligachev, and technocrats such as Prime Minister Ryzhkov, found themselves increasingly disillusioned with Gorbachev during this stage of his leadership. Their alienation from Gorbachev's evolving definitions of *perestroika* only deepened as the general secretary permitted civil liberties to expand in the areas of religion, travel, emigration, speech, and mass media.[3] As the bounds of the permissible grew, so too did the boldness of journalists, academics, writers, artists, and political activists. Their actions, and the autonomous social organizations they helped to create or enlarge, pushed beyond the degrees of freedom of speech and association that Gorbachev had formally and publicly sanctioned. Increasingly, Gorbachev's unwillingness to draw and enforce limits alienated those members of the Central Committee who had always assumed that the alternative to order would be anarchy.

There is a striking parallel between Khrushchev's behavior in 1958–1960 and that of Gorbachev during 1987–1989. In both periods, these men achieved positions of ascendancy within the leadership. Both of them put forth comprehensive programs for attaining a hugely ambitious goal based on a progressive, transcendant vision.[4] Khrushchev, like Gorbachev, expanded the arenas of politics and the scope of generalizable criticism of the system in order to overcome entrenched obstacles to change.

The content of their visions was quite different, however. Khrushchev advocated and promised no less than the "full-scale construction of communism,"

---

[3] See Nikolai Ryzhkov, *Desiat' let velikikh potriasenii* (Moscow: Assotsiatsiia "Kniga. Prosviashchenie. Miloserdie," 1995), pp. 77, 86, 185–8, 200. Yegor Ligachev (*Inside Gorbachev's Kremlin: The Memoirs of Yegor Ligachev* [New York: Pantheon, 1993]) devotes many pages to denunciation of Politburo member Aleksandr Yakovlev as an evil force within the Politburo who was pushing Gorbachev's reforms in increasingly radical and unacceptable directions. On Ligachev's alienation, see also Anatoly Chernyaev, *Shest' let s Gorbachevym* (Moscow: Progress, 1993), pp. 97, 201–5; on Ligachev's and Ryzhkov's joining together against certain forms of radicalization, see ibid., p. 236. Ryzhkov (*Desiat' let*, p. 199) also writes that in 1987 there were passionate meetings of the Politburo, "hot, ferocious (*iarostnykh*), endlessly long" meetings that "went as far as cussing (*do rugani dokhodivshikh*)."

[4] For the argument that, throughout Soviet history, ascendant leaders have been driven by an ideological urge to "transcend" real-world constraints, see Stephen E. Hanson, *Time and Revolution: Marxism and the Design of Soviet Institutions* (Chapel Hill: University of North Carolina Press, 1998).

based on "overtaking and surpassing capitalism" in growth and consumption indicators, as well as a decisive shift in the international "correlation of forces" in favor of socialism and, before too long, the "full and final victory of socialism" on a global scale. But Khrushchev did not seek to bridge, much less cross, the divide between Leninism and procedural democracy. He sought only to make the Leninist system somewhat more open and significantly less bureaucratized, which, he claimed, would energize the population and help to build a society of material abundance and political consensus. There was no room in his programs of 1958–1960 for competitive, secret elections, publicity for anti-system criticism, pluralism as an ideal, or voluntary associations that were independent of Party control. Khrushchev's vision was of a process of sociopolitical and socioeconomic homogenization, whereas Gorbachev was endorsing and expanding pluralism and heterogeneity (though not individualism per se) in these spheres. Khrushchev's vision of politics was plebiscitarian and populist, with himself as the uncontested leader. Gorbachev's was institutional and representative, with Gorbachev as the leading political broker and guarantor of progress – but not someone who should be treated as immune to criticism or challenge.

Both men recognized that reforming the system required organizational and ideological challenges to the heritage within which they were operating. But only Gorbachev was ready to synthesize Leninism with a variant of procedural democracy by subjecting officialdom to autonomous mechanisms of public accountability.[5] And only Gorbachev was ready to abandon the "anti-imperialist struggle" abroad.

JUSTIFYING AND STEERING DOMESTIC TRANSFORMATION

During 1987–1989, Gorbachev transformed both the ideology and organization of Soviet politics – what I have called the language and arenas of politics. He radicalized and elaborated the reformist concepts that he had advanced only gingerly during 1984–1986. Now he criticized "the dogmatic,

---

[5] Khrushchev would move in an even more radical direction – though nothing approaching Gorbachev's level of radicalism – during his last years in office, when he was politically embattled and searching for ways simultaneously to make the system work and to keep potential rivals off balance. See, for example, Alexander Yanov, *The Drama of the Soviet 1960s: A Lost Reform* (Berkeley: University of California, Institute of International Studies, 1984), and William Zimmerman, *Soviet Perspectives on International Relations, 1956–1967* (Princeton, NJ: Princeton University Press, 1969), pp. 99–101, 152, 196–205, 222ff., 259–69.

bureaucratic and voluntaristic inheritance"[6] and basically gave notice to those who were unable or unwilling to adapt to a new sociopolitical order.[7] But he did not jettison those components of his public statements that had appealed to puritans and technocrats. Nor did he ignore other officials who had internalized Marxist–Leninist categories and assumptions but who accepted the need for significant change in light of the crisis in which the country found itself. Instead, Gorbachev shifted the weights among these emphases within his speeches, consistently trying to demonstrate that, while a reformist, he remained faithful to the ideological tradition. In a sense, he did a remarkable job of appearing to straddle, but not cross, the divide between Leninism and procedural democracy.

One way in which Gorbachev did this was by articulating a vision of a reformed Soviet socialist society: one that remained faithful to traditional, Marxist socialism, to the romantic Leninism of "State and Revolution" (published in 1917), and to the reformist Leninism of the "New Economic Policy" (1921–1927) but that broke with the elitist and dictatorial features of the system as it had developed since then. Thus, his speeches and writings during 1987–1988 consistently extolled and quoted Lenin to justify his most radical proposals. In equal measure, they extolled the virtues and potential of "socialism" – a potential, he claimed, that his policies would reveal and realize. At times, this resulted in formulations that, to an outside observer, might have appeared to be arcane and convoluted: "The essence of *perestroika* lies in the fact that it unites socialism with democracy and revives the Leninist concept of socialist construction both in theory and in practice."[8] But to members of the Central Committee, these words could have lent a familiar ring to a potentially threatening policy.

Such familiarity might not have resulted in enthusiasm for the changes among those officials who were nervous about the implications of public criticism, decentralization, and competitive elections. But that familiarity may have allowed many officials, already somewhat intimidated by Gorbachev's assertiveness and lacking in self-confidence to begin with, to rationalize that the processes being unleashed were in principle controllable. It also allowed

---

[6] Mikhail S. Gorbachev, *Izbrannye rechi i stat'i*, vol. 6 (Moscow: Izdatel'stvo politicheskoi literatury, 1987), p. 64 (February 1988 Central Committee Plenum). "Voluntaristic" here refers to the ability of Party officials to conduct themselves with impunity; it implies the need to make them formally accountable for their actions.

[7] See e.g. ibid., p. 394 (June 1988 CPSU Conference).

[8] Mikhail Gorbachev, *Perestroika: New Thinking for Our Country and the World* (New York: Perennial, 1987), p. 22.

them to rationalize that Gorbachev himself was committed to holding those processes within bounds. Gorbachev sought to reassure them: the intent, he averred, was to "deepen people's socialist self-government.... We are not talking about, obviously, any kind of sabotage (*lomka*) of our political system. We must use all of its possibilities with maximal efficiency."⁹ Democracy, after all, was to be *socialist* democracy; pluralism was to be *socialist* pluralism. Nothing he was proposing was meant to invalidate the "socialist idea" and the Soviet peoples' "socialist choice."

Gorbachev also assured his audiences that he respected the achievements of Soviet history – even as he was seeking a "sharp break" with past practice – and would preserve the best features of the inherited system. Thus, alongside his calls for criticism of the past and the filling in of "blank spots" in history and literature, he defended the historical record of the Party under very difficult circumstances (World War II, the Cold War) and lauded Soviet accomplishments.¹⁰ He presented his reforms as a continuation of the earlier efforts of progressive forces within the Party who had attempted unsuccessfully to realize the potential of socialism back in 1953, 1956, and 1965.¹¹ In like manner, when discussing decisions during the *perestroika* period, he always referred to them as collective, not individual, decisions by the leadership. And he reassured his audiences, using Marxist language, that the leadership remained firmly in charge of an evolutionary process that would not get out of control:

I want to emphasize ... that *perestroika* is not a negation, and even if it is a negation, it is a dialectical one. Affirming our line for acceleration, for *perestroika,* we stand not on some slippery swamp, but on firm ground that has been formed through the efforts of many generations of Soviet people, as a result of our struggle as pioneers (*pervoprokhodtsy*).¹²

For the technocrats, Gorbachev also had choice ways of framing the changes he proposed. He appealed to scientific rationalism, which has deep roots in both Marxism and Soviet history. Reminiscent of Lenin's fascination with

---

⁹ Gorbachev, *Izbrannye,* vol. 4, p. 317 (speech at January 1987 Plenum of Central Committee). For representative examples of Gorbachev's extolling of socialism and Leninism in 1987–1988, which marked almost every speech he gave, see Gorbachev, *Perestroika,* pp. 18–19, 22, 36, 72, 82; Gorbachev, *Izbrannye,* vol. 5, p. 411 (November 1987 anniversary speech); vol. 6, pp. 61–7 (February 1988 Plenum of Central Committee), and pp. 335, 394, 395 (June 1988 CPSU Conference).

¹⁰ Gorbachev, *Izbrannye,* vol. 4, pp. 373–4 (February 1987 meeting in Central Committee).

¹¹ Ibid., vol. 6, pp. 351, 383, 399–400 (June 1988 CPSU Conference).

¹² Ibid., vol. 5, p. 210 (July 1987 meeting in Central Committee); see also vol. 4, p. 327 (January 1987 Central Committee Plenum).

American efficiency and industrialization, he proclaimed that *perestroika* "is the attachment to socialism of the most modern forms."[13] Modernity had institutional forms, but socialism had political and cultural content! *Perestroika* would "attach" one to the other without corrupting the essence – the soul – of the system. Similarly, "*Perestroika* means a resolute shift to scientific methods .... It means the combination of the achievements of the scientific and technological revolution with a planned economy."[14]

Gorbachev's emphasis on a "law-based state" (*pravovoe gosudarstvo*) could also have been appealing to would-be rationalizers of the Soviet economy. These people yearned to create a more predictable, procedural grounding for public administration. And, like their puritan brethren, they viewed official corruption and arbitrariness as enemies of administrative rationalization. Both puritans and technocrats wanted to avoid a return to autocratic leadership of the Politburo – whether Stalinist despotism or Khrushchevian arbitrariness. To the extent that legality constrained arbitrariness among their leaders (i.e., "provided reliable guarantees against a return to the cult of personality," as both Khrushchev and Gorbachev put it), it too was desirable.[15] A law-based state, to technocrats and puritans, was not intended to replace an authoritarian regime with mass democracy. But, to the extent that legal codification fosters administrative rationalization and nonarbitrary leadership, these types of officials could find something appealing in Gorbachev's democratization program.[16]

Even as he defined *perestroika* as a revolution, Gorbachev spoke the language of evolution, defining change as a long-term process that requires acclimatization to continuous change. Leninists must be creative, he would say, just as Lenin was. On the one hand, he was providing reassurance that the system would not collapse but would instead "realize its potential." On the other hand, he insisted that accommodation to the "stagnation" of the late-Brezhnev era was unacceptable and was in fact a surer recipe for systemic demise. Progressive change was an idea that also had deep roots in the Marxist and Leninist traditions. Indeed, those traditions were rooted in a theory of

---

[13] Ibid., p. 410 (November 1987 anniversary speech).

[14] Gorbachev, *Perestroika*, p. 21.

[15] This is the phrase Khrushchev used at the Party Congress in 1961 to justify intensification of the anti-Stalin campaign. Gorbachev broadened the idea to encompass guarantees of *perestroika* as a whole against regression. Thus, at the 19th Party Conference in June 1988, he averred: "the task of renewal requires guarantees .... We need such guarantees, to strengthen them" (Gorbachev, *Izbrannye*, vol. 6, p. 392).

[16] On the law-based state, see Gorbachev, *Perestroika*, pp. 91–5; Gorbachev, *Izbrannye*, vol. 6, pp. 354–7, 373–6 (June 1988 CPSU Conference).

historical change, within which stasis was viewed as regressive and change was treated as the normal condition of human affairs.[17] To be sure, the ideological tradition assumed that the transition from one system to another (as from capitalism to socialism) would require a violent revolution from below. But Gorbachev did not define *perestroika* as that kind of a transition; instead, socialism was still "developing" and *perestroika* would assist in the realization of socialism's potential. It would result not in a new historical system but rather in a more progressive, moral, and liberating variant of socialism.[18]

Gorbachev's comprehensive program was premised on the notion that culture must be transformed even more quickly than political and economic organization if structural changes were to take root and result in new patterns of behavior. This was the rationale for his emphasis on what he called "the human factor," which he had brought up already in December 1984 and on which he elaborated at the 27th Party Congress in February 1986.[19] In April 1986, he argued that cultural change – among both the elite and the masses – was a precondition for successful economic reform: "We have to begin, first of all, with changes in our attitudes and psychology, with the style and method of work.... I have to tell you frankly that, if we do not change ourselves, I am deeply convinced that there will be no changes in our economic and social life."[20] This was an argument that resonated positively during the stage of political succession, for it appealed to the puritans and technocrats as well – as long as the content of the proposed changes in attitude and style of work were not specified. The Soviet tradition had included a stage and concept of "cultural revolution." And the CPSU had always been touted as an organization whose activists would continuously educate and mold (*vospitat'*) the less-conscious masses. Hence, when Gorbachev called for more attention to the consciousness of the masses and to the role this might play in forging a more vibrant, dynamic, and efficient society, he struck a chord that was familiar to officials of the Party–State.

---

[17] Robert C. Tucker, *The Marxian Revolutionary Idea* (New York: Norton, 1969); Hanson, *Time and Revolution.*

[18] See Gorbachev, *Izbrannye,* vol. 4, pp. 370, 371 (February 1987 meeting in Central Committee); vol. 5, pp. 410–11 (November 1987 anniversary speech); vol. 6, p. 63 (February 1988 Central Committee Plenum), p. 395 (June 1988 CPSU Conference); Gorbachev, *Perestroika,* p. 37 ("*Perestroika* is a revolutionary process for it is a jump forward in the development of socialism, in the realization of its essential characteristics"). Brown quotes from an interview Gorbachev gave in 1992 in which he described the process of *perestroika* as having been intended to be "revolutionary in its essence but evolutionary in its tempo" (Brown, *The Gorbachev Factor,* p. 94).

[19] Gorbachev, *Izbrannye,* vol. 3, p. 217.

[20] Gorbachev speech, April 8, 1986, as quoted in Dusko Doder and Louise Branson, *Gorbachev: Heretic in the Kremlin* (New York: Viking, 1990), p. 137.

During his stage of ascendancy, Gorbachev would retain the commitment to cultural change but give it a radical, transformative content. Now the educated masses were treated as the source of wisdom, not simply clay to be molded by Party officials. Now officials would be held formally accountable to the conscious public, with secret-ballot elections and multiple candidacies. Now a "pluralism of opinions" and systemic criticism were defined as healthy phenomena that would better assist society as a whole to discover "truth." *Glasnost'* and democratization now implied an equalization of status between officials and masses as well as a process of formal accountability of those officials to the masses. It was difficult to disguise the threatening implications of these ideas and practices to officials of a Leninist regime, whatever their orientation. Gorbachev tried to reduce opposition by instituting procedures that allowed officials a disproportionate influence over the nomination process and that ensured a certain degree of corporate representation in the new parliament. Yet Gorbachev also obscured the more radical implications behind a veil of continuity.

One way he did this was periodically to declare that criticism and mass initiative, while prerequisites for the success of *perestroika,* were not absolutes. The goal must be "conscious discipline."[21] Criticism must combine "bravery" with a "principled orientation" – that is, *printsipial'nost',* which in Soviet lexicon means respect for the "correct [Party] line."[22] In February 1987, he addressed the issue of how far criticism should go in the era of *perestroika.* He declared that it must not be baseless; it must be "*partiinoi* (Party-minded), based on truth ... the sharper it is, the more responsible it should be."[23] A "law-based" (*pravovoe*) state creates a framework for "responsible" citizenship, not for unlimited license.[24] In like manner, Gorbachev echoed his predecessors' commitment to normative definitions of the public interest: "we support and will continue to support that which serves socialism, and will reject everything that is against the interests of the people."[25] This was a far cry from the tenets of *liberal* democracy, for it presumed that the public interest had to be defined by an enlightened elite and defended by that elite against citizens who were not principled, disciplined, or responsible.

---

[21] Gorbachev, *Perestroika,* p. 18.
[22] Gorbachev, *Izbrannye,* vol. 4, p. 326 (January 1987 Plenum).
[23] Ibid., p. 371 (February 1987 meeting in Central Committee); see also ibid., p. 359 (January 1987 Central Committee Plenum), and vol. 5, p. 415 (November 1987 anniversary speech).
[24] Gorbachev, *Perestroika,* pp. 93–4.
[25] Gorbachev, *Izbrannye,* vol. 6, p. 61 (February 1988 Central Committee Plenum); see also vol. 4, p. 327 (January 1987 Central Committee Plenum), and vol. 6, p. 393 (June 1988 CPSU Conference).

Gorbachev also reassured members of the Central Committee that, as long as they themselves got on the *perestroika* bandwagon, they had nothing to fear from the masses. The people, he argued repeatedly, are loyal to the Party, to *perestroika,* and to the system. They have been well educated by Soviet institutions and therefore have much expertise to offer. They need not be distrusted. Their activation need not be feared.[26]

For those who doubted the loyalty of the masses, Gorbachev provided assurance that a mighty and fundamentally legitimate Party–State, led by a determined general secretary, remained willing and able to enforce limits: "Is it possible that we, with such a powerful Party, such a patriotic people, which is dedicated to the ideas of socialism, to its Motherland, will not be able to cope if someone decides to use the wide-ranging *glasnost',* the democratic process for self-serving and anti-societal aims, for the aim of blackening?"[27] Considering that the cohesion and capacity of the KGB and other control mechanisms remained high during Gorbachev's stage of ascendancy, many officials of the Party–State must have found this assurance to be credible.

In addition to reassurance, Gorbachev played upon the elite's lack of self-confidence to intimidate fence-sitters into cooperating with his policies. In his December 1984 "campaign" speech, he had defined the need for fundamental change as a national security imperative if the USSR was to "enter the 21st century as a great power," and he had implied that the country was on the brink of a prerevolutionary situation.[28] Once in power, he toned down such dire warnings, but they reappeared as his program became more radical. "We are living in a critical time," he warned in September 1986.[29] The "destiny of socialism" hinges on avoiding a repetition of the mistakes of the 1970s and early 1980s.[30] There is "no alternative"; *perestroika* is simply "an objective necessity."[31]

The result of these efforts, Gorbachev assured his audiences, would be satisfying and familiar to those who joined the *perestroika* bandwagon. He

---

[26] Gorbachev, *Izbrannye,* vol. 2, p. 235 (27th Party Congress of February 1986); vol. 4, pp. 35–6, 50–1 (July 1986); vol. 4, p. 359 (January 1987 Central Committee Plenum); vol. 5, p. 130 (June 1987 Central Committee Plenum); vol. 6, p. 70 (February 1988 Central Committee Plenum); vol. 6, pp. 394–5 (June 1988 CPSU Conference). See also Gorbachev, *Perestroika,* pp. 54–7.

[27] Gorbachev, *Izbrannye rechi,* vol. 4, p. 358 (January 1987 Central Committee Plenum).

[28] Ibid., vol. 2, p. 86.

[29] Ibid., vol. 4, p. 88.

[30] Ibid., p. 300 (January 1987 Central Committee Plenum); see also vol. 5, p. 130 (June 1987 Central Committee Plenum); vol. 6, p. 77 (February 1988 Central Committee Plenum); vol. 6, pp. 326, 394 (June 1988 CPSU Party Conference: "The fate of the country, the fate of socialism is at stake. We are obligated to make clear the sharpness of the situation to those who have yet to acknowledge it" [p. 394]).

[31] Ibid., p. 300 (section heading of address to January 1987 Central Committee Plenum).

could not specify in detail what that system would look like. But he assured them that it would meet the highest ideals of the Marxist tradition. As he put it toward the end of his speech to the June 1988 Party Conference:

Yes, we do reject everything that deformed socialism in the 1930s and led it to stagnation in the 1970s. We want the type of socialism that has been cleansed from the encrustations (*nasloenii*) and perversions of past periods, but that retains everything that is best that came from the founders of socialist teaching.... We see socialism as a system of high culture and morality. It retains and reproduces the best accomplishments of the spiritual development of humankind, its rich moral experience. This is a society in which the life of working people is saturated with material and spiritual fulfillment, rejecting consumerism, lack of spirituality, and cultural primitivism.[32]

Although men like Ligachev and Ryzhkov were increasingly alienated by Gorbachev's radicalization, their ability jointly to oppose Gorbachev's initiatives was inhibited by the fact that they were alienated by different features of his program. Puritans were most concerned about affirming the leading role of the Party – and of orthodox values – in culture, politics, and administration. Technocrats were most concerned about rationalizing public administration by getting Party officials to interfere less in the workings of the ministerial bureaucracy and by rationalizing plan indicators. Thus, taking Chernyaev's informative memoir as a guide, we learn that Ryzhkov and Ligachev squared off in a December 1986 Politburo meeting about the desirability and necessity of retail price increases.[33] We also learn that, in November 1987, Ryzhkov blew up at Ligachev over economic reform policy: "Yegor Kuzmich personalizes the gross output, slave-driving, shock-work approach .... [T]he prime minister's reaction is understandable, he blew up.... It's been obvious for some time now that he [Ligachev] elicits a deep and barely concealed personal hostility, and not only from Ryzhkov."[34] And Ryzhkov delivered "the most forcefully emotional speech" against Ligachev over the Nina Andreeva affair (Spring 1988). Ryzhkov "even suggested relieving Ligachev of his control of ideology."[35]

But Ryzhkov's memoirs also reveal his alienation from both Ligachev and Gorbachev over an issue that is key to technocratic thinking: the calculation of what is possible. Ryzhkov denounces the anti-alcohol campaign as an example of a policy that placed ideology over practical considerations: "The tragedy of the campaign was in attempting to speed up and bring about the [immediate] achievement of what should have been a long-term program.

---

[32] Ibid., vol. 6, pp. 395, 396.
[33] Chernyaev, *Shest' let*, pp. 122–3.
[34] Ibid., p. 202.
[35] Ibid., pp. 205–6; see also Ryzhkov, *Desiat' let*, pp. 96–7, 102.

This demonstrated the personalities of Gorbachev and Ligachev – to solve problems immediately and quickly, without regard for real possibilities."[36] Yet it was Gorbachev's sponsorship of a campaignist approach to all of his policies, including *perestroika,* that made him appear to embody less of a break with the past than he would prove actually to be. As a result, during 1987–1989, Gorbachev was able to position himself as a liaison among shifting coalitions of supporters and dissenters within the Politburo. By shifting his political support among reformists, puritans, and technocrats, Gorbachev was able to forestall the creation of a stable coalition of opponents to his domestic policies.

JUSTIFYING A CONCESSIONARY FOREIGN POLICY

A similar pattern of justification of fundamental changes by cleverly linking them to the Marxist–Leninist tradition, and by presenting himself as an enlightened Marxist, can be found in Gorbachev's authority-building strategy in the realm of foreign policy.

Gorbachev used his proclaimed "new thinking" about international relations as justification for a concessionary foreign policy. The new thinking amounted to a new theory of international relations – one closer to liberal internationalism than to power politics, isolationism, or proletarian internationalism, which were its main competitors behind the scenes. The premises of the theory allowed Gorbachev to argue that his policies were not a sellout but a salvation, that they amounted to concessions to *reality* but not concessions to the imperialists per se. Given the cognitive and emotional condition of the elite, Gorbachev's audiences were predisposed to entertain these explanations as, at least, plausible. The plausibility of the claims, then, allowed Gorbachev to seize the initiative from rivals who argued that he was selling out the ideological heritage of the regime.

The power of the new thinking as justification can best be appreciated by comparing it to the "old thinking." Bear in mind that the Brezhnevite theory of international relations had been deployed to justify a nonconcessionary foreign policy, one that sought to collaborate and compete simultaneously – and to do each from a position of relative strength (or at least acknowledged equality) vis-à-vis the "imperialists." This was the meaning of the idea that "peaceful coexistence" was a form of class struggle. The collaborative urge under Brezhnev had been genuine, but it was not intended or allowed

---

[36] Ibid., p. 102.

to supplant or compromise the commitment of the Soviet leadership to the "anti-imperialist struggle," to Soviet hegemony in Eastern Europe, or to the continued division of Europe. What Gorbachev sought to justify was a policy that decisively subordinated or even abandoned the anti-imperialist struggle to the higher imperatives of great power collaboration, a policy that sought to eliminate inter-bloc competition on the European continent – indeed, to create a community of friendly states "from Vancouver to Vladivostok."

The basic tenets of the "old thinking" justified combining inter-bloc competition with collaborative management of the nuclear relationship.[37] However much Soviet doctrine had evolved since the death of Stalin, it was still based on a two-camps (or two-blocs) image of the international system in which an ongoing struggle between imperialist and anti-imperialist forces was shaping the future of international relations and was fostering – at some indeterminate point in the future – the "final crisis of capitalism." Class interests, though set within the existing state system, were still the driving force of international politics. Peaceful coexistence was a necessary concession to the realities of the nuclear age, but it sought to create a safe umbrella under which the competitive struggle could proceed and not to sacrifice class struggle on the altar of collaboration. Peaceful coexistence, then, was meant to make the world safe for the spread and defense of socialist values.

All of this was consistent with the two primary normative commitments that had been embedded in the Leninist–Stalinist heritage since 1918. The Bolshevik Party had a historical responsibility to maintain the power of the CPSU in the USSR *and* to assist the eventual global victory of socialism over imperialism. In practice these desiderata often conflicted with each other. In the nuclear age, they led to a constant wariness of the escalatory potential inherent in competitive or confrontational initiatives. However, with the possible exception of Khrushchev in 1963–1964,[38] they never led to the abandonment of one or the other normative commitment.

The commitment to anti-imperialist struggle was sustained, despite periodic setbacks and sobering experiences, by philosophical assumptions built

---

[37] Studies that specify the content of foreign policy doctrine under Brezhnev include: John Lenczowski, *Soviet Perceptions of U.S. Foreign Policy* (Ithaca, NY: Cornell University Press, 1982); R. Judson Mitchell, *Ideology of a Superpower* (Stanford, CA: Hoover Institution, 1982); Franklyn Griffiths, "The sources of American conduct: Soviet perspectives and their policy implications," *International Security*, vol. 9, no. 1 (Fall 1984), pp. 30–50; Zimmerman, *Soviet Perspectives*; Richard D. Anderson, *Public Politics in an Authoritarian State: Making Foreign Policy during the Brezhnev Years* (Ithaca, NY: Cornell University Press, 1993); S. Neil MacFarlane, *Superpower Rivalry and 3rd World Radicalism: The Idea of National Liberation* (London: Croom Helm, 1985).

[38] See Zimmerman, *Soviet Perspectives*, pp. 99–101, 152, 196–205, 222ff., 259–69.

into the ideological heritage. A Marxist–Leninist treated conflict and change as the normal conditions of international politics, as indeed of history and matter more generally. Hence setbacks and struggles were to be expected, but discouragement was prevented by the assumption that time is on the side of socialism and that eventual victory is assured. This assumption did not have to be demonstrated empirically. Indeed, the philosophy of knowledge on which the ideology was based presumed that, in any given era, only the process of struggle itself would reveal the scope of currently attainable gains. This reinforced the commitment to struggle, just as belief in the inevitability of eventual victory served to maintain morale. Once that belief was irretrievably lost, morale – or the stomach for sustained anti-imperialist struggle in the face of rising costs – plummeted as well.

Gorbachev's new thinking was crafted in this context of lost belief and damaged self-confidence. It substituted for the old precepts a quite different perspective on international politics.[39] In place of two-camp struggle based on class interests, Gorbachev touted the "interdependence" of the world community, the commonality of interests among states of North America, Europe, and the USSR, and the transcendant threats to "all-human interests" posed by nuclear competition, the militarization of international relations, the proliferation of weapons of mass destruction, Third World poverty, and environmental hazards. Peaceful coexistence, his spokespersons argued, must no longer be viewed as a form of class struggle. Rather, it is an end in itself, essential to avert threats to the survival of humankind inherent in unrestrained competition. It was therefore imperative that the great powers, and especially the superpowers, put an end to their military competition and collaborate on the resolution of transnational existential threats.

The new thinking was especially critical of the use of military force as a means of dealing with threats to states. Since violence contains the greatest escalatory potential in interstate relations, and since global interdependence ensures that violent disruptions may reverberate throughout the international order, demilitarization of relations among states was a priority. From this it followed that great-power relations could not be built upon mutual intimidation; rather, the goal was a "mutual security" in which neither side tried to base its own security on the other side's insecurity.

---

[39] Studies of the doctrinal content of Gorbachev's new thinking include: Allen Lynch, *Gorbachev's International Outlook: Intellectual Origins and Political Consequences* (Boulder, CO: Westview, 1989); Margot Light, *The Soviet Theory of International Relations* (New York: St. Martin's, 1988); V. Kubalkova and A. A. Cruickshank, *Thinking "New" about Soviet New Thinking* (Berkeley: University of California, Institute of International Studies, no. 74, 1989); Robert D. English, *Russia and the Idea of the West: Gorbachev, Intellectuals and the End of the Cold War* (New York: Columbia University Press, 2000).

An important tactical component of the new thinking was the entreaty to "deny the imperialists their 'enemy image'." On this score, the new thinking proclaimed that, in order to build a collaborative relationship with the West, it was necessary to reshape the politics of foreign policy decisionmaking in the West. If hardliners remained ascendant in Western capitals, then Soviet overtures would not be reciprocated and the prospect of great-power collaboration would not be realized. Accordingly, the USSR's historical responsibility was to make offers the West could not refuse in order to delegitimize the hardliners' claim that the communist enemy could never be trusted. Thus, Soviet policies would assist the transformation of both public and elite opinion in Western countries, helping thereby to create the political basis for the kind of sustained collaboration required to defuse threats to civilization.

As we documented in Chapter 3, Gorbachev's speeches of December 1984 had already endorsed concepts associated with new thinking and new thinkers in foreign relations. However, as in his address to the 27th Party Congress in February 1986,[40] such endorsement had coexisted – not very peacefully – with traditional rhetoric about the "world revolutionary process" and the "anti-imperialist struggle." At that time, new themes were present but not prominent in his speeches. In 1987, however, Gorbachev largely eliminated the traditionalist rhetoric. Themes of the new thinking occupied center stage in his major address of February 1987 to an international conference of peace activists gathered in Moscow.[41] Implications of the new thinking were elaborated extensively in the book Gorbachev published that year, which was intended for both internal and external audiences.[42]

SELLING SALVATION OR SELLING OUT?

In what ways could these doctrinal substitutions justify a concessionary foreign policy? How could they gain credibility among audiences beset by self-doubt concerning their own political staying power at home and abroad? Perhaps most striking about the content and tone of the new thinking was its resonance with certain features of the Marxist–Leninist ideological heritage, which allowed many "romantic Leninists" to relate to it even if they were ambivalent about its content. Thus, as Kubalkova and Cruickshank have nicely demonstrated,[43] the new thinking, like the Leninist heritage in Soviet foreign policy, was highly moralistic, missionary, and self-righteous in presenting the

---

[40] *Izbrannye,* vol. 3, esp. pp. 245–52.
[41] *Izbrannye,* vol. 4, pp. 376–92.
[42] Gorbachev, *Perestroika.*
[43] *Thinking "New."*

Soviet Union as a beacon for world public opinion. It presented the image of a radiant future to be brokered by a progressive USSR that possessed special insight into historical necessity and was mobilizing global social forces to discredit militarist "old thinkers" in all countries. In this respect, the new thinking could appeal as well to "Soviet patriots," who were primarily interested in Western acceptance of the USSR as a co-equal great power; they were being promised a future in which their country would play a leading role in the promised transformation of international relations.

This perspective fed nicely into traditional Soviet optimism as well as Leninist ontology. It presented the newly defined radiant future as a potential that is latent within the current international system – but a potential that can be realized only through conscious action and determined consciousness-raising. In this respect, global interdependence and a "common European home" were latent conditions and also policy goals. At the same time, the new thinking presented interdependence as an autonomously growing trend within international relations, one that could be resisted only at growing cost and with potentially catastrophic consequences. All of this echoed precisely a key philosophical premise of Marxism–Leninism: the inevitability of the desirable. The victory of socialism at home and abroad was historically inevitable, but only if enlightened elites struggled to realize the socialist potential latent within the current order of things.

The idea of "robbing the imperialists of their enemy image" was also an ingenious update of a traditional Soviet perspective on East–West competition. Leninist and Stalinist foreign policy had always looked to influence or ally with potentially progressive forces in Western societies against militarist elites within those countries. After Stalin, this tendency continued but was supplemented by a more differentiated image of Western elites, which led Khrushchev and Brezhnev at times to urge policies that would help the "moderates" or "bourgeois realists" in their policy struggles with the "madmen."[44] Thus, Gorbachev's strategy of helping to raise the consciousness of global masses about the need for transnational cooperation, as well as his strategy of undercutting the credibility of hardliners in policymaking circles, resonated with important tactical components of the Leninist heritage.

In a practical sense, Gorbachev's deprecation of the utility – and magnification of the dangers – of the military instrument in global affairs provided a justification for undercutting the political weight of powerful constituencies

---

[44] Zimmerman, *Soviet Perspectives*; Franklyn Griffiths, "Images, politics, and learning in Soviet behavior toward the United States" (Ph.D. dissertation, Columbia University, New York, 1972).

in contemporary Soviet politics. Moreover, his redefinition of security as having to be "mutual" challenged the unilateralism and self-sufficiency inherent in Soviet military doctrine. Surely, elite audiences who lacked self-confidence about their ability to continue in the old way, who were intimidated by the prospect of another arms race, and who realized to their chagrin that the arms buildup under Brezhnev had not, after all, shifted the correlation of forces to the advantage of socialism, were susceptible to an alternative way of thinking about global politics. Similarly, conservative elites who realized that repeated Soviet invasions had not reduced the endemic instability of East European regimes were susceptible to an alternative vision of political order on the European continent. Gorbachev's redefinitions could provide solace to these audiences even as they angered the unreconstructed militarists.

To a lesser degree (but still substantially), this redefinition also resonated with the Leninist heritage, for the "correlation of forces" doctrine had roots in a tradition that never measured power in purely military terms. In contrast to some balance-of-power notions in Western "realist" thought, the Leninist correlation of forces insisted that the sources of power are multidimensional. Gorbachev was thus plausibly emphasizing some of those other dimensions, including moral authority. Then too, the correlation of forces doctrine was always explicitly *dynamic* in its thrust; as Seweryn Bialer has noted, it focused on the correlation of *trends*.[45] Hence audiences who had a sense of foreboding about the future could receive reassurance from the new thinking. Its emphasis on other sources of power, and on conscious struggle to realize the potential latent within the international system, could shift the correlation of trends back to the advantage of the Soviet Union in world affairs – or at least could stop the anti-Soviet tide. The outcome might not be socialist revolution or victory in the anti-imperialist struggle, both of which Gorbachev either wrote off or downplayed, but it would be a new era of Soviet co-leadership in world affairs that would help to avert catastrophes facing the global village.

Another strength of the new thinking as an act of political salesmanship was that elements of it had already been legitimized in Soviet politics in earlier decades. The dangers of nuclear war, and the implicit "all-human" stake in avoiding it, had been central to doctrinal innovations that Malenkov (and, later, Khrushchev) had introduced in the 1950s and 1960s.[46] Those doctrinal changes survived Khrushchev's overthrow more or less intact, facilitating the

[45] Seweryn Bialer, *Stalin's Successors: Leadership, Stability, and Change in the Soviet Union* (Cambridge University Press, 1980), p. 246.

[46] In addition to Zimmerman, *Soviet Perspectives,* and Griffiths, "The Sources," see Evangelista, *Unarmed Warriors.*

détente of the early 1970s. Likewise, notions of global interdependence had entered official Soviet rhetoric, albeit tentatively, under Khrushchev and even before him, as these notions had typically been emphasized for tactical purposes during traditional Soviet "breathing spells" in foreign policy. To be sure, Gorbachev was now elaborating these concepts to an unprecedented extent and was drawing conclusions for Soviet global power that by far exceeded those of his predecessors. Yegor Ligachev, for example, was correct to complain in 1988 that the regime's Leninist identity was threatened by the recent substitution of "all-human interests" for class interests as the top priority of Soviet foreign policy.[47] But precisely because the concepts were familiar ones, and because they could be used to justify either a breathing spell or a more fundamental reevaluation, they afforded Gorbachev the tactical advantage – whether he planned it this way or not – of postponing awareness among the fence-sitters and ambivalents in the Central Committee of the full implications of what he was doing.

There was more than just formal doctrinal change involved in the process of justifying Gorbachev's giveaways. There were also tactical maneuvers with which he supplemented the new doctrine. Consider, for example, his behavior in Washington, D.C., in December 1987, when he made concessions that allowed him and President Reagan to finalize and sign the INF Treaty. After the signing, Gorbachev and Shevardnadze stood up, beaming, and raised their arms straight up in a victory gesture.[48] Victory? Gorbachev, in the course of 1987, had abandoned every negotiating position upon which Soviet leaders had been insisting since 1979. But this was victory according to a different set of criteria. Moscow had made Reagan an offer he could not refuse and robbed him of his "enemy image" of the USSR. Gorbachev had delivered the presumably irreconcilable author of Star Wars missile defense and "evil empire" rhetoric to the temple of negotiation and collaboration. Gorbachev and Shevardnadze had proven that one could do business with Reagan – or better, that Reagan could be induced to do business with them. The U.S. missiles would not be deployed after all!

This was an entirely different set of "success indicators" from those traditionally employed by Soviet negotiators. Until then, the cost of achieving the goal had been the issue; but as Gorbachev redefined the game, the cost was to be downplayed if not ignored. The goal of delivering Reagan and of ending the deployment of Pershing and cruise missiles on land in Europe had been accomplished.

---

[47] *Pravda*, August 6, 1988, p. 2.
[48] "The CBS Evening News," December 8, 1987.

This conception of reciprocity – and of equivalence of exchange in the East–West relationship – was new to Soviet bargaining behavior. It could only have been sold in terms that played to the elite's loss of self-confidence. At the theoretical level, the new thinking did just that, making a virtue of proclaimed necessity. Yet even below the level of theory, at the very practical level of everyday political rhetoric, Gorbachev played to the loss of self-confidence with the much-applied proclamation: "there is no alternative!"[49]

Consider the implications of this claim. In effect, it argues that the appropriate success indicator for judging Soviet negotiating behavior is not conformance of the deal to some preconceived notion of equal sacrifice by each superpower. "There is no alternative" is an implicitly dynamic concept, one that invites the audience to consider the consequences of intransigence and of the failure to reach agreement. It stands in contrast to the static conceptions of quantitative parity and equivalent exchange that marked U.S.–Soviet negotiations throughout the 1970s. Gorbachev was telling his audiences that intransigence would allow the emergence of a reality still more disagreeable than the reality he proposed to negotiate with the United States. In the INF negotiations, for example, the implication was that the deployment of Pershing and cruise missiles in Europe, faced by a large and growing Soviet arsenal of SS-20s and by other countermeasures against the U.S. deployments (and then by U.S. reactions to those countermeasures), would be more disagreeable than intrusively verified elimination of all these missiles by both sides.[50]

When we consider tactical advantages, no catalog of the times would be complete without mention of the term "new thinking." The connotations of the phrase squared with a climate of opinion that was eager to "get the country moving again" after the geriatric leadership's debacles of the early 1980s. But the term also facilitated seizure of the political initiative and disabling of one's opponents by its progressive and optimistic connotations. Doubters were waved off as "old thinkers." New thinking was a sign that you had understood the requirements of historical necessity, that you recognized the

---

49 Already in April 1985, Gorbachev had been arguing that "there is no other way" when proclaiming that a decisive break with Brezhnevism was needed (Gorbachev, *Izbrannye*, vol. 2, p. 155; see also p. 212 [May 1985]). The argument, of course, had been implicit in his December 1984 speech, when he suggested that Russia could lose its great-power status or could face a revolutionary situation at home if it did not change course. What changed in 1987 was the application of the claim ("there is no alternative") to a specified, transformational program for breaking out of the constraints of the culture and institutions (ideology and organization) bequeathed by Brezhnev.

50 Although speculative, it is not difficult to imagine discussions in which Gorbachev countered the defiant negotiating proposals of militant colleagues with the challenge: *"nu, i potom, chto?"* ("yes, and what *then?*").

direction in which history was moving. Old thinkers had allowed themselves to become myopic about their "historical responsibility." Who would want to be so dubbed?

None of this is to claim that clever argumentation alone was sufficient to sell a concessionary foreign policy. Surely, both the message and the messenger had an impact. Gorbachev built up his power base before launching his foreign policy revolution. Moreover, his strong personality, capacity for complex debate in small groups, and magnificent sense of political timing and surprise during his rise to ascendancy (though not thereafter) reinforced the image projected by his power – thereby giving his audiences a motivation to follow him, or at least not to defy him. The content, tone, and form of the new thinking then became an important reinforcement of both power and personality, helping Gorbachev to build his authority as a foreign policy decisionmaker even as (by traditional standards) he was "giving away the store."

Thus, in both domestic and foreign policy, Gorbachev built authority by first consolidating his power while cultivating the image of a "responsible" innovator and then pushing to the fore with a comprehensive, radical program that he managed to present as a novel synthesis of Leninism and procedural democracy: "socialist democracy." This strategy was ingenious as long as his political audiences were unable to calculate the magnitude of the threats to their interests and identities that lurked below the surface. It did not take long before these became obvious.

5

Gorbachev on the Political Defensive

The twelve months between mid-1989 and mid-1990 were one of those turn-ing points in a leader's administration when suddenly things start to go very wrong. Khrushchev experienced this from mid-1960 to mid-1961. For Brezh-nev, the tide did not turn so suddenly; his domestic program faltered in 1972, his foreign policy only during 1974–1976. For Gorbachev, as for Khrushchev, one year highlighted the contradictions within both his domestic and for-eign policy programs. This also meant that both men suddenly experienced a crisis of credibility. Both of them had promised a great deal and had pushed themselves to the fore as sponsors of a transformative vision.[1] Hence, they could not credibly diffuse responsibility for failure onto the leadership collec-tive. Their authority was on the line. In Gorbachev's case, he found himself at the mercy of domestic and international forces he himself had unleashed as he introduced an autonomous public arena into Soviet politics and as he pursued a conciliatory foreign policy. This chapter analyzes the vulnerabili-ties of Gorbachev's domestic and foreign policies and his efforts to retain and recoup his political authority as those vulnerabilities became obvious.

VULNERABILITIES OF *PERESTROIKA*

During 1988–1989, the contradictions within Gorbachev's program for *pere-stroika* started to become obvious. His strategy of giving the official class a

---

[1] Khrushchev's transformative vision of 1959–1960 was of a Leninist system that had achieved its utopian goal. Since Khrushchev was not seeking to destroy the Leninist system, however, I have been referring to his leadership as "reformist" and to Gorbachev's as "transformational." This should not be confused with my use here of "transformative vision" to refer to both men's programs during their stages of ascendancy.

stake in the new order by only gradually shifting authority from Party executive organs to soviet legislative organs, while a boon for democracy, created a situation in which officials of the Party and the state had both the incentive and the opportunity to instead "steal the state": privatizing and stealing the assets of their agencies and contributing thereby to a collapse of public administration that was becoming increasingly evident in 1990.[2] Similarly, his strategy of giving officials the opportunity to become businessmen, while it gave them a stake in the new order, also gave them the opportunity to use their continuing official power to monopolize business activity in the budding private sector that they were entering.

Glasnost' revealed the contradictions between Leninism and liberalism. Gorbachev had attempted to expand the functions of *glasnost'* from a limited "searchlight" role – selectively exposing incompetence and malfeasance among officials – to a broader, more systemic critique. But he tried to do so gradually in order to avoid driving moderates into the ranks of the extremists on both ends of the political spectrum. Indeed, during 1987–1988, while increasingly removing the shackles of censorship, he also tried to keep journal and newspaper editors from going too far, tried to strike a balance between the old and the new in his public statements, and tried to maintain the fiction of there being a "correct Party line" to which agents of the regime were expected to conform.[3]

All of this was easier said than done. During 1988–1989, the forces of radicalism within the cultural intelligentsia, the journalistic community, and the Academy of Sciences were publishing increasingly bold and systemic critiques; they did so within the very public arenas that Gorbachev had created for them.[4] Whereas Gorbachev was willing to criticize Stalin, they were willing to criticize Lenin also. Whereas Gorbachev was willing to denounce the

[2] Steven L. Solnick, *Stealing the State: Control and Collapse in Soviet Institutions* (Cambridge, MA: Harvard University Press, 1998).

[3] See, for example, his speech on the 70th anniversary of the 1917 Bolshevik Revolution, November 7, 1987 (Mikhail Gorbachev, *Izbrannye rech'i i stat'i* [Moscow: Izdatel'stvo politicheskoi literatury, 1987], vol. 5, pp. 386–436).

[4] For studies of the evolution of *glasnost'* and of this tension between Gorbachev and the radicals, see Alec Nove, *Glasnost' in Action: Cultural Renaissance in Russia* (Boston: Unwin Hyman, 1989); Roy Medvedev and Giuletto Chiesa, *Time of Change: An Insider's View of Russia's Transformation* (New York: Random House, 1989); Stephen F. Cohen and Katrina vanden Heuvel, *Voices of Glasnost: Interviews with Gorbachev's Reformers* (New York: Norton, 1989); William & Jane Taubman, *Moscow Spring* (New York: Summit, 1989); Andrei Melville and Gail W. Lapidus (Eds.), *The Glasnost Papers: Voices on Reform from Moscow* (Boulder, CO: Westview, 1990); Jack F. Matlock, Jr., *Autopsy on an Empire* (New York: Random House, 1995).

corruption of many officials and the Party apparatus for acting as a "braking mechanism" on the implementation of *perestroika*,[5] the radicals were willing to argue that the system of single-party rule itself was the problem – that it created and protected a class of corrupt officials and that it was incapable of being reformed. Whereas Gorbachev countenanced a far-reaching yet only partial review of the crimes of Soviet history, the radicals insisted on a complete review of that history. Whereas Gorbachev was willing to institute parliamentary elections, the radicals called for public election of the president and an end to the exclusive nominating procedures employed during the first parliamentary elections. Gorbachev, both to protect his power and to regulate the process of transformation in order to keep it peaceful, wanted to retain the ability to modulate free expression. The radicals wanted an absolute commitment to free speech. As a result, the rate of radicalization of the active, mobilized public during 1989–1990 was decidedly outpacing Gorbachev's strategy for maintaining a balance between the "moderate right" and the "moderate left" while retaining for himself an indispensable political role as balancer between the two poles.[6]

In economic policy, Gorbachev moved cautiously and with half-measures, thus heightening the contradictions. He reduced the prerogatives of ministries and central planners, but went slow on (or entirely avoided) the construction of market institutions, de-monopolization of the economy, and liberalization of prices. The consequence was that, by 1989–1990, the capacity of the command system to coordinate exchange relationships within the economy had been crippled, but a market economy had not yet been created as a substitute. Perhaps Gorbachev rationalized that opening the economy to the world market, as he began to do with his unprecedented joint-ventures legislation in January 1987, would offset these deficiencies. But that would take time as well as a further loosening of restrictions on joint ventures. In the near term, this left the economy with the worst of both worlds, suffering from extreme disequilibrium and lack of coordination.

---

[5] Mikhail Gorbachev, *Perestroika: New Thinking for Our Country and the World* (New York: Perennial, 1987), pp. 97–8.

[6] For a penetrating analysis of the contradictions that emerged as political space was opened to autonomous political expression, see Michael Urban (with Vyecheslav Igrunov and Sergei Mitrokhin), *The Rebirth of Politics in Russia* (Cambridge University Press, 1997), chs. 3–6. For other excellent case studies of this rebirth of political society, see Kathleen E. Smith, *Remembering Stalin's Victims: Popular Memory and the End of the USSR* (Ithaca, NY: Cornell University Press, 1996); Jane I. Dawson, *Eco-nationalism: Anti-Nuclear Activism and National Identity in Russia, Lithuania, and Ukraine* (Durham, NC: Duke University Press, 1996); M. Steven Fish, *Democracy from Scratch: Opposition and Regime in the New Russian Revolution* (Princeton, NJ: Princeton University Press, 1995).

For example, Gorbachev's strategy of gradually increasing the opportunities for private commercial activity, while leaving such activities only semi-legitimized and under heavy regulatory restrictions, provided the opportunity for corrupt officials and organized crime to extort from, and ultimately control, the budding, small-scale private sector – and to ensure against the emergence of a truly competitive market. Moreover, Gorbachev's refusal to tackle macroeconomic stabilization by liberalizing price controls led him to borrow money abroad and spend money desperately to counter disequilibria in the economy, which exacerbated hidden inflation, shortages, and a severe budgetary shortfall. By mid-1990, the shelves of foodstores were largely empty in Moscow at a time when people had the newfound freedom to complain loudly and to seek electoral revenge against Party officials for the situation.[7]

This points to still another contradiction. Gorbachev, consistent with the Marxist tradition, defined Soviet socialism as a salvageable system. He promised to realize the potential of that system by demonstrating that a "good" society (a "socialist democracy") lay latent within Soviet society. In order to accomplish this, he needed to mobilize the "human factor" – the young, the educated, and the idealistic – by removing the shackles imposed on them by a corrupted Party apparatus. Like Khrushchev earlier, Gorbachev argued that Party activists, not Party bureaucrats, would become the leadership core of a future socialist society. They would lead by example, and they would help to bring out the best in people. Gorbachev argued that cultural transformation would be a product of persuasion and inspiration and that conscious mobilization of the population, led by the best and the brightest among Party activists, was the route toward that end. By contrast, the regulatory institutions and incentive structures typical of highly competitive, capitalist societies were based on the assumption that human beings can be motivated only by coercion and greed – that human nature is ultimately egoistic and invidious, and that discipline needs to be imposed from without. Instead, Gorbachev's program was based on the premise that human beings in a socialist society are essentially charitable and collectivistic, if properly inspired.

Such an optimistic vision may or may not be intrinsically realistic, but that is beside the point. In the Soviet case, it is clear that realization of the vision required both time and improvements in everyday material conditions. However, Gorbachev found himself with very little "political time" on his hands. He could not demonstrate the collectivistic potential latent within Soviet citizens on short order (if ever). And, given the contradictions in his

---

[7] On the contradictions within Gorbachev's approach to economic reform, see Marshall I. Goldman, *What Went Wrong with Perestroika* (New York: Norton, 1991).

economic policy, material conditions deteriorated. Hence, many Soviet citizens, anxious about material conditions and unshackled by *glasnost'*, became cynics and/or critics, rapidly losing faith in *perestroika* and becoming vocal opponents of Soviet leaders in Moscow. Gorbachev could hardly recoup his authority in 1990–1991 by pointing to this mobilized opposition (such as the "Democratic Russia" movement) as an example of the new socialist citizen, for they were already rejecting him as insufficiently radical.

In 1989–1990 as well, centrifugal forces within the federation at large threatened to reach a point of no return. Secession was already on the front burner in the Baltic states, inter-ethnic violence was starting to sweep the Caucasus and portions of Central Asia, and the Nagorno–Karabakh issue between Armenia and Azerbaidjan had already resulted in open warfare. Here Gorbachev fell victim to his program's lack of appreciation of the depth of nationalist sentiment in the republics. *Glasnost'* had created an autonomous public arena in which to press nationalist and secessionist demands. Disintegration of the command economy undercut the ties that bound together the economies of the republics within the Soviet Union. Economic nationalism reinforced growing civic and ethnic nationalism in those union republics. Democratization introduced competitive elections to republican legislatures that fundamentally undermined the centralized system of cadre control that Gorbachev had inherited. Henceforth, republic-level officials would know that their political careers hinged as much, and perhaps more, on satisfying constituents "below" as on catering to political bosses "above" in Moscow. The combination of all these policies, together with Gorbachev's reluctance to use force to define strict limits to republican initiatives, further angered and demoralized officials of the military and the KGB – the very institutions that would be needed to prevent disintegration from resulting in dissolution of the USSR. In sum, the weakening of central control and the transformative policies embraced by Gorbachev brought to the fore a series of contradictions within Soviet ethnofederalism, contradictions that Soviet leaders had previously managed through a combination of strict political controls and economic benefits to the politically conformist.[8]

---

[8] On the evolution of tensions between the republics and the center during 1988–1990, see Gail W. Lapidus, "Gorbachev and the 'national question': Restructuring the Soviet Federation," *Soviet Economy*, vol. 5, no. 3 (July–September 1989), pp. 201–50, and Gregory Gleason (Ed.), *Federalism and Nationalism: The Struggle for Republican Rights in the USSR* (Boulder, CO: Westview, 1990). On the contradictions within Soviet ethnofederalism, see Ronald Suny, *The Revenge of the Past: Nationalism, Revolution, and the Collapse of the Soviet Union* (Stanford, CA: Stanford University Press, 1993), and Valerie Bunce, *Subversive Institutions: The Design and Destruction of Socialism and the State* (Cambridge University Press, 1999).

Gorbachev had no realistic strategy for keeping nationalism within bounds once his policies removed both the incentives and the threats on which Soviet central power had rested. He assumed that negotiations among leaders of the republics, plus a nationwide referendum, would lead to a middle ground on which a stable federation would rest. He further assumed that he could rein in the forces of both reaction and secession. He proved capable of doing neither, though he did prevent a full-blown reactionary backlash against centrifugal tendencies. But he was unwilling or unable to join forces fully with either extreme to save his political hide.

Thus, Gorbachev's policies crippled the ability of the old system to defend itself *as a system* against the very social forces his policies had unleashed. The result was not the creation of a stable equilibrium on which a middle way could rest. Instead, the result was systemic disintegration, public mobilization of opposition to that system, and a relentless slide toward collapse. Gorbachev never advocated abolition of the Communist Party or collapse of the Soviet Union. But that is what he got, and the speed with which this occurred discredited his leadership, leaving him little time to recoup his political authority.

VULNERABILITIES OF THE NEW THINKING

Even as Gorbachev's domestic policies were foundering, one could discern vulnerabilities within the new thinking that would make it susceptible to counterattack. Here, in the foreign policy realm, contradictions were increasingly being revealed between the new thinking's idealistic liberal internationalism and the *realpolitik* that still informed the foreign policies of the United States. The new thinking, as a way of conceptualizing international politics and thereby of justifying Soviet concessionary behavior, was both intrinsically vulnerable and losing credibility in light of events abroad.

One such vulnerability was intrinsic to the tension in Marxist–Leninist theory between the potential and the actual. Khrushchev and Brezhnev had touted the traditional Leninist claim that the twentieth century was indeed the era of the "final crisis of capitalism" and that the global correlation of forces was shifting in favor of socialism. It was the historical responsibility of the USSR to assist those forces that would effect the final crisis and the decisive shift. But one could not know in advance whether such assistance was on the verge of making the difference. It remained only an article of faith that victory was "inevitable."

In like manner – but with very different purposes and much greater urgency – Gorbachev had predicted that the contemporary world was becoming so interdependent and dangerous that all reasonable people would recognize the need for an anti-militarist, cooperative world order. He further predicted that, as a result of Soviet concessionary foreign policies, international public opinion and (accordingly) the leaders of major governments would acknowledge the moral force of the USSR and treat that country as a leading power within the emerging world order. Having based his foreign policies on this prediction, Gorbachev had to search for evidence that the potential he so loudly touted was indeed being realized. He had to worry about his ability to demonstrate that his concessionary behavior was in fact helping to transform the adversary (by robbing him of his "enemy image") and helping to actualize the potential for a new world order inherent in the "fact" of global interdependence. (This authority-maintenance imperative was, I take it, in part responsible for his triumphant posturing at the December 1987 summit in Washington.) Thus, the credibility of Gorbachev's authority-building strategy in the foreign policy realm was hostage to the behavior of the United States and to events (in Afghanistan, Europe, the United States, and elsewhere) that were largely beyond his control.

Unfortunately for Gorbachev, he was not able to demonstrate much more actualization of potential than the willingness of Ronald Reagan and George Bush to sign deals that involved Soviet acceptance of maximal U.S. terms. Nor was Gorbachev able to claim that his idealistic, self-denying internationalism was being reciprocated by the United States. The U.S. invasion of Panama in 1989 and the Persian Gulf confrontation (1990) and war (1991), although not threatening to Soviet national security, provided fuel for arguments that U.S. politics were not changing at all, that *realpolitik* remained the driving perspective behind U.S. foreign policy, that military force remained the primary instrumentality of U.S. foreign policy, and that the U.S. goal was a unipolar world, not an East–West collective security system. The Persian Gulf war demonstrated this contradiction at work. On the one hand, Gorbachev accepted and endorsed the use of military force against Saddam Hussein if the Iraqi leader did not withdraw his troops from Kuwait. On the other hand, Gorbachev tried desperately to avoid the war, attempting last-minute Soviet mediation of the conflict between Washington and Baghdad. It was a measure of the political dilemma in which he found himself that the Soviet leader left town (Moscow) when President Bush expressed irritation at Soviet efforts and launched the ground offensive against Iraq.[9]

A further vulnerability of the new thinking revealed itself in Eastern Europe during 1989. Gorbachev assumed that an all-European security community

---

[9] *Pravda*, February 25, 1991, p. 1, and March 1, 1991, pp. 1–2.

could eventually emerge as the Soviet Union and the socialist states of Eastern Europe transformed themselves into socialist democracies and sought a joint, Soviet-backed rapprochement with Western Europe and the United States. Toward this end, he even encouraged reformist forces within Eastern Europe to assert themselves against recalcitrant communist elites – in the faith that this would lead to the construction of socialist democracies rather than revolutionary overthrow of the entire political order. Just as Gorbachev assumed that a democratic–internationalist equilibrium could develop in interrepublican relations within the USSR, so he assumed that such an equilibrium could develop in Eastern Europe. Both assumptions proved illusory. The alternative to state socialism in Eastern Europe was not socialist democracy and a foreign policy of equal friendship with both East and West. Rather, it was either revanchist nationalism or liberal democracy and an effort to join Western Europe at the expense of relations with the USSR. Gorbachev's search for a stable equilibrium was frustrated by a cascade of revolutions against both Communist Party rule and alliance with the USSR.

The collapse of communism in Eastern Europe not only discredited Gorbachev's promise to reconcile transformation and stability, it also undercut his promise to reconcile transformation with Soviet national security. Gorbachev's eagerness to claim that traditional definitions of national security had become obsolete was here put to its most severe test. Panama and Iraq damaged the credibility of Gorbachev's claims about the broader international order. But events in Eastern Europe hit even closer to home: collapse of the Warsaw Pact, reunification of Germany within NATO, demands from Poland, Hungary, and Czechoslovakia that Soviet troops depart their country as soon as possible, a Conventional Forces in Europe Treaty in which the West secured asymmetrical deep cuts in Soviet armed forces, and the sudden emergence of Western rhetoric about "victory" in the Cold War. All these events cascaded in less than a year, between late 1989 and late 1990. They bolstered the credibility of counterclaims that the international order had not essentially changed for the better and that the shifting correlation of trends internationally actually posed a direct threat to Soviet national security and, indeed, to the survival of the USSR as a state.

Such a critique was compelling, as communist states collapsed *seriatim* throughout Eastern Europe during the second half of 1989. But Gorbachev could not bring himself to use force to stem the tide. In his mind, the prospective costs of doing so exceeded by far the costs of living with the consequences of these anti-communist revolutions. Gorbachev had built his authority at home *and abroad* by arguing against the continued militarization of state–society relations and relations among states. By 1989, he would have had to renounce everything he had stood for publicly if he had sent the tanks back into

Eastern Europe. This would have cost him the good relations he had developed with Western leaders as well as the prospects of material benefit and international integration ("Europe – our Common Home") that those relations held. Remilitarization would also have undercut the stated rationale for continued democratization of his own country. Of course, it would also have deeply undercut his credibility as a leader among the audiences to which he had directed his authority-building appeals. Furthermore, by 1989, it might also have run counter to the self-image and values he had internalized during 1985–1989.[10]

Hence, Gorbachev acquiesced in the East European revolutions and tried to make the losses more palatable to his political audiences. He negotiated a deal with the United States and Germany that provided for substantial material assistance to the USSR and for a phased (rather than precipitous) withdrawal of Soviet troops from eastern Germany. In exchange, he accepted what had fast become a fait accompli: the reunification of Germany within NATO. But material assistance, in the eyes of most Soviet politicians, was scant compensation for national humiliation and national-security perils. Not surprisingly, when Foreign Minister Shevardnadze resigned in December 1990, he complained specifically about those deputies who were accusing him of a sellout in the Persian Gulf and Eastern Europe.[11] Thus, well before the collapse of the USSR and the end of Gorbachev's days in power, both nationalists and advocates of *realpolitik* had defected from the dominant foreign policy coalition or had become more vocal in expressing their ambivalence.

How did Gorbachev respond to the growing gap between promise and performance? Simultaneously, he sought to reconsolidate his political power and to recoup his depleted credibility and authority as leader.

THE RECONSOLIDATION OF POLITICAL POWER

A Soviet Party leader could not take his power for granted; he was not elected to a fixed term of office and had to begin his years in office in the midst of a struggle for power. (By contrast, the succession struggle in electoral regimes precedes the assumption of formal power.) For this reason, Soviet leaders did not present comprehensive programs until their stage of ascendancy, following their victory in the power struggle. In the meantime, they sought not only to shape the climate of opinion within the Central Committee in their favor but also to build networks of supporters within the Central Committee, its apparatus of rule, and regional Party organs.

---

[10] For a masterful demonstration of how Gorbachev came to be incapable of bringing himself to use force in Eastern Europe, see Jacques Lévesque, *The Enigma of 1989: The USSR and the Liberation of Eastern Europe* (Berkeley: University of California Press, 1997).

[11] *Izvestiia*, December 29, 1990.

Gorbachev followed this conventional route during the first stage of his administration. During 1985–1987, he placed supporters in the Politburo, the central Party apparatus, and the regional Party organs, while purging many incumbents from those institutions. He also replaced the editors of major media outlets and the directors of major cultural institutions (Union of Writers, Union of Theatre Workers, etc.). These outlets and institutions were the instruments of *glasnost'* that bolstered his ability to mobilize a social base for significant change.

Although Gorbachev consolidated his power exceptionally quickly by historical Soviet standards, the radical policies he adopted during his stage of ascendancy undermined the loyalties of his erstwhile clients within the Party apparatus. The democratizing policies he enacted in 1988 clearly (and predictably) threatened the material interests of Party officials, who were sensitive to being criticized in public and completely unaccustomed to being replaced through public elections. The radicalization of Gorbachev's policy program, therefore, led him to both weaken and purge the institutions through which he had prevailed in the succession struggle. Thus, in October 1988, he abolished almost all the branch economic departments of the Central Committee, diminished the role of the Central Committee Secretariat in top-level decisionmaking, and set up six new Central Committee commissions (of dubious power) to perform functions previously exercised by the Secretariat. In April 1989, Gorbachev pressured 98 members and candidate members of the Party's Central Committee to resign from that body; several of these were Politburo-level holdovers from the old regime, including former Foreign Minister Andrei Gromyko and former Prime Minister Nikolai Tikhonov.

But even as Gorbachev was sapping the very bodies of the Party apparatus within which he enjoyed the power of patronage allocation, he was building up the power of alternative institutions within which he did not have such hierarchical powers. His program called for the steady transfer of political power from the Party apparatus to newly created legislative institutions. The Congress of People's Deputies was founded by competitive, popular election in April 1989. It chose a Supreme Soviet as its primary working body. Gorbachev was elected chairman of that Supreme Soviet by a vote of the deputies.

Gorbachev had taken the step of undermining the institutions through which he had consolidated his power only two years earlier. He had then sponsored the creation of an institution in which accountability of the parliamentarians would be to the people, rather than to a political boss at the top of the political hierarchy. His chairmanship of this institution, and his effort to foster the image of a strong leader within that institution (through cajoling as well as persuasion), were attempts to build alternative sources of power through which he could ensure that democratization, which was genuine, did not lead to his overthrow.

Such was also the case ten months later (in February 1990) when Gorbachev asked the Central Committee to abrogate Article 6 of the Soviet Constitution, which stipulated that the CPSU play the "leading role" in the political order. This was a move long since demanded by radical political movements under the umbrella of Democratic Russia, which mobilized tens of thousands of supporters in public demonstrations. Abrogation of the CPSU's right to be the only legal political Party was a precondition for legalization of multiparty (not just multicandidate) competition in the electoral process. Gorbachev compensated for this further weakening of the Party by engineering his own selection as president of the USSR. Rather than submit to a public election, he allowed himself to be elected president by a vote of the Congress of People's Deputies. And rather than resign as Party leader, which he feared would cede the entire Party structure to hostile forces that might deploy resources of the institution to undermine both him and his reforms, he decided to serve simultaneously as general secretary of the CPSU and president of the USSR.[12]

Thereafter, Gorbachev continued to weaken the central organs of the Party. He purged and reorganized the Politburo in July 1990, after which he called meetings of that body with decreasing frequency. He set up two new bodies for top-level deliberations – a "Presidential Council" and a "Federation Council" – neither of which had independent sources of power through which to defy him. The new Politburo became a marginalized policymaking body. Without seats for leaders of the state, military, or police bureaucracies, the Politburo ceased to be an oligarchy of elites that could pretend to dictate policy in all sectors or that could attempt to subject Gorbachev to the discipline of the collective leadership. With a trusted deputy in charge of day-to-day Party affairs, Gorbachev could concentrate on affairs of state, confident that the Politburo could not become either a unified or an assertive force. Finally, by having himself elected general secretary by the Party Congress, not the Central Committee, Gorbachev established the precedent that he would not be held accountable to the Central Committee.

We should not succumb to the impression that Gorbachev was oblivious to the need for a reserve of raw power to fend off political enemies. He was not so naïve as to believe that a high-wire act of persuasion and rhetoric could continue to "balance" opposing forces in the political elite and society. The wild card in his mind may have been the KGB, which he treated gingerly during 1985–1989 (perhaps recalling the key role that the KGB played in the

---

[12] For documentation of Gorbachev's reasoning at the time, based on the memoirs of associates, see Brown, *The Gorbachev Factor*, pp. 195–6.

removal of Khrushchev).[13] His purges and restructuring of the Party, ministerial, and military commands did not extend to the KGB, though he did replace the chairman of that organization in 1988 after Chebrikov supported the
Nina Andreeva manifesto against *perestroika*. Although many KGB officials
lamented the "excesses" of *glasnost'* and democratization, their functions
were actually expanded in other areas: foreign intelligence and counterintel-
ligence and especially economic intelligence-gathering.[14]

In sum, Gorbachev tried to strengthen the legislative organs of the state
as he weakened the executive and legislative organs of the Communist Party,
simultaneously bolstering his formal executive powers within each and relying on the KGB as insurance against the collapse of the state. In the case
of the new legislative structures, however, his ability to protect himself from
defiance was complicated by his lack of patronage powers within those institutions. Gorbachev had initiated and then accelerated the transfer of power
from "kings" (the Party) to "people,"[15] and he thus made his formal power
increasingly dependent on his capacity to maintain legitimacy and credibility
as a problem solver and politician. This was perilous for a leader who was
already suffering a crisis of authority. The KGB command proved faithful to
him only as long as he strengthened that institution to prevent the collapse
of the USSR. Once Gorbachev swung back into an alliance with the radicals
in spring 1991, KGB Chairman Kriuchkov initiated preparations for the coup
attempt of August 1991.[16]

THE REDIRECTION OF GORBACHEV'S MANAGEMENT STYLE

Whatever their strategies for building authority and consolidating power, Soviet leaders can also be distinguished by the extent to which they exercise

---

[13] See William J. Tompson, *Khrushchev: A Political Life* (New York: St. Martin's, 1995), ch. 10.

[14] On Gorbachev's relations with the KGB during 1985–1989, see Amy Knight, *The KGB: Police
    and Politics in the Soviet Union* (Boston: Unwin Hyman, 1990); Alexander Rahr, "Gorbachev
    and the post-Chebrikov KGB," *Radio Liberty Report on the USSR*, vol. 1, no. 51 (December
    22, 1989), pp. 16–20.

[15] I borrow the image from Reinhard Bendix, *Kings or People* (Berkeley: University of California
    Press, 1978).

[16] Gorbachev's behavior in fall 1990 is usually referred to as a swing to the "right," and his
    switch in April 1991 as a move back to the "left." I have tried thus far to avoid left–right ter-
    minology, but it becomes increasingly difficult as the political situation polarizes. Hence, let
    me clarify my use of the terms. In Soviet history prior to Gorbachev, Soviet literature used
    "right wing" to refer to the reformists (e.g. Bukharin) and "left wing" to refer to the ortho-
    dox Leninists. In Western literature during the Gorbachev era, however, the Soviet political
    scene was assimilated to Western categories of analysis: the "right" referred to traditional-
    ists of one kind or another who were opposing Gorbachev's radicalization; the "left" referred
    to those seeking democratization and marketization at home and accommodation abroad. I
    will use the Western parlance in this book.

personalistic leadership vis-à-vis their advisors and the collective leadership. Stalin's personalism was the extreme case: despotic and deadly. Khrushchev's personalism was arbitrary and nonconsultative, but it was neither despotic nor deadly. At all stages of his administration, Khrushchev frequently announced public initiatives without consulting the collective leadership and occasionally humiliated other members of the Politburo in public. By contrast, Brezhnev – while "first among equals" (because of the powers of his office) and while exercising leadership that steadily enhanced his status within the collective – behaved more like a chairman of the board than like a personalistic leader. He worked through, rather than around, the collective.

Where does Gorbachev fit along this spectrum from a highly personalistic to a highly executive operating style? For the first two stages of his administration (1985–1989), I would place him somewhere in the middle of the continuum but closer to the executive end. His radical associates and aides claim that he displayed a relatively consultative style of leadership and tolerance of criticism.[17] Even though he exercised innovative leadership, he respected the norms of collective leadership by subjecting himself to the discipline of the collective – for example, by having speeches and policy initiatives cleared in advance. Gorbachev combined self-confidence and egocentricity with self-control, prudence, and restraint; he exhibited both personal assertiveness on policy and deference to the leading role of the Politburo. He did not generally succumb to impulse and did not humiliate members of his Politburo in public. His capacity to hide his real thoughts and to lead diverse members of the leadership to believe he supported them was manipulative but nonconfrontational. He often mediated tensions within the Politburo. In December 1986, for example, Gorbachev adjourned a meeting of the Politburo without decision, claiming that the debate had become so heated that he feared a split in the Politburo. Sometime after the Nina Andreeva affair of spring 1988, Ligachev was being so harshly criticized in a Politburo meeting that Gorbachev started to defend him and to "try to reconcile the two sides."[18]

At the same time, we would expect also to find personalistic elements in Gorbachev's leadership style. We know (from his biography) that he was a natural leader in his Komsomol days, self-confident and assertive but also a good listener. His self-confidence and egocentricity may account for some of the more paternalistic components of his private discourse once he became general secretary. Thus, Gorbachev typically used the informal "*ty*" ("you")

---

[17] Archie Brown, *The Gorbachev Factor* (Oxford & New York: Oxford University Press, 1996), p. 389, fn. 9.

[18] Anatolii Chernyaev, *Shest' let s Gorbachevym* (Moscow: Progress, 1993), pp. 122–3, p. 207.

in addressing colleagues, subordinates, and even people he did not know.[19] He frequently referred to himself in the third person.[20] These practices plainly irritated associates and aides who later parted company with Gorbachev, and they led his main rival (Yegor Ligachev) to conclude that Gorbachev was attracted to the aura of an "enlightened monarch."[21]

Memoirs by Gorbachev's aides and associates, both hardliners and moderates, agree that he often would play people off against each other.[22] Gorbachev is said (by a close supporter) to have pitted Ligachev against Yakovlev and vice versa: they were each given about half of the responsibility for doctrinal affairs that, until January 1982, had been held by Mikhail Suslov.[23] In like manner, Gorbachev allegedly preferred to have others do kamikaze work for him; they were assigned to advocate policies and then take the political heat, while Gorbachev sat back and assessed the situation, deciding whether to intervene on their behalf or disown them.[24] He also preferred to have several teams working in parallel on the same task.[25] Consistent with these tactics was Gorbachev's tendency to dissimulate. Boldin claims that, on difficult issues, Gorbachev almost never said a definite "yes" or "no" to his associates. Rather, his tactic was to resort to interjection (*mezhdometie*), silence, or changing of the topic.[26] All these elements of his operating style were manipulative, but they were not manifestations of arbitary rulership.

Yet the political system, and the policy circumstances under which he came to power in Moscow in 1985, demanded of Gorbachev that he be more than

---

[19] Ibid., p. 7; V. I. Boldin, *Krushenie p'edestala: Shtrikhi k portretu M.S. Gorbacheva* (Moscow: Respublika, 1995), pp. 221–2; Fyodor Burlatskii, *Glotok svobody,* vol. 2 (Moscow: RIK Kul'tura, 1997), p. 126.

[20] Chernyaev, *Shest' let,* p. 104; Andrei Grachev, *Kremlevskaia khronika* (Moscow: EKSMO, 1994), p. 181. The practice appears as well in Gorbachev's memoirs, written after his forced retirement (Mikhail Gorbachev, *Zhizn' i reformy,* vol. 1 [Moscow: Novosti, 1996], pp. 269, 281, 369, 371).

[21] Yegor Ligachev, *Inside Gorbachev's Kremlin* (New York: Pantheon, 1993), pp. 98, 124.

[22] Grachev, *Kremlevskaia,* p. 132; Boldin, *Krushenie,* pp. 163, 208, 240. These authors differ, however, in their interpretation of Gorbachev's motives. Grachev sees this as a means of gaining multiple sources of information and interpretation; Boldin views it as a way of avoiding personal responsibility for failure. I do not find the two interpretations to be mutually exclusive, as I assume that politicians seek, when they can, to reconcile rational decisionmaking with political self-interest.

[23] Grachev, *Kremlevskaia,* p. 95.

[24] On this point as well, Grachev (a supporter of Gorbachev) and Boldin (a protagonist in the coup of August 1991) are agreed; see ibid., p. 133, and Boldin, *Krushenie,* p. 208. See also Ligachev, *Inside Gorbachev's Kremlin,* p. 307, on Gorbachev's allegedly opportunistic use of Yakovlev in the Nina Andreeva affair of spring 1988.

[25] Grachev, *Kremlevskaia,* p. 132.

[26] Boldin, *Krushenie,* p. 17. Many coup plotters claim that Gorbachev gave them mixed signals in 1991, leading them to believe that he would welcome their imposition of emergency rule as long as Gorbachev himself could not be implicated (ibid., p. 19).

just a skilled and manipulative chairman of the board. The political system encouraged both power consolidation by the Party leader and adulation of the general secretary as the font of wisdom and initiative. Gorbachev tried to resist such adulation and even denounced it in one public forum, fearing that a traditional "personality cult" would undermine public belief that his democratic reform program was serious.[27] But bolstering the image of the Party leader went hand-in-hand with far-reaching policy innovations – and Gorbachev was expected to provide leadership to a demoralized political elite. Hence, at televised meetings of the Congress of People's Deputies in 1989, Gorbachev used the powers of the podium to criticize and praise speakers, projecting the image of a founding father who was responsible for ensuring that the children did not get out of control. This behavior did not win him points with those who disagreed with his policies, but it did convey the message that, democracy or not, Gorbachev considered himself indispensable as a leader.

Once Gorbachev was thrown onto the political defensive, personalistic elements in his management style increased proportionately. His reconsolidation of political power effectively neutered the Politburo as a check on the behavior of the general secretary. He consulted less and less with advisors like Chernyaev, who had stood with him throughout the first stages of his administration. Indeed, in 1990–1991, he lamented to his aides that he could trust only two men: Defense Minister D. Yazov and KGB Chairman V. Kriuchkov.[28] Ye. Primakov, a top advisor to Gorbachev, advised him at the time that he ought not trust information received from the KGB as much as he did.[29] Both his radical and reactionary associates felt betrayed as he manipulated them constantly into believing that he agreed with them. In the end, Gorbachev's heightened personalism lacked both the raw power and the political credibility to head off his demise.

GORBACHEV'S AUTHORITY-MAINTENANCE DILEMMA

During 1989–1990, Gorbachev became increasingly defensive about the policies he was advocating and about his performance as a leader. Under growing challenge from critics on the left and the right, Gorbachev tried to maintain his authority by arguing that his basic conception of the middle way remained the only desirable and feasible alternative to either totalitarian restoration or

---

[27] Dusko Doder and Louise Branson, *Gorbachev: Heretic in the Kremlin* (New York: Viking, 1990), pp. 119–20.

[28] Boldin, *Krushenie*, p. 386; Chernyaev, *Shest' let*, p. 401.

[29] Chernyaev, *Shest' let*, p. 452.

systemic collapse and anarchy. He struggled to maintain his image as an effective leader, and he frequently reminded political audiences of the price he would *not* pay in seeking to transform the Soviet Union.

From 1988 onward, critiques of *perestroika* appeared in increasingly autonomous public arenas: the mass media, Central Committee meetings, the Party Conference of June 1988, the Party Congress of July 1990, the Supreme Soviet, the Congress of People's Deputies, demonstrations in the streets of Moscow, the newfound (1990) Communist Party of the RSFSR (i.e., Russia), and wildcat strikes by coal miners throughout the country (1989 and 1991). Although many of these criticisms and events stemmed from the very social forces that Gorbachev had unleashed in order to drive forward the process of transformation, he now felt the need to define limits. He strove to balance transformation with traditional values and political stability.

Thus, at the First Congress of People's Deputies (1989), at which some speakers defined the Communist Party as the main obstacle to democratization, Gorbachev called the Party "the guarantor of this revolutionary process" (i.e., *perestroika*) and its defender against "both conservative and ultra-leftist elements."[30] When *glasnost'* was becoming radicalized in 1988, he told representatives of the media that "we need order, responsibility, and initiative as we need the air we breathe" and proclaimed that *"glasnost'* in the interests of the people and socialism should be without limits. I repeat – in the interests of the people and socialism."[31] In the face of challenges to the Communist Party's "leading role," he proclaimed that "without the Party, without its fundamental influence on every aspect of social life, *perestroika* will not succeed."[32] In the same speech, he summed up his position as follows:

We say that *perestroika* means renewal but not dismantling of socialism. We say that *perestroika* is a revolutionary transformation, remedying deformations of socialism but not amounting to a restoration of capitalism. We say that *perestroika* is the revival of creative Marxism, the fresh realization of Lenin's ideas, the assertion of new approaches and methods of work.[33]

Similarly, when republics were defying Moscow's authority by passing laws on sovereignty that conflicted with those passed by central authorities, Gorbachev insisted on the importance of "the Union," held together by a

---

[30] M. K. Gorshkov, V. V. Zhuravlev, and L. N. Dobrokhotov (Eds.), *Gorbachev–Yel'tsin: 1500 dnei politicheskogo protivostoiania* (Moscow: Terra, 1992), p. 131. This book is a compendium of speeches by Gorbachev and Yeltsin from 1986 to 1991.

[31] *Pravda*, September 25, 1988 (Gorbachev, *Izbrannye*, vol. 6, pp. 572, 575).

[32] *Sovetskaia Rossiia*, September 30, 1989.

[33] Ibid.

"transformed Communist Party."[34] When leaders of the Russian republic demanded sovereignty from the center's diktat, Gorbachev argued that "an isolated Russia" is not the solution.[35] When radicals called for abolishing Party cells in the army and in security organs, Gorbachev insisted that communists had the "right" to organize autonomously.[36] When radicals pushed for the legalization of private land ownership, Gorbachev declared his opposition and argued that collective and state property should limit the scope of purely private enterprise.[37] Even after the coup of August 1991, Gorbachev returned to Moscow and urged that the sins of the Party apparatus not be visited on the millions of rank-and-file Party members.[38] He also insisted that the "socialist choice" and the "socialist idea" had not been discredited and that these remained the core of both his political philosophy and of the only viable, good society.[39]

Throughout 1990–1991, as centrifugal pressures grew, Gorbachev warned repeatedly that the Soviet Union, in some renegotiated form, simply had to be preserved. After April 1991, he became more tolerant of confederal formulas as he observed that federalism ("strong center–strong regions") was no longer acceptable to regional leaders, whether or not he believed, in his heart, that confederalism could ever constitute a stable equilibrium. "New, unprecedented" forms of statehood were tolerable, even desirable, as long as they avoided formal secession and disassociation of the constituent units of the pre-existing state. Anything to retain formal continuity and the juridical existence of the state; anything to avoid formal disintegration and the conflicts that, he claimed, would ensue; and, of course, anything to retain the office he occupied and the state without which his office would cease to exist.[40]

---

[34] Gorshkov et al., *Gorbachev–Yel'tsin*, pp. 208–9; see also *Sovetskaia Rossiia*, September 30, 1989.

[35] Gorshkov et al., *Gorbachev–Yel'tsin*, p. 209.

[36] Ibid., pp. 215–16, 221.

[37] *Izvestiia*, August 19, 1990; *Sovetskaia Rossiia*, September 22, October 9, and December 1, 1990. See also TASS, September 17, 1990: "Not the nationalization of all and sundry, but the creation of free associations of producers, joint stock companies, production and consumer cooperatives, associations of leaseholders and entrepreneurs – that is the high road to a genuine socialization of production on the principles of free will and economic expediency. It is here that the roots of the true socialization of our economy lie."

[38] *Pravda*, August 23, 1991.

[39] Ibid.; see also *Sovetskaia Rossiia*, May 25, 1990, and October 9, 1990.

[40] Gorbachev's emphasis on (indeed, obsession with) statehood runs through his speeches even when his logic comes across as forced. On March 29, 1991, he warned that calls to close down the Communist Party would mean the "disruption of all elements of statehood" (Moscow Radio Rossii Network, March 29, 1991). On July 24, 1991, he warned representatives of the republics against confrontations that could lead to "the breakdown of Soviet statehood" (TASS, July 24, 1991). On August 2, 1991, shortly before the abortive coup, he justified the new Union Treaty as "a reform of Soviet statehood" and pointed to the institutional mechanisms it would

Gorbachev's defense of Soviet statehood contained more than just the defense of a political–organizational form; it also contained advocacy of a valued political community. He clearly articulated a conception of political community that was internationalist and ethnically inclusive and that constituted a "unique civilization" with a "common fate." His rhetoric both extolled the Soviet Union as a civilization worth preserving and warned of the dire consequences of trying to decouple the components of an organic entity. Retention of common statehood, then, was a prerequisite for binding together the peoples residing in the USSR. As he remarked in February 1991:

> In approaching the referendum and thinking about our position, each of us should understand that, essentially, what is at stake is the fate of our state and of each of its peoples, our common fate.... One can justifiably say that a unique civilization has developed in this country, one that is the result of many centuries of joint efforts by all of our peoples.[41]

When he resigned from office begrudgingly on December 25, 1991, Gorbachev spoke to the nation about his greatest fears: "The worst aspect of this crisis was the collapse of statehood. I am alarmed at our people's loss of their citizenship of a great country – the consequences of this could be severe for everybody."[42]

In Defense of Transformation

During this period, Gorbachev also felt the need to respond to a reactionary challenge, for this threatened to scuttle *perestroika* and to halt the processes of

---

provide for combining division of powers with coordinating functions (Moscow Central Television Network, "Vremia," August 2, 1991). On November 20, 1991, Gorbachev complained that one consequence of the coup had been to destroy the prospects for signing the Union Treaty. Hence, the authorities would have to start over in the face of "the threat of destruction of our statehood" (Moscow All-Union Radio Maiak, November 20, 1991). Two weeks later (*Izvestiia*, December 3, 1991), he declared to the Supreme Soviet that the number-one issue is the "crisis of our statehood," which is paralyzing official action while threatening the economy and morality. He placed his hopes in revival of the Union Treaty to save the country from disintegration. The Union Treaty would offer a "new, unprecedented statehood," but "any loss of time may be catastrophic." (See also Moscow Central Television Network, December 5, 1991: "the question of statehood is the vital question.") As late as December 18, Gorbachev sent a message to leaders of the "sovereign states" (before a scheduled December 21 meeting) in which he urged an emphasis on continuity as they move to "the creation of a new form of statehood" (TASS, December 19, 1991).

[41] *Pravda* and *Izvestiia*, February 7, 1991; see also Moscow Central Television Network, First Channel, "Vremia," August 2, 1991.

[42] *Nezavisimaia gazeta*, December 26, 1991. Throughout 1990–1991, Gorbachev had spoken in apocalyptic terms about the consequences of collapse of the Soviet Union, calling it a "crime" with consequences that would be "ruinous" and that would result in escalating civil conflict. For examples, see *Pravda*, February 15, 1990; *Pravda*, June 20, 1990; *Pravda*, December 11, 1990; *Pravda*, December 18, 1990; TASS, March 16, 1991; *Pravda*, April 27, 1991.

transformation entirely. Thus, he rejected the rationality of those people who have "panicked" in the face of increasingly autonomous social forces, who claim that "democracy and *glasnost'* are all but a disaster," who "are losing confidence and surrendering their positions," who "see a threat to social-ism," who "regard these changes as the downfall, disintegration and collapse of everything – as a real apocalypse," or who have succumbed to "needless fear."[43]

As Gorbachev explained it, such people did not understand that *pere-stroika* is the roadmap to a more just, humane system in which the most cherished goals of socialism would be achieved and sustained. But the Com-munist Party could only retain its leading role – de facto, if not de jure – if it transformed itself. A consensus on behalf of such a leading role could only be reached if the Communist Party changed its methods of rule. Such self-transformation would ensure that the Party and its cadres retain their hegemony within the political order.

Now, when all of society is on the move, when the process of democratization has ex-panded in depth and in breadth, when it is bringing to the surface of public life both new strengths and new problems that require discussion and resolution, on this path we more and more often run into the inertia of old thinking, into a desire to resort to old methods, to slow down the processes that are under way. This is where the con-tradiction arises.

Some people are even beginning to panic, all but seeing a threat to socialism, to all our gains, from the development of democratic processes in the country.

No, comrades, today we should not concern ourselves with slowing popular initia-tive and grass-roots activity. The Party's task is to head up the process of the growth of the people's public activeness, to set the tone of this process and to strengthen its constructive elements in the interests of the revolutionary renewal of socialist society, in the interests of restructuring. This is the heart of the matter.[44]

The stakes were high. If the Party proceeded along this path, it "will re-ceive even more support from the working people." If it failed to do so, then "irreparable damage will be done."[45] In response to those who viewed this as a weakening of the Party's leadership role, Gorbachev was blunt:

The dialogue between the Party and the working people is not a weakness, not the transformation of the CPSU into a debating club. If it is a weakness to conduct a dia-logue with all strata of society, then I do not know what courage is.... We must not

---

[43] *Pravda*, September 25, 1988 (Gorbachev, *Izbrannye*, vol. 6, p. 568); also, vol. 7, p. 477, 487–90 (April 25, 1989); TASS, September 17, 1990; *Pravda*, December 18, 1990.
[44] Gorbachev, *Izbrannye*, vol. 7, pp. 489–90 (April 25, 1989: concluding speech to the CPSU Central Committee Plenum).
[45] Ibid., p. 490.

operate according to the pattern: permit or not permit, allow or not allow. All that is in the past.[46]

Gorbachev employed the same logic with respect to economic reform. Facing audiences of Party cadres, he insisted that the transition to a market economy simply had to be accelerated. This would not constitute a restoration of capitalism; nor would it forsake socialist values. It was an objective necessity if the standard of living was to rise. And it could not wait.

We regard an accelerated transition to a regulated market economy as a way out of the current situation. We should finally overcome fluctuations in this respect.... We need the transition to the market not for its own sake but in order to reach new forms of economic life.... We should understand well the essence of the transition to a market economy and agree on this issue. There is no other choice ....

Attempts are being made to impose an opinion on society that *movement* towards the market means a return to capitalism. One could not have invented anything more absurd.[47]

But even as Gorbachev warned the radicals not to tolerate secession from the USSR, he also warned reactionaries and conservatives that the Soviet Union could no longer afford to remain a unitary, totalitarian state. An intermediate solution, he told the Ukrainian Communist Party in September 1989, would defuse many inter-ethnic tensions. That solution would have to be based on "democracy and equality, mutual respect and free development of peoples"; it would have to "shape a new image of our Soviet federation that harmoniously combines the interests of national sovereignty and development and the common interests of the union of peoples of our country."[48] Stopping the conflicts that threatened to tear the country apart required "accelerating the radical transformation of the Soviet federation" – combined, he admitted, with "resolute measures" (i.e., coercion in the face of violence).[49]

Gorbachev as Embattled Centrist: The 28th Party Congress, July 1990

Gorbachev had built his authority by claiming the ability to bridge moderate forces on the left and right wings of the Soviet political spectrum. As the

[46] Ibid., p. 491; for similar statements, see also *Sovetskaia Rossiia*, September 30, 1989 (speech to Ukrainian Party Plenum); *Pravda*, December 13, 1989; *Pravda*, June 20, 1990 (speech to Conference of RSFSR Communist Party); *Pravda*, December 18, 1990 (speech to Congress of People's Deputies).

[47] *Pravda*, June 20, 1990; see also TASS, September 17, 1990; *Pravda*, April 27, 1991.

[48] *Sovetskaia Rossiia*, September 30, 1989.

[49] *Pravda*, February 15, 1990. For later examples of this intermediate position, see Gorbachev in *Pravda*, December 18, 1990; TASS, March 16, 1991; *Pravda*, April 27, 1991.

level of political polarization rose and as more and more centrists defected to the more extreme wings of the political spectrum, Gorbachev's political base grew weaker. It was in his interest as a politician to create the perception that there was no desirable alternative to the continued existence of a strong, centrist coalition. The 28th Party Congress of July 1990 illustrated Gorbachev's efforts (a) to prevent a formal split in the Communist Party, in order to retain his centrist role, and (b) to move the Party and its policies in a more radical direction in order to keep pace with the growing polarization.

The delegate selection process had been dominated by regional Party committees, yielding a Congress that was far more conservative than the Party membership as a whole. As a result, during the first days of debate, Gorbachev and his reformist allies were subjected to widespread, frequent, and harsh criticism, while Yegor Ligachev led the conservative charge. When viewed in light of the reactionary tide that had dominated the Congress of the RSFSR Communist Party just one month earlier, it appeared to outside observers that Gorbachev might be forced to abandon his plans to further restructure the Party's leading organs. It even appeared that he could be forced out as general secretary, or have to share power with a hardline opponent. At a minimum, it appeared that hardliners would consolidate their power to obstruct Gorbachev and his transformational agenda.

By the end of the Congress, however, Gorbachev had stemmed and reversed the conservative tide. He was overwhelmingly reelected as general secretary, and his chosen candidate, V. A. Ivashko, trounced Yegor Ligachev for the position of Deputy Chairman of the CPSU. The Politburo was totally reconstructed – expanded to include the first secretary of every republic plus a series of nonentities. Ligachev retired to Siberia after failing even to win reelection to the Central Committee. One exultant delegate concluded: "The monster of conservatism has been slain!"[50]

At the same time, Gorbachev appeased conservatism by refusing to abolish democratic centralism, to disband Party cells in the workplace, army, and police, or to accede to other such demands of the Democratic Platform, a radical faction within the CPSU and Congress. The result was that Boris Yeltsin and many radical deputies, including the mayors of Moscow and Leningrad, withdrew from the CPSU in order to challenge the Party order from without.

Gorbachev had apparently hoped to avoid the defection of the radicals. His tactic called for neutralizing or purging the puritans and technocrats, as represented and rallied by Ligachev, moving the Party's center of gravity to the center-left and encouraging the radical left to believe that he would use

---

[50] Roy Medvedev, as quoted in *The Pittsburgh Press,* July 15, 1990, p. A4.

his new powers to the benefit of radicalizing reforms. He succeeded on the first two scores but lost the radicals in the process. Still, if there really existed a threat that conservative forces would dominate this Congress, then the first two purposes were more important to Gorbachev than the third.

As for the substance of policy, this Congress reflected a struggle among three major organizational tendencies within the Party. One tendency, represented by Ligachev, was willing to fight to maintain the *monopolistic* position of the Party in society, economy, and polity. A second tendency, represented by Boris Yeltsin, was *abolitionist*, demanding that the Party abdicate its leading role, politically and organizationally, by dissolving Party cells in nonpolitical institutions and by ceding the Party's organizational resources to an autonomous state that would redistribute them to diverse social and political forces. Gorbachev adopted the centrist position: anti-monopolistic *and* anti-abolitionist. As he put it, "[t]he question of whether there should or should not be Party organizations at enterprises can be answered very simply: there should be. This naturally fully applies to members of other parties." [51] Gorbachev was calling for the Party to adopt a *competitive* posture and for the population to decide which organizations to join. "Let society decide," seemed to be his message. In the meantime, he would retain his posture and his political role as an *antidisestablishmentarian*.

In both his opening and closing speeches, and in shorter statements in between, Gorbachev played upon the dominant fears of conservative and uncommitted delegates: that society would decide against them, and deal with them accordingly, in the absence of successful reform. This was a credible warning, coming as it did on the heels of the collapse of communism in Eastern Europe. Gorbachev presented himself as the sole indispensable leader who could steer the Party and country away from such a fate. When delegates threatened a vote of "no confidence" in the leadership, Gorbachev warned them that such a rebellion could so divide the Party that it would never recover: "If you want to bury the Party, to divide the Party, just continue this way. But think seriously about it!" [52] Leninists in particular understood this principle of political life – that division within the elite invites challenges from below. When wrapping up his reelection as general secretary, Gorbachev made clear his demand that the Party allow further radicalization of reform. The only real choice lay between de-monopolization and marginalization: "The Party's success depends on whether it realizes that this is already a different society. Otherwise other political forces will crowd it out and we

[51] TASS, July 2, 1990; *The New York Times,* July 3, 1990, p. A5.
[52] TASS, July 7, 1990; *The New York Times,* July 8, 1990, p. A4.

will lose our position."[53] He called on delegates to "put an end to this monopoly forever."[54] This posture likely helped to foster a bandwagon effect among Congress delegates, who apparently more feared a marginalized future without Gorbachev than a radicalized, competitive future with him at the helm. By contrast, for radical democratizers within the Party, the fear of staying inside apparently exceeded their fear of being isolated from the Party's organizational resources.

Gorbachev in Defense of his Leadership Capacity

Gorbachev was more than a national problem solver, scientifically seeking the happy medium that would balance transformation and stability as well as new goals and selected traditional values. He was also a politician, faced with defending his authority against those who could argue that the growing contradictions in society proved his incompetence and liability – and even his dispensability – as a leader.[55] Like his predecessors, Gorbachev had built his authority by trying to present himself as an indispensable problem solver and builder of political coalitions. As the vulnerabilities of his program unfolded, he had to worry, like any politician, about the impact of those contradictions on his political credibility. This preoccupation was evident in his speeches during 1989–1991, the third stage of his administration, when (like his predecessors) he was on the political defensive. It took the form of ongoing efforts to defend himself against accusations that he had made a mess of things.

During 1988–1989, Gorbachev frequently defended *perestroika* against its critics on the right and the left. But it was only in 1990 that a tone of genuine alarm entered Gorbachev's speeches, reflective of the growing polarization that posed a threat to both social peace and Gorbachev's political standing. In his speech to the first Conference of the Communist Party of the RSFSR (a hostile, reactionary audience) in June 1990, Gorbachev felt the need to justify himself and his policies quite fully. He began by expressing alarm at the growth of political polarization:

Some favor *perestroika,* while others already anathematize it. But this is not all. The desire is being witnessed recently to go over from statements to actions. Attempts

---

[53] Radio Moscow, July 10, 1990; *The Wall Street Journal,* July 11, 1990, p. A10.
[54] *The New York Times,* July 11, 1990, p. A6.
[55] In the given time period, Gorbachev was no longer *building* his authority. Rather, he was desperately trying to *recoup* it.

are being made to muster dissatisfaction ... and to exploit the acuteness of the situation as a ram against *perestroika*.... No matter from what positions such attacks are launched, their true purpose is destructive.[56]

However, Gorbachev followed these warnings with a more defensive summary of the successes of his administration. The basic theme was: Look how much we have accomplished in such a short period of time!

Within just one year, 1987, we created prerequisites for reforms that greatly surpass everything achieved previously. And then, within two years of the implementation of the reform, we have actually finished a "preparatory school" which brought us to the shaping of a market economy, regulated in its social aspects. Thus, within three years we have fully achieved everything that has been debated and experimented with for more than thirty years.

And now, two years since the 19th Party Conference, we have achieved what the most progressive people of our country have been striving for for decades. The Party has decided not to assume the functions of the state any longer. The division of power is now actual fact. Elections have become truly free. We are actually on the threshold of true political pluralism. *Glasnost'* has become an effective tool of progress. The notion of "social democracy" is no longer a mere propaganda phrase. It is a reality ....

We can say now that what whole generations were striving for and could not achieve has been achieved in the ideological and political sphere within five years. Thus, despite all drawbacks, extremes, negative phenomena and losses, including those of an ideological and moral nature, the way has been cleared for the spiritual rebirth of man and society.[57]

Gorbachev did not leave it at that. He was willing to admit, in the spirit of "self-criticism," that he had made mistakes. Rather than revert to the traditional Soviet tendency to blame dysfunctions on local cadres and "anti-state behavior," he accepted some of the responsibility himself.

Speaking of recent years, the Party, its Central Committee and Politburo were unable to avoid miscalculations and even mistakes, as they sought to overcome the heavy

---

[56] *Pravda,* June 20, 1990. For subsequent, analogous expressions of alarm, see Gorbachev in *Pravda,* December 11, 1990; *Pravda,* December 18, 1990 ("We are in a dire situation"); *Trud,* December 21, 1990 ("the main thing is not to panic"); TASS, March 16, 1991; TASS, April 7, 1991 (in Japan); *Pravda,* April 27, 1991; and sources cited in note 12. In his speech of April 26 to the Central Committee Plenum, published in *Pravda* the next day, Gorbachev portrayed himself as a latter-day Lenin: "The situation resembles the social and psychological atmosphere that arose within the Party during the period when V. I. Lenin had abruptly turned the Party and the country towards NEP .... Lenin was accused of reneging on the cause of October and the interests of workers and peasants and of deviation from the principles of socialism .... In the end, the Stalinist dictatorship with all the well-known consequences asserted itself in the Party and the country .... So let us all together try to prevent emotions from pushing our plenum away from positions of political common sense" (*Pravda,* April 27, 1991).

[57] *Pravda,* June 20, 1990; see also *Pravda,* December 18, 1990.

legacy of the past and launched transformations to renew society. We did not always catch up with developments or find unequivocal political solutions to various problems ....

As a matter of self-criticism, one has to admit that we underestimated the forces of nationalism and separatism that were hidden deep within our system and their ability to merge with populist elements, creating a socially explosive mixture.[58]

After 1989, Gorbachev was also on the defensive about the results of his foreign policies, but he appears to have been less embattled in this realm. For one thing, he was being attacked from only one end of the political spectrum – the reactionary extreme. The radical democratic forces generally approved of his concessionary foreign policies and the "new thinking" about international relations. For another thing, the spectre of civil conflict within the USSR or of the country's dissolution was far more threatening than even such foreign policy setbacks as the collapse of communism in Eastern Europe. Hence, Gorbachev's foreign policy commentary during this period lacked both the sense of alarm and the self-criticism that marked Gorbachev's defense of his record on domestic policies. Instead, the Soviet leader simply insisted that the new thinking was working, that the world was still conforming to the expectations inherent in the new thinking, and that the potential latent within the international order was being realized – in good measure because of the leadership he had supplied.

For example, on August 1, 1989, Gorbachev reported to the USSR Supreme Soviet on his recent trips to the West and the recent meeting of Warsaw Pact countries. He noted the importance of his own role as a leader in helping to build a new world order: "I sense how quickly our relations with the Western world are changing .... As is now clear to everyone, the personality element is of enormous importance for present-day politics."[59] Speaking to the Conference of the RSFSR Communist Party in June 1990, Gorbachev proclaimed that "[p]rofound transformations in international relations are quite apparent and widely known. The epoch of exhausting and pointless confrontation is over. As a result, the entire world situation has improved considerably. Our security has been strengthened and conditions have been created for cutting our defense spending in order to use those funds to improve people's standard of living." Lest there be any talk of these changes having reduced Soviet security by emboldening would-be antagonists, Gorbachev added: "we shall never allow anyone to interfere in our affairs." And lest this hardline audience forget

---

[58] *Pravda,* June 20, 1990. For subsequent, analogous self-criticisms, see Gorbachev in *Pravda,* December 18, 1990; Associated Press, September 10, 1991.

[59] BBC, August 3, 1989.

the basic principle of "mutual security" and unilateral restraint that underlay the "new thinking," Gorbachev continued: "we unconditionally recognize the same right of choice of every people."[60] Compared to the growing alarm in Gorbachev's speeches about domestic matters, however, this was tepid fare.

PENDULAR DEFENSE OF AUTHORITY

Gorbachev's apparent victory at the 28th Party Congress in July 1990 was Pyrrhic. He had managed to defeat the conservatives and to strengthen his control over the top-level organs of power, but leaders of the most radical wing of the CPSU (Boris Yeltsin, A. Sobchak, G. Popov) handed in their Party membership cards. Moreover, reactionary forces concentrated on capturing the newfound Communist Party of the RSFSR. The CPSU had actually split after all, despite Gorbachev's best efforts.

Surely, the days of a radical transformational leader employing "centrist" political tactics were numbered if the level of political polarization reached the point that there were few "centrists" (i.e., moderates) remaining in the political establishment and among mobilized social forces.

Within these limits, however, Gorbachev tried to cope with the polarization taking place around him. Earlier, during the initial stages of his authority crisis (late 1989 to mid-1990), he had made ongoing concessions to radicalism while trying to hold those concessions within bounds. He had been a reluctant accommodator. After the 28th Party Congress, Gorbachev's advisors presented him with a program for radical reform of the Soviet economy and for the creation of a functioning market economy within 500 days. Other advisors, however, presented him with a counterproposal for reform that did not go as far in the direction of decentralization and that had less chance of reinforcing centrifugal forces within the union republics. After deliberating several days, Gorbachev told the dueling teams of economists to work together to reconcile their proposals with each other: an intellectual and practical impossibility.[61] In the absence of such reconciliation, Gorbachev was unwilling to push through any radical program for economic reform.

This was a sign that Gorbachev was shifting tactics, perhaps in confusion as to what might work. He decided that he had cast his lot too fully with the radicals. Thus began the pendular phase of Gorbachev's authority-maintenance

---

[60] *Pravda,* June 20, 1990; see also Gorbachev's address to the Fourth Congress of People's Deputies (*Pravda,* December 18, 1990).

[61] For Gorbachev's comments on earlier and later versions of these plans, see Official Kremlin International News Broadcast, September 4, 1990, and TASS, September 17, 1990.

tactics. He now sought to shore up the power of conservatism. He fired several of his most liberal advisers and associates and appointed conservatives in their place, many of whom would help to organize the coup against him in August 1991. It was in this context that Eduard Shevardnadze resigned, in December 1990, after making an impassioned speech in which he charged that reactionary forces were seizing the initiative and after criticizing Gorbachev for not having done enough to protect him against their accusations.[62] Gorbachev also reinforced conservatism in his approach to maintaining the cohesion of the Soviet Union. He broke with the radicals with whom he had been negotiating a decentralized union and adopted a hold-the-line posture there as well. Whether he was complicit in the use of violence against separatists in Latvia and Lithuania in January 1991 remains a matter of historical dispute.[63] But it is probably not coincidental that this happened during Gorbachev's course correction of September 1990–April 1991. For if he did not order it himself – which is plausible, given his distaste for the use of force – then he certainly created a political context in which those more inclined to use force felt at greater liberty to do so behind his back.

Gorbachev admitted to this shift of political strategy in his speech to the Fourth Congress of People's Deputies in December 1990. It was time, he argued, to strengthen executive power at all levels of the system and to restore order:

The most essential thing needed to get over the crisis is to restore order to the country. This hinges on the issue of power. If we have strong government, tight discipline, and control over the fulfillment of decisions, then we shall be able to ensure normal food supplies, rein in crime and stop inter-ethnic strife. If we fail to achieve this, a greater discord, the rampage of dark forces and a breakup of statehood would be inevitable ....

It is precisely for the sake of attaining these goals that a strong executive power at all levels is necessary – from the head of state to executive committees in town and countryside – an executive power able to secure the observance of laws, the implementation of decisions and to maintain proper and discipline ....

The president bears full responsibility for the country's security.

None of this furthered the cause of either economic reform or maintenance of cohesion within the USSR. Instead, Gorbachev's move to the right only infuriated the radicals and reinforced centrifugal forces in both the center and the republics. A "war of laws" intensified between the center and the

---

[62] *Izvestiia*, December 29, 1990.
[63] Brown (*The Gorbachev Factor*, pp. 279ff.) makes the case for Gorbachev's noninvolvement in these decisions.

periphery concerning who had legal jurisdiction in the republics and regions. In March 1991, Gorbachev sponsored a nationwide referendum to register popular sentiment on whether maintenance of the union should remain a top priority. And while he secured majority support in all voting republics for the ideal of retaining the USSR, the wording of the referendum was so misleading that many radicals claimed it to be a poor measure of the public's actual preferences.

Then, suddenly, Gorbachev decided that his swing to the right had been ineffective, perhaps even counterproductive. In April 1991 he swung back to the left on the issue of the union (but not on economic reform), making common cause with the radicals and this time on their terms. Thus, rather than move back toward a middle-of-the-road position and try to broker a compromise between extremist forces, as he might have done in 1989–1990, Gorbachev instead rejoined negotiations for a confederal relationship between the center and the republics. This meant "strong regions–weak center," a major retreat from his earlier defense of a more balanced, federal formula.

Gorbachev remained consistent in his strategic determination to maintain the existence of the USSR, to search for a "third way" between state socialism and capitalism, and to synthesize collectivistic and individualistic conceptions of democracy. What changed during his last year and a half in office was his perception of the political strategy required to maintain his power and recoup his authority while pursuing these goals. In the face of a rapidly polarizing situation, he reverted to a pattern of allying himself sequentially with those extreme forces that he viewed to be ascendant at the moment.

We had earlier seen this pattern of pendular swings as a means of recouping authority. Khrushchev embraced one political base in 1961–1962 but abandoned it after October 1962, when the shock of the Cuban Missile Crisis led him to reevaluate the risks, both at home and abroad, of continuing down that road. He then swung in the opposite direction, confronting the military–industrial complex at home and pursuing a concessionary détente with the United States. Similarly, Gorbachev abandoned the hardline coalition when he concluded that the risks of a prolonged alliance were too great, and the rewards too few, in the context of a rapidly polarizing society and a rapidly disintegrating USSR. He rejoined the camp of the radicals in hopes of salvaging a confederal compromise.

It was two years before Khrushchev's revised strategy failed; he was ousted by a cabal of his associates in October 1964. Things moved more quickly in 1991. Within four months of Gorbachev's shift back to the left, a cabal of his reactionary associates placed him under house arrest and seized the reins of government.[64] The coup failed ignominiously within three days. When Gorbachev returned to the capital, he spent several months trying to restore an effective political role for himself and working to prevent dissolution of the USSR.

But events overtook him. In Ukraine, polarization had advanced so far that, on December 1, 1991, an overwhelming majority of the population voted for independence. Shortly thereafter, the presidents of Russia (Yeltsin), Ukraine (Kravchuk), and Belorussia (Shushkevitch) met in the forest outside Minsk and plotted the formal dissolution of the USSR. Gorbachev learned about it after the fact; he was furious but helpless. He accepted the inevitable and resigned his office on December 25, 1991. Like Khrushchev, he had been forced out of office by a conspiracy. But Gorbachev's case was unique in that he was the victim of two conspiracies – one from the right and one from the left. First he suffered house arrest by the "establishmentarians" and later he suffered abolition of his country and his political office by the "disestablishmentarians." This sequence of cabals was a vivid reflection of the degree of polarization made possible by Gorbachev's policies. It also mirrored the declining size of the centrist political base on which Gorbachev had rested his political authority.

---

[64] Most of the coup plotters claim that Gorbachev misled them into believing that he wanted them to impose a state of emergency, from which he would dissociate himself but from which he would also eventually benefit. This was a theme argued by several of the coup plotters who were interviewed in Moscow in June 1999 at a conference in which I participated. Some Western scholars also believe that Gorbachev was no innocent victim of the coup; see, for example, Amy Knight, *Spies without Cloaks: The KGB's Successors* (Princeton, NJ: Princeton University Press, 1996), pp. 12–37, and John B. Dunlop, *The Rise of Russia and the Fall of the Soviet Empire* (Princeton, NJ: Princeton University Press, 1993). But Brown, *The Gorbachev Factor* (pp. 294ff.), persuasively refutes these claims, as does Anatolii Chernyaev in his "Afterword to the U.S. Edition" of the English-language Anatolii Chernyaev, *My Six Years with Gorbachev* (University Park: Pennsylvania State University Press, 2000), pp. 401–23; see also the "Foreword" to this edition by Jack F. Matlock, Jr., then U.S. Ambassador to the Soviet Union (ibid., pp. vii–xiv).

6

Yeltsin versus Gorbachev

The collapse of Gorbachev's efforts to steer a middle course toward a mixed system at home and abroad was in large measure a product of the social forces his policies had unleashed in the USSR and Eastern Europe. But if there was one individual who acted as an independent causal force in the unfolding of this process, it was Boris Yeltsin. Initially, during 1986–1988, Yeltsin merely complicated Gorbachev's authority-building efforts. During 1989–1991, however, he effectively scuttled Gorbachev's attempts to recoup lost credibility. When Gorbachev first tapped Yeltsin for a leadership position in Moscow in 1985, raising him from the ranks of first secretary of the Sverdlovsk Party organization, he had little idea of the trouble he was buying. Gorbachev's authority-building strategy at that point was still fairly conservative, and in 1986–1987 it would come to combine radicalization with a *controlled* and *evolutionary* pace of change. It sought to expand the arenas of politics and transform the language of politics, but at a pace to be dictated by the general secretary. Yeltsin, it turned out, found the pace in each realm to be intolerably slow.

YELTSIN, GORBACHEV, AND THE STAGE OF POLITICAL SUCCESSION, 1985–1986

The Politburo brought Yeltsin to Moscow in April 1985, appointing him first as head of the Central Committee construction department and then as Central Committee secretary for construction. By his own admission, he hated the experience, for the central Party apparatus left him much less leeway to run things as he saw fit. Though he worked long, hard hours and drove his staff to distraction with his workaholic tendencies, he felt like a caged animal at this desk job.[1] Gorbachev and Ligachev learned of Yeltsin's dissatisfaction and decided to reassign him. They saw to his appointment, in December 1985, as first secretary of the Moscow city Party committee, one of the most powerful positions in the country; simultaneously, they made him a candidate member of the Politburo. Run for many years by Viktor Grishin, the Moscow Party organization had sunk into a swamp of corruption during the Brezhnev years. Gorbachev wanted someone in that job who could purge the Grishin political machine and turn the Moscow Party into a force for administrative and political rationalization. Yeltsin's track record in Sverdlovsk suggested he could do just that.

Yeltsin took to the job with the alacrity of the turnaround artist he imagined himself to be. Though self-conscious about being a provincial bumpkin in elite circles of the country's capital,[2] he did not let this deter him; he was determined to turn Moscow around. He was given the job, he would write later, because Moscow was "in need of a rescue operation."[3] According to Yeltsin, Gorbachev "knew my character and must have felt certain I would be able to clear away the old debris, to fight the mafia, and he knew that I was tough enough to carry out a wholesale cleanup of the personnel." And Gorbachev was right, because "[w]e had to rebuild practically from zero" for "[a]bsolutely everything was in a state of neglect."[4] It is far from clear whether Gorbachev or Ligachev wanted Yeltsin to turn Moscow upside down. But Gorbachev did signal that he was looking for a no-nonsense turnaround artist.[5] Ever the passionate "stormer," Yeltsin tackled the job at full throttle.

Yeltsin's leadership style in Moscow mimicked his populist style in Sverdlovsk, though his populism became still more far-reaching – and threatening to traditional values – in the context of Gorbachev's policy of "acceleration." He rode the busses and subways, raided stores in search of goods being hoarded under the table, and held public meetings with lengthy question-and-answer periods. He dragged around the city members of the municipal Party and

---

[1] Boris Yeltsin, *Against the Grain: An Autobiography*, trans. by Michael Glenny (New York: Summit, 1990), p. 91; see also the lengthy memoir by nine of Yeltsin's former advisors, staff members, and government ministers: Yu. M. Baturin, A. L. Ilin, V. F. Kadatskii, V. V. Kostikov, M. A. Krasnov, A. Ya. Livshits, K. F. Nikiforov, L. G. Pikhoia, and G. A. Satarov, *Epokha Yel'tsina: Ocherki politicheskoi istorii* (Moscow: Vagrius, 2001), pp. 40–1.

[2] Yeltsin, *Against the Grain*, p. 90; Baturin et al. (*Epokha*, p. 41) report that he was widely referred to by Moscow officials as *chuzhak* (stranger, interloper, alien).

[3] Yeltsin, *Against the Grain*, p. 108.

[4] Ibid., pp. 109, 110, 114, 118–25.

[5] Gorbachev said in July 1986 that Moscow needed "a large bulldozer to clear the way" (as quoted in Leon Aron, *Boris Yeltsin: A Revolutionary Life* [London: HarperCollins, 2000], p. 134).

governmental leadership, both on inspection tours and to respond to questions from the public. He called for more unrestrained, public criticism of shortcomings. He even publicized the fact that he was using a public health clinic for his medical services, rather than the Kremlin hospital to which he was entitled.[6] In these ways, the provincial puritan signaled that a "man of the people" had arrived in town, one who did not accept the traditional ways of doing things, one who would not treat politics as an entirely private affair, one who did not accept the system of privilege through which the loyalty and cohesion of the ruling elite had been purchased, and one who did not accept the notion that Moscow's corrupt nobility of Party and state officials was entitled to immunity from exposure and accountability. This was new for Moscow and was a breath of fresh air for those of its citizens who were hoping for a new deal. It was also combustible political material that went beyond what Gorbachev was saying and doing during his stage of political succession.

Yeltsin's populism as leader in Moscow was Leninist, analogous to that which Khrushchev had embraced after the death of Stalin. In Chapter 2, reflecting on Yeltsin's earlier life and tenure of rule in Sverdlovsk, I noted many similarities between Khrushchev's and Yeltsin's leadership styles. Yeltsin's rule in Moscow further highlights the similarities. Both men were a distinctive personality type within a Leninist system: the "stormer." The stormer professes to hate bureaucracy, deplores the ability of lower-level officials to evade responsibility for nonperformance, attempts to solve problems by intensified pressure on (and purge of) cadres, and uses a combination of controlled publicity and mass mobilization to expose underachieving or corrupt officials. In a position of political leadership, the stormer becomes responsible for getting things done, which only increases his sense of urgency about delivering results. That sense of urgency leads him to become increasingly autocratic, to try to galvanize people in pursuit of seemingly unattainable plan targets, to reorganize bureaucracies with abandon, and to seek panaceas for the solution of practical problems. In the end, as was the case of both Khrushchev's Soviet Union and Yeltsin's Moscow, the stormer eventually discovers the limited ability of such methods to improve systemic performance or to deliver the goods.[7]

Khrushchev came to power prepared to shake things up and to force the *nomenklatura* to change their ways. In the process, during 1953–1956, he displayed many of the tendencies just described. So, too, did Yeltsin in Moscow

---

[6] Timothy Colton, *Moscow* (Cambridge, MA: Harvard University Press, 1997), pp. 572–8; Aron, *Boris Yeltsin,* pp. 135–70.

[7] Aron (*Boris Yeltsin,* p. 170) sums up six-month results of Yeltsin's storming: "the yield was startlingly, pitifully, and confoundingly puny." The result was little better on most fronts after eighteen months (ibid., pp. 197–8).

in 1986–1987.[8] Each man used storming additionally as a means of intimidating associates in the leadership to do things his way. Thus, Khrushchev
would go out among the people and urge them to be more demanding of public officials; then he would return to official meetings of the elite and urge
them to adopt his policies lest they face the wrath of the people – who, he
said, had become more demanding![9] So too with Yeltsin, who told a meeting
of the city's Party elite in January 1986 – one month after his appointment as
Moscow's Party first secretary – that the people of Moscow "are no longer
simply complaining. They are indignant."[10] Such allusions to the threatening mood of the masses were risky and incendiary tactics. They could raise
consumer expectations, deepen popular alienation, and be interpreted as invitations to the people to assert themselves against the regime. But such a
strategy was one option for getting things done and building one's political
leverage in a Leninist system.

Both Khrushchev and Yeltsin were a particular type of stormer: the egalitarian populist. They were both inexhaustible workaholics who despised
routine deskwork and preferred to be out among the people, urging them on
and even working alongside them. They also professed to despise corruption,
invoked the egalitarian rhetoric of the ideological heritage, and criticized the
socioeconomic privileges accorded to underachieving officials.[11] A stormer of
this type has the potential, when frustrated, to become a critic of the *nomenklatura* system itself. Both Khrushchev and Yeltsin, albeit under very different
circumstances, evolved in this direction – though Khrushchev, unlike Yeltsin,
never crossed the line.

Yeltsin's efforts to revitalize Moscow presaged (as with Khrushchev) a
search for ways to circumvent the corrupt bureaucracy by enlisting the broader
public against the bureaucrats. Calls for greater criticism amounted to calls
for the public to expose wrongdoing. Yet such calls, in and of themselves, were
unlikely to shatter or even jar the wall of mutual protection that shielded entrenched officials, so a leader might feel the need to go farther: to expand

---

[8] In a parallel with Khrushchev that is striking for its unreality, Yeltsin in 1986 "pledged, by
1990, to have telephones installed within a year of request … [and] … promised to double the
length of the Metro routes in the next five years" (Aron, *Boris Yeltsin*, p. 149).

[9] George W. Breslauer, *Khrushchev and Brezhnev as Leaders: Building Authority in Soviet Politics* (London: Allen & Unwin, 1982), pp. 37–8.

[10] John Morrison, *Boris Yeltsin: From Bolshevik to Democrat* (New York: Dutton, 1991), p. 47;
see also Aron, *Boris Yeltsin*, pp. 136–8.

[11] "Egalitarian" here refers to revulsion at the extremes of *nomenklatura* privileges. It does
not mean endorsement of a radical egalitarian "leveling" approach to worker compensation,
though it often means a preference for collective material rewards over purely individual material rewards.

both the scope of criticism and the arenas in which it took place. In Khrushchev's case, the initial calls for criticism ran into immediate resistance from self-protective officials. Khrushchev responded by launching his anti-Stalin campaign; then he started publishing the proceedings of Central Committee meetings and inviting non–Party members to attend. At the same time he launched a campaign for transferring functions to public organizations independent of officialdom. There followed his more radical doctrinal innovations ("Party of all the people"), his policy of limiting the tenure of Party officials to a fixed term in office, and his tentative consideration of multi-candidate elections.[12]

Yeltsin soon discovered the limits of what he could accomplish by traditional methods. Gorbachev had charged him with cleaning out Grishin's large network of corrupt political clients. That was fairly straightforward. Yeltsin immediately started firing high-ranking officials of Moscow's municipal Party apparatus. But the more people he fired, the more people he claimed needed to be fired. Networks stretched throughout the city in both vertical and horizontal directions. One man's client was another man's patron at a lower level or in a different bureaucracy. A corrupt director of a retail outlet had to have many protectors in different sectors and levels of the Party and state apparatus. Within a year and a half Yeltsin had purged about 60 percent of all district Party chiefs in the large Moscow Party organization – a staggering figure.[13] At a public meeting in April 1986, Yeltsin revealed his dismay that, despite the purges, corruption was proving to be a bottomless pit as well as a problem more tenacious than he had anticipated. He would fire people and replace them, and then the replacements would turn out to be corrupt as well.[14] In this forum, Yeltsin did not go so far as to define corruption as a systemic problem, but an observer could have reached that conclusion. Instead, Yeltsin simply expressed his dismay as well as his determination to keep purging all those people who succumbed to temptation.

Yeltsin had already sensed that there were deeper causes to the problem, ones that would require qualitatively new policies to eliminate. In Sverdlovsk he had conducted limited campaigns against both corruption and the socioeconomic privileges of officialdom. These privileges allegedly offended his conception of social justice and ran counter to his own way of living; he

---

[12] Breslauer, *Khrushchev and Brezhnev*, chs. 2, 4, 5, 6.

[13] Mikheyev, *Russia Transformed* (Indianapolis, IN: Hudson Institute, 1996), p. 57; Aron, *Boris Yeltsin*, p. 166.

[14] "Vypiska iz vystupleniia t. Yeltsina B.N. pered propagandistami g. Moskvy," Radio Liberty, Arkhiv Samizdata, no. 5721 (April 11, 1986); for Yeltsin's retrospective account, see Yeltsin, *Against the Grain*, pp. 115–19.

claimed to be uninterested in personal material luxuries.[15] He may or may not have understood fully the link between privilege and corruption, though doing so did not require much of an intellectual leap.[16] Institutionalized privilege was a system of rule. It ensured both the loyalty of the elite *and* the impunity of officialdom against challenge from below. By contrast, corruption was not officially sanctioned; it was treated as deviant in principle, even when the leadership in Moscow cast a blind eye to it. But the corruption of officialdom under Brezhnev became so entrenched precisely because the Politburo protected officials against challenges to their prerogatives and perks. Were a new leader to allow attacks on the privileges of the elite, it would signal an end to that impunity. Hence, it was not accidental that, even as Khrushchev was expanding the arenas and scope of criticism in order to undercut the bureaucracy and increase his own political leverage, he was also adopting policies to reduce the socioeconomic privileges of the *nomenklatura*.

If not in Sverdlovsk, then quickly in Moscow, Yeltsin drew the link between the two. And he did not hesitate to express it in the highest and most public of Party forums. His speech at the 27th Party Congress in February 1986, only two months after he was appointed head of the Moscow Party organization, was the most iconoclastic of all the speeches delivered at that meeting.[17] Like Khrushchev in February 1956, and like Gorbachev in December 1984, he not only criticized "some cadres" for poor performance (which would have been routine) but also generalized the criticism to imply that the problem went beyond "some cadres" and was more of a systemic deformation that needed to be confronted: "an inert layer of time-servers with Party cards." But unlike Gorbachev at the time, Yeltsin was prepared as well to strike at the privileges that allowed this "layer" to be "inert time-servers." Yeltsin made this incendiary issue – what was being called at the time the issue of "social justice" – the centerpiece of his address to the Party Congress and warned that, if problems were not overcome, political stability could not be guaranteed.[18]

Rooting out corruption and reducing official privileges in Sverdlovsk was hard enough; doing so in Moscow was a virtually insurmountable challenge. Moscow was much larger and was located in the midst of the central organs of power. The Central Committee's apparatus, headquartered in Moscow,

---

[15] Boris Yeltsin, *Ispoved' na zadannuiu temu* (Sverdlovsk: Sredne-Ural'skoe knizhnoe izd-vo, 1990), p. 87 (the claim is greatly tempered in the English-language version of this book [*Against the Grain*, p. 90]); *Toronto Star*, November 12, 1987.

[16] Baturin et al. (*Epokha*, pp. 43–4) suggest that Yeltsin well understood this link and that this understanding contributed to his zeal.

[17] *Pravda*, February 27, 1986, pp. 2–3.

[18] Aron, *Boris Yeltsin*, p. 143.

could easily protect its political clients against a maverick leader of the Moscow Party organization. Yeltsin was accustomed to being fully in charge and, as noted in Chapter 2, chafed in positions of subordination.[19] He soon learned that appeals to the apparatus of the Central Committee and to patrons within the Politburo could actually help the corrupt bureaucrats evade his thrusts or reverse his decisions. This might explain why his speech at the Party Congress also included a demand that the Central Committee apparatus "butt out" so that Yeltsin could do his job. This was a less incendiary remark than his other ones, because it was not a form of systemic criticism. But it was not likely to win Yeltsin many allies within the Politburo and Central Committee apparatus as then constituted. And it was sure to alienate the very man – Central Committee Secretary Yegor Ligachev – who had been instrumental in having Yeltsin promoted to a position in Moscow in the first place.

This may have been the point at which Gorbachev and Ligachev realized that they had misjudged the man from Sverdlovsk. Gorbachev, who combined reformist and puritanical traits, might have been comfortable in principle with what Yeltsin was saying, and he might have found it politically useful to have someone push for radicalization without the general secretary himself having to take responsibility should a backlash set in. But Gorbachev might have wondered whether Yeltsin would push the process of public radicalization faster than he and the Politburo could control. Gorbachev might also have worried that the measured introduction of radical ideas and doctrines, which was his strategy at the time, would be discredited by Yeltsin's extension of them into a prematurely systemic critique.

Even more so than Gorbachev, however, Ligachev must have realized that the man for whom he had expressed such enthusiasm in September 1984 was not cut from the same cloth as he. They both fit the puritanical mold of the ascetic anti-corruption fighter who found ways to make the system work better while maintaining social stability. They both possessed the mentality of a stormer who places inordinately high pressure on subordinates to get things done. But Ligachev had little patience for systemic critiques that might undercut the public legitimacy of the leading role of the Party.[20] In his personal life, Ligachev might have been an ascetic, but he understood that the system

---

[19] Former Politburo member Aleksandr Yakovlev reportedly said that, as a candidate member of the Politburo, Yeltsin did not have much of a presence, adding: "He is energetic when he is first, but if he is not first he goes sour right away" (quoted in Sergei Filatov, *Sovershenno nesekretno* [Moscow: Vagrius, 2000], p. 418).

[20] Although he does not discuss Yeltsin in his memoir, Ligachev does note that he himself supported *perestroika* and *glasnost'* until it started to allow systemic critiques in public forums (Yegor Ligachev, *Inside Gorbachev's Kremlin* [New York: Pantheon, 1993], pp. 91, 96–7, 131,

of institutionalized privilege could not be challenged without potentially undercutting the larger system of *nomenklatura* domination.[21] Indeed, in his own speech to the Party Congress, Ligachev criticized the CPSU's daily newspaper, *Pravda,* for publishing an article that aired popular discontent with the socioeconomic privileges of the *nomenklatura.*[22]

Moreover, Ligachev could not have been happy to be advised that the central Party apparatus, of which he was the top-ranked Central Committee secretary, should abdicate its right to intervene in the affairs of the most important regional Party organization in the country! Ligachev was a puritan and could cooperate during this early stage with those technocrats (such as Ryzhkov) who appeared to respect a system based on central planning and control and also to respect official privileges.[23] Hence, he considered himself a "reformer" and endorsed *glasnost'* and *perestroika* in principle; but he was not an egalitarian populist. Yeltsin was pushing well beyond Ligachev's conception of tolerable reform.

YELTSIN AND GORBACHEV'S STAGE OF ASCENDANCY, 1987–1989

Once Gorbachev began to radicalize his program in late 1986, Yeltsin would feel vindicated and emboldened by the new direction and pace of policy change. *Glasnost'* and democratization looked to Yeltsin like the kind of societal self-expression required to outflank the bureaucracy and mobilize new energies to revitalize the country. *Perestroika* suggested a license to rethink authority relationships between the Party and the state, between the central and regional Party apparatuses, and between the central planners and regional executives. Yeltsin did not yet possess a complete, anti-systemic critique, much less a crystallized vision of what might replace the Leninist system. By his own testimony, he was still very much a Leninist in 1986, a man who saw no clear alternative to the leading role of the Party and state ownership of production. But Yeltsin – like Gorbachev, Shevardnadze, and Yakovlev

287, 295); notable in this regard is Ligachev's contention that iconoclasm in policy was more tolerable than iconoclasm about the public interpretation of the history of the USSR.

[21] Ligachev's personal asceticism is amply evident from his memoir; it is also noted in Fyodor Burlatskii, *Glotok svobody,* vol. 2 (Moscow: RIK Kul'tura, 1997). I have also been told that a former Soviet cultural figure who toured the country and performed in Tomsk, where Ligachev was then *oblast'* first secretary, was taken to see Ligachev, who began by taking the measure of his interlocutor thusly: "Do you smoke? Do you drink?" An aide of Ligachev told this cultural figure that, if either question was answered in the affirmative, Ligachev had no further use for the person. But on Ligachev's preference for keeping the system of privileges for *nomenklatura* officials, see *The Washington Post,* March 3, 1986.

[22] *Pravda,* February 28, 1986.

[23] Ligachev, *Inside Gorbachev's Kremlin,* pp. 350–1.

in 1984 and like Khrushchev in 1956 – had concluded that "we cannot go on like this" and was searching for more radical measures to deal with the manifold obstacles to change.

Initially, Yeltsin was both enthusiastic about the radicalization of Gorbachev's program and admiring of Gorbachev for having done so.[24] Moscow started to experience a cultural renaissance, as scores of voluntary associations ("informals") emerged to claim their right to space in an autonomous public arena. Cautiously, but with determination, the informals challenged official dogmas and asserted their right to dramatize demands in public arenas not dominated by Soviet officialdom. Yeltsin did not cause this renaissance to happen, but he also did little to discourage it. He was neither a democrat nor a cultural eccentric, but he understood that it would be impossible simultaneously to resist both the corrupt bureaucracy and the awakening society. He cast his lot with the latter.

The puritans and the technocrats, however, experienced such an awakening with apprehension. They appreciated the utilitarian approach to *glasnost'*: as an instrument for exposing malfeasance and for providing a safety valve for pent-up public frustrations with Brezhnevite stagnation. But members of the educated, activated public did not care to be used for such limited purposes. They soon pushed for still further expansion of the public arena and the scope of critical public discourse. All this was taking place to the greatest extent in Moscow itself, within eyesight and earshot of the Kremlin. Yeltsin was willing to tolerate it and even allowed a congress of informal associations to meet in Moscow – a major event in those tenuous, early days of *glasnost'*. Ligachev presumably was not amused.

Nor was Ligachev likely to have been amused by Yeltsin's continuous purges of the Moscow Party organization, withdrawal of socioeconomic privileges from people who worked for him, and public criticism of the central Party apparatus for obstructing these efforts. There was, of course, truth to Yeltsin's complaints about the Central Committee Secretariat's intervention on behalf of some of the people he had targeted.[25] But there was also something quixotic about his reaction to the frustration of his initiatives. Like Khrushchev in 1961, who experienced similar frustrations in trying to combine frequent and far-reaching purges and administrative reorganizations with an insistence on quick results, Yeltsin had a short fuse and a penchant for turning up the heat in response to resistance. Occasionally, he complained at

---

[24] Yeltsin, *Against the Grain*, p. 139; Aleksandr Korzhakov, *Boris Yel'tsin: Ot rassveta do zakata* (Moscow: Izd-vo "Interbuk," 1997), pp. 52, 64–5; Aron, *Boris Yeltsin*, p. 192.

[25] Baturin et al., *Epokha*, p. 48.

Politburo meetings about his frustrations. He also complained privately to Gorbachev, on the assumption that Gorbachev would be both sympathetic and a potential ally. But within months, and despite a January 1987 Central Committee plenum at which Gorbachev launched his radical program for "democratization," Yeltsin began to conclude that Gorbachev was a compromiser who would never throw down the gauntlet against those who were obstructing or slowing *perestroika*.[26]

Later, in retrospect, Yeltsin would write bitterly about meetings of the Politburo during this period. He criticized Gorbachev for being long on words and short on actions, for dominating the formal sessions of the Politburo with long-winded speeches that resulted only in (what he considered to be) half-measures. It galled him that he was only a candidate member of this Politburo (unlike his predecessor, Viktor Grishin), without the full voting rights of those – Gorbachev and Ligachev – who were his contemporaries but who had risen much farther and faster than he and now dominated the proceedings. Indeed, these pages of Yeltsin's first memoir read like they were written by a newly elected member of a board of directors who has been emboldened by his membership but has not yet learned that the most critical decisions are made not by the board but rather by the executive committee of the board.[27]

Yeltsin's memoir of this period hardly does justice to the unprecedented radicalism of Gorbachev's program of democratization. Perhaps Yeltsin was alienated by the fact that, at the January 1987 plenum, Gorbachev settled for a closing resolution that was less radical about intra-Party democratization than Gorbachev had proposed in his opening speech. Perhaps he was upset that Gorbachev's public rhetoric was still somewhat less iconoclastic than was his own. Perhaps Yeltsin was so focused on problems inside Moscow that the gap between central Party resolutions and actual changes on the ground was foremost in his mind. Or perhaps Yeltsin was galled by, indeed obsessed with, Ligachev's ability to frustrate some of his initiatives behind the scenes. Whatever the precise cause, in 1987 Yeltsin was apparently torn between concluding that Gorbachev was insufficiently committed to change and concluding that Gorbachev simply lacked the courage to confront Ligachev and abandon his "go slow" tactics. Yeltsin was not seeking to bring Gorbachev down in early 1987; he was seeking rather to bring him around. He wanted Gorbachev to become as bold as he in publicly challenging the sclerotic organs of the Party and the state at all levels. He was trying to stiffen Gorbachev's spine.

[26] Burlatskii, *Glotok svobody*, vol. 2, pp. 129–30, 193.
[27] Yeltsin, *Against the Grain*, pp. 130–1.

In the face of continuing frustration, however, Yeltsin came to the conclusion that his leadership of the Moscow Party organization was a lost cause. He felt like an isolate within the Politburo[28] and decided to resign. When Gorbachev failed to accept his resignation and was unavailable to discuss the matter further, Yeltsin's frustration grew.

Just before adjournment of a meeting of the Central Committee membership – called on October 21, 1987, to discuss Gorbachev's proposed draft of his important anniversary speech – Yeltsin let his impulses get the best of him and asked to speak. He had not gone into the meeting determined to do so, and he had only a few notes written down in case he did. But, as the meeting was about to conclude, this lifelong risk-seeker (see Chapter 2) could not resist the temptation. He then delivered a disjointed but utterly blunt attack on the slow pace of *perestroika,* on the obstructionist behavior of Yegor Ligachev and the central Party apparatus, and even on Gorbachev's allegedly hesitant, self-congratulatory leadership of the entire process. He reiterated his criticisms of Party privilege and his warning that political stability was at risk if conditions did not improve. *Perestroika,* he was suggesting, was not only insufficiently radical and far-reaching; it was threatening to mire the country again in stagnation. He repeated his offer to resign from the Politburo.[29]

Only a speech delivered before the mass public would have been more of a challenge to the leadership. As it was, this challenge was great enough, not just for what it said but also for where and when it was delivered. Yeltsin was denouncing the Politburo in front of the "Party public," the 300-odd members of the Central Committee to whom the Politburo was nominally (but not actually) accountable.[30] This was a challenge both to the leaders being criticized and to the Politburo as an institution. It was a breach of institutional discipline in that it was not discussed by the collective leadership beforehand in private session and approved in advance for discussion before the broader clientele. It was an unsanctioned effort to force an expansion of the arenas and language of legitimate criticism far beyond those Gorbachev had already sanctioned. It was the very definition of "loose cannon" behavior within the Leninist institutional context. Only a direct appeal to the mass public would have been more intolerable.

---

[28] Baturin et al., *Epokha,* p. 48.

[29] For the text of Yeltsin's speech, see M. K. Gorshkov, V. V. Zhuravlev, and L. N. Dobrokhotov (Eds.), *Gorbachev–Yel'tsin: 1500 dnei politicheskogo protivostoianiia* (Moscow: Terra, 1992), pp. 23–5.

[30] For the concept of Party members as the "citizens" and "public" of Leninist regimes, see Ken Jowitt, "An organizational approach to the study of political culture in Marxist–Leninist systems," *American Political Science Review,* vol. 68, no. 3 (September 1974), pp. 1171–91.

In response, Gorbachev opened the floor to denunciations of Yeltsin by reformists and conservatives alike. If, before this, Gorbachev might have rationalized that Yeltsin could be useful within the leadership as a counterweight to those opposed to the further radicalization of *perestroika,* now he saw Yeltsin as someone who might actually discredit the cause of radicalizing reform.[31] Politburo members Eduard Shevardnadze, Aleksandr Yakovlev, and perhaps Vadim Medvedev were pushing the cause of radicalization within the leadership, but they were doing so largely at the pace demanded by Gorbachev. The general secretary presumably did not want to frighten the puritans and technocrats into mobilizing against his program. Apparently, he wanted them to think, for as long as possible, that there was a legitimate place for them in the new order and no need to become obstructionist. Yeltsin's behavior, however, was threatening to give them a case in point of what further radicalization might engender, much as Dubček's Czechoslovakia in 1968 worked to the disadvantage of reformists within Brezhnev's Politburo and Central Committee. At least within the Party, Yeltsin's penchant for egalitarian populism and his disrespect for the norms of proper procedure might prematurely antagonize the "centrists" and fence-sitters on whom Gorbachev was banking for support. The cruel and sustained hazing of Yeltsin – especially later on, in the Moscow Party organization meeting at which Gorbachev saw to his removal from office – was apparently Gorbachev's concession to his own perceived coalition-maintenance needs.

Perhaps because he felt guilty about the cruelty of the exercise (Gorbachev had had Yeltsin dragged from his hospital bed after a heart seizure to experience a vicious verbal assault by associates in the Moscow Party organization), Gorbachev gave Yeltsin a dignified position within the state bureaucracy as deputy minister for construction.[32] But he also advised Yeltsin privately that he would never let him back into politics.[33] There followed a period of many months during which Yeltsin put himself through a wrenching self-examination. He was determined to draw fundamental conclusions from what he had been through.[34] He had experienced the full force of an

---

[31] Archie Brown, *The Gorbachev Factor* (Oxford & New York: Oxford University Press, 1996), p. 171.

[32] The chorus of denunciations at the meeting of the Moscow city Party committee was especially vicious, perhaps more so than Gorbachev had anticipated. Aron (*Boris Yeltsin,* p. 215), based on memoirs by and interviews with participants, writes: "As the meeting progressed, Gorbachev began to look strangely uncomfortable, even 'embarrassed.' He fidgeted. He grew red in the face. His eyes crisscrossed the hall 'restlessly.' A few times, he shook his head, as if 'struck by the fury and the spite he had unleashed.' By contrast, next to him Egor Ligachev sat with arms crossed on his chest staring 'triumphantly' at the hall below."

[33] Burlatskii, *Glotok svobody,* p. 135; Yeltsin, *Against the Grain,* p. 14.

[34] Yeltsin, *Against the Grain,* pp. 204ff.

inquisition by the Party apparatus, unlike anything seen within the Central Committee since 1961, and had even been denounced by some people he thought were his friends. He had fought against the corruption and privilege of the Party apparatus as a whole and against the domination of regional Party and state organs by the central Party apparatus. Instead of being thanked for his efforts to improve the situation in Moscow, he was purged and nearly driven to his death. Despite all this, he continued to believe (in principle at least) in the "leading role of the Party" and a better future for the Soviet people under the leadership of the CPSU.[35] How could he reconcile these conflicting beliefs? Never one to shirk a personal challenge, Yeltsin was searching for answers. He had not yet realized that he would have to jettison one or the other set of beliefs.

This agonizing reappraisal was taking place in a political context that was changing by the month. The battle between radical reform and "hold the line" conservatism was heating up. The Nina Andreeva affair of March 1988, supported by Yegor Ligachev, was a blatant effort by those opposed to further radicalization to dramatize their conviction that *perestroika* was turning out to be a threat to the entire system of Party rule.[36] Radical reformists within the leadership, supported by Gorbachev, counterattacked and managed to throw the conservatives back onto the defensive. In the meantime, radical reformist editors of journals and newspapers were allowing or encouraging further expansion of the scale of criticism – to the extent that many of the things Yeltsin had said at the 27th Party Congress were by now standard fare in large-circulation publications. The informal organizations were growing exponentially in number and assertiveness. The Soviet intelligentsia, including young and old alike, was losing its fears and inhibitions and was increasingly acting on its convictions, confident in its growing strength as a social movement. A huge public demonstration on Yeltsin's behalf took place in Sverdlovsk. Some people demanded publicly to know what had happened in the Central Committee meeting at which Yeltsin had defied the Politburo. Letters of support reached him from around the country, greatly bolstering his spirits,[37] and perhaps also influencing his intellectual development. Yeltsin had earlier viewed societal awakening as a healthy manifestation of vitality and a useful ally against the bureaucracy, but now he was starting to realize also that "the people" might become the core of a political strategy through which he could resurrect himself politically.

---

[35] On the timing of Yeltsin's final break with these beliefs, see Aron, *Boris Yeltsin,* p. 366.

[36] Nina Andreeva, a chemistry teacher from Leningrad, published in a nationwide Party newspaper a manifesto denouncing *perestroika* as a betrayal of Soviet history. The publication was facilitated, if not instigated, by Yegor Ligachev.

[37] Aron, *Boris Yeltsin,* p. 227.

The June 1988 Party Conference provided an unanticipated forum for Boris Yeltsin to continue his struggle with the Party's establishment. He had decided to resume the battle for his political resurrection and rehabilitation, as well as for his increasingly radical vision for the future of the Soviet political order. And the circumstances of this conference – its televising nationwide – allowed him to turn what had been an intra-Party war into a public battle. This forum would allow Yeltsin's grievances to be aired before an audience of all the people, not just the Party citizenry or the nobility of the *nomenklatura* that sat within the Central Committee. Gorbachev, too, was trying to expand both the scope and the arenas of criticism as a way of transforming the Soviet system into a more democratic form of political organization. He had his own reasons for doing so, unrelated to the challenge from Yeltsin. He did not intend for Yeltsin to speak at the conference, but the irrepressible Boris Nikolaevich forced his way to the podium toward the very end of the conference and Gorbachev, for reasons best known to himself, allowed Yeltsin to speak. Gorbachev also allowed Yegor Ligachev to respond, and the combative Politburo member took up the challenge.

Millions of television viewers were provided, for the first time, with a close-up view of uncensored intra-Party debate and struggle. It was both an enlightening and a mesmerizing experience for most of them. They witnessed the diverse orientations toward Party life that were put on display: the puritan who was proud of "building socialism" during the so-called "era of stagnation"; technocrats discussing the limits of economic decentralization and market-oriented reforms; radical reformers seeking a fundamental democratization of the Party. They also witnessed Boris Yeltsin: not yet clear as to what democracy looks like, and humbly begging the Party to rehabilitate him, but increasingly convinced that the Party apparatus was the problem and not the solution.[38]

At least as important as the conference debate were the resolutions of the conference that called for creating a national legislature based on nationwide elections to be held in March 1989. Yeltsin had about six months to survey the political landscape and decide whether this was a channel of political mobility he might wish to exploit. At some point, he decided that it was. Consistent with both his lifelong search for huge challenges and his determination to show Gorbachev and the Politburo that he was their equal, Yeltsin refused to run for parliament in his home town of Sverdlovsk. That would have been too easy a win. If he was to reemerge as a national figure in politics and not

---

[38] For Yeltsin's speech at the conference, see Gorshkov et al., *Gorbachev–Yel'tsin*, pp. 75–82; for a brilliant analysis of how Yeltsin's rhetorical style at the conference may have resonated with the Russian mass public, see Aron, *Boris Yeltsin*, pp. 245–6.

just as one of several thousand parliamentary deputies, then he would have to beat the greatest of odds. Yeltsin decided to run for the citywide seat in the city of Moscow itself.[39] This was by far the largest electoral district in the USSR, which greatly increased the vote's importance as a bellwether of public opinion.

Officials in control of nominating processes did their best to obstruct Yeltsin's running and then threw their weight behind the director of a large limousine factory as his opponent. They smeared Yeltsin in the newspapers with charges that were variously political and personal. Nothing worked. The more they smeared him, the more his popularity and credibility rose. Yeltsin ran on a program that condemned corruption and privilege and called for radical democratization of the Party.[40] In the end, he blew away his opponent, winning an astonishing 89.4 percent of the vote.

At some point during late 1988 or early 1989, Yeltsin's personal reevaluation of his political philosophy led him to a conclusion that the founders of liberal democratic theory had reached hundreds of years earlier: democratization requires a transfer of power and authority from "kings" to "people."[41] In the case of the communist system in its post-Stalin era, the "king" was the Party, a collectivity that claimed a secular variant of "divine right." Whereas once Yeltsin had been a true believer in the right of the Party to embody and express truth and legitimacy, now he transferred those traits to another collectivity: the "people." And whereas once the Party spoke *for* the people, now that Party would answer *to* the people, and Yeltsin would be their standard-bearer. Gorbachev's reforms made this possible. To Gorbachev's surprise and distress, Yeltsin seized the opportunity to get back into politics – precisely what Gorbachev had warned him he would never allow – and to turn those new arenas against the Party and, later, against Gorbachev. Whereas Gorbachev viewed these new channels (elections and a parliament) as an expansion of the public arena that would result in a form of democratic socialism, Yeltsin treated them as instruments for destroying the power of the Party apparatus. Whereas the new language of politics under Gorbachev now routinely included amalgams of socialist and liberal democratic precepts (e.g., "socialist pluralism" and "socialist market"), Yeltsin used the new public forums to reject those amalgams as unworkable and to trump them with both liberal democratic and anti-system doctrines. The stage was set for Yeltsin to

---

[39] Yeltsin writes about his reasons for running in Moscow in Yeltsin, *Against the Grain,* pp. 83–5.
[40] See, for example, the campaign speech that was reprinted in *Moskovskaia pravda,* March 21, 1989.
[41] Reinhard Bendix, *Kings or People* (Berkeley: University of California Press, 1978).

seize the political initiative at the very moment at which Gorbachev, for reasons other than Boris Yeltsin, had been thrown onto the political defensive.[42]

GORBACHEV DECLINING, YELTSIN RISING, 1989–1991

There is general agreement among observers that 1989 was the year during which Gorbachev lost control of the social forces that his policies of *glasnost'*, *perestroika*, and *demokratizatsiya* had unleashed. That is to say, at about this time the mobilization of anti-system forces by sociopolitical organizations (such as *Democratic Russia* in Russia and the ethno-national popular fronts in other republics) was pushing for radicalization of policy at a rate that exceeded Gorbachev's preferences and efforts. Earlier, Gorbachev had followed a strategy that sought to push policy in a radical direction but without driving moderates into opposition. Now he found himself in a position of trying simultaneously to keep up with rapidly radicalizing social forces (to avoid losing his radical base) and of restraining them as best he could (to avoid losing the moderates). Gorbachev's main fear, as we shall see, was irretrievable polarization. It frightened him as a citizen because he believed that it presaged social instability; but it also should have frightened him as a politician, for it threatened to make him irrelevant as a political actor. His distinctive political competence lay in his tactical skills as a bridge between the wings within the Communist Party. Total polarization would mean collapse of the center of the political spectrum, in which case no such bridging would be possible: the wings would be too far apart from each other. The political role with which he had built his authority would become irrelevant.

Yeltsin, by contrast, would play a polarizing role by catering to and gathering around him the very anti-system forces that Gorbachev was seeking to restrain. To the extent that Yeltsin succeeded in building his authority by embracing the forces of radical maximalism, Gorbachev's task would become harder and perhaps impossible. In sum, Yeltsin was building his authority with a platform that, if successful, might diminish the probability that Gorbachev would succeed in recouping his own political authority. Both Khrushchev and Brezhnev had been thrown onto the political defensive and had sought to recoup authority by redesigning their programs. In both cases they faced intra-Party skeptics and low-key critics who wondered whether their latest initiatives were any more likely than previous ones to succeed at an

---

[42] Yeltsin was certainly ambitious. But it is not my purpose to determine whether his policy positions were driven by pure political ambition or by genuine belief. Leaders seeking to build their authority are not required necessarily to believe in the ideas they are propagating.

acceptable price. But Gorbachev's situation was unique, precisely because he had opened up Soviet politics to *public* political competition. He now faced an open political struggle, one marked by mobilized mass constituencies that included anti-communist social forces and explicit counter-elites. This was no longer "Leninist politics." But it was a variant of competitive politics that contained its own logic of authority building and authority maintenance and its own stages of development. Gorbachev's stage of decline was coterminous with Yeltsin's stage of political succession, during which the latter would strive to consolidate a new political base.

Yeltsin rose steadily to prominence in the new public arenas. Within the USSR Congress of People's Deputies, he had a forum for his speeches that was initially televised to a nationwide audience. He was elected to membership in the policymaking Supreme Soviet, which was scheduled to meet in continuous session. Within the Supreme Soviet he became a prominent member of the In-terregional Group of Deputies, chaired initially by the distinguished physicist and dissident democrat, Andrei Sakharov, and then by Yeltsin himself after Sakharov's sudden death in December 1989. In March 1990, Yeltsin won pub-lic election as a delegate to the newly created parliament of the RSFSR and became a member of its Supreme Soviet. One month later, in May 1990, he won a tense, close battle for chairmanship of the Supreme Soviet. In July 1990, he announced to the 28th Congress of the Communist Party of the So-viet Union that he was turning in his Party card; he then dramatically marched up the aisle to the exit. In March 1991, using his position as Chairman of the Supreme Soviet, he engineered a public referendum that endorsed the es-tablishment of a Russian presidency freely elected by the citizens of Russia. Three months later he won that election in a landslide. Thus, Gorbachev's ef-forts to recoup his political standing took place in a context in which a rising political star, more radical than Gorbachev himself, was increasingly domi-nating the very public arenas that Gorbachev had created to channel public initiative and to control the rate of polarization.

Yeltsin played a polarizing game of politics during these last two to three years of Gorbachev's leadership. No matter what Gorbachev proposed in domestic policy, Yeltsin criticized the Party leader for conservatism and half-measures. He supported centrifugal forces in the union republics at a time when Gorbachev was trying to contain them through a combination of threats and rewards. He defined the "center" (i.e., the Kremlin and the Soviet author-ities in Moscow) as the main obstacle to Russia's achieving a decisive tran-sition to a new political and socioeconomic order. He initiated a "war of laws," contesting or blocking the enforcement of Soviet laws on the territory of the Russian republic. He sponsored a declaration of Russian "sovereignty" and supported other republics that were doing the same. He dictated terms for a proposed "Union Treaty," being negotiated throughout 1990–1991, that would have turned the USSR into a confederation of largely independent states – leaving the center with few powers that the republics did not explicitly and consensually cede to it. He sided with the coal miners who suddenly rose up in strikes against economic conditions (1989) and, later (1991), against Gorbachev and the communist regime itself, endorsing the legitimacy of their demands and taking the opportunity to have jurisdiction over the mines transferred to the Russian republic. He told representatives of Russia's regions, who were also declaring their "autonomy" in relation to central power *in Russia,* to "take all the autonomy you can swallow." [43]

When Gorbachev accommodated radicalizing forces, Yeltsin typically upped the ante by endorsing a still more radical option. And when Gorbachev moved back toward the center of the political spectrum – seeking compromises between gradualist and rapid programs for economic reform, and between federalist and confederalist terms in the Union Treaty – or when the regime used violence against anti-system forces in Georgia, Azerbaidjan, or the Baltics, Yeltsin denounced Gorbachev for being conservative, reactionary, or worse. It was a classic polarizing game, designed to put Gorbachev in "no-win" situations and to create the conditions for a decisive break with the old order. Yeltsin, over time, became increasingly determined to destroy both Gorbachev's authority and the Kremlin's powers.

Yeltsin was not the only major political actor mobilizing against Gorbachev during this period. In response to such shocks as the collapse of communism in Eastern Europe (1989), miners' strikes, removal of the leading role of the Communist Party from the Constitution (1990), disintegration of all-union power structures (1990–1991), proto-secessionist tendencies in Russia, Ukraine, the Caucasus, and the Baltics, and the apparent unwillingness of Gorbachev to stand up against the tide, the forces of conservative reaction began to mobilize in public and behind the scenes. Gorbachev initially tried to accommodate them and, as we have seen, moved partially to the right on domestic policy during the period from September 1990 to April 1991. But this was little more than a holding action, for the social forces that held the

---

[43] Foreign Broadcast Information Service, Daily Report, Soviet Union (hereafter, FBIS-SOV), August 13, 1990, p. 84; seven months later, however, he qualified this admonition: "the autonomies can take as much sovereignty as they can administer. We can agree to all of that. But they will have to answer independently, of course, for the well-being of their people. We make one condition: they will have to take part in a federation treaty with Russia. I underline: we will not let anyone pull Russia down" (*Komsomol'skaia pravda,* 14 March 1991). My thanks to Philip Roeder for this citation.

initiative in day-to-day politics were the radical, anti-system forces – or at least those forces whose behaviors furthered the disintegration of the system. Gorbachev could prevent the promulgation of a radical and rapid decentralization of the economy, but he could not impose a gradualist program of reform when the leadership of the Russian republic refused to implement it. He could prevent the adoption of a confederalist Union Treaty, but he could not impose a federalist alternative when the major republics, including Russia, refused to honor it. In the meantime, the economy was experiencing a steady decline in performance that was commensurate with a steady decline in the cohesion of public administration.

When, in April 1991, Gorbachev decided to shift camps once again and to negotiate the transformation of the USSR into a confederation, he predictably infuriated the conservatives and reactionaries who had joined his government in recent months and who expected some reassertion of the Kremlin's authority over the country. When instead Gorbachev scheduled a ceremony in August 1991 for signing the radical version of a Union Treaty, leaders of all-union institutions – the KGB, military, and central planners – took things into their own hands. Their coup of August 19, 1991, was hastily and poorly planned, had only limited support among military commanders, and was not energized by any collective sense of self-confidence. Moreover, while the plotters had succeeded in holding Gorbachev under house arrest in his vacation home far from Moscow, they had not succeeded in so isolating Boris Yeltsin. This was Yeltsin's finest hour. He risked his life by standing on a tank and demanding, as the duly elected president of Russia, that the troops not take part in this anti-democratic infamy, warning that they would be held accountable if they cooperated with the treasonous plotters.

The subsequent history of Russia, and perhaps also of the Soviet Union, might have been quite different had Yeltsin not survived his defiance. It would have taken but one sniper's bullet to end his life as he stood on that tank. And it would have taken just one determined platoon commander to open artillery fire on the White House and to kill off much of the leadership of the anti-system forces assembled there that day. Although mobilized social forces may push a country's politics in a given direction, they do not always determine how far the push will go and how long it will last. Yeltsin's role in further polarizing Russian politics, and in frustrating Gorbachev's efforts to recoup his political role, is undeniable. Absent Yeltsin after August 1991, and even if the coup had ultimately failed after such a bloodletting, the political landscape would have been quite different. But the flip side is also true: Yeltsin's successful defiance of the coup plotters turned his high popularity into a condition of almost legendary charisma. Seemingly, he had single-handedly faced down the coup, a feat at least as large and awe-inspiring as his successful political resurrection through electoral politics in 1989.[44]

Yeltsin had performed a seeming miracle, which is precisely what charismatic leaders are viewed by their followers as capable of doing. Thereafter, he had Gorbachev at his mercy – and he was rarely merciful, much less magnanimous. Yeltsin may not have decided until November–December 1991 to work behind the scenes with the leaders of two other republics to dissolve the Soviet Union and to transfer the Kremlin (and the all-union institutions it controlled) to the jurisdiction of the Russian republic. He may not have decided in August–September whether he preferred to replace Gorbachev as leader of a new, confederal Union of Sovereign States. But it was increasingly clear by fall of 1991 that Gorbachev was finished as a serious political force and that the future of Russia would be shaped by the decisions of President Yeltsin.

THE POLITICS OF "INBIDDING" AND OUTBIDDING

In established democratic regimes in which levels of social conflict and polarization are relatively low, and when the electoral contest is "winner-take-all," political competitors on the campaign trail typically compete for the votes of the moderate middle of the electorate. When social conflict and polarization rise, a reverse process sets in. The moderate middle declines in size and candidates must compete for the allegiances of the swelling extremes of the political spectrum. Under such conditions, the language of politics becomes more extremist in both directions. Moreover, competitors on the same side of the ideological spectrum often seek to outbid each other for the allegiances of the extremist voters. In contexts marked by polarizing ethnic or racial conflict, the reactionary strategy is sometimes referred to as "playing the ethnic (or race) card." This will take a dual form: denouncing one's ideological opponents for their position on the issue and outbidding one's rivals on the same side of the political spectrum by showing that one is more intensely committed to the value than they are.

In situations of rising electoral polarization, competitors on each side of the political spectrum may attempt to seize the initiative from rivals within their ideological camp by trumping each other's policy advocacy – or, to use still other metaphors from card games, by "upping the ante," "raising the

---

[44] This, in any case, was the public perception. There are those who argue that Yeltsin was not in danger of losing his life during the coup – that the plotters chose not to try to kill him. I leave the resolution of this matter to future historians.

stakes," or "outbidding each other." This often takes the form of trying to exaggerate the competitor's compatibility with the opposite wing of the political spectrum. Whether this proves to be a winning strategy depends on the type of election in question (party primary versus general election), the electoral rules (proportional representation versus winner-take-all), and the size and dispositions of the "moderate" bloc among the voting public. In Yeltsin's case, the special circumstances created by Gorbachev's reforms provided him a propitious opportunity for building his political standing through such outbidding.

Soviet politics before Gorbachev was certainly not electoral politics, but it was a form of competition for the allegiance of intra-elite constituencies. In this competition, the higher the level of issue polarization within the establishment, the greater the temptation to up the ante in order to seize the initiative from rivals. This was the case during the political succession struggle that followed Stalin's death and before the "Stalin question" had been resolved. It was Khrushchev who successfully played the game of outbidding. The post-Stalin consensus called for breaking with the terroristic atmosphere and improving the consumer situation. But Khrushchev threw his rivals onto the political defensive with his unexpected denunciation of Stalin. In socioeconomic policy, he accused his rivals of failing to understand the magnitude of the food emergency, as he sponsored a campaign (the "Virgin Lands" project) for rapidly cultivating new lands in order to alleviate the grain shortage – thus trumping Malenkov's more sober (and more expensive) long-range plan for the further development of traditional agricultural regions. Khrushchev then upped the ante further, touring the country and calling on peasants to commit to extraordinary levels of meat and milk production within a three- to four-year period. Khrushchev's rivals in the leadership were consistently caught flat-footed by this intentional effort to raise popular consumption expectations and to shatter political icons. By the time they tried to oust Khrushchev in 1957, however, his patronage network in the Central Committee had grown to the point that he was able to turn the tables and purge his competitors instead.

When Khrushchev was finally ousted in 1964, the leadership was far more consensual than it had been after Stalin's death. The anti-Stalin campaign was brought to a halt to prevent the intelligentsia from continuing to cast doubt on the wisdom of the Communist Party and its "correct line." Khrushchev's extraordinary promises about the "full and final victory of communism" in the USSR and about "overtaking and surpassing the United States" in industrial production and standard of living were also tacitly retracted. Collectively, the leadership had developed a better appreciation of the incapacity of the system to deliver on such promises. Given these changes, the level of issue polarization within the leadership had declined to the point that "inbidding," or building a coalition that coopted the moderate middle of the political spectrum, became the winning formula. Khrushchev most recently, and Stalin before him, had demonstrated to the political leadership the dangers "from above" when a leader gains too much power and can use it against his nominally "collective" leadership. Under such circumstances, political competition under Brezhnev became constricted: confined within narrower arenas of politics and always sensitive to the need to avoid challenges to the political prerogatives of the Party leadership, whether from "above" (an autocrat) or "below" (forces outside the Party–State). Maintenance of a façade of unity within the leadership was a way of heading off such challenges; it interacted with, and reinforced, the moderate issue consensus within the leadership. The result was that political competition became more a matter of inbidding than outbidding. This went on for some twenty years and contributed to a condition that Gorbachev and his allies would characterize as "stagnation."

Gorbachev, like Khrushchev, faced a situation in which the climate of opinion within the political establishment had shifted toward a diffuse sense that "we cannot go on like this." There was no consensus regarding how to cure the malaise, but there was a widespread yearning for change. The stand-pat mentality of Brezhnev's and Chernenko's heirs (Tikhonov, Grishin, Romanov, Kunaev, et al.) was the analog of the neo-Stalinist sentiment in 1953 – and was as easily outflanked. Gorbachev's "campaign speech" of December 1984 was analogous to Khrushchev's de-Stalinization campaign. It threw down the gauntlet and announced that continuing in the old way was no longer acceptable. After consolidating his power base in 1985–1986, Gorbachev again seized the initiative by beginning a process of continuous radicalization of policy, which found expression in his *glasnost'* and *demokratizatsiya* programs of 1987–1988. But in sponsoring these initiatives, Gorbachev was not trying to outbid rivals within the leadership. Those who agreed with his program, such as Shevardnadze and Yakovlev, were not his rivals but his allies; he did not need to outbid them. Gorbachev was simply trying to lead the country in the direction he preferred. He preferred to radicalize in piecemeal fashion, trying to keep social forces from pushing too far and too fast in a direction that might bring down the system or create a powerful backlash by forces within the establishment.

These were the conditions under which Yeltsin tried to outbid Gorbachev, first in order to force him to radicalize more fully and more quickly (1986–1987) and then in order to outflank Gorbachev in the struggle for the allegiances of newly mobilized social forces (1988–1991). Yeltsin lost the first of these struggles because it took place within the confines of the Party establishment and at a time when the level of issue polarization within the Politburo and Central Committee was still relatively low. However, he won the second struggle because it took place in a public arena that extended to a newly empowered (and quickly radicalizing) electorate. In effect, Yeltsin was able to outbid Gorbachev once two conditions obtained: (1) political polarization had risen greatly; and (2) the game of political competition was taking place in new arenas and with new rules – arenas and rules that, ironically, had been called into being by Gorbachev himself.

At the 27th Party Congress (February 1986), Yeltsin revealed that he was now more radical than any other member of the Politburo, criticizing the central Party apparatus and the socioeconomic privileges of the *nomenklatura* and doing so in front of a broad Party membership in a speech that would be published in *Pravda* the next day. Yeltsin did much the same in a number of Politburo meetings, where he criticized the pace of *perestroika* (and thereby criticized Gorbachev's leadership), causing Gorbachev at one point to storm out of the meeting.[45] At some points in time, Gorbachev might have found it convenient to have a Politburo member advocating things that were even more radical than what Gorbachev was advocating. That would enhance Gorbachev's image as a *responsible* reformer and, at least temporarily, increase the puritans' and technocrats' sense of dependence on Gorbachev for political protection against "wild-eyed radicals" within the elite.

But when, in 1987, Yeltsin took his critique of *perestroika*, Ligachev, privilege, and Gorbachev's leadership to a meeting of the Central Committee – and did so without clearing his speech in advance with the Politburo – he had violated some of the most cherished rules of Politburo politics. He was tearing down the façade of unanimity that the Politburo preferred to show to broader audiences, even those within the political establishment, and was seeking to mobilize members of the Central Committee against his rivals within the Politburo. He was, in short, trying to discredit Gorbachev by "reporting" him to the Central Committee, accusing him of lack of courage and accusing Ligachev of seeking to sabotage *perestroika*. The vitriolic denunciation he received for his efforts, and his subsequent firing from positions in the Politburo and regional Party leadership, were demonstrations that outbidding in a still-Leninist regime is best conducted from a position of strength. Lacking a strong constituency for his views within the Central Committee, and lacking the institutional channels through which to mobilize a broader public constituency, Yeltsin's challenge was easily beaten back.

---

45 Yeltsin, *Against the Grain,* pp. 128–9.

Such was not the case in 1988–1989, when Yeltsin seized the opportunity to outbid Gorbachev before broader, more sympathetic audiences. The process began at the televised 19th Party Conference of June 1988, which was precisely the forum at which Gorbachev introduced his most radical proposals. Absent Yeltsin's intervention, Gorbachev might have left this conference with a public image as a great democratizer. Instead, Yeltsin's unscheduled speech, for which he literally had to force himself to the microphone, raised the stakes to the point that Gorbachev came away looking like a moderate – or, at worst, like a conservative – in the eyes of the most radical forces. Some of Yeltsin's criticisms and proposals were merely tactical and could well be characterized as carping, as follows.[46]

- The Party Conference should have taken place much earlier.
- The election of delegates to the conference was not always conducted in a democratic fashion.
- Current members of the leadership who served under Brezhnev and who were tolerant of stagnation and corruption should be dismissed from the Politburo.
- When a general secretary leaves office, many other members of the Politburo should depart with him.
- The designers of *perestroika* did not prepare the ground for it properly; they did not sufficiently analyze the reasons for "stagnation."

But other proposals and criticisms staked out a more radical and egalitarian conception of democratization.

- Gorbachev's proposal to combine the functions of first secretaries of Party committees and heads of soviet delegations should be put to a popular referendum.
- The general secretary should also be subjected to direct, secret-ballot public election.
- Leaders of all political institutions should have term limits of two terms for each office and an age limit of 65 years.
- The Politburo should produce accounts of its activity – the biographies of its members, how much money they earn, what they do, etc.
- The budget of the Central Committee should be discussed openly.
- Corruption and privileges among the upper *nomenklatura* are intolerable and a violation of "social justice"; access to resources should be based on

---

[46] The following proposals are found in Yeltsin's speech as reprinted in Gorshkov et al., *Gorbachev–Yel'tsin*, pp. 78–82.

the principle that material shortages must be experienced by everyone, including officials of the Party apparatus.
• The Party apparatus is too large and strong; it can frustrate democratization. Reduce the apparatus of regional Party organizations by 2–3 times and of the Central Committee by 6–10 times, and liquidate various departments of the Central Committee apparatus.
• Socialism has failed "to resolve the main issues – to feed and clothe the people, to provide for the service sector, to solve social problems."

By any definition of the term, both Gorbachev and Yeltsin were proposing radical, democratizing changes in June 1988, beyond anything heard in Party forums since the 1920s. Soviet doctrine under Brezhnev had justified the hegemony of the CPSU by claiming that only the Party was capable of aggregating interests in society and of preventing tensions within society from becoming "antagonistic contradictions." Competitive elections and a multi-party system were not needed, so the doctrine read, because only the CPSU had sufficient understanding of the public interest to mediate and contain social conflict. It was unnecessary to expand the political rights of the masses, since such rights were only needed in systems in which an antagonistic relationship obtained between the interests of the "people" and the interests of their rulers.[47]

When Gorbachev began trying to introduce new mechanisms of intra-Party democracy in 1987 and new mechanisms of official electoral accountability in 1988, he marched well beyond the previous doctrinal limits. For he was now claiming that the Party, as constituted, could not be trusted to smooth contradictions, to aggregate interests properly, and to defend the public interest rather than solely the personal interests of the official class. Hence, genuine accountability to "the people" required more than merely a stated commitment to be responsive to popular needs; it required that one give power to the people directly to sanction or remove unresponsive officials.

Boris Yeltsin's egalitarian populism while Party first secretary in Moscow had led him toward an antagonistic view of the relationship between the *nomenklatura* and the populace. At the time, he thought of the *nomenklatura* as a set of corrupted officials in need of being replaced. After 1987, however, he came increasingly to define the *nomenklatura* in systemic terms: not as an

---

[47] For fuller discussion and documentation, see Breslauer, *Khrushchev and Brezhnev*, pp. 174–5; for the work of an intra-establishment liberal who was trying to extend the Brezhnevian definition of political participation to include "expanded political rights," see Fyodor Burlatskii, *Lenin, gosudarstvo, politika* (Moscow: Nauka, 1970).

aggregate of individuals but as a system of rule. This was consistent with Gorbachev's public statements at the time. But Yeltsin pushed things farther and faster than Gorbachev on the theoretical plane. His outbidding was both an expression of his evolving beliefs and an act of political competition that motivated him to seek increasingly radical positions to endorse.[48]

By June 1988, what distinguished Gorbachev from Yeltsin was not the endorsement of democratization but rather the degree to which each man defined democratization as consistent with maintenance of the "leading role of the Party." Both men continued formally to endorse the desirability and necessity of the Party's leading role. But Yeltsin was increasingly defining the Party apparatus as standing in antagonistic *and irremediable* contradiction to the public interest. Gorbachev's proposals would have made Party officials increasingly accountable to an electorate; Yeltsin's proposals would have done this and, additionally, would have made the daily operations of the Party apparatus more open to public scrutiny and more easily subject to angry public mobilization. Yeltsin, then, was one large step closer than Gorbachev to the position that the CPSU needed to be abolished because it was incapable of being transformed.

After June 1988, as Soviet democrats pushed to further radicalize the reforms, Gorbachev accommodated the pressures. Until fall 1990 he acceded incrementally, and often with protest, to increasingly radical demands – either because he believed in radicalization as an end in itself or because he calculated that the cost of resistance exceeded the cost of acquiescence. He was playing a political game of selective accommodation while trying to contain the pace of political polarization.

Yeltsin, however, was playing a different game, using newspaper interviews and public speeches to dog Gorbachev by continuously outbidding him for the allegiance of the people and, in the process, further radicalizing the perspectives and perceptions of the populace. If Yeltsin's public statements had had no impact on the rate of polarization, we would not need to refer

---

[48] Outbidding is a calculated act of political competition. In any given case, it may or may not be hypocritical. Yeltsin's beliefs radicalized over time in response to learning, as during his trip to the United States in September 1989 (Aron, *Boris Yeltsin,* ch. 7). But Yeltsin's "views" also happened to radicalize at key points in the political competition with Gorbachev – in the run-up to the 1989 and 1990 parliamentary elections, for example. Given the speed with which human beings are able to rationalize their behavior as being in line with their principles, it may be a futile exercise to try to determine the degree to which Yeltsin's radicalization was opportunistic. Nor is it a necessary exercise, for the approach to authority building and political competition employed in this book focuses largely on impression management and the public presentation of self. It is enough to demonstrate the process of outbidding and to consider its impact on political audiences.

to this as outbidding; we would simply argue that he chose a different constituency than did Gorbachev within a rapidly polarizing electorate. Under
such circumstances, Yeltsin's behavior would have mimicked the rate of social polarization, not influenced it. We would need an ambitious and careful
study of the interaction between Yeltsin's actions and the behavior of social
forces to decide the matter conclusively. But the available evidence suggests
to me that Yeltsin in 1988–1989 became a focal point for social forces.

To be sure, there were forces more radical than he. But the bulk of the
population that came eventually to support him had not developed a revolutionary consciousness by 1988–1989. Yeltsin articulated for them, in intelli-
gible form, that which they felt in their guts. He helped them to explain the
precise sources of their condition. He raised their consciousness about what
was necessary to reverse their misery. And, importantly for a focal point,
he demonstrated by his succession of political victories that peaceful revolutionary change was not only desirable and necessary but also *feasible*. This
set him apart from deputies in several public forums who advanced proposals
that were fully as radical as his were. Yeltsin was able to outbid Gorbachev because he did so persistently and on all domestic issues,[49] in numerous venues,
and with a plausible claim to compete with Gorbachev for the allegiance of
the populace (whether he denied this intent or not).

We have already witnessed Yeltsin's outbidding of Gorbachev at the televised June 1988 Party Conference. But the conference ended with numerous
speeches that roasted Yeltsin for his iconoclasm, and the leadership rejected
his request to be "rehabilitated" by the Party. All this caused him to fall into
prolonged despondency.[50] Yet after absorbing the lessons of the Party Conference and buoyed by a torrent of letters and telegrams of support, Yeltsin
decided to run for a seat in the new parliament, the Congress of People's
Deputies, elections to which would be held in March 1989. The intellectual
and emotional bruising he had recently suffered – combined with the prospect
of a political competition in which he could settle scores and regain power –
caused him to up the rhetorical ante still further. In his electoral platform,
published in *Moskovskaia pravda* on March 21, 1989,[51] Yeltsin called for a
comprehensive decentralization of power to all those who wished to receive it:
the "people," the soviets, enterprises, would-be landowners, even republics.

---

[49] I discern no pattern of outbidding on foreign policy issues, unless one chooses to define inter-
republican relations as such.
[50] Aron, *Boris Yeltsin*, p. 249.
[51] *Moskovskaia pravda*, March 21, 1989, reprinted in Gorshkov et al., *Gorbachev–Yel'tsin*; cited
demands are on page 118.

Although Yeltsin did not yet articulate a coherent alternative to the existing system, he was moving in that direction. This platform implied (though it did not say it) that "the leading role of the Party" in the country's political, economic, and cultural life should be abolished.

Similarly, at the televised First Congress of People's Deputies on May 31, 1989, Gorbachev referred to the CPSU as the "guarantor of democracy," whereas Yeltsin characterized the Party as the main obstacle to democratization.[52] Yeltsin also demanded "greater political rights, greater economic and financial independence ... for each republic of the USSR," and he supported a deputy's proposal that some republics be allowed to have two state languages.[53] In a clearly demagogic bid for support of the "little man," Yeltsin suggested that Gorbachev's years in power had been a "do-nothing" period: "Even at this congress we should solve at least one concrete question, otherwise people will not understand us. For example, institute free supply of medications and free [public] transport in the cities for invalids and people living below the poverty line, solve the question of pensions, at least in part."[54] Yeltsin claimed that in one realm, however, Gorbachev had done too much. He had concentrated too much power in his own hands: "We could find ourselves again, without realizing it, in the grip of a new authoritarian regime, a new dictatorship." Yeltsin proposed a yearly popular referendum on the question of trust in the chairman of the Supreme Soviet of the USSR.[55]

Two months later, in a published interview, Yeltsin commented that the congress should abolish Article 6 of the Constitution (which protected the monopoly role of the Communist Party in the political system), with power being exercised only by organs elected by the people.[56] In the same month, he called for a "drastic reduction" in the KGB, a topic on which Gorbachev continued to exercise reserve in public comments.[57] In December 1989, his speech at the Congress of People's Deputies upped the ante on economic reform, calling for a more complete economic decentralization than he had ever advocated before and demanding a *rapid* transition to the market – much more rapid than the six years that the Ryzhkov government was proposing.[58] In the same month, a rare direct exchange took place between Gorbachev and

---

[52] Ibid., p. 134.
[53] Ibid., p. 138.
[54] Ibid., p. 139.
[55] Ibid.
[56] Ibid., p. 146.
[57] Soviet television, July 14, 1989 (FBIS-SOV, July 17, 1989), as noted in Marc Zlotnik, "Yeltsin and Gorbachev: The politics of confrontation" (unpublished manuscript, 1999).
[58] Soviet television, December 15, 1989 (FBIS-SOV, December 18, 1989).

Yeltsin regarding their political identities. Yeltsin told a Greek newspaper: "Those who still believe in communism are moving in the sphere of fantasy. I regard myself as a social democrat." Gorbachev responded several days later at a meeting of the Supreme Soviet: "I am a Communist, a convinced Communist. For some that may be a fantasy. But for me it is my main goal."[59]

Matters continued to escalate thereafter. The year 1990 saw the outbidding encompass: (1) matters of intra-Party reform (should the CPSU split into two parties? Should the conservatives be purged and the Party turned into a social democratic party? Should a multiparty, liberal democratic political order replace the current system?); (2) direct attacks on Gorbachev's fitness to continue in power; (3) relations between Moscow and the republics of the USSR; and, most consequentially, (4) the right of Russia to run its own affairs, irrespective of the wishes of the Soviet "center." This extension of outbidding, which both mirrored and further emboldened radicalizing forces in society, set the USSR on a course toward its eventual dissolution.

In January 1990, Yeltsin told a Latvian youth newspaper that the Baltic republics needed real sovereignty; he also accused Gorbachev of having become a rightist in view of his reluctance to pass fundamental laws on property, land, and the media and of his "unconcealed wish" to retain Article 6 of the Constitution.[60] In an interview eleven days later, Yeltsin implied his intention to split the Party at its forthcoming Congress unless there is "a serious renewal."[61] At the Central Committee plenum on February 5, 1990, Yeltsin elaborated on the meaning of such a renewal. Morrison summarizes it well:

His demands included the abandonment of democratic centralism and a guarantee of freedom of opinion for individual members; the abolition of the full-time *apparat*; a multiparty system; the formal recognition of internal Party factions; the abolition of article six of the Soviet constitution ...; a change in the Party structure from vertical to horizontal; democratic Party elections; an end to the *nomenklatura* system of Party control over appointments; decentralization of the Party finances; the transformation of the Party into a federal structure of parties from individual republics, including Russia ....[62]

On February 17, Yeltsin declared that Russia should be "autonomous in internal and international relations."[63] On February 20, he declared that the

---

[59] The exchange is noted and translated in Morrison, *Boris Yeltsin*, p. 108.

[60] Gorshkov et al., *Gorbachev–Yel'tsin*, pp. 164–5.

[61] Ibid., p. 169.

[62] Morrison, *Boris Yeltsin*, p. 118.

[63] Moscow radio, February 17, 1990 (FBIS-SOV, February 20, 1990), as depicted in Zlotnik, "Yeltsin and Gorbachev."

purpose of his seeking the chairmanship of the soon-to-be-elected Supreme Soviet of Russia was to force a "radicalization of all reforms."[64] In the course of this election campaign, Yeltsin made explicit what he had only hinted at earlier: that the USSR needed a liberal democracy based on total freedom of choice, without the limits that Gorbachev continued to advocate.[65] Yeltsin was making a virtue of the centrifugal forces that were straining the seams of the Soviet Union, endorsing them without equivocation and, in effect, equating disintegration with "freedom of choice" and "democracy." Gorbachev, by contrast, was defining centrifugal forces as portents of anarchy and trying to rein them in and buy them off.

In May 1990, things escalated further – again at Yeltsin's initiative. At the First Congress of People's Deputies of the Russian Federation, where he was elected as chairman by a narrow margin, Yeltsin defined "sovereignty" for the republics as the right to decide what rights the "center" should enjoy. Legally, he argued, the Russian constitution should supersede the all-union constitution. On May 30, he announced that laws were being prepared for the popular election of a Russian Federation president.[66] In June 1990, Gorbachev and Yeltsin polemicized with each other on the matter of republican sovereignty, with Yeltsin supporting "strong republics" and Gorbachev upholding the importance of the union (an "isolated" Russia is not the solution, Gorbachev insisted).[67] In July 1990, the fateful 28th Party Congress took place at which (as we have seen) Yeltsin took an abolitionist position concerning the organizational powers of the CPSU and Gorbachev countered with a position that was both anti-monopolistic and anti-abolitionist. This did not satisfy Yeltsin, who raised the stakes once again by exiting the congress and handing in his Party card.

And so it went, on issue after issue. Gorbachev would move incrementally in more radical directions and then Yeltsin would trump him, denounce him for caution or lack of commitment, and force a public confrontation. As revolutionary forces within the intelligentsia and within the union republics gained strength, Yeltsin ensured that he kept up with them (or stayed ahead of them), leaving Gorbachev in the unenviable position of trying to restrain them and being denounced as a conservative – or, alternatively, of casting his lot with hardline forces within the Party. Thus, Yeltsin, in summer 1990, forced Gorbachev prematurely to endorse the 500-day program for radical reform

[64] *Sovetskaia Estoniia*, February 20, 1990, as quoted in Aron, *Boris Yelstin*, p. 364.
[65] See Aron, *Boris Yeltsin*, pp. 366–70.
[66] Gorshkov et al., *Gorbachev–Yel'tsin*, p. 200.
[67] Ibid., pp. 204–9.

of the economy by threatening to implement it within Russia. In January 1991, Yeltsin called on Russian soldiers sent to the Baltics to consider refusing to follow the illegitimate orders of their commanders.[68] The next day, Yeltsin announced that Russia, Kazakhstan, Belorussia, and Ukraine might sign a four-sided treaty – ahead of the Union Treaty being negotiated at the time – that other republics and the center would be welcome to sign later on.[69] On February 19, 1991, Yeltsin for the first time called on Gorbachev to resign.[70] In March, when Gorbachev sponsored a nationwide referendum on whether Soviet citizens wanted to maintain the union, Yeltsin inserted onto the Russian republic's ballot the question of whether a popularly elected Russian presidency should be created. After Yeltsin's election as president, he signed a decree ending the activity of political parties within Russian state organs, an action that provoked both the communists and Gorbachev.[71]

Yeltsin began the year 1991 with a public position that sought to reconcile Russian autonomy with maintenance of a confederal variant of the USSR. It was not initially a call for Russian secession from the existing state. Indeed, on March 17, 1991, he called upon voters to *endorse* Gorbachev's referendum on behalf of a "renewed union." Yet in contrast to Gorbachev's position, Yeltsin called simultaneously for "the strengthening of Russia's statehood." Moreover, he defined such strengthening as a prerequisite for effective membership in the proposed "Union of Sovereign States." He discussed the ambiguities publicly:

I support the union. But only one that the republics would join of their own free will and not by force.... Even today there are several republics that have declared their intention to secede from it.... The only power that is strong is power based on the support of the people. Therefore, we believe that the president of Russia should be elected not by a narrow circle but by all citizens of the republic, by the whole people. The introduction of the post of president will make it possible to strengthen the sovereignty of the republic.... The election of a president of Russia by means of a vote of all the people is only the start of the strengthening of executive power in the republic.... I view your "Yes" [vote] as support for reforms in our republic, as your personal contribution toward strengthening Russian statehood, which will enable Russia to be a full participant in a renewed union of sovereign states.[72]

Yeltsin got what he had asked for: a presidential election in Russia that he won handily in June 1991. He was now in a position to act upon his calls

[68] Ibid., p. 295.
[69] Ibid., p. 296.
[70] Ibid., p. 314.
[71] Ibid., pp. 375–7.
[72] Moscow Radio Rossii Network, March 17, 1991.

for "strengthening executive power in the republic" as a means of further "strengthening Russian statehood," albeit within the context of a "renewed union." As events unfolded, it became clear that Yeltsin's commitment to a renewed union was far weaker than were his commitments to executive power within the republic and independence of the republic from any imperative co-ordination by the union's central authorities. At the same time, while unwilling publicly to advocate dismemberment of the USSR, he depicted a Russian state that would be the core of a redefined union of sovereign states.[73]

As time went on, events would force Yeltsin to choose between this flowering of Russian executive power and statehood relative to the union "center" on the one hand and, on the other hand, his avoidance of publicly advocating dissolution of the USSR. That would lead to his final act of outbidding Gorbachev, in December 1991, when he conspired reluctantly (but successfully) to abolish both the Soviet Union and Gorbachev's presidency.

CONCLUSION

In sum, Gorbachev's reforms unleashed forces that eventually he could not control. He was playing a political game that required him to maintain support among moderates even as he tried to push those moderates toward increasingly radical positions. However, the level of polarization among politically mobilized citizens was increasing more rapidly than Gorbachev had anticipated. Into this breach jumped an aggrieved and determined Boris Yeltsin. He sensed intuitively that the USSR was experiencing a peaceful revolution, not a controlled transformation. He sensed that the winning political strategy in such a situation was to keep up with – and stoke the passions of – radicalizing forces and simultaneously to frustrate the efforts of political rivals to contain the pace of change. He played this game relentlessly, perhaps relishing the opportunity to gain revenge against Gorbachev for the agony of 1987.

This explains why occupying the middle ground in competitive politics is viewed sometimes as a rational strategy and sometimes as folly. When the level of issue polarization among those with the right to participate in politics is low, and when "moderates" predominate numerically within the active (s)electorate, occupying the middle ground can be a winning strategy. But when the level of polarization is high and rising, when "moderates" are moving toward one or the other extreme, and when counter-elites raise the

---

[73] See, for example, his statement at a press conference on June 26, 1991 (Official Kremlin International News Broadcast, June 27, 1991).

expectations of popular audiences, occupying the middle ground becomes a losing strategy: one gets caught in a cross-fire, accused by both extremes of selling them out.

Gorbachev had risen skillfully within the Soviet political establishment. Once in the position of general secretary, he had demonstrated his capacity to initiate a peaceful transformation of the system. But in the end, and precisely because of the institutions Gorbachev had created, Yeltsin was able to play the game of public politics better than Gorbachev himself. Gorbachev proved more skilled at authority building within a Soviet political structure. Yeltsin proved more skilled at exploiting the public politics that Gorbachev had called into being.

7

Yeltsin Ascendant

Yeltsin had won the power struggle. He would now enter his own stage of ascendancy, when he would be expected to take political responsibility for solving the problems facing Russia – in particular, a collapsing state and an economy on the verge of collapse. The expectations of him were shaped in large part by the public image he had forged in the course of outflanking Gorbachev. Yeltsin had built his authority and seized the political initiative on the basis of an expanding but largely negative program: anti-corruption, anti-privilege, anti-Party apparatus, anti-communist, anti-Gorbachev, and, finally, anti-"the center" (i.e., the Kremlin's Soviet authority). The apogee of this accumulation of authority came in August 1991 when, in the eyes of many citizens, he assumed almost legendary heroic status by mounting a tank in front of the White House and facing down the coup plotters, seemingly through the sheer force of his will. The positive features of Yeltsin's program were real, but they were neither elaborated nor implemented at the time. Throughout 1991 and especially during his presidential election campaign of Spring 1991, Yeltsin promised Russia that he would build a market economy on the Western model, integrate the country into the global capitalist economy, and see Russia take its place among the "normal" and "civilized" liberal democracies of the world. But he did not have to specify a strategy for accomplishing all this, since Russia was not yet autonomous of the Kremlin's dictates.

All he needed to do in order to win the power struggle (no mean feat, of course) was to identify himself publicly with these visionary goals and lambaste Gorbachev at every turn for failing to adopt a program that would accomplish them swiftly on a nationwide basis. During the period of radicalization and revolutionary polarization made possible by Gorbachev's transformation of Soviet politics, this was a winning strategy. It allied Yeltsin with the most mobilized, self-confident, and energetic forces within society: anti-system voters and protesters in all republics; educated, urban youth; and "Westernizers" among the technical and critical intelligentsia. It permitted him to paint his main rivals as either spent forces (Gorbachev), conservatives (Ligachev), or restorationists (the coup plotters). It allowed him to build his own authority by playing the revolutionary's game of undercutting the authority of incumbents and state institutions alike. And it allowed him to accumulate political support without having to specify a positive program and take responsibility for policy results.

Each of the Soviet leaders on whom we have focused – Khrushchev in 1958–1959, Brezhnev in 1970–1971, and Gorbachev in 1986–1987 – followed his victory in the political succession struggle with a brief period during which he emerged ascendant within the leadership and had the authority and power to sponsor a comprehensive program for change in domestic and foreign policies. This was the leader's "honeymoon" period, when his authority was at its greatest and many skeptics deferred to his right to specify a vision.[1] Yeltsin, too, emerged ascendant after his victory in the Russian presidential election of June 1991, and his authority soared even higher after August 1991. Moreover, in many ways he was even more unconstrained at this point than the earlier leaders had been, both because he had secured a huge electoral mandate and because there was no longer a powerful collective leadership – backed by clients within a Central Committee apparatus – to which he had to report. And in October of that year, his parliament (the Russian Supreme Soviet), which would later become antagonistic to his program, accorded him special powers to rule by decree for a one-year period. His honeymoon had begun, but like his predecessors', it would not last long.

RUSSIA'S POST-SOVIET POLICY AGENDA

Yeltsin's ascendancy took place in a context that looked quite different from those that Khrushchev, Brezhnev, and Gorbachev faced at analogous stages of their administrations. The Communist Party no longer enjoyed a "leading role" or the opportunity to impose its "correct line" on the country; instead, it was struggling to avoid expropriation of its assets and abrogation of its right to exist. Politics, of course, was no longer a private affair; instead, the mass public was now the arena for contested electoral politics, while civil liberties – freedom of speech, religion, organization, press, and movement – were

---

[1] Gorbachev, however, faced more resistance to his domestic policy radicalization in 1987 than had Khrushchev and Brezhnev at comparable points in time.

widespread. The command economy had been destroyed, though an institutionalized free market had not been created. Internationally, communism had ceased to rule in Eastern Europe, the Warsaw Pact had been dissolved, and there was no longer a Soviet Union to serve as ideological and organizational center of the world communist movement.

Whatever program Yeltsin intended to forge, it was not going to be Leninist. At the analogous stage of their administrations, his predecessors in the Kremlin had come forth with programs that sought to adapt, reform, or transform the Party–State apparatus; Yeltsin instead faced a crumbling Party–State and the challenge of building a new one. His immediate predecessor sought to transform the Communist Party; Yeltsin proposed to destroy it and to replace it with new bases of political organization and ideology. Gorbachev had sought to transform the command economy; Yeltsin sought not only to cope with a rapidly disintegrating, no longer commanding economy but also to *build* an economic system to replace it. His predecessor had tried to define a new mission and ethos for the "Soviet people"; Yeltsin had to cope with the disorientation and identity void following the collapse of Soviet civilization while helping to build a Russian nation to replace it. Gorbachev had been challenged to provide a formula for dealing with the "nationalities problem" within the USSR; Yeltsin had to define a strategy for ordering Russia's now-foreign relations with the fourteen other successor states of the former Soviet Union. His predecessors had to specify a program for simultaneously maintaining or extending the global power of the USSR and keeping the peace between the two nuclear superpowers. Yeltsin had to define from scratch what were to be *Russia's* roles and responsibilities in the post–Cold War international system. In sum, Yeltsin was challenged to be simultaneously a state builder, a nation builder, the designer of a new economic order, and a statesman. He had built his authority as an oppositional leader but would have to maintain it as a creator.

In fall 1991, when Yeltsin began to anticipate and prepare for his country's independence from Soviet authorities, the Russian leader set to work on these general issues as well as on the numerous practical matters that still faced him in the rush of daily decisionmaking. The latter were not inconsiderable. He still had to deal with Gorbachev, who was working furiously to recoup some political standing following the August 1991 coup and its aftermath and who put much of his energy into trying to save the Soviet Union from extinction. Yeltsin also had to put together a team of advisors, aides, and cabinet members to help him design new programs. He had to decide how to handle autonomist pressures in Russia's regions, now that some were starting to claim greater sovereignty than most politicians in Moscow could countenance; indeed, the Chechen-Ingush Republic formally announced its secession from Russia in November 1991. Yeltsin had to decide whether to allow new local elections to take place as scheduled in Fall 1991 or rather to alter the schedule of elections in light of new political realities. He had to respond, one way or the other, to pressures on him to call unscheduled elections for the Supreme Soviet and to sponsor a "presidential political party" to compete in those elections – in order to seize this unique opportunity to elect a more radical deputy corps within the legislature. And he had to decide whether to capitalize on his charismatic authority to increase the formal powers of his office.

Whereas Gorbachev in 1988–1989 had come forth with a comprehensive program for transforming the Soviet Union without inducing systemic collapse, Yeltsin now had to deal with the aftermath of a collapse he had helped to bring about. He also had to come forth with a comprehensive program for transforming newly independent Russia into the kind of "normal," "civilized" country that he had been touting. Gorbachev had tried to transform the Soviet system on the territory of the USSR; Yeltsin now had to replace that system on the territory of Russia, presumably in ways consistent with the vision he had propounded on his way to the top. There was, at this point, plenty of room for political creativity. Yeltsin's personal preferences could hold sway – at least for the moment – as he decided how to attain the vision. Constraints would pile up soon thereafter, however, as the costs of his policy initiatives became evident.

YELTSIN AS STATE BUILDER

Several weeks after the abortive coup of August 1991, Yeltsin held a press conference for foreign journalists (September 7) at which he said the following about his image of what kind of a state Russia needed:

The country is now devoid of all "isms." It isn't capitalist, nor communist, nor socialist; it's a country in a transitional period, which wants to proceed along a civilized path, the path along which France, Britain, the United States, Japan, Germany, Spain and other countries have been and still are proceeding. It's an aspiration to proceed precisely along this path, that is, the decommunization of all aspects of society's life, the deideologization of all aspects of society's life, an aspiration to democracy ....[2]

Four days later, at the Conference on Security and Cooperation in Europe (CSCE), he would add still more evocative imagery: "Our democracy is like

---

[2] Moscow Russian Television Network, September 7, 1991 (FBIS-SOV-91-174, p. 66).

a sickly child. But the main choice has already been made. We have the determination to go the whole way, climbing up the ladder to civilization."[3]

Yeltsin proposed to emulate Western "civilization" in many of its specifics. At the news conference, he indicated that a new presidential service had to be created and, toward that end, his associates were studying the organization of the White House staff in the United States, "where this system has simply been refined right down to the details...."[4] Subsequently, he spoke of the need for creating an independent judiciary and legal profession,[5] the normality of political opposition[6] and of mutual criticism between the executive and legislative branches,[7] the need to create a rule of law,[8] the desirability of allowing Gorbachev to retire from office "with dignity,"[9] the "shaping and development of a civil society," "a strong and united democratic federative state," and the need for civil service reform and the rooting out of corruption.[10]

But how to bring these about? How to root out corruption, build a reliable civil service, and foster rule of law? How to protect the independence of the judiciary? How to create a strong civil society? And precisely what form of representative democracy did he have in mind? What degree of separation of powers between the executive and legislative branches – and how much criticism of himself and his policies – would he put up with? What would be the relative powers of the federal authorities and the regions of Russia?

Yeltsin depicted strong executive power as a prerequisite for building a new order on the ruins of the old. The man who had chafed in positions of subordination, and who would admit that he always wanted to be the "boss,"[11] was prepared to capitalize on his extraordinary political momentum by maximizing his powers to the extent possible. Thus, he demanded (and received) from the Supreme Soviet emergency powers to rule by decree for twelve months. He moved quickly to bring the military and secret police under the control of trusted associates. He brought in former associates from Sverdlovsk to run his presidential administration.[12]

---

[3] Moscow Radio Rossii Network, September 11, 1991 (FBIS-SOV-91-177, p. 1).
[4] Moscow Russian Television Network, September 7, 1991 (FBIS-SOV-91-174, p. 69).
[5] Moscow Radio Rossii Network, October 17, 1991.
[6] Ibid.
[7] Moscow Russian Television Network, February 19, 1992.
[8] Deutschlandfunk Network, November 17, 1991; *Der Spiegel,* November 18, 1991, pp. 253–62.
[9] Moscow All-Union Radio Maiak Network, December 23, 1991.
[10] Moscow Russian Television Network, April 5, 1992 (FBIS-SOV-92-066, p. 23).
[11] Boris Yeltsin, *Against the Grain: An Autobiography,* trans. by Michael Glenny (New York: Summit, 1990), pp. 72–3.
[12] When asked about this in a televised interview on February 19, 1992, he denied that this is untoward ("it is one-tenth the number Bush brought from Texas") yet then argued that it

But Yeltsin depicted strong executive power as more than a way to maximize his personal political security. He also depicted it as a prerequisite for holding Russia together as a territorial entity. Thus, he announced that autonomist pressures in the regions would be offset by the appointment of presidential representatives to serve as "heads of administration" in each region. He postponed plans for new local elections and the election of regional governors. And when the Chechen-Ingush Republic declared its independence, he tried to use military force to overturn the decision, though his action was rescinded by the parliament.[13]

Yeltsin's approach to executive power was plebiscitarian. In fall 1991 he did more than demand that parliament accord him the power to rule by decree; he also rejected the request of leaders of Democratic Russia that he sponsor a presidential party, opting instead to be president of "all the people." The "people" had been his ticket to resurrection in 1989; they had validated him further as president in June 1991; he had appealed to them in August 1991. His state-building and authority-building strategies would rest on his capacity to mobilize popular support directly without the mediation of a partisan political organization.[14]

Moreover, Yeltsin presented himself as a man who possessed the unique set of skills required to steer Russia through the difficult passage before it. Whereas he described Gorbachev as timid and inclined toward "half-measures," Yeltsin depicted himself as possessing "the courage to take this severe step" (i.e., the unfreezing of prices).[15] His image was that of a tough, self-made man who demands of others that they be willing to tackle the Herculean challenges he

---

was necessary in light of the political insecurity surrounding him: "Do you think I want to find myself in Gorbachev's position? At such a difficult moment on 19 August everyone from his personal bodyguard to the prime minister acted as traitors. They all betrayed him. I do not want to find myself in that position" (Moscow Russian Television Network, February 19, 1992 [FBIS-SOV-92-034, p. 51]). He repeated the latter rationale in an interview televised on June 11, 1992, while adding that his strategy had already proven itself: "if you recall the time of the putsch, on 19 and 20 August, none of the comrades in arms selected by me defected" (Moscow Russian Television Network, June 11, 1992 [FBIS-SOV-92-114, p. 22]).

[13] On October 28, 1991, several weeks before the fiasco in Chechen-Ingushetia, he proclaimed to the Congress of RSFSR People's Deputies: "there is a point beyond which we cannot go under any conditions. This point is Russia's territorial integrity and its state and legal unity. We cannot allow and will not allow the breakup of Russia, or its fragmentation into dozens of principalities that are at war with each other" (Moscow Russian Television Network, October 28, 1991 [FBIS-SOV-91-209, p. 54]).

[14] See Lilia Shevtsova, *Yeltsin's Russia: Myths and Reality* (Washington, DC: Carnegie Endowment, 1999), p. 16; Peter Reddaway and Dmitri Glinski, *The Tragedy of Russia's Reforms: Market Bolshevism against Democracy* (Washington, DC: U.S. Institute of Peace, 2001), ch. 6.

[15] Moscow Russian Television Network, October 28, 1991.

himself was willing to tackle.[16] He was a man of action who depicted himself as a revolutionary hero. Following the anti-communist revolution, he presented himself as the man who would cure Russia of its diseases and then lead it along the road to "civilization."

YELTSIN AS NATION BUILDER

State building requires the formal definition of constitutional relationships and the construction of formal institutions. Nation building, by contrast, is a more symbolic process of instilling in a population a sense of "we feeling" that is based on a common sense of history and destiny. But it also has a formal dimension in that building a nation-*state* (as opposed to an oppositional social movement) also entails constitutional specification of the boundaries of the political community: who "the people" are and what their rights and obligations are as citizens. In Russia, for example, where prior notions of a "Soviet people" no longer applied, do "the people" include all residents of the Russian Federation, regardless of ethnicity, or only those of Russian ethnic ancestry? Whichever definition is chosen, what will be the terms of responsiveness between the people and the state? Will this relationship be defined in civic and procedural terms that are based on universalistic and liberal democratic conceptions of accountability to empowered individuals? Or will the legitimacy of the state be based on more exclusive and substantive criteria, such as the material and symbolic goods that it "delivers" to the population?

Yeltsin's emphasis on gaining Russia's independence coexisted in his political rhetoric with a liberal definition of the people whom those institutions would serve. He eschewed nostalgic, invidious, imperial, and ethnic designations of the character of the state and promoted instead a non-ethnic definition of citizenship within Russia. While his state-building rhetoric can justifiably be depicted as endorsing civil liberties, strong executive authority, and plebiscitarian accountability, his approach to Russian nationhood can be characterized as liberal, de-ethnicized nation building.

Yeltsin's rhetoric on this score was consistent during both the struggle with Gorbachev and his subsequent period of ascendancy. He addressed the issue in terms that contrasted sharply with those of both ethnic nationalists and imperialist restorationists within Russian politics. His speeches eschewed references to *Rus'* (the lands of the Russians), in favor of *Rossiia* (the country, Russia). He referred consistently to *Rossiiskie,* not *Russkie,* state interests.

[16] See interview in *Trud,* December 14, 1991 (FBIS-SOV-91-241, p. 36).

He referred to citizens of Russia as *Rossiiane* (citizens of the country, Russia), not *Russkie* (ethnic Russians). He referred to the people as the *narod* (people), not the *natsiia* (nation, a term used largely by the most extreme nationalists).

A corollary of this choice of vocabulary was Yeltsin's consistent underscoring of the multinational character of the Russian Federation. When not referring to the secularized entity of "the Russian (*Rossiiskii*) people," he referred to "the interests of the peoples of the state of Russia."[17] Yeltsin cautioned against any policies that could stoke inter-ethnic strife, and he warned frequently of the need to construct a political order within which all the peoples of the country would feel represented.[18] In this connection he explicitly renounced the Russian imperial heritage and rejected the notion of a tyranny of the ethnic majority: "Russian statehood, which has chosen democracy and freedom, will never be an empire, or a big or small brother, it will be an equal among equals."[19] Ethnic minorities within Russia and their constituent republics within the Russian Federation, he averred, possessed laws of their own that Moscow was obliged to "respect."[20] One of his "priorities," he proclaimed to a nationwide television audience, was "the revival of the traditional values of all the peoples of Russia and the development of their culture."[21] The state, he later declared, must not "impinge on the spiritual and cultural specificity of nations [within Russia]." Indeed, that same state has an obligation to "assist in preserving the native language, culture, and traditions of the peoples of Russia." But lest he be accused of ignoring the concerns of the majority ethnicity within the Russian Federation, he added: "That fully applies to the Russian (*russkii*) people as well."[22]

Yeltsin also attempted to refute his opponents' appropriation of Russian history. He insisted that Russia's historical traditions were not necessarily antithetical to the new values of freedom and democracy, citing the democratic experiments in Russian history as the traditions to be revived. In the late nineteenth and early twentieth centuries, he declared,

Russia was confidently modernizing herself; she was moving toward the market and democracy, and her culture was forcefully asserting common human values, while

[17] Moscow Domestic Service, "Congress Diary," June 22, 1990.
[18] Moscow Domestic Service, December 11, 1990; TASS, March 29, 1991; Moscow Russian Television Network, October 6, 1992; Moscow Ostankino Television Network, November 9, 1993.
[19] TASS, September 3, 1991; see also Moscow Central Television, "Vostok," December 29, 1991.
[20] TASS, March 29, 1991.
[21] Moscow Russian Television Network, April 5, 1992 (FBIS-SOV-92-066, p. 23).
[22] Moscow Ostankino Television Network, November 9, 1993.

naturally retaining national specifics. [As a result], it is all the more strange to hear accusations of our betraying the national tradition.[23]

Yeltsin's imagery of Russia as a nation was of a wounded country with an unspecified, spiritual sense of unity based on geography, history, and the very multinational character of its citizenry.[24] He defined these features as strengths to be mobilized in order to heal the wounds of the past and construct a revitalized, but new, nation. He called for "patriotism" and "pride" but warned against chauvinism and restoration.[25] He refurbished the Kremlin to restore the unifying, historical symbols of statehood.[26] He proposed a role for the Russian Orthodox Church in helping to unify Russia, but without either exclusionary or invidious references to other religions.[27]

Yeltsin combined this conception with his oft-stated vision of a civic political order. The Russian people were depicted in his speeches as a collectivity of individuals who possessed democratic rights derived from universal principles of human rights: "Neither the Communist Party, nor the nation, nor any other party, but rather the individual himself, is the supreme value."[28] He declared to the United Nations in February 1992 his intention to renounce all statist and coercively collectivist ideologies in favor of "democracy, human rights and freedoms, legal and moral standards, and political and civil rights."[29] Later that year, Yeltsin declared to the Supreme Soviet that "we do not need a new 'ism'" to solve Russia's problems.[30]

Nevertheless, recurrent themes in Yeltsin's speeches loosely described the new order as predicated on certain substantive ideas other than the procedural commitment to "democracy" and "individualism." In the same speech to the Supreme Soviet, Yeltsin defined these as a "sense of duty and patriotism."[31] Indeed, in defending his economic reforms earlier that year, Yeltsin

---

[23] *Rossiiskie vesti,* April 21, 1993; see also Moscow Russian Television Network, June 7, 1993, where he defined the past pillars of Russian statehood as Novgorod, Peter I, Alexander II, and the *zemstva* [local councils], concluding that procedural democratic statehood is therefore not at all at odds with the traditions of Russia.

[24] See Moscow Domestic Services, December 4, 1990; Radio Rossii, April 1 and June 4, 1991; Moscow All-Union Radio Maiak, August 29, 1991; Moscow Russian Television Network, April 7 and November 30, 1992; and *Rossiiskie vesti,* April 21, 1993.

[25] TASS, September 3, 1991; Moscow Central Television, "Vostok," December 29, 1991.

[26] TASS, September 1, 1992.

[27] TASS, October 6, 1992, and February 5, 1993.

[28] TASS, November 2, 1991; see also Radio Rossii, May 21 and June 1, 1991, as well as *Rossiiskaia gazeta,* February 3, 1992.

[29] *Rossiiskaia gazeta,* February 3, 1992.

[30] TASS, October 6, 1992.

[31] Ibid.

had argued that those reforms were compatible with his own "vision of patriotism," a view of a "united, revitalized Russia ... a civilized country capable
of providing high standards of living and strict observance of human rights
for its citizens."[32]

When we combine these rhetorical positions with Yeltsin's plebiscitarian
approach to executive power, we conclude that Yeltsin was offering the office
of the presidency, and himself as its occupant, as the symbol and protector
of that proud, multi-ethnic nation. To be sure, the president must be regularly accountable to the people and must justify their trust. He must respect
the laws that restrict the discretion of the state vis-à-vis its citizens. But as a
centralized symbol, in both rhetoric and constitutional wording, Yeltsin offered the president as the personification of the Russian (*Rossiiskii*) people.
Moreover, he defined the Russian people as unified by their common sense of
duty and by the loose binding power of a democratic patriotism – not by their
ethnicity.[33]

DEFINING THE BOUNDARIES OF THE RUSSIAN NATION AND STATE

Two specific dilemmas of state building and nation building arose immediately upon the collapse of the USSR. One concerned the territorial borders
of the new Russian state. The Russian Federation had been a circumstantial
construction of Soviet power. The borders of the heartland of the Russian
empire in 1913 and 1917 were not identical to the borders of the Russian
Federation in 1991. Adjustments had been made at numerous times, including (most recently) Khrushchev's whimsical transfer of Crimea to Ukraine in
1954. Hence, there remained plenty of reason for competing politicians to
differ credibly over the desirability and feasibility of again revising the borders of the Russian Federation.

A second dilemma concerned the obligations of the Russian state to the
20–25 million ethnic Russians living in the newly independent former republics of the Soviet Union. Formally, they were now residents or citizens
of other sovereign states. But given the role Moscow had played for at least
sixty years in protecting their interests and guaranteeing their security, they
seemed to warrant treatment by the Russian state somewhat different from
the relative lack of interest accorded twentieth-century Russian diasporas in
distant lands. Did Russia's protection or proselytizing of this newest diaspora constitute interference in the internal affairs of independent states?

---

[32] *Rossiiskaia gazeta*, April 7, 1992.
[33] In this respect, Yeltsin's position was consistent with Soviet-era ideology, which embraced
"Soviet patriotism" and eschewed ethnic "nationalism."

Alternatively, were these Russians in the "Near Abroad" tacit or would-be citizens of the Russian state? And if the latter, should the boundaries of Russia be redrawn to incorporate those lands currently occupied largely by Russians?

Boris Yeltsin was both consistent and insistent in presenting a de-ethnicized and civic conception of the political order he promised to construct within the Russian Federation. However, the question of how to define Moscow's obligations to Russians in the Near Abroad was one that split the democratic camp immediately upon the collapse of the USSR. Angry rhetoric emanated from the mouths of some individuals, such as St. Petersburg mayor Anatolii Sobchak, who had been leaders of the anti-communist and democratic revolution in Soviet and Russian politics.[34] At the other end of the political spectrum, both ethnic nationalists and imperial restorationists could use the issue as justification for the most revanchist proposals, while imperial institutions – such as the Soviet Army, which remained entrenched in the Near Abroad – could serve as an instrument for revanchist actions. Whatever his predispositions in such a context, it would have been difficult for Yeltsin to avoid eventual political isolation if he advocated a policy of laissez-faire toward governments in the successor states or if he ignored the alleged plight of new Russian diaspora.

Yeltsin responded by attempting to combine the universalism of his state-building and nation-building strategies within Russia with a qualified defense of Russians in the Near Abroad. It was a tense and, in some respects, incompatible coexistence of policy orientations, a reflection of one of the most intractable dilemmas of democratic nation building in a post-imperial and diasporic context. From late 1990 onward, more than a year before the dissolution of the USSR, Yeltsin spoke out clearly on behalf of the ethnic Russian and "Russian-speaking" populations in the increasingly autonomous, and then independent, republics of the USSR.[35] Clearly and consistently, he articulated concern for these "compatriots" (*sootechestvenniki*) and committed the Russian government to protect their rights against discrimination or persecution.[36]

---

[34] In an interview with *Le Figaro* on December 4, 1991, responding to the recent Ukrainian vote for independence, Sobchak stridently opposed "the threat of forced Ukrainianization in Crimea, with its Russian majority." He argued that Russia "would immediately raise territorial claims" if Ukraine refused to join in a political union (*Report on the USSR*, December 13, 1991).

[35] See TASS, November 13, 1990; *Argumenty i fakty*, no. 3, 1991, pp. 4–5; TASS, February 9, 1991; Reuters, September 30, 1991; *Komsomol'skaia pravda*, May 27 and July 3, 1992; *Trud*, October 6, 1992; TASS, March 17 and March 22, 1993.

[36] See *Pravda*, September 26, 1990; *Izvestiia*, December 25, 1990; *Krasnaia zvezda*, June 11, 1992; TASS, September 7, October 6, and November 5, 1992.

He held a centrist (i.e., moderate) position within the debate of the time. He insisted, in contrast to the extreme nationalists and imperial restorationists,[37] that pursuit of the rights of compatriots should take place through "legal" and "political" means.[38] Rhetorically, he rejected the use of armed force and indicated his desire that Russians in the Near Abroad stay put, rather than emigrating back to Russia.[39] He treated the issue of the political rights of Russians within those countries as one to be negotiated through state-to-state bargaining and the conclusion of interstate treaties.[40] He appealed to Western governments and international organizations to join in protecting these allegedly stranded and persecuted populations, invoking international conventions on human rights as justification.[41]

There were, to be sure, counter trends within Yeltsin's own cabinet. Defense Minister Grachev made occasional vitriolic statements that stretched or contradicted the moderation of Yeltsin's remarks.[42] Furthermore, Moscow's actual policies in the Near Abroad occasionally leaned on the threat or use of force and material coercion.[43] Yeltsin himself wavered between an ethnic

---

[37] See Official Kremlin International News Broadcast, September 20, 1991; *Literaturnaia Rossiia,* no. 42, 1991; Russian Press Digest, December 11, 1991; *Komsomol'skaia pravda,* January 17, 1992; TASS, January 17, 1992, January 21, 1992, February 27, 1992, July 1, 1992, October 8, 1992, October 15, 1992, October 17, 1992, January 31, 1993, and February 20, 1993; *Moskovskie novosti,* February 12, 1992; Reuters, February 13, 1992; Official Kremlin News Broadcast, January 28, 1993. For example, just after the Soviet collapse, Vladimir Lukin (chair for foreign affairs of the Russian Supreme Soviet) wrote a letter to Supreme Soviet Chair Ruslan Khasbulatov in which he argued that Ukraine should give up either the Black Sea Fleet or Crimea (*Toronto Globe and Mail,* January 23, 1992).

[38] See *Izvestiia,* December 25, 1990; Reuters, September 30, 1991; *Komsomol'skaia pravda,* May 27, 1992; *Krasnaia zvezda,* June 11, 1992.

[39] *Pravda,* September 26, 1990; TASS, November 13, 1990; *Argumenty i fakty,* no. 3, 1991; *Komsomol'skaia pravda,* May 27, 1992.

[40] See *Krasnaia zvezda,* January 15, 1991; *Argumenty i fakty,* no. 3, 1991; TASS, February 9, 1991; *The New York Times,* June 22, 1992; *Trud,* October 6, 1992; and TASS, June 29, 1993.

[41] See TASS, July 10, 1992, April 30, 1993, June 29, 1993; see also Reuters, November 6, 1992.

[42] As early as mid-June 1992, Grachev declared that the use of force against Russians would be answered with force (*The New York Times,* June 22, 1992). By late 1993, Kozyrev had articulated the possibility of a strong response. He stated that Russia would "protect the Russian population and Russia's interests in a tough manner wherever it is needed and whoever is concerned, even if it be our friends" (Reuters, November 24, 1993). Given Kozyrev's known views on interstate relations, however, we may assume that Kozyrev was posturing when he made this statement. Nonetheless, the fact that he felt the need to posture is a good indicator of the changing climate of opinion within Russian politics.

[43] For example, Russia stopped delivery to Estonia of natural gas, for which Estonia is completely dependent on Russia (*The New York Times,* June 26, 1993). While the nominal reason was Estonia's backlog of unpaid debt, the move closely followed the introduction of Estonia's new Law on Foreigners, which, Yeltsin stated, "crudely violates the legal, civil, property, social and vital interests of Russians and the Russian-speaking population" (TASS, June 25, 1993).

definition of the purported constituency within the Near Abroad and a definition that included many millions of non-Russians (the "Russian-speaking population") as well.[44]

Thus, there was a continuous tension between Yeltsin's extension to ethnic Russians and Russian speakers in the Near Abroad of tacit rights to protection by Russia and his simultaneous insistence that, within Russia, citizenship was to be defined in territorial, not ethnic, terms. The tension reflected the intellectual and political dilemmas of fashioning a de-ethnicized strategy of nation building within this post-imperial context of dispersion and competing nation-building strategies. It might have been the best amalgam of incompatible premises that any liberal politician at the time could have hoped to come up with. But Yeltsin promised to balance and manage those tensions as he pushed to the fore.

BUILDING A NEW ECONOMIC ORDER

One of the most urgent challenges that Yeltsin faced in the fall of 1991 was to decide on his strategy for rescuing the sinking Russian economy. He interviewed several economists and economic administrators, seeking their advice and evaluating their credentials for positions in his administration. He settled on a previously obscure economist named Yegor Gaidar, who sold him on the idea that, without strong medicine, the Russian economy would collapse. Gaidar offered to prevent that collapse with a strategy for rapid transformation that had been called "shock therapy" when adopted in Latin America and Poland. He proposed to end price controls, balance the state budget through severe cuts in subsidies to industry and agriculture, and de-monopolize the economy through rapid privatization of state-owned assets. The result, he argued, would be economic "stabilization," the introduction of a competitive market economy, and the eventual production in large quantities of goods that consumers actually wanted to buy. Such was the theory.[45]

Yeltsin bought it – for reasons that may have been personal and political. He was a witness to the economic disarray in the country at the time, but he was also attracted to a breakthrough strategy for building a new economic

---

[44] Yeltsin regularly interspersed his more numerous references to "Russian-speaking populations" (see TASS, February 9, 1991; *Komsomol'skaia pravda*, May 27 and July 3 1992; *Trud*, October 6, 1992; Reuters, October 8, 1992; TASS, October 27, 1992; Reuters, November 6, 1992; TASS, March 17, April 30, and June 25, 1993) with references to "ethnic Russians" (see *Argumenty i fakty*, no. 3, 1991; Reuters, September 30, 1991; TASS, March 17, 1993; Reuters, April 4, 1993).

[45] See Gaidar's account of his fall 1991 job interview with Yeltsin in Yegor T. Gaidar, *Dni porazhenii i pobed* (Moscow: Vagrius, 1996), p. 105.

order in Russia. Shock therapy promised quick results at the macroeconomic level, with none of the procrastination and compromise he had criticized in Gorbachev's policies.[46] It was consistent with the campaignism, command-ism, and "struggle" that had been common features of the Stalinist and post-Stalinist administrative cultures in which Yeltsin grew up and that had defined his leadership style in both Sverdlovsk and Moscow. As Fyodorov notes, it filled the cognitive vacuum left by the disappearance of any confidence in the previous ideology and also appealed to the campaignist mentality: it was simple, was clear-cut in its principles, and required resolve and political deci-siveness to implement.[47]

Moreover, shock therapy was reductionist in that it focused attention on transformation of the individual citizen; it promised to "cure" Russians of the lethargy into which they had fallen. As much as the strategy was a pre-scription for macroeconomic stabilization, it was also based on an implicit theory of behavioral and cultural change. It was a cultural revolution of sorts. If people were put in situations where survival depended on their exercising entrepreneurial initiative, and if the state ended its practice of dictating to people what kind of initiative to exercise,[48] then they would finally overcome their lethargy and search for those opportunities. As Yeltsin put it in retro-spect: "Sometimes it takes a sharp break or rupture to make a person move forward or even survive at all";[49] this observation was based on personal ex-perience, for he had put himself through such a wrenching cognitive and value transformation during 1988 after being purged from the Soviet leadership.[50] Presumably, sustained behavioral change would ultimately lead attitudes to conform with the new behavior, transforming the culture of lethargy and envy into one of initiative and achievement.

---

[46] As he put it in introducing the reform (*Sovetskaia Rossiia,* October 29, 1991): "The time has come to act decisively, firmly, without hesitation.... The period of movement with small steps is over .... A big reformist breakthrough is necessary" (as quoted and translated in Anders Åslund, *How Russia Became a Market Economy* [Washington, DC: Brookings Institution, 1995], p. 64).

[47] Valentin Fyodorov, *Yel'tsin* (Moscow: "Golos," 1995), pp. 27–8, 55. See also Gaidar, *Dni,* p. 105; Yu. M. Baturin, A. L. Il'in, V. F. Kadatskii, V. V. Kostikov, M. A. Krasnov, A. Ya. Livshits, K. F. Nikiforov, L. G. Pikhoia, and G. A. Satarov, *Epokha Yel'tsina: Ocherki politicheskoi istorii* (Moscow: Vagrius, 2001), pp. 173–4.

[48] Yeltsin called this "freedom ... from the bureaucratic straitjacket" (Moscow Russian Televi-sion Network, October 28, 1991 [FBIS-SOV-91-209, p. 47]).

[49] Boris Yeltsin, *The Struggle for Russia,* trans. by Catherine A. Fitzpatrick (New York: Random House, 1994), p. 149.

[50] Yeltsin, *Against the Grain,* pp. 203–10; 216–39. Observation of this parallel between soci-etal shock therapy and his own personal reappraisal was noted in Dmitry Mikheyev, *Russia Transformed* (Indianapolis, IN: Hudson Institute, 1996), p. 89.

As Yeltsin presented it, cultural transformation would also be a product of generational change. Those who would not (or could not) adapt to the stringent new requirements would be replaced by the new generations reaching their twenties and thirties in the 1990s. He projected himself as the leader of a revolution that would bring those new generations into positions of authority in the polity, economy, and society. For the most part, he assumed the older generation of citizens to be relatively hopeless as would-be capitalists, having been ruined by the old system. But his candor also revealed his Leninist "campaign" mentality. As head of the Moscow City Committee, for example, Yeltsin says he strove to replace compromised workers in Moscow shops with "young, 'uninfected' (*nezarazhennaya*) staff."[51] When he discusses shock therapy in the second memoir, he praises tough, independent, ambitious young people who possess "an entirely new psychology."[52] Russia's backwardness cannot be overcome until generational change has taken place: "We must finally admit that Russia comprehends democracy poorly – not merely for global, historical reasons but for rather prosaic ones: the new generation cannot break its way into power. The Socialist mode of thinking has left its imprint on all of us .... The new generation must come to the forefront as quickly as possible."[53] There are no fortresses that "uninfected" young people cannot storm, once you give them an electoral voice, hire them in large numbers, liberate them from the command economy, and allow money to be the focus of economic ambition and exchange.

Yeltsin knew that he was running a huge risk. This breakthrough strategy promised to impose severe pain on the population in the near term, and at a time when institutions of democratic accountability existed that could subject Yeltsin to public criticism, legislative censure, impeachment, or electoral defeat. Moreover, for all his charisma and for all the legal authority garnered

---

[51] Yeltsin, *Against the Grain*, p. 118 (the Russian original is in Boris Yel'tsin, *Ispoved' na zadannuiu temu* [Sverdlovsk: Sredne-Ural'skoe knizhnoe izdatel'stvo, 1990], p. 112). On the other hand, it should be noted that, in both the Russian and English versions, Yeltsin was sufficiently self-conscious about the connotations to put the word "uninfected" in quotation marks.

[52] Yeltsin, *The Struggle*, p. 146.

[53] Ibid., pp. 290–1. For other references in Yeltsin's memoirs to the crucial role of the younger generation, see *Against the Grain*, pp. 183, 234, 253; *The Struggle*, pp. 126–7, 151–2, 291; Boris Yeltsin, *Midnight Diaries* (New York: Public Affairs, 2000), pp. 23, 27, 28, 39, 63, 79–83, 103, 114, 274. Shortly after the August 1991 coup, Yeltsin proclaimed as follows: "no matter how difficult it is, each of us should aim to do whatever we can to restructure ourselves in a fundamental way, so that we can follow a civilized road. This will be difficult, very difficult .... It will be easier for young people, whose hearts, minds, and heads have not been drawn into the system" (news conference for Russian and foreign journalists hosted by Russian President Boris Yeltsin at the Russian Soviet Federated Socialist Republic House of Soviets in Moscow on September 7, 1991, as transcribed in FBIS-SOV-9-174, p. 68).

from his victory at the polls in June 1991, Yeltsin knew that Russia's nascent democracy was a fragile one. In August 1991, after all, a coup d'etat had been attempted. Although he had defeated the attempt, Yeltsin continued to govern under a pall of uncertainty about the possibility of another coup attempt, this one perhaps more successful than the last. He had been told by the architect of the shock therapy (Gaidar) that the pain would be severe, and that he – Gaidar – might have to be sacrificed politically as a result.[54] One could observe the apprehensions of Yeltsin in late 1991, therefore, when he repeatedly tried to reassure audiences that the pain from shock therapy would last only six months, or one year at most.[55]

YELTSIN AS STATESMAN

The emergence of an independent Russia forced Yeltsin also to address East–West relations and their relationship to both Russian security and Russian prosperity. He inherited a drastically altered position in the world, as Russia was shorn of the USSR's East European alliance system and its global power status. Gorbachev's concessionary foreign policy had tried to make the best of this situation by making a virtue of necessity, by attempting to integrate into Western multilateral organizations, by doing the bidding of the West on most issues in contention, and by seeking as much economic assistance from the West as he could hope to secure. Yeltsin, while in opposition to Gorbachev, did not dissent from these aspects of his foreign policy.[56] He did not try to outbid Gorbachev on East–West relations.

But after the August coup, when Yeltsin started to define an independent foreign policy for Russia, he went beyond what even Gorbachev had advocated. He called for "substantial cuts in defense expenditures," cuts that soon (1992) assumed enormous magnitudes.[57] He volunteered to adopt "a more radical stance on the destruction of nuclear, bacteriological, and chemical weapons, on the ending of underground testing of nuclear weapons."[58] He

---

[54] Gaidar, *Dni,* p. 105.

[55] *Sovetskaia Rossiia,* October 29, 1991; Official Kremlin International News Broadcast, November 20, 1991; Moscow Central Television, November 20, 1991.

[56] With the exception of the Kurile Islands dispute with Japan, on which Yeltsin insisted in 1991 that Gorbachev no longer had authority to negotiate the return to Japan of territory that was formally part of the Russian Republic; see Tsuyoshi Hasegawa, *The Northern Territories Dispute and Russo-Japanese Relations,* 2 vols. (Berkeley: University of California, International and Area Studies, 1998), vol. 2, pp. 374f.

[57] Moscow Central Television First Program Network, September 3, 1991 (FBIS-SOV-91-171, p. 10); Åslund, *How Russia Became,* p. 66.

[58] Moscow Russian Television Network, September 7, 1991 (FBIS-SOV-91-174, p. 66).

curried favor with European audiences by announcing that Russia would move toward full repeal of the death penalty.[59] In December 1991, Yeltsin publicly announced Russia's interest in joining NATO.[60] He accepted the applicability to Russia of the terms of the Conventional Forces in Europe Treaty (1990), even though the restrictions had been tailored to the geography of the Soviet Union, not Russia.

After January 1992, when Russia was formally an independent state, Yeltsin established a firmly pro-Western foreign policy. He outdid Gorbachev's arms-reduction race, announcing in June 1992 that Russia had already begun unilaterally destroying SS-18 intercontinental ballistic missiles. He ended his country's continuing – and very large – subsidies to Cuba and Afghanistan.[61] Yeltsin's Russia assumed responsibility for Soviet debt, supported U.S. containment of Iraq, stated that it was willing to renegotiate the Anti-Ballistic Missile Treaty and to consider developing a joint global ballistic missile defense with the United States, agreed to ambitious cooperation in space exploration, and opened secret archives to Americans investigating prisoners of war and the downing of Korean Air Lines flight 007.[62]

In June 1992, Yeltsin addressed a joint session of the United States Congress, where he received thirteen standing ovations and promised that "the idol of communism, which spread social strife, enmity, and unparalleled brutality everywhere, which instilled fear in humanity, has collapsed. It has collapsed never to rise again. I am here to assure you. We shall not let it rise again in our land."[63]

Yeltsin was not subtle. The explicit quid pro quo for this consistent support of U.S. foreign policy objectives was financial aid. Democracy in Russia, Yeltsin told the joint session, has only one chance:

there will be no second try.... The reforms must succeed.... If we [that is, you Americans] do not take measures now to support Russia, this will not be a collapse of Russia only, it will be a collapse of the United States, because it will mean new trillions of dollars for the arms race.[64]

---

[59] Moscow Radio Rossii Network, September 11, 1991.

[60] Press conference in Rome, TASS, December 23, 1991.

[61] In fall 1991, he had already declared his intention to do this.

[62] Baturin et al. (*Epokha*, p. 467) write that Yeltsin and his foreign minister, Andrei Kozyrev, largely continued Gorbachev's and Shevardnadze's course in foreign policy, adding: "There was even a kind of competition between the two teams – who can appeal to the West the most."

[63] Michael Dobbs, "Yeltsin Appeals for American Aid," *The Washington Post*, June 18, 1992, p. 1.

[64] Ibid.

Back at home, Yeltsin sold his foreign policies as the harbinger of Russia's integration into the civilized, Western world, which would also provide the financial aid and security umbrella that Russia would need during this transition.

During the days immediately following the dissolution of the USSR, Yeltsin presented the "Commonwealth of Independent States" (CIS), which he co-founded in December 1991, as a sign that Russia was breaking decisively with the imperial past and behaving like a "normal, civilized" state, even as it sought responsibly to offset the political and economic disarray caused by the dissolution of the USSR. When, on December 12, he discussed the CIS at Russia's Supreme Soviet, he explained that the choice of Minsk (Belarus) as the center of the CIS did not mean that city was the capital of a new union "but – and this is very important – it does mean the end of speculation that Russia aspires to take the place of the union center and cherishes some kind of imperial ambitions."[65] Two days later, in an interview in *Trud*, he explained that this was the civilized way to handle relations among friendly states: "There was only one way – to unite, but not within the framework of a single state but within a community of states. Just as, for example, the European countries are now doing." In a speech to the Russian Supreme Soviet on December 25, Yeltsin also made clear that there was an important practical rationale for such a decentralized organization as the CIS: "The Commonwealth of Independent States is today the optimum and perhaps the only option to preserve stability both in Russia and in the other states. Our principle is: Not the states for the sake of the Commonwealth but, on the contrary, the Commonwealth for the sake of the peoples, citizens and states."[66]

BIG PROMISES AND MEASURES OF PROGRESS

Leaders during periods of transformation or crisis typically try to mobilize support for their visions by holding out the prospect of a better tomorrow, to be made possible by near-term exertions and/or the endurance of considerable pain. Winston Churchill promised that wartime victory would follow the expenditure of much "blood, sweat, and tears." Closer to home, Khrushchev promised the full-scale construction of communism if all Soviet citizens exerted themselves to the fullest in the directions and ways he had specified. Gorbachev promised a third way between capitalism and statist socialism if

---

[65] Moscow Russian Television Network, December 12, 1991 (FBIS-SOV-91-239, p. 40).
[66] Moscow Radio Rossii Network, December 25, 1991 (FBIS-SOV-91-248, p. 38).

all citizens restructured themselves psychologically and responsibly exercised the rights he was extending to them. Yeltsin propounded a vision of a free, peaceful, and prosperous society, integrated into Western civilization. But he never said it would be easy.

The metaphorical structure of Yeltsin's speeches in fall 1991 is indicative of his effort both to legitimize a great leap forward and to warn his audiences of how far they had to go, especially with regard to economics. Not coincidentally, this also served to protect him against accusations that he was inflicting unnecessary pain. We might call this the "from hell to heaven" metaphor, based on an image of ascent from the lowest depths. Thus, in a speech of September 11, 1991, he announced that Russia was about to "begin the process of the most difficult ascent to normal life"; to understand the magnitude of the challenge, one "has to take account of the abyss in which we found ourselves." But, with courage and endurance, "we have the determination to go the whole way, climbing up the ladder to civilization."[67] Doing so requires freedom from communism, which had put people in a "bureaucratic straitjacket."[68] Only such freedom will permit the country finally "to get on its feet" in order to begin the ascent.[69] A related metaphor was that of illness and life-threatening conditions, which require strong medicine and bold action to bring the patient back from the brink. The legacy of communism, he argued, had left the country "sick."[70] "We have undertaken these actions in order to save ourselves from drowning."[71] Given the gravity of the condition, "there was no other way" than to adopt such measures.[72]

But lest his apocalyptic rhetoric be interpreted as unnecessarily frightening, Yeltsin also reassured his audiences that the pain would be rewarded. At the metaphorical level, he continued the imagery of disease but classified the

---

[67] Moscow Radio Rossii Network, September 11, 1991 (FBIS-SOV-91-177, p. 1). Other examples of the metaphor include: "we will finally begin to haul ourselves out of the quagmire that is sucking us in deeper and deeper" (Moscow Russian Television Network, October 28, 1991 [FBIS-SOV-91-209, p. 47]); and "we have a chance to climb out of this ditch in which we have found ourselves" (Moscow Central Television, "Vostok," December 29, 1991 [FBIS-SOV-91-250, p. 27]).

[68] Moscow Russian Television Network, October 28, 1991 (FBIS-SOV-91-209, p. 47).

[69] Moscow Radio Rossii Network, September 11, 1991 (FBIS-SOV-91-177, p. 1).

[70] Moscow Radio Rossii Network, September 11, 1991 (FBIS-SOV-91-177, p. 2).

[71] *Trud*, December 14, 1991, pp. 1–2, as translated in FBIS-SOV-91-241, p. 36. See also "Russia is gravely ill, its economy is ill" (Moscow Central Television, "Vostok," December 29, 1991 [FBIS-SOV-91-250, p. 29]).

[72] Ibid. Not coincidentally, "there is no alternative" was also an argument that Gorbachev used against conservatives who were skeptical of his political radicalization.

present disease as curable: "as distinct from human ailments, there are no in-
curable diseases in the economy."[73] At the concrete level, Yeltsin hastened
to assure his audiences that the pain would be relatively short in duration:
"If we embark on this path," he announced on October 28, 1991, "then we
will see real results by the autumn of 1992 .... Everyone will find life harder
for approximately six months. Then, prices will fall and goods will begin
to fill the market. By the autumn of 1992, as I promised before the elections, the economy will have stabilized and people's lives will gradually get
better."[74]

Or so Yeltsin promised and, presumably, hoped. In interviews toward the
end of the year, he was very eager – too eager – to convince journalists that
the pain would be short-lived. "Six months, six months," he repeated.[75] He
was in the difficult situation of trying to protect himself politically by shaping the indicators by which his success as a political leader would be judged.
Yeltsin was also aware of both the unpredictability of the situation and the
link between his promises and his political authority. As he declared on February 19, 1992: "I believe that the reforms will win and this year this victory
will already be obvious. There is no doubt about it. I will not go back on my
word, which I gave during the election campaign. I will not go back on it!"[76]

During the months following defeat of the August 1991 coup, Yeltsin
worked feverishly both to undercut Gorbachev and to formulate a comprehensive program for independent Russia. He succeeded on both scores, but
the program was filled with vulnerabilities. Like the programs of all his predecessors at the helm in Moscow, and like many a comprehensive program put
forward by presidents and prime ministers in liberal democracies, Yeltsin's
program was extremely ambitious, quickly met reality, and was in need of
adjustments. From mid-1992, Yeltsin began making those adjustments. He
did not abandon the basic premises for which he had stood; he only reconsidered the costs and risks, shifting his politics somewhat toward the center.
After taking two steps forward, Yeltsin took one step back while continuing
to point the country in the general direction he had promised all along.

---

[73] *Trud*, December 14, 1991, pp. 1–2, as translated in FBIS-SOV-91-241, p. 38; see also Yeltsin's
December 29, 1991, State of the Republic Address (televised by Moscow Central Television)
for the same argument. And, continuing the metaphor, one year later he would refer to bankruptcy as a sometimes useful "surgical procedure" (December 1, 1992 address to 7th Congress
of the Congress of People's Deputies).

[74] Moscow Russian Television Network, October 28, 1991 (FBIS-SOV-91-209, p. 48).

[75] Moscow Central Television, November 20, 1991.

[76] Moscow Russian Television Network, February 19, 1992 (FBIS-SOV-92-034, p. 53).

Backlash Sets In .

The crunch hit very soon, as the abolition of most price controls in January 1992 led to an immediate tripling and quadrupling of prices, a continuing inflation, and the wiping out of the value of the life savings and pensions of many Russian citizens.[77] The spectre of civil unrest hung over the country as spiraling inflation rapidly impoverished a people who had for decades been accustomed to price stability. In like manner, the sharp cuts in budget subsidies to enterprises led to a howl of protest from enterprise directors, their lobbying organizations, and their patrons in the Supreme Soviet. These hardships induced a widespread anti-Yeltsin mobilization within the Supreme Soviet itself, led by former Yeltsin ally and parliamentary speaker Ruslan Khasbulatov and soon thereafter joined by Aleksandr Rutskoi, Yeltsin's own vice-president.

Moreover, a "red-brown" coalition of Russian nationalists, neocommunists, and imperialist restorationists began to coalesce during 1991–1992, even as Yeltsin had his hands full dealing with the daily conflicts with parliament over politics and policy. The red-browns were united in their support for authoritarianism and their opposition to building a Westernized liberal democracy. They denounced democratic proceduralism, unbridled individualism, and a secular, civic definition of the Russian state. For them, the state was a moral community, not simply a set of formal organizations and procedures. This gave them an advantage in the struggle with liberals, who found it difficult to integrate liberal nationalism and the virtues of individualism with a moral content that transcended the democratic proceduralism itself. Yeltsin's definition of the nation as "multinationality" plus "democratic individualism," his insistence that Russia did not need a new collectivist ideology, and his apparently self-serving definition of himself as the guarantor of the new secular nation allowed opponents rhetorically to seize the initiative on the issue.

In the realm of interstate relations, a growing chorus of voices started to be heard – even among many earlier supporters of Gorbachev's "new thinking" – calling for some hard-headed thinking about Russia's "national interest." Now that Russia and the Soviet Union had made unilateral concessions and asymmetrical deals on almost all foreign policy issues, where was the government prepared to draw the line? Of that which remained, what would it *not* give away? If Russia was a reemerging nation-state and no longer either

---

[77] The first round of savings wipeouts, however, had occurred in spring 1991 under Gorbachev's prime minister, Valentin Pavlov, whose "reforms" had no redeeming positive consequences.

a Russian or a Soviet empire, what were the national interests it was to pursue as it made its own place in the world? Groups of policy influentials and parliamentarians discussed and debated these issues in 1992, producing memoranda and publications that insisted upon the need for Russia to craft an international identity – other than that of a supplicant – and to take a stand in defense of that identity and the interests that flowed from it. The phrase that invariably accompanied these elaborate and intelligent pronouncements was that Russia is, and must be treated as, a "great power" (*derzhava*). The people associated with this "realist" perspective on international affairs came to be known as "statists" (*gosudarstvenniki*). While most of the statists were not part of the emerging red-brown coalition, they were a powerful dissenting voice from the concessionary foreign policy that Yeltsin had intensified after the collapse of the USSR.

"... And One Step Back"

In a speech delivered on April 5, 1992, we see the first signs that Yeltsin had perceived the need for an adjustment. He defended his economic reforms and predicted that, at the forthcoming meeting of the Congress of People's Deputies, "an attempt at revanche will be made [which must receive] a decisive rebuff."[78] But he also conceded that his government had made mistakes and that corrections were now in order:

Not even the most precise calculations and the most well thought-out models are capable of taking into account all the very complex areas of life with its multifarious surprises. Not a single program can be implemented if it is not constantly subjected to adjustments and corrections. The past months have taught the government a great deal.[79]

But a correction was not the same thing as abandonment of previous policy:

If we stop the reforms, we'll never emerge from poverty. To achieve a breakthrough is incredibly difficult .... Only one path today has the right to existence – that of the continuation of radical reforms .... I will not shift from that path. And, in my opinion, there is simply no other way.[80]

In the same speech, Yeltsin rebuffed the nostalgics among the defeated communists and nationalists:

---

[78] Moscow Russian Television Network, April 5, 1992 (FBIS-SOV-92-066, p. 20).
[79] Ibid.
[80] Ibid.

We will not have a continuation of the isolation of our country under the pretext of preserving Russia's original character. That would mean once again driving Russia into a historical impasse, condemning it to backwardness and its people to a meager existence.[81]

Yeltsin closed by reiterating that the matter of Russia's Westernization was not an issue for negotiation: "History cannot be turned back."[82] He repeated many of these themes in his speech the next day to the Congress of People's Deputies.

Having admitted that he had made mistakes, Yeltsin also felt the need to alter the concrete indicators of success by which his effectiveness as a leader would be judged. In November 1991, he had promised six months of pain to be followed by a turnaround. On May 27, 1992, he altered the assessment. Asked whether he wished to retract any of his earlier promises, he said "No" but revised what those promises had actually been:

I said back at the time of the Russian presidential campaign that the end of 1992 would see the beginning of stabilization in the economy. I did not simply say that the situation would improve. First, you get the stabilization of the economy and then, as a consequence, improvement in people's lives.[83]

Yeltsin then went on to elongate the time frame under which his success should be judged:

The reform cannot be completed in a single year.... [We] are seeking to ... define the stages: What can be done now, what in three years' time, and what is possible only after ten years. We have had to go through this most critical period of 1992. And I think we are now perhaps past the most dangerous point.[84]

Being now "past the most dangerous point" was of course a prediction, but it bought time. As time went on and economic hardships deepened, Yeltsin's political rhetoric turned to still other justifications of his record. In his August 19, 1992, televised speech on the anniversary of the putsch attempt, he congratulated the government and the nation for merely surviving the treatment: "Over the past six months, Russia has developed the basis of a market system. As the saying goes, we stepped into the water without knowing how to swim. But we have not choked in water or drowned."[85] He went on immediately to lengthen still further the time frame for judgment of results: "It is

[81] Ibid., p. 23.

[82] Ibid.

[83] *Komsomol'skaia pravda,* May 27, 1992, p. 2, as translated in FBIS-SOV-92-103, May 28, 1992, p. 28.

[84] Ibid.

[85] Moscow Russian Television Network, August 19, 1992 (FBIS-SOV-92-162, p. 19).

precisely now that we are gaining the unique experience that will benefit us and even more so our children and grandchildren."[86] Thereafter, as his confrontation with parliament escalated, so too did his explanations for failure evolve. On April 14, 1993, he declared that "it is the legislature that is responsible for the hardships associated with reforms";[87] later, he further broadened his attribution of responsibility, defining the culprit as the institutional and cultural legacy of communism.[88]

Yeltsin did not merely change his rhetoric; he also made concrete changes in policy. In spring 1992, about five months after the initiation of Gaidar's program, Yeltsin shuffled his cabinet and appointed four representatives of the managerial and defense lobbies to key positions. He also tolerated the pumping of new monies into the economy in order to maintain subsidies that would prevent bankruptcies of major enterprises that might trigger social unrest among the newly unemployed. He embraced a mass privatization program ("we need millions of owners and not hundreds of millionaires" – April 7, 1992, and August 19, 1992) that was nonetheless biased toward selling most shares to insiders (managers and workers of the enterprise) rather than to outside investors (whether domestic or foreign), in order to prevent mass layoffs (which would threaten social stability) and the large-scale dismissal of managers (which would threaten Yeltsin's ties with the managerial lobby).

The conflicting goals of Yeltsin's economic policy were coming into focus. He pursued macroeconomic stabilization through freeing prices and slashing the budget, and he rapidly privatized the economy – including a strong push to get parliamentary approval for privatization of land. But he pushed further with his reforms in ways that least threatened social stability or the interests of the "Red Directors." This was the meaning of his newfound incantation, beginning in June 1992, that the "principal task" is "to halt the drop of production."[89] Such a hybrid policy would not lead to a great deal of enterprise restructuring or many bankruptcies,[90] but it could provide a bulwark against communist restoration by creating a widespread stake in the prevention of re-nationalization. And it could be sustained only if new infusions of loans and credits from the International Monetary Fund, the World Bank, and foreign governments allowed Moscow to buy off discontent at home.

---

[86] Ibid.
[87] Moscow Ostankino Television First Channel Network, April 14, 1993 (FBIS-SOV-93-071, p. 13).
[88] *The Herald* (Glasgow), April 30, 1993, p. 4.
[89] *Vreme*, June 15, 1992, as translated in FBIS-SOV-92-132, p. 35.
[90] See Joseph Blasi et al., *Kremlin Capitalism* (Ithaca, NY: Cornell University Press, 1997), ch. 4.

But those loans and credits were not easy to secure, for the conditionality attached to them actually increased the risk of social instability in Russia. Hence, on July 4, 1992, in a televised news conference in the Kremlin, Yeltsin adopted the mantle of protector of the Russian people against unreasonable and dangerous demands by Russia's benefactors and creditors:

I will state plainly that during discussions there were voices calling for us to freeze wages. Of course, this would have produced great exhilaration at the International Monetary Fund, but we cannot embark on this. You see? Then, by this step, we will immediately open up, I would simply say, some local conflicts, or ones at the level of industries or regions. There will definitely be tension. There will definitely be dissatisfaction among people. There will definitely be quite widespread strikes....

If we free fuel prices today, there will be a tenfold increase in all other prices, including prices for bread and food products and so on. Will the people bear it? They will not.... When the people's patience snaps, their trust in the president will be exhausted and then chaos will begin.[91]

Yeltsin was willing to admit that he was backtracking: "we resorted to a certain moderation of the reforms, even when it meant the loss of a certain dynamism."[92]

His July 4, 1992, lecture also permitted Yeltsin to assume a nationalist mantle and thereby blunt some of the criticism coming from statists and nationalists:

So today, Mr. Camdessus ... will insist on us freeing fuel prices. This is now the main subject of disagreement between us. We cannot embark on this and I will tell him so today.... If that's the case, we can do without the 24 billion, all the more so because it is not some sort of charity handout. We will have to pay for it later. The sum is a credit, civilized credit. We should not be forced onto our knees for it. No, Russia is a great power and will not allow itself to do that....[93]

We know the mood of the people. But the International Monetary Fund and Mr. Camdessus do not know the limits of the people's tolerance.[94]

DEFENDING THE NATIONAL INTEREST

This effort to assume a nationalist mantle was indicative of the direction in which Yeltsin was edging in other realms of policy. In response to the efforts

---

[91] Moscow Russian Television Network, July 4, 1992 (FBIS-SOV-92-129, p. 24).

[92] *Vreme*, June 15, 1992 (FBIS-SOV-92-132, p. 35).

[93] Moscow Russian Television Network, July 4, 1992 (FBIS-SOV-92-129, p. 25).

[94] Ibid.; see also his June 15, 1992 interview with *Vreme*, in which many of these themes are previewed. In the latter he had also said: "It is our principal task to halt the drop of production before the end of the year.... The main condition for achieving that goal is preservation of stability in society."

of statists and chauvinists alike, Yeltsin sought to counter radical nationalism not by adopting its message but rather by attempting to supplement his liberal internationalism with a nonprovocative and nonexclusionary state centrism.

In response to criticisms of Russia's concessionary foreign policy, Yeltsin shifted toward the center. In 1992–1993, Yeltsin moved Russia toward a more assertive position. He canceled his visit to Japan and shelved the idea of making concessions on return of the southern Kurile Islands. Moscow began to insist on a special status for Russia within the Partnership for Peace, organized by Washington as an omnibus military adjunct to NATO that included all post-communist states. Moscow became more insistent on Western deference to its association with Serbian interests in the Yugoslav civil war. Both politically and militarily, Russia became more assertive on the ground in the Near Abroad, and it announced to the West that the CIS was an area of exclusive Russian interest. As noted previously, the Russian government used economic coercion and military threats against Estonia in response to its discriminatory citizenship law of 1992. A push began in 1993 for CIS states to allow "dual citizenship" to their ethnic Russian populations and to increase the range and depth of economic and political integration within the Commonwealth. In February 1994, the Foreign Ministry drafted a program for the protection of Russian speakers in former republics that included the use of economic sanctions to protest rights violations. According to a Foreign Ministry spokesperson, that measure was included because "we feel that diplomatic measures are not enough."[95] Thus, in response to the discrediting of idealist thinking about international relations, Yeltsin moved toward a *realpolitik,* spheres-of-influence approach to Russia's international "neighborhood" and toward a somewhat more insistent posture in the Far Abroad.

Yet beyond these shifts Russia remained a cooperative partner with Western Europe and the United States in arms control and other realms of East–West relations. Yeltsin was furthermore decidedly accommodative in relations with the two largest successor states after Russia: Ukraine and Kazakhstan. The correction of 1992–1993 was a search for a synthesis of liberal internationalism and realist statism – or, put differently, a search for a relationship based on elements of both cooperation and competition. Yeltsin's hope was that such a combination would satisfy Russia's statists while retaining good will in Western capitals. The dominant goal of his East–West policy remained: to enlist maximal Western cooperation in easing the socioeconomic, political, and military transitions within Russia.[96]

---

[95] *Rossiiskaia gazeta,* February 18, 1994; *Moscow Times,* February 18, 1994.
[96] He reiterated the goal many times and was gushing about the prospects for European integration in a speech in Brussels on December 9, 1993.

CONSTITUTIONAL CRISIS AND THE STATE-BUILDING CONUNDRUM

The one realm in which Yeltsin did not change his position concerned his relations with parliament and the power of the presidency. True, during much
of 1992 he tried to reach accommodations with the Congress of People's
Deputies, but to little avail.[97] By fall 1992, Yeltsin's extraordinary powers to
rule by decree had expired; the parliament was disinclined to renew them and
was even seeking to scale back the president's formal powers. Some deputies
were also calling for Yeltsin's impeachment.[98]

That seems to have been a point of no return in Yeltsin's eyes. He had built
his authority as an advocate of benevolent but personalistic leadership. He
had in fact pushed himself hard to build coalitions and forge compromises
among disparate forces while serving as Chairman of the RSFSR Supreme
Soviet in 1990–1991,[99] but that behavior reflected the narrow (four-vote) margin by which he had been elected chairman in a closed, intra-parliament vote.
Once Yeltsin had received validation of his leadership by the mass public (in the
June 1991 presidential election), he asserted himself. Opposition to his leadership during 1992 from the Congress of People's Deputies – and from his own
vice-president, who joined the anti-Yeltsin forces – threatened his political authority and contradicted his definition of the principles of political order. The
Congress, he argued, was a holdover from Soviet days that had never been
subjected to a truly free and fair election. It was all the more intolerable that,
because of the constitutional impasse, the Supreme Soviet claimed to be the

---

[97] The scholarly literature on the battles of 1992–1993 is divided over whether Yeltsin or the parliament and its speaker (Ruslan Khasbulatov) was more to blame for the impasses – or whether
this was an impersonal, inter-institutional conflict that was bound to escalate to a schism.
For the "institutional" argument, see Yitzhak M. Brudny, "Neoliberal economic reform and
the consolidation of democracy in Russia: Or why institutions and ideas might matter more
than economics," in Karen Dawisha (Ed.), *The International Dimension of Post-Communist
Transitions in Russia and the New States of Eurasia* (Armonk, NY: M.E. Sharpe, 1997), pp.
297–321, and Nikolai Biriukov and Viktor Sergeyev, *Russian Politics in Transition* (Aldershot, U.K.: Ashgate, 1997), pp. 176–87. Leon Aron (*Boris Yeltsin: A Revolutionary Life* [New
York: HarperCollins, 2000], pp. 495, 510) blames the deadlock on Khasbulatov's personality;
Jerry F. Hough (*The Logic of Economic Reform in Russia* [Washington, DC: Brookings Institution, 2001], pp. 138–42, 159–61) blames the outcome on Yeltsin's personality; and Lilia
Shevtsova (*Yeltsin's Russia: Myths and Realities* [Washington, DC: Carnegie Endowment,
1999], pp. 38–40, 59–61, 76, 90) assigns equal responsibility to both sides, blaming individuals and bemoaning missed opportunities – not treating the gridlock as an inevitable product
of institutional rivalry. For a riveting, on-the-spot journalistic account of the siege of parliament in September–October 1993, see Veronika Kutsyllo, *Zapiski iz Belogo doma* (Moscow:
"Kommersant," 1993).

[98] *The Independent* (London), September 24, 1992; *Los Angeles Times*, December 2, 1992.

[99] Associated Press, July 16, 1990; see also the observations of John Morrison, *Boris Yeltsin:
From Bolshevik to Democrat* (New York: Dutton, 1991), ch. 13.

"supreme authority" within the polity, as written in the banal but still unre-pealed Brezhnev Constitution of 1977. The "people" were the supreme author-ity, according to Yeltsin's plebiscitarian conception of authority, and he – but not the parliament – had passed that test.[100] Hence, when parliamentarians began to call for his impeachment, the Russian president was ready to rumble.

In a speech delivered on February 11, 1993, Yeltsin admitted that the eco-nomic reform policies of 1992 had been marked by "quite a few mistakes."[101] But rather than getting defensive about his personal responsibility, Yeltsin shifted the blame to the legislative branch: "growing tension in the sphere of government inflicted huge damage last year, including economic damage. To-day, this is liable simply to blow up the country, to torpedo any, even the very best, action program."[102] The following week, he railed about the intolerabil-ity of the standoff between the legislative and executive branches, demanding a new constitution and a public referendum.[103] On February 28, his strategy was becoming clear. He pushed his political rhetoric to the extreme, defining the choices as binary oppositions. He accused the Supreme Soviet of trying to impose a "return to the absolute power of the Soviets." This stood in sharp contrast to the "normal division of power [between executive and legislative branches] that is accepted throughout the world." The result of this split was political paralysis, which threatened "an explosion of counterrevolution in the country ... which would ruin not only the reforms and democracy, but Russia itself." His conclusion was predictable, but stated for the first time in public: "I can no longer tolerate such a situation."[104]

But Yeltsin was not willing to isolate himself politically. In the same speech, he appealed to his audience – the middle-of-the-road coalition of industrial-ists, "The Civic Union" – to join him in a broad centrist coalition that would isolate the extremists.[105] He reiterated the theme in a televised interview on March 7, 1993.[106] Four days later, at the 8th Congress of People's Deputies, he insisted that Russia must be a presidential republic and warned that "the Con-gress must choose between consensus or confrontation – one or the other."[107]

---

[100] Of course, the "people" are the font of legitimacy in any notion of popular sovereignty, be it plebiscitarian or representative. But as Yeltsin presented it, only he had received true valida-tion by all the people in a free and fair election.

[101] Ostankino Television First Channel Network, February 11, 1993 (FBIS-SOV-93-029, p. 18).

[102] Ibid.

[103] Moscow Russian Television Network, February 18, 1993 (FBIS-SOV-93-032, pp. 13–15).

[104] Moscow Russian Television Network, February 28, 1993 (FBIS-SOV-93-038, p. 20).

[105] Ibid., pp. 21–2.

[106] Moscow Ostankino Television First Channel Network, "Itogi," March 7, 1993 (FBIS-SOV-93-043, pp. 9–12).

[107] Moscow Ostankino Television First Channel Network, March 11, 1993 (FBIS-SOV-93-046, p. 18).

Yeltsin apparently decided to further polarize the situation by demonizing his opponents, thereby presenting himself as the man who would take the measures required to save the country from reactionary restoration and inevitable destruction. In a televised address to the Russian people on March 20, he defined the Congress of People's Deputies as a holdover from the "former Bolshevik, anti-popular system ... that aspires again today to recoup its lost authority over Russia."[108] He described the recent 8th Congress as "a dress rehearsal of revenge on the part of the former Party *nomenklatura*."[109] Moreover, "imperial ideology reigned supreme at the Congress."[110] If allowed to run the country, such forces would foment "armed conflicts with all the former Union republics,... a return to the arms race, growing military expenditures, and a global confrontation with the whole world."[111] Reverting to the "hell to heaven" metaphor, Yeltsin reversed the direction of travel, warning that, if the revanchists came back to power, "this would be plunging into the abyss."[112] As the elected representative of all the people and the guardian of Russia's well-being, Yeltsin announced that he was signing a decree suspending the authority of parliament, giving the president emergency powers to rule, scheduling a public referendum – on support for the president, the Congress, and Yeltsin's social policies – and anticipating new parliamentary elections. Yeltsin was going the plebiscitarian route once again. As he put it on March 26, "I leave my fate in the hands of the most just and supreme judge: the people."[113]

Within days, Yeltsin rescinded his threat to impose emergency rule. But he got the public referendum he had been seeking, and he got the public validation as well, winning the plebiscite (held in late April) rather handily. Although he had rescinded the emergency regime, he still felt the need to resume negotiations with the parliament over the terms of a new constitution and federation treaty. In subsequent months, these negotiations remained deadlocked over incompatible conceptions of executive–legislative and center–periphery relations. Yeltsin grew increasingly impatient. He escalated the rhetoric once again, accusing parliament and its local soviet branches of seeking to restore communism ("a process of repression against dissidents

---

[108] Moscow Ostankino Television First Channel Network, March 20, 1993 (FBIS-SOV-93-053, p. 13).

[109] Ibid.

[110] Ibid.

[111] Ibid.

[112] Ibid., p. 14.

[113] This quotation is from Russian Television Network, March 26, 1993 (FBIS-SOV-93-057, p. 23); see also Official Kremlin International News Broadcast, April 15 and 16, 1993; *Rossiiskie vesti*, April 16, 1993; *Argumenty i fakty*, April 22, 1993.

within the whole system of the soviets is under way. The aim is to exterminate everything that is alive"[114]). Finally, in September 1993, he did what he had been contemplating all year.[115] He dissolved the Supreme Soviet by decree and announced that new elections would take place in December. This was an acknowledged violation of the existing Constitution, which specifically prohibited any attempt to dissolve or even suspend the Russian parliament. But Yeltsin justified the action as a national-security imperative: "These measures are essential to protect Russia and the whole world against catastrophic consequences of the disintegration of Russian statehood, again recurring in a country that has an enormous arsenal of nuclear weapons."[116]

In early October 1993, when deputies refused to leave the parliament that Yeltsin had declared dissolved, the situation turned violent. This is not the place to assign degrees of responsibility for the escalation; clearly, from a humanitarian standpoint, both sides share in the blame. Yeltsin turned off the electricity in the parliament; not long thereafter, armed and unarmed resistance to the dissolution triggered violence on the streets of Moscow between pro-executive and pro-parliament supporters. After a tense period of several days, Yeltsin managed to convince military commanders to support him. He brought in overwhelming – some would say disproportionate – military force and used powerful artillery against the parliament building to ensure the exit and arrest of deputies lodged therein. Hundreds of Russian citizens are said to have died during those days of violence. But Yeltsin prevailed. This cleared the field for Yeltsin to define the terms of the new Constitution and to call elections for a new parliament.[117]

Those elections took place in December, along with a referendum on whether or not the country should adopt Yeltsin's preferred constitution. That constitution reflected the strong version of the position that Yeltsin had been fighting for throughout 1992–1993. It was super-presidentialist in the relations among branches of government in Moscow. The president was accorded wide powers to rule by decree, while the parliament and the constitutional court enjoyed only limited powers. The proposed constitution provided for no vice-presidency, so that no future VP could turn against the president the way Yeltsin's vice-president, Aleksandr Rutskoi, had done during 1992–1993.

---

[114] Moscow Maiak Radio Network, August 12, 1993 (FBIS-SOV-93-154, p. 14).

[115] Aleksandr Korzhakov (in *Boris Yel'tsin: Ot rassveta do zakata* [Moscow: Izd-vo "Interbuk," 1997], pp. 158–9) claims that Yeltsin had made preparations for the parliament to be gassed and seized by the army in the spring of 1993 had it supported his impeachment at that time.

[116] Moscow Ostankino First Channel Network, September 21, 1993 (FBIS-SOV-93-182-S, p. 2).

[117] For divergent assessments of responsibility for the violent outcome, contrast Aron, *Boris Yeltsin*, pp. 540–50, with Reddaway and Glinski, *The Tragedy of Russia's Reforms*, pp. 370–429.

Moreover, by the terms of the constitution, it was almost impossible to impeach the president and equally difficult to amend the constitution itself. The constitution reflected Yeltsin's "boss" mentality and plebiscitarian conception of accountability. The document was designed to ensure that the president would be by far the highest authority in the land, largely unaccountable to institutions and primarily answerable only to the voters at the subsequent presidential election.[118]

As for center–periphery relations, the new Constitution was based on a mix of unitary and federal principles. This, too, was the strong version of the position Yeltsin had been pushing during 1992–1993 in negotiations over the Federation Treaty. The task had been complicated by both the powerful centrifugal forces at play in 1990–1991, which Yeltsin had encouraged at the time, and the institutional legacy of Soviet rule. There remained a hierarchy of status that differentiated among the territorial units within Russia and accorded some of them (the ethnic "republics") greater autonomy, privilege, and political rank than others. During the negotiations, republics sought to maximize their autonomy from the center while provinces (oblasts and krays) sought to attain no less autonomy than republics would be granted. Yeltsin's constitution sought to rein in both of these tendencies, to define both republics and provinces as equally "subjects of the Federation," and to expand the formal powers of the center to impose its will on the regions. At the same time, in a significant bow to federal principles, it gave the regions formal representation by their leaders in the upper house of the new parliament and scheduled the direct election of regional governors. This mix of unitary and federal principles stood in sharp contrast to the de facto confederalism (strong regions–weak center) that existed at the time.[119]

Thus, as a state builder, Yeltsin's democratic rhetoric of 1989–1991 evolved thereafter toward a mix of liberal and illiberal principles. He attached low priority to construction of a strong system of political parties, to a balanced separation of powers between the executive and legislative branches, to checks and balances among the branches of government, and to the further encouragement of regional autonomy. Instead, super-presidentialism,

---

[118] Yeltsin's chief of staff at the time reports that Yeltsin personally edited a draft of the constitution only days before it was to be made public; perhaps his most significant revision, according to Filatov, concerned the status of the presidency: "additions that specify that presidential decrees are normative and that the president may chair government sessions" (Sergei Filatov, *Sovershenno nesekretno* [Moscow: Vagrius, 2000], p. 329).

[119] Filatov (ibid., pp. 333–4) quotes Yeltsin as saying, at the time of finalization of the draft constitution, that the adjective "sovereign" should no longer be attached to "republics" in that document because "the position of the president is to protect the rights of nations, on whatever part of the territory of Russia they happen to live, not to protect the rights of 'sovereign' national states."

plebiscitarianism, populism, and a center strong enough to prevent regions from ignoring the writ of Moscow were the features of Yeltsin's evolving program of state building. Civil liberties and electoralism in state–society relations, and a still-to-be-negotiated relationship between center and periphery, remained as the principal liberal features of his state-building program.

CONCLUSION

During his period of ascendancy, Yeltsin worked out programs in the major realms of policy that were geared toward transforming independent Russia into a new, decisively post-Soviet polity, economy, and international actor. The program unfolded over the course of 1992–1993. Yeltsin broadened his coalition beyond the intense but narrow political base on which he had built his authority during the struggle for power of 1989–1991. That anti-communist and anti-statist political base supported his "shock therapy" for the economy, his liberal strategy of nation building, his willingness to dissolve the USSR, and his concessionary foreign policies. But already in mid-1992, as the costs of these policies were rising, it became clear that Yeltsin was making adjustments to accommodate forces and ideas that otherwise might be mobilized against him.

From mid-1992 through the end of 1993, Yeltsin fashioned an appeal that promised: (1) to sustain his economic reform efforts while averting threats to social stability; (2) to build a secular Russian nation without sacrificing Russian ethnic traditions or the interests of the Russian diaspora in the Near Abroad; (3) to integrate Russia into Western international organizations without sacrificing Russia's autonomy as an international actor or its ability to defend its national interests as a "great power"; (4) to maintain the territorial integrity of Russia without resorting to military force against the regions; and (5) to construct a presidential republic in which the president would be the guarantor of the accomplishment of all these goals.

Yeltsin made the transition from a predominantly oppositional figure within Soviet politics to the president of an independent Russian state, and he forged a comprehensive program for leading his country into the promised land. That program was a complex mix of orientations, but each realm of policy excluded deference to the unreconstructed communists and extreme nationalists. Yeltsin settled on a formula for co-opting the center of the political spectrum while continuing to pursue the agenda he had laid out in late 1991. It was by no means clear that such an amalgam of policies would yield the intended results. If it did not, Yeltsin would find himself on the political defensive once again, and he could not diffuse responsibility for failure. His personalistic leadership style – and his insistence on being granted emergency powers to rule by decree – meant that others could not credibly be blamed if the synthetic program failed. If he wanted credit for accomplishments then he would also have to accept responsibility for failure. Or so people would judge him, whether he accepted their judgment or not. As with Khrushchev and Gorbachev before him, that is precisely what happened.

8

Yeltsin on the Political Defensive

In December 1993, Yeltsin should have been riding high. He had eliminated the old Supreme Soviet and imprisoned his nemeses, Ruslan Khasbulatov and his former vice-president, Aleksandr Rutskoi. He had secured passage of his Constitution, which accorded him extraordinary powers vis-à-vis all other political institutions, made him virtually unimpeachable, and enshrined the approach to center–periphery relations and nation building for which he had been pushing. But that is not quite how Yeltsin saw it. Although he celebrated passage of the Constitution, he was apparently surprised by the results of the elections to the Duma: the anti-regime nationalists and communists won a substantial plurality. Yeltsin did not comment on the December 12 election results until ten days later. Then he criticized the "democrats" for their disunity, the opposition for their extremism, the government for the way in which it had implemented policy, and himself for having lost touch with the people.[1]

The memoir literature gives us a fuller understanding of Yeltsin's reaction to this frustration. The Russian president was very pleased with his accretion of formal powers and with the adoption – at long last! – of his preferred Constitution. But he was distressed by the dramatic deflation of his popularity with the mass public. He had exerted great energy to gain military support for subduing the Supreme Soviet by force – and even then it was a close call. He knew that he might not be able to count on such support in the future. Moreover, public opinion polls revealed a backlash against him for having used military force in October 1993.[2] The Duma elections brought

---

[1] Moscow Ostankino Television First Channel Network, December 22, 1993 (FBIS-SOV-93-244, pp. 1–8).

[2] Associated Press, October 30, 1993.

into power another set of oppositional forces (radical nationalists and communists), this time mobilized by political parties better organized than the parliamentary factions that had supported Khasbulatov and Rutskoi. Within two months, the new Duma declared an amnesty for all those political figures arrested in October 1993 and for the coup plotters of August 1991 as well.

Yeltsin was enraged by the amnesty and by the failure of his staff to prevent it, apprehensive about the loyalty of the military, and disappointed by the electoral verdict. He disappeared for several weeks in January 1994 and, in the eyes of some of his staff members, returned a changed man. Memoirs reveal that his most immediate reaction to these frustrations, other than depression and hitting the bottle, was to retreat into a more authoritarian and reclusive management style. Study of the evolution of his leadership reveals that his always personalistic operating style had earlier been accessible, open to suggestion, and consultative. After 1993, however, Yeltsin allowed an exclusionary and neo-tsarist component, which I will refer to as "patriarchal," to reign ascendant in relations with his staff. He retreated into himself.[3] The present chapter focuses on Yeltsin's behavior during this stage of political defensiveness. I first examine the transformation of Yeltsin's management style in dealings with his staff and cabinet and then analyze the change in Yeltsin's authority-maintenance strategy after 1993.

YELTSIN AS PATRIARCH

I noted in Chapter 5 that the management styles of Soviet leaders varied from highly personalistic to "executive," as measured by the degree to which they worked through (or, alternatively, around and over) their "cabinets" and staffs. Gorbachev combined some personalistic traits with a largely executive style of management. But after he was thrown onto the political defensive, he became more arbitrary and less consultative than he had been before. Yeltsin had always been much more of a personalistic leader than Gorbachev, but he became even more so when on the political defensive.

---

[3] I first developed this periodization and conceptualization in George W. Breslauer, "Boris Yeltsin as patriarch," *Post-Soviet Affairs*, vol. 15, no. 2 (April–June 1999); since then, several books have appeared that examine this period using diverse methodologies (interviews, documents, memoirs, and insider information). It is reassuring to note that they all point to a turn of this sort after December 1993 and they all view Yeltsin as having reverted at this time to a more reclusive, monarchical style of leadership. See Leon Aron, *Boris Yeltsin: A Revolutionary Life* (New York: St. Martin's, 2000), pp. 564–77; Lilia Shevtsova, *Yeltsin's Russia: Myths and Realities* (Washington, DC: Carnegie Endowment, 1999), pp. 99–100; Peter Reddaway and Dmitri Glinski, *The Tragedy of Russia's Reforms: Market Bolshevism against Democracy* (Washington, DC: U.S. Institute of Peace, 2000), ch. 8.

Personalism is not necessarily the same as despotism – though all despots are, by definition, personalistic. Personalism is a form of rule in which the leader is not held accountable – formally, regularly, and frequently – to institutions that can substantially constrain his discretion. Beyond that, personalistic rulers *can* be generous, proper, and temperate; they are not necessarily tyrannical, capricious, or corrupt. Patriarchalism is a form of personalism that treats the political community as a household within which the leader is the *pater familias*; patriarchs typically rely on tradition, rather than charisma or rational–legal norms, to validate their right to rule as they please.[4] But the concept does not prejudge how the ruler distributes benefits, be these material or honorific, and whether he is generous or stingy and responsive or unresponsive to his staff's personal feelings.

Examination of the memoir literature, bolstered by the author's personal interviews with some of Yeltsin's subordinates, offers insight into the nature of Yeltsin's self-conception as a leader. As shown in Chapter 2, Yeltsin always ruled over his administrative domains like a tsar and master; Yeltsin always had a patriarchal self-image as well. Thus, even before 1994, within his inner circle he viewed himself as head of the household, as a leader who demanded total loyalty to himself and his commands, and who had the right to exercise maximal discretion over the public and (at times) private lives of his subordinates. There was nothing impersonal about these relationships, nothing based on procedural propriety or the prerogatives of office – except his own. The staff and officials of the presidential administration were his retainers, not his lieutenants. He treated his entourage as a family with himself as its head rather than as a corpus of professionals of which he was chief executive. This is not a mere academic distinction; it had striking behavioral consequences.

Yeltsin compelled his subordinates to try to improve themselves along the lines he dictated. According to Bonet's research on Yeltsin's tenure in Sverdlovsk, he insisted that all his assistants wear formal clothes.[5] When they were not dressed formally enough for him, he made them return home to change their clothes. He also "turned the obkom [the regional Party committee] into a

---

[4] Max Weber, *The Theory of Social and Economic Organization* (New York: Free Press, 1947), p. 346; Reinhard Bendix, *Max Weber: An Intellectual Portrait* (Garden City, NY: Doubleday, 1960), pp. 330–60; H. E. Chehabi and Juan J. Linz (Eds)., *Sultanistic Regimes* (Baltimore: Johns Hopkins University Press, 1998), ch. 1. Note that, as used by Weber and his followers, patriarchs are male; however, this usage does not correspond to the usage in current feminist literature, which treats male domination of women as a product or distinguishing characteristic of patriarchy. In the usage employed in this article, a patriarch is a leader who dominates subordinates of both sexes.

[5] Pilar Bonet, "Lord of the manor: Boris Yeltsin in Sverdlovsk oblast'," Occasional Paper no. 260 (Washington, DC: Kennan Institute), 1995, p. 8.

volleyball league," dividing it into five teams in which members of the provincial Party committee (*obkom*) were required to participate, both to foster bonhomie and to improve the physical fitness of his political elite.[6] As president of Russia, Yeltsin continued the pattern. After the August 1991 coup, he ordered a house to be built where he, his wife, and his daughters' families, as well as all the top officials in his administration and their families, would reside. He insisted that one apartment be held in common by residents of the apartment building, so that joint celebrations could be held there. Similarly, Yeltsin insisted that members of his entourage share his passion for playing tennis and that they display proper deference by losing to him on the court. He organized a "Presidential Club" into which members of his staff and cabinet were selectively initiated. He demanded that, in his presence or at the Presidential Club, associates not use swearwords.[7]

Former press secretary Vyacheslav Kostikov notes in his memoirs that Yeltsin considered himself "something like the father of an extended family (*semeystvo*)." He enjoyed flaunting his patriarchal authority and liked it when he had the opportunity to demand that somebody apologize for a bureaucratic inadvertence: "ask Papa for forgiveness." He liked a good meal with vodka, during which he would offer long toasts and enjoy his role as head of the family.[8]

Memoirs by associates – as well as Yeltsin's own memoirs – are laced with additional examples of this attitude. Kostikov affirms that Yeltsin harbored a great deal of sentimentality, almost love, for Gaidar and says that, for Yeltsin, Gaidar was his "alter ego" (*vtorym ya*).[9] Yeltsin is reported to have referred to Chubais and Nemtsov as being "like sons to me."[10] Yeltsin's ghost-writer (and eventual chief of staff) Valentin Yumashev appears in a photograph with Yeltsin in one memoir; the caption reads: "For the President, V. Yumashev is almost like a son. It is not for nothing that his patronymic is Borisovich."[11]

---

[6] Pilar Bonet, "Nevozmozhnaia Rossiia: Boris Yel'tsin. Provintsial v Kremle," trans. by G. Luk'ianova, in *Ural* (Yekaterinburg), no. 4 (April 1994), pp. 80–3; Fyodor Burlatskii, *Glotok svobody* (Moscow: RIK Kul'tura, 1997), vol. 2, p. 123.

[7] On the communal apartment building, see Korzhakov, *Boris Yel'tsin*, pp. 134–50; on tennis, see Yeltsin, *The Struggle*, pp. 234–6; on Yeltsin's need to win on the court, see Korzhakov, *Boris Yel'tsin*, p. 61; on the Presidential Club, see Viacheslav Kostikov, *Roman s prezidentom: zapiski press-sekretaria* (Moscow: Vagrius, 1997), p. 319, Korzhakov, *Boris Yel'tsin*, pp. 24–5, and Yeltsin, *The Struggle*, pp. 236–7; on swearwords, see Yeltsin, *The Struggle*, p. 237, and Korzhakov, *Boris Yel'tsin*, p. 309.

[8] Kostikov, *Roman*, pp. 8, 25.

[9] Ibid., pp. 157, 278.

[10] *Financial Times*, September 16, 1997.

[11] Valerii Streletskii, *Mrakobesie* (Moscow: Detektiv-Press, 1998), last page of book (unnumbered). Note also the following observation by a Russian journalist: "Presidential policy has

Kostikov's memoir (1997) is entitled *Love Affair with a President*. An inter-viewee and former Yeltsin aide avers that, in the early 1990s, Yeltsin "loved" his young advisors and they "loved" him in return.[12]

During the 1980s, Yeltsin's relationship with his bodyguard, Aleksandr Korzhakov, was intimate to the point that the two exchanged blood from their fingers on two occasions to affirm their eternal loyalty to each other as "blood brothers."[13] (Yeltsin was in his mid-fifties at the time.) Korzhakov refers to a vacation that he and Yeltsin took in 1986 as our "honeymoon."[14] Yeltsin was the designated "wedding patriarch" at the marriage of Korzhakov's daugh-ter.[15] Streletskii writes of the psychology of those responsible for guarding Party and governmental officials under Yeltsin: "bit by bit they are turned into 'members of the families' of those they are guarding."[16] Tellingly, when Yeltsin rebuked Korzhakov in May 1996 for getting involved in politics, the blood brother proclaimed to Yeltsin's daughter that "it would be mild to say that I do not love Boris Nikolaevich." Tatyana flew into a rage at this statement.[17]

In such an administrative context, the key to both political longevity and political influence was to capture the attention and the ear of the leader. But this had to be done with all proper deference. Indeed, when seven members of Yeltsin's staff wrote a joint letter to their boss in 1994 – urging him not to repeat his embarrassing and apparently drunken performance in Berlin – Boris Nikolaevich was livid. His reaction, however, was that of a patriarch, not an executive: he demanded that each of them, individually, admit to him their "guilt" and express "repentance."[18]

Yeltsin's patriarchal self-conception extended beyond his immediate en-tourage and economic ministers. It also encompassed members of the mili-tary leadership. On this score, the detailed study – part memoir, part research project – by Baranets (1998) is useful and has an air of credibility, though of course it is only a single source and was written by a man quite alienated by

      long been a family business, in which Yumashev is admitted with the rights of a relative"
      (Aleksandr Gamov, in *Komsomol'skaia pravda*, July 8, 1998); see also Baturin et al., *Epokha*,
      pp. 732, 780.
[12] See also Oleg Poptsov, *Khronika vremyon "Tsaria Borisa"* (Moscow: Sovershenno sekretno,
      1996), p. 269.
[13] Korzhakov, *Boris Yel'tsin*, p. 223.
[14] Ibid., p. 63.
[15] Ibid., p. 243.
[16] Streletskii, *Mrakobesie*, p. 24.
[17] Korzhakov, *Boris Yel'tsin*, p. 358.
[18] Ibid., pp. 220–3; Kostikov, *Roman*, pp. 328–31. Yeltsin eventually calmed down, however; see
      Baturin et al., *Epokha*, pp. 523–4.

Yeltsin's treatment of the Russian military. Here too we encounter the use of intimate, familial metaphors. Defense Minister Grachev "loved" Yeltsin, and the two men once declared their "eternal friendship and love" for each other.[19] When he awarded Grachev a special presidential gold medal in a public ceremony, Yeltsin declared that this "is my personal gift to you."[20]

The Patriarch as Abusive Parent

The language of familial intimacy and love is one discursive indicator of a patriarchal self-conception. But Yeltsin, like Khrushchev, also reserved to himself the right to abuse verbally members of the executive branch. As Baranets documents, in October 1993, when Yeltsin sought military support against the Supreme Soviet, one of the participants at the meeting remarked that "[w]e were sitting there and feeling as if our strict and enraged father had come to our school in order to listen to the principal's complaining about our bad behavior."[21] Several years later, after having decided to fire Defense Minister Igor Rodionov and Chief of the General Staff Viktor Samsonov, Yeltsin first harassed them verbally in front of their subordinates.[22]

Nor were the military the only victims. Other members of Yeltsin's cabinet were subjected to open, verbal abuse: Foreign Minister Kozyrev, Interior Minister Yerin, and Nationalities Minister Yegorov are specifically mentioned in memoirs as having gotten the treatment, while Kostikov implies that Prime Minister Viktor Chernomyrdin was victimized as well.[23]

Yeltsin also felt at liberty to be physically abusive. He could be very cruel to the most loyal of his aides, especially when he had been drinking. Whatever the foibles of presidents and prime ministers elsewhere, it is difficult to imagine them "playing the spoons" on the heads of their ranking assistants and, when the others in the room responded with laughter, increasing the speed and force of the spoon-pounding, as well as the number of heads being pounded.[24] It is also difficult to imagine them emulating Yeltsin's behavior on a boat on the Yenisei River, when he lost patience with the interruptions of his press secretary and ordered his bodyguards to toss the man overboard.

---

[19] V. N. Baranets, *Yel'tsin i ego generaly: zapiski polkovnika genshtaba* (Moscow: "Sovershenno sekretno," 1998), pp. 170, 230.

[20] Ibid., pp. 248–9.

[21] Ibid., p. 26.

[22] Ibid., pp. 77, 122.

[23] Yegor T. Gaidar, *Dni porazhenii i pobed* (Moscow: Vagrius, 1996), pp. 107–8, 333–4; Korzhakov, *Boris Yel'tsin,* pp. 52–3; Kostikov, *Roman,* p. 347.

[24] Korzhakov, *Boris Yel'tsin,* pp. 81–2.

When his bodyguards hesitated, on the assumption that he was kidding, he reiterated that he was serious and saw that the hapless press secretary went over the side.[25]

Nor did Yeltsin's abuse of his most dependent and servile subordinates cease at the boundary of the Russian executive and presidential branches. We also learn that he played the spoons on the head of the president of Kyrgyzstan, Askar Akayev![26] Unless this was mutual, good-natured play (not clear from the memoir account), it is a stunning indicator of the extent to which Yeltsin may have considered portions of the Commonwealth of Independent States (CIS) to be part of his political household.

The Patriarch as Generous Benefactor

Although Yeltsin frequently abused his subordinates and those most dependent upon him, he could also be generous toward members of the political family. He enjoyed giving gifts (usually expensive watches) to his staff.[27] The gestures reached beyond the inner circle as well. He became the focus of innumerable requests for special favors – tax exemptions, in particular – from representatives of regional and sectoral interests. Reportedly, he found it difficult to say "no" in the face of opportunities to assist friends, maddening his budget-conscious economics minister in the process, though he also used such dispensations as a conscious strategy of "buying" political support.[28] Moreover, such tendencies extended beyond the borders of the Russian Federation. Yegor Gaidar reports in his memoir his fear that Yeltsin, if left alone with the leaders of Belarus, would concede more than Russia could afford in economic policy.[29] An interviewee added that such fears were well-founded, but not because of Yeltsin's (very real) ignorance of economics or an ideological

---

[25] Ibid., pp. 253–4.

[26] Ibid., p. 82. This was corroborated by others (none of them admirers of Korzhakov) interviewed by me in Moscow in June 1998.

[27] Ibid., p. 54. As Korzhakov notes, this notion of *shef darit* (the chief or patron gives a gift) was one that Yeltsin enjoyed practicing in his Sverdlovsk days as well.

[28] Kostikov, *Roman*, pp. 216–17; Baturin et al., *Epokha*, pp. 339, 340, 435. See also Eugene Huskey, *Presidential Power in Russia* (Armonk, NY: M.E. Sharpe, 1999), pp. 137–8; Anatol Lieven, *Chechnya: Tombstone of Russian Power* (New Haven & London: Yale University Press, 1998), p. 171; Victor M. Sergeyev, *The Wild East: Crime and Lawlessness in Post-Communist Russia* (Armonk, NY: M.E. Sharpe, 1998), pp. 117–18. Huskey reports that Finance Minister Livshits lamented that Yeltsin does not understand the economy "and tries to help everyone ... but some people need to be imprisoned rather than helped" (p. 57) and that Economics Minister Yasin complained that Yeltsin has "his favorite directors who can open any doors" (p. 137).

[29] Gaidar, *Dni*, pp. 183–4.

commitment to CIS integration. Rather, what drove Yeltsin in such conversations was paternalism and a sense of communalism. As this interviewee put it, Yeltsin's expressed sentiment was: "We're a family here. Let's dispense with the formalities! Why should we wrangle? Here, I'll give you this!" This extended beyond the Russia–Belarus relationship, according to this insider, and helps to explain Russia's flexibility in relations with Ukraine and Kazakhstan (the latter regarding Caspian Sea oil). The same interviewee averred that, in CIS relations, Yeltsin "could be generous to a fault."[30]

Yeltsin also thought in generous patriarchal terms about his relationship with the Russian population, even as his policies caused great suffering to a majority of the population. He thought of himself in 1992–1993 as "Director of all of Russia" whose election as president had validated his right to interpret the will of the people.[31] Because of his overwhelming victories in confrontations with the old system and in free elections, he believed that he didn't have to account, or explain himself, to anyone.[32] But he also thought of himself as a "people's tsar": benevolent and caring, though strict when necessary.[33] When he would offer reassurances to the populace that their pain would shortly ease, he felt like a Russian priest lifting the spirits of his flock.[34] On a tour of Russia in 1992, he brought along hundreds of millions of rubles for "gifts to the working people." He knew that this violated the prevailing economic policy, "but he considered it possible for himself to make tsarist gestures."[35]

The Evolution of Yeltsin's Management Style

Yeltsin entertained a personalistic self-conception throughout his political career; he always wanted to be "in charge." He was an extremely demanding boss, one who expected all his subordinates to work and play as hard as he did.

---

[30] Although I have no evidence on the matter, such an attitude may have informed Yeltsin's relations with Tatarstan's President Shaimiev and the generous terms Yeltsin offered to secure the treaty of February 1994, which accorded that republic substantial autonomy within the Russian Federation. For an admission that many people accuse him of being too generous to the CIS leaders – and for his self-justification for doing so, see Boris Yeltsin, *Midnight Diaries* (New York: Public Affairs, 2000), pp. 247–8.

[31] Kostikov, *Roman*, pp. 306–7; Poptsov, *Khronika vremyon*, p. 283.

[32] Kostikov, *Roman*, p. 304.

[33] Burlatskii, *Glotok svobody*, vol. 2, p. 315.

[34] Kostikov, *Roman*, pp. 21–2.

[35] Ibid., pp. 42–3. In *Presidential Power*, Huskey argues that Yeltsin conceived of the presidency as "the country's primary institutional patron" (p. 119) and of the president as standing above all branches of government and sending "emissaries" (p. 81) to them. The evidence displayed in this chapter supports Huskey's characterizations.

In Sverdlovsk, he expected subordinates to give up their weekends to play volleyball or to go fishing and hunting whenever he so demanded.[36] In Moscow, they were called to the tennis court. But Yeltsin's operating style evolved over time. He always combined personalism with a patriarchal self-conception; a reclusive, monarchical style became dominant only after 1993. Memoirs by two of his close aides from the late 1980s, while he was an oppositional leader in Gorbachev's Soviet Union, make little mention of the traits I have been emphasizing to this point, stressing instead Yeltsin's charismatic personalism at the time.[37] Several memoirs by people who worked with Yeltsin both before and after 1993 distinguish between the early President Yeltsin and the late President Yeltsin, with the breakpoint coming sometime in late 1993. Before then, Yeltsin was a populist who, these memoirists claim, was confident of his ability to mobilize the masses against his political adversaries. He also enjoyed enormous charismatic authority within his entourage and rational–legal authority derived from his public election as president in June 1991. In addition, within his inner circle, while demanding the deference due a patriarch, he was also accessible, consultative, and receptive to a range of policy advice.

By late 1993, however, Yeltsin had lost confidence in his ability to rally the masses, a conclusion reinforced mightily by the results of the December 1993 parliamentary elections.[38] This was not only a blow (presumably) to his ego; it was also a threat to his authority-maintenance strategy. For a plebiscitarian approach to getting one's way assumes that "the people" will side with the leader against his political enemies. In 1988–1989, Yeltsin had turned to the people for defense against the Communist Party–State. In 1989–1992, he had risen to ascendancy on waves of popular affirmation and reaffirmation. In 1993, the costs of his policies were piling up and the populace lost faith in their hero. Yeltsin was still in power – formally, stronger than ever – but found himself in new political territory.

Gaidar writes that, around this time, Yeltsin began to present himself as a benevolent tsar surrounded by a huge court.[39] Increasingly over time, Kostikov reports, Yeltsin referred to himself in the third person.[40] According

---

[36] Burlatskii, *Glotok svobody,* vol. 2, p. 123.

[37] Lev Sukhanov, *Tri goda s Yel'tsinym* (Riga: "Vaga," 1992); Viktor Yaroshenko, *Ya otvechiu za vsyo* (Moscow: Vokrug sveta, 1997).

[38] Kostikov, *Roman,* pp. 151–2; Gaidar, *Dni,* pp. 230–1, 313–14; Korzhakov, *Boris Yel'tsin,* p. 330.

[39] Gaidar, *Dni,* p. 295.

[40] Kostikov, *Roman,* p. 308.

to Korzhakov, Yeltsin began to be heavily preoccupied with his personal security.[41] He also narrowed the circle of those to whom he would turn for advice and allowed the security personnel in his entourage to have a major influence on policy.[42] As Kostikov lamented, "we ['democrats'] were pained that, in relations with Boris Nikolaevich, a steady disappearance of democratism, accessibility, and relations of trust was occurring."[43] One former associate explains this trend as a joint product of the physical pain and exhaustion Yeltsin experienced at this time and the emotional anguish of having "lost" the December 1993 parliamentary elections after having expended so much energy to prevail over the Supreme Soviet in 1993. He had been expending so much "negative energy" for so many years that, by 1994, his entourage could bring him "bad news" only when it was packaged with three times as much "good news."[44]

The change led Gaidar to remark to Kostikov in January 1994 that "we must return Yeltsin to Yeltsin," which meant that they must find a way to curb Yeltsin's authoritarian impulse, reinforce his consultative strain, and prevent him from relying excessively on alcohol as an escape.[45] Yeltsin had evolved from a "people's tsar"[46] into an increasingly reclusive monarch. His personalism − though a constant throughout his years as president − had evolved from a populist, consultative, and accessible variant into a more reclusive and exclusionary one.

The Patriarch as System Manager

Yeltsin's sense of political vulnerability and his withdrawal into a more exclusionary operating style were accompanied by a demonstrable shift in his authority-maintenance strategy as well. From 1994 onward, Yeltsin presented himself publicly as a leader whose primary goal was to consolidate the new

---

[41] Korzhakov, *Boris Yel'tsin*, p. 133.

[42] Gaidar, *Dni*, p. 300.

[43] Kostikov, *Roman*, p. 322. Yeltsin's chief of staff at the time, Sergei Filatov, reports that Yeltsin became relatively reclusive and traveled little around Russia in 1994–1995 (*Sovershenno nesekretno*, p. 401).

[44] Interview by the author, Moscow, June 1998; see also Korzhakov, *Boris Yel'tsin*, p. 251.

[45] Kostikov, *Roman*, p. 296. In his post-retirement memoir, Yeltsin admits that alcohol got the best of him during 1994–1995 (Yeltsin, *Midnight Diaries*, pp. 318–19), though he denies being an alcoholic either before then or since then; for a somewhat different view of Yeltsin's reaction to the December 1993 votes, see Baturin et al., *Epokha*, p. 402. Curiously, the "author's collective" that produced *Epokha* included V. Kostikov.

[46] Burlatskii, *Glotok svobody*, vol. 2, p. 315.

order he had built and to manage the contradictions within that new order. He presented himself more as a system manager than a system builder. The change led him to distance himself further from the radical reformers and to shore up his ties with the centrists. This was consistent with his earlier reactions to political challenge.

When his popularity fell and criticism rose after the economic reforms of early 1992, he shifted toward currying support from centrists in many realms of policy. After his military victory over the parliamentarians and their paramilitary allies in October 1993, but before the elections of December, Yeltsin began to emphasize the theme of "normalization" and the need for a long-term process of cultural adaptation to the new system.[47] At his press conference following the elections, he declared that "the whole of Russia craves stability. Russia needs peace."[48] The memoir he signed for publication in early 1994 ends with the prosaic promise to give the Russian people "stability and consistency in politics and the economy" and with the declaration that "the only definite guarantor of calm is the president himself."[49] After he calmed down following his anger at the amnesty of February 1994, Yeltsin proposed and brokered a "memorandum on social accord" geared toward inducing all moderates to agree formally to work within the system, to avoid inflaming public passions, and to help him isolate the extremists within the Duma.[50] The Constitution, he suggested, had put an end to the contradictions of dual power, and it would open up a civilized basis for lasting peace and rational development.

Structural transformations were no longer the leitmotif of Yeltsin's administration. The emphasis would now fall on consolidation of gains, rationalization of administration within the new structural context, political isolation of anti-system forces, and popular adaptation to the system as constructed.[51]

A good indicator of the change in policy priorities was the newfound emphasis in Yeltsin's speeches on consolidative themes and a relative downplaying of the transformative themes that had predominated in 1992–1993. His first

---

[47] Interview in *Izvestiia,* November 16, 1993.
[48] Moscow Ostankino Television First Channel Network, December 22, 1993, as transcribed in FBIS-SOV-93-244, p. 2.
[49] Yeltsin, *The Struggle,* p. 292.
[50] Also, in an interview on April 5, 1994, he made clear that another priority had entered his goal-set: "I believe that one of my main accomplishments by 1996 will have been to create the guarantee that prevents the country from falling into totalitarianism .... Our shared duty is to isolate the extremist forces in parliament (*La Republica,* April 5, 1994, p. 14 [FBIS-SOV-94-065, pp. 11–12]).
[51] See Baturin et al., *Epokha,* pp. 16–17, 379–80, 397, 412.

speech to the Federation Council, on January 11, 1994, stressed the need to firm up the market economy by giving it a legal infrastructure.[52] On February 24, his landmark "State of the Federation" address to the Federal Assembly was titled "On Strengthening the Russian State" and declared: "The important stage of Russia's transformation into a democratic state is now coming to a close. A democratic system of power is being shaped on the basis of the Constitution."[53] The section on economic reform itself, the priority in earlier days, was now located in the middle of a long address. This speech and subsequent ones – while still touting the need to continue and deepen the reform process – placed much greater emphasis on the maintenance of social peace (that is, among "all healthy forces in society") and the creation of order, with new attention to courts, crime, social programs, administrative reliability, an orderly relationship between Moscow and the regions, the population's long-term adaptation to the new system, and the need for civil service reform as a means of reducing the level of corruption. Following the amnesty, Yeltsin summarized the new orientation nicely in a speech to the government on March 4, 1994: "Today in Russia democracy means first and foremost stability, order, cooperation."[54] Gaidar sensed the shift coming and resigned from his position as a member of the government's cabinet in January 1994.[55]

Yeltsin had been a competent manager and Party leader in Sverdlovsk from the 1950s through the 1970s, when he had been undisputed master of his domain and when the communist system enforced a social peace and political conformity that kept conflict within bounds. He had then evolved into a tactically brilliant revolutionary figure during Gorbachev's last years in power.

---

[52] Moscow Radio Rossii Network, January 11, 1994.

[53] *Rossiiskaia gazeta,* February 25, 1994, p. 1, as translated in FBIS-SOV-94-039, p. 37.

[54] Moscow Maiak Radio Network, March 4, 1994 (FBIS-SOV-94-043, p. 16).

[55] In an interview published in *Izvestiia* on March 26, 1994, Yeltsin was challenged to explain the fact that he had noticeably distanced himself from the "democrats and radical reformers." He denied that he had done so, claiming that he had instead "broadened the spectrum of cooperation.... Precise, thorough, patient work is essential here. Passions must not be further intensified.... The main idea ... – strengthening the state on the basis of the Constitution – is cherished by everyone whose common sense has not failed them.... I feel that the main demand now being voiced by people and by all strata of society is that stability is strengthened and our life rendered more peaceful" (*Izvestiia,* March 26, 1994). In August 1995, he went even further: "Time is changing the meaning of the word 'democrat.' Until recently it had been used primarily for radicals, hardline opponents of the former system, and dedicated rally participants. Now, in my view, it primarily refers to professionals able to create. People who recognize only the constitutional method of coming to office and leaving office. Democrats are the people who are prepared to ensure that the country moves toward a normal life" (*Komsomol'skaia pravda,* August 19, 1995).

As president of independent Russia he had led the country, for better or for worse, through a radical rupture with the legacy of communist institutions. But now – weakened by age, illness, and the sheer fatigue of having battled for so long – Yeltsin faced still another social role: the leader as system manager.

The course of the privatization program reflected this new stage in Yeltsin's administration. As previously scheduled, a second round of privatization, based on a new set of rules, took place during 1994–1995. Whereas the rules governing the first round ("voucher privatization" in 1992–1994) favored insider workers and managers, the second round amounted to one of the largest and most blatant cases of plutocratic favoritism imaginable. Huge industries, potentially worth many billions of dollars, were "sold" to a few wealthy individuals for a nominal sum – in some cases, less than one percent of their real value. It is doubtful that Yeltsin either understood the intricacies or cared to learn them. As he confessed in his second memoir, "I do not pretend to understand the philosophy behind our economic reforms."[56] But his advisors convinced him that rapid transfer of large assets into the hands of monopoly capitalists would help create a class of wealthy property owners who would be potent allies in the ongoing struggle against communist restoration. Those capitalists would then have a great deal to lose from the communists coming back to power and would accordingly be willing to use all means to prevent that from happening. And, with the presidential election only one year away, their financial and political (i.e., media) support for Yeltsin would be assured. Yeltsin, in this stage of political defensiveness, could thus use the new round of privatization simultaneously to shore up his personal power and to redefine his authority-maintenance strategy by presenting himself as the guarantor against communist restoration, whatever the price.

In December 1994, Yeltsin made the fateful decision to invade the republic of Chechnya. I will discuss the rationale for that decision in Chapter 9. In this chapter, I will briefly examine the aftermath as an indicator of Yeltsin's reaction to the frustration of his policies. Following the invasion, members of the political, military, and journalistic establishments criticized Yeltsin forcefully. They challenged him to justify his strategy for maintaining the integrity of Russia. The goal itself was unobjectionable, and he touted it in his State of the Federation speeches of February 1995 and February 1996; indeed, in the 1996 speech, he defined the most important accomplishment (the "first success") of four years of reform as prevention of the disintegration of Russia.[57]

---

[56] Boris Yeltsin, *Zapiski prezidenta* (Moscow: Ogonyok, 1994), p. 235; the admission was omitted from the English-language version, *Struggle,* p. 145.

[57] TASS, February 23, 1996.

But beyond that, how could he justify the price paid in Chechnya to achieve that goal? How do you convince Russians that it is worth losing thousands of soldiers to keep largely Muslim Chechnya within the ostensibly liberal Russian Federation and yet not worth a drop of blood to protect ethnic Russians in the so-called Near Abroad? Yeltsin did not have a ready answer, a reflection of the (perhaps intractable) dilemma of nation-state construction in a post-imperial but diasporic context.

Instead, Yeltsin fell back on nationalistic discourse. He lectured journalists about their alleged obligation to promote the spiritual and religious rebirth of Russia,[58] much as Gorbachev and Khrushchev had tried to keep journalists from going too far in response to the campaigns for *glasnost'* and de-Stalinization. Yeltsin called on the younger generations not to "disgrace the glory of their fathers," to appreciate the importance of defending the Motherland.[59] He publicly courted Cossack organizations – both to secure their loyalty and to make rhetorical use of their historical and current roles in guaranteeing Russian statehood and nationhood.[60]

Yeltsin also took the opportunity to crack down on the most extreme anti-system forces among the Russian nationalists. On March 23, 1995, he issued a decree against "fascist" organizations and activities.[61] This was an effort to lay down the law, to establish boundaries to anti-regime activity, to construct a right-wing enemy of the Russian nation, and to warn that the Yeltsin

---

[58] Moscow Russian Television Network, February 16, 1995; *Rossiiskaia gazeta,* February 20, 1995.

[59] TASS, June 13, 1995.

[60] It seems that the first war in Chechnya (1994–1996) triggered a growing romance between Yeltsin and Cossack organizations. When the war began, Cossacks were drawn in immediately, as historically Cossack villages came under fire and were destroyed. Self-organized battalions immediately volunteered their services, and on January 30, 1995, Cossack leaders asked Yeltsin to "severely punish" Chechen president Dudaev for bringing conflict into Russia and pledged their assistance in protecting Russian territorial integrity (TASS, January 30, 1995). In May 1995, the Extraordinary Council of Cossack Atamans declared its readiness to serve loyally and to defend the security and territorial integrity of Russia (TASS, May 19, 1995). Yeltsin reciprocated with a decree "On the state registry of Cossack societies" (*Moskovskie novosti,* August 25, 1995) and later with the decree "On the main directorate of Cossack troops under the President of the Russian Federation" (TASS, January 20, 1996), both of which recognized the Cossacks officially and also organized them for state service. In September 1995, Yeltsin publicly praised the role of Cossacks in Russian history (TASS, September 7, 1995). In 1996, he expressed his confidence that the Cossacks would continue to set a good example by "defend[ing] the borders and interests of Russia as in ancient times" (TASS, April 17, 1996). Correspondingly, he noted that he would continue to assist the irreversible revival of the Cossack community, a "pillar of Russian statehood" (TASS, June 6, 1996).

[61] It was published in *Rossiiskaia gazeta* on March 25, 1995.

government was willing and able to defeat that enemy. Thus, as all radical nationalists had long warned, this decree acknowledged that the "nation" was under threat, but it uniquely declared the nation to be under threat from the most extreme nationalists themselves. And the decree pointed to Yeltsin's government as the force that would save the nation from that threat.

Nonetheless, Yeltsin resisted ethnicization of the rhetoric of nation building. Thus, in appealing for unity behind his Chechnya policy, he proclaimed that "the citizens of Russia, regardless of their nationality [read: ethnicity], are dying there."[62] Moreover, Yeltsin supplemented his remarks about citizen obligations with a reiteration of the democratic principles of freedom of speech and freedom of the press. His anti-fascism decree was apparently aimed at those radical nationalists who were prepared to call militias into the streets, rather than at the Ziuganovs, Baburins, and others who were expressing their opposition within the legitimate political institutions created by the December 1993 Constitution.

In sum, Yeltsin redefined his priorities and political strategies after December 1993. But the transition from system builder to system manager did not relieve him from having to manage the contradictions built into that system of rule.

THE SYSTEM MANAGER AS STATESMAN

Yeltsin's pro-Western foreign policy of 1992 came under criticism at the time, leading the Russian president to explore the possibility of synthesizing a pro-Western, liberal international policy with one that attempted to advance and defend Russia's national interest as a "great power." After the Duma elections of 1993, however, Yeltsin felt the need to respond with ever greater sensitivity to perceived setbacks or shortfalls on the international scene. In 1994, Yeltsin became less of an assertive leader who was building bridges to the West and more the defensive manager of a fragmented and often incoherent foreign policy. Initially, he had oversold his pro-Western foreign policy. Thereafter, he promised the best of both worlds. By 1994, Western powers were acting in ways quite divergent from the ways Yeltsin had promised they would. Critics – led by Zhirinovskii's Liberal Democratic Party of Russia and the Communist Party, which held sway in the newly elected Duma – turned up the rhetorical heat on Yeltsin for allegedly kow-towing to the West and to the United States in particular.

Yeltsin the authority builder had created unrealistic expectations. Now his critics, combined with his personal isolation and unhelpful international

---

[62] TASS, February 23, 1996.

events, made his optimistic vision of a Russia–West "marriage" seem both less desirable and less feasible. The result of this process was the transformation of Yeltsin into a defensive statesman who was struggling not only to manage the contradictions between these expectations and reality but also to defend his political authority as an effective foreign policymaker.

Russia and the West, 1994–1996

A search for Western assistance to help finance the Russian transition had been a constant throughout Yeltsin's years as president of the Russian Federation. In the early years, hopes were high in Moscow that the rich democracies would provide huge sums, both in appreciation of the anti-communist credentials of the Yeltsin government and in fear of what might replace it. Those hopes were soon disappointed, and the "game" thereafter became one of playing upon Western fears of Russian revanchism to induce the extension of whatever credits, loans, guarantees, and policy concessions the West might be persuaded or cajoled to deliver. Jerry Hough, in a recent study, demonstrates how Yeltsin and his government played upon the Western identification of Yeltsin's political survival with the continuation of something called "reform." The rhetorical characterization of opponents within Russia, and the timing of alleged threats to "reformism," often coincided with moments when the International Monetary Fund was deliberating the extension of new loans. Those loans, Hough argues, were largely counted upon to help pay the wages of workers in the urban state sector of the economy and thereby to avert potential social unrest.[63]

Clinton and Yeltsin met in Moscow in January 1994. In the news conference held jointly with Clinton, Yeltsin, though upbeat and ebullient, gave voice to a long list of Russia's concerns about U.S. deficiencies as a partner of Russia in international affairs, complaining of discriminatory trade restrictions and the treatment of Russians in the Baltics ("There should be no double standards here, whether it is taking place in Haiti or in the Baltic area").[64] In his dinner toast to Clinton following the summit, Yeltsin extended the laundry list of complaints, signaling irritation and impatience with his American partner and suggesting that the United States was not doing its part to help Russia.[65]

---

[63] Jerry Hough, *The Logic of Economic Reform in Russia* (Washington, DC: Brookings Institution, 2001).

[64] Moscow Russian Television Network, January 14, 1994 (FBIS-SOV-94-011, p. 7).

[65] ITAR-TASS, January 14, 1994 (FBIS-SOV-94-011, pp. 12–13); "we need to be sincerely supportive of each other's success .... It is not enough to mouth these values. It is necessary to bring one's actions into line with them" (ibid., p. 13).

After the pro-Western romanticism of early 1992 had worn off, Yeltsin felt the need to elicit Western financial support without giving away too much in return. His revised authority-building strategy called for him to manage the contradictions among an array of goals. In his State of the Federation address on February 24, 1994, Yeltsin went farther than ever before in identifying the sheer number of conflicting goals he was promising to advance:

It is in Russia's interests to create favorable external conditions for the country's development. This must be achieved by a proper and friendly but at the same time firm and consistent foreign policy, in which the desire for cooperation does not conflict with the country's national interests and Russian citizens' sense of national pride.[66]

That was a tall order, indeed!

Issues other than trade, credits, and arms reductions also conspired to complicate the realization of this vision. Most immediately at the time, the war in former Yugoslavia caused a crisis in U.S.–Russian relations. Beginning in late 1993, NATO threatened to bomb Serbia if it failed to respect United Nations "safe havens." However, Serbian President Slobodan Milosevic proved recalcitrant. When NATO responded by bombing the Bosnian Serbs – despite Russia's protests and without the imprimatur of the UN Security Council – Yeltsin temporarily postponed his State of the Federation address and thereafter complained repeatedly in public about both a Western double standard in Yugoslavia and Western unilateralism.[67] After much international maneuvering, Russian troops served side-by-side with NATO troops, but under UN command, in what proved to be a failed attempt to secure the safe havens from attack. However, they did so with mixed support from Russia's Ministry of Defense. The NATO leaders became increasingly frustrated with Milosevic and were poised to begin airstrikes on the night of February 17, 1994. But that day the Russians surprised NATO by unilaterally brokering a cease-fire and landing Russian troops in and around Sarajevo. Yeltsin released a statement that touted the Russian "triumph," and he later called for a Russia-led summit of the United States, Britain, France, and Germany to resolve the Serb–Bosnian crisis. The summit never took place.

Coterminous with the Yugoslav crisis was the matter of NATO's enlargement, which held out the prospect of adding East European states to the

---

[66] "Poslanie Prezidenta Rossiiskoi Federatsii Federal'nomu Sobraniiu: Ob ukreplenii rossiiskogo gosudarstva. (Osnovnye napravleniia vnutrennei i vneshnei politiki.)," *Rossiiskaia gazeta,* February 25, 1994, pp. 1, 3–7, quoted from p. 1.

[67] Moscow Ostankino Television First Channel Network, October 4, 1994 (FBIS-SOV-94-193, pp. 7–10), quoted from p. 9; *Rossiiskaia gazeta,* August 10, 1995, p. 1; Moscow Radio Rossii Network, September 8, 1995; ITAR-TASS, September 8, 1995.

alliance. The issue further complicated Yeltsin's efforts to deliver on the multiple goals of his redefined foreign policy vision, and it reinforced the credibility of anti-Western forces within Russia's political establishment and intelligentsia. Several compromises were offered by the Western powers: a "Partnership for Peace," in which Russia and all formerly communist states would participate; a temperate pace of NATO expansion, sensitive to Yeltsin's political predicament; and, ultimately, a NATO–Russia Charter, institutionalizing forms of cooperation between an enlarged NATO and an excluded Russia. Even though these compromises were ultimately agreed upon, they were viewed in Moscow as little more than palliatives. The issue of NATO's enlargement eastward (which Moscow could not prevent) and of Moscow's likely exclusion from membership severely complicated Yeltsin's authority maintenance throughout 1994–1996.

In October 1993, U.S. Secretary of State Warren Christopher presented to Yeltsin the idea of the Partnership for Peace, which Yeltsin misunderstood to be an *alternative* to NATO expansion. Christopher recalled the misunderstanding in his memoir:

Yeltsin became quite animated when I described the Partnership proposal. The Russians had been very nervous about the NATO issue in the run-up to our visit .... He called the Partnership idea a "stroke of genius," saying it would dissipate Russian tensions regarding the East Europeans and their aspirations toward NATO .... "This really is a great idea, really great," Yeltsin said enthusiastically. "Tell Bill that I am thrilled by this brilliant stroke." In retrospect, it is clear that his enthusiasm was based upon his mistaken assumption that the Partnership for Peace would not lead to eventual NATO expansion.[68]

Within months, however, it became clear to Russian officials and to Boris Yeltsin that they had either misunderstood or been misled. Foreign Minister Kozyrev did his best during 1994 to push for a revitalized Organization for Security and Cooperation in Europe in lieu of an expanded NATO.[69] But during the second half of 1994, the United States intensified its efforts to build support for NATO enlargement.[70] Moscow reacted with indignation. At a meeting of European heads of state in Budapest in December 1994, Yeltsin and Kozyrev angrily denounced NATO expansion and refused to sign on to the Partnership for Peace.[71] At a Clinton–Yeltsin summit meeting in Moscow

[68] As quoted in James M. Goldgeier, *Not Whether but When: The U.S. Decision to Enlarge NATO* (Washington, DC: Brookings Institution, 1999), p. 59.
[69] *Segodnia,* February 25, 1994; TASS, March 2 and June 22, 1994; UPI, March 10 and August 17, 1994; Official Kremlin International News Broadcast, August 17, 1994.
[70] Goldgeier, *Not Whether,* pp. 71–5.
[71] Ibid., pp. 85–7.

in May 1995, the rhetorical heat subsided but no final agreement was reached, as "Clinton and Yeltsin agreed to disagree on enlargement" and Clinton rebuffed Yeltsin's demands for a substantial delay in the admission of new members to NATO.[72] Although Clinton thought he had persuaded Yeltsin at that summit to join the Partnership for Peace,[73] it was not until December 1996 that Kozyrev's successor, Yevgeny Primakov, agreed for the last time to join NATO's Partnership – and even after that, Russia participated only fitfully.

Given this thicket of contradictions, during 1994–1995 Yeltsin found it increasingly difficult to reconcile with reality his previous vision of friendly and benevolent U.S.–Russia relations. After a September 1994 summit with Clinton, Yeltsin declared: "There are people in my country, though few, who say that our relationship with the U.S. is transient and that an era of confrontation will return. But I would like to tell you that we have never fought the U.S. and I believe, and I can say as President of Russia, that we will never fight the U.S."[74] By that December, Yeltsin was less optimistic, warning of a "cold peace" in place of the Cold War.[75] In spring 1995, Foreign Minister Kozyrev announced that "[t]he honeymoon is over" in U.S.–Russian relations.[76]

Of course, Yeltsin very often put a positive spin on the "results" of his meetings with leaders of the rich democracies. In his news conferences and dinner toasts at summits, he frankly summarized the remaining areas of disagreement and often sternly lectured his Western counterpart on the deficiencies of his policies. But he also spoke of the progress made in discussions and in mutual understanding of each other's positions. And he frequently spoke ebulliently of their personal relationship. This was an important component of his authority-maintenance strategy. If he could not deliver concrete, laudatory results on issues like Yugoslavia, NATO, trade, and the like, he could at least hold out the prospect of future progress that would result from continuation of his close, personal relationships with Western leaders. This was the likely rationale for his constantly referring to "my friend Bill," "my friend Helmut," and, later, even "my friend Ryu," the Japanese leader whom he was meeting for the first time. Thus, in January 1996, after a one-hour telephone conversation with Clinton, Yeltsin proclaimed a "second honeymoon" in U.S.–Russia relations, proudly declaring that "I remained loyal to my friend and he remained loyal to me."[77] The message was consistent. Russia and the

[72] Ibid., p. 92, 93.
[73] Ibid., p. 93.
[74] *Financial Times*, September 24, 1994.
[75] *Los Angeles Times*, December 6, 1994.
[76] *Financial Times*, March 24, 1995.
[77] *The Washington Post*, January 28, 1996.

West might be as far apart as ever on the issues that divide them, but Boris Nikolaevich can still manage this as a disagreement among close friends – and can hold out the prospect of bridging the divide in the future.[78]

The Commonwealth of Independent States

Already in 1993, Russia had begun to move toward an increasingly interventionist policy in the Near Abroad. Progress toward some degree of economic reintegration of states of the former Soviet Union became a goal of Russian foreign policy. Better yet, demonstration of enhanced political and military cooperation among those states, coerced or otherwise, became a means by which Yeltsin tried to assuage his nationalist critics. Thus, as early as January 1994, the *Financial Times* reported that Russia was negotiating a secret deal to merge its economy with that of Belarus.[79] Yeltsin confirmed these rumors in a speech in February, when he also publicly signed a military cooperation treaty with Georgia.[80] In ensuing months, Yeltsin announced several treaties and agreements deepening ties with Belarus, Georgia, Kazakhstan, Ukraine, Tadjikistan, and Armenia. During 1993–1995, Russia pressured states of the Commonwealth to adopt "dual citizenship" laws. Yeltsin also made increasingly nationalistic statements about Russia's "moral and political" responsibility to provide security and currency for CIS countries,[81] turned up the rhetorical heat on European governments to punish Estonia and Latvia for their restrictive citizenship laws (which disadvantaged resident Russians), and proclaimed Russia's right to police the Near Abroad when threats of instability on Russia's borders appeared.[82] Kozyrev ratcheted up the patriotic rhetoric in parallel, announcing by April 1995 that Russia was prepared to use force to "defend our compatriots abroad."[83]

Much of this rhetoric proved to be bluster. Economic and political unions with Belarus were on the Russian policy agenda from 1991 onward, yet none were implemented to a degree that would force Moscow to pay significant

---

[78] In his post-retirement memoir, Yeltsin discusses his final summit meetings with Western leaders in precisely these terms. He presents himself as a great leader who brought the world back from the precipice by forgiving Western leaders their challenges to Russian security and pride (*Midnight Diaries*, ch. 23).

[79] *Financial Times*, January 7, 1994, p. 1.

[80] ITAR-TASS, February 3, 1994.

[81] Radio Free Europe/Radio Liberty Daily Report, no. 126, Part I, June 29, 1995.

[82] Moscow Russian Television Network, January 14, 1994 (FBIS-SOV-94-011, pp. 6–7); *Rossiiskaia gazeta*, February 25, 1994 (section on foreign policy); *Rossiiskaia gazeta*, April 29, 1994, p. 3; *Izvestiia*, July 21, 1994, pp. 1, 3.

[83] *Izvestiia*, April 20, 1995.

material costs. Yeltsin and presidents Kravchuk and Kuchma of Ukraine announced several compromise resolutions of their conflicts over control of the
Black Sea Fleet during 1994–1996, only to see these resolutions fall apart
and the negotiations reopened. The issue of dual citizenship was quietly
dropped when widespread governmental resistance to the idea arose in the
Near Abroad.[84] European pressure on Estonia resulted in a change in that
country's laws, as a result of which Russia withdrew her troops by the announced deadline. Throughout, Russian officials tried to increase the level
of economic integration within the Commonwealth, but they avoided using
a heavy hand and typically backed off when they met resistance. On the
other hand, Russian military assertiveness, both covert and overt, intensified
in the affairs of the more defenseless successor states: Georgia, Moldova, and
Tadjikistan.

Yeltsin used the prospect of CIS integration to co-opt nationalist sentiment and maintain his broad, centrist coalition. His commitment to defend
Russians in the Near Abroad may or may not have been genuine, but his
hardline rhetoric was certainly an easy way to score points with nationalist
constituencies. He declared his preference that Russians in those countries
not emigrate back to Russia and that the issue never torpedo his relations
with the rich democracies. Similarly, Yeltsin was attentive to instability along
Russia's borders. He declared it right and proper that Russia use its military,
political, and economic leverage to reduce or contain the instability in ways
that were consistent with Russia's long-term interests. Yet when discussing
these issues with European and U.S. leaders, he was willing to balance his
"spheres of influence" approach with invitations to European institutions to
provide peacekeeping forces and good offices on the territory of the former
Soviet Union.

CONCLUSION

When Yeltsin's initial promises lost credibility, he tried to deepen his appeal
to moderates and centrists in order to expand his coalition. His "system management" posture constituted a step back from the transformative thrust of
his comprehensive program; it represented an effort to consolidate gains. One
of his main, stated priorities now came to be the (negative) goal of isolating
the extremists and preventing communist restoration. Toward that end, he
tried to maintain his appeal to the broadest possible range of moderate forces.

---

[84] Igor Zevelev, "Russia and the Russian diasporas," *Post-Soviet Affairs*, vol. 12, no. 3 (July–
September 1996).

This choice, while rational as a means of retaining power, forced Yeltsin to present himself as a man who could manage the contradictions within both his domestic and foreign policies. It required him to demonstrate simultaneously that consolidation did not mean stasis and that continued reform did not mean a radical disruption of the lives of the people. Similarly, on the international front, he had to demonstrate that cooperation with the West did not mean capitulation and that the advancement of Russia's interests abroad would not lead the rich democracies to deny economic and political assistance to Russia. It was a precarious balance to strike. None of Yeltsin's predecessors had managed to recoup their authority and realize their policy priorities once their comprehensive programs faltered. Yeltsin kept trying, for he had a mechanism – popular reelection – that was unavailable to his predecessors. But that reelection was imperiled by a momentous decision Yeltsin had made in December 1994: the decision to invade Chechnya.

9

Yeltsin Lashes Out

The Invasion of Chechnya (December 1994)

Yeltsin's political defensiveness and his search for means to recoup lost authority were decisive determinants of the fact and timing of his decision to invade Chechnya. By late 1994 – with his personal approval ratings plummeting, the economy in a precarious state after the crash of the ruble on October 11, 1994, a hostile (albeit less powerful) Duma, charges of corruption swirling around his government, powerful centrifugal forces still asserting themselves in the regions of Russia, Western assistance and investment at a small fraction of earlier expectations, integration into Western institutions proceeding at a snail's pace, and NATO expansion on the table – Yeltsin found himself severely challenged to justify the quality of his leadership. He was very much on the defensive politically, even though he had secured popular ratification of a Constitution that, formally at least, largely shielded him from threats of impeachment or legislative vetoes of his decrees. Moreover, already in 1995, "election season" would begin in anticipation of parliamentary elections scheduled for December 1995 and presidential elections scheduled for June 1996.

It was in this context that Yeltsin tackled the Chechnya problem. His first State of the Federation address, in February 1994, was significantly entitled "The Strengthening of the Russian State."[1] A treaty relationship was struck with Tatarstan in February 1994 that gave that region within Russia an exceptional level of autonomy, far more than that accorded regions within Switzerland, Spain's Catalonia, or states within the United States. But the president

---

[1] "Poslanie Prezidenta Rossiiskoi Federatsii Federal'nomu Sobraniiu: Ob ukreplenii rossiiskogo gosudarstva. (Osnovnye napravleniia vnutrennei i vneshnei politiki.)," *Rossiiskaia gazeta*, February 25, 1994, pp. 1, 3–7.

of Chechnya would not accept the same terms; he insisted on independence from Russia and on pursuing policies that threatened Russia's internal security. In May 1994, Yeltsin gave a speech to officers of the border guards in which he proclaimed that "we will firmly defend the territorial integrity of the Russian Federation. We do not have any spare, unneeded land in Russia!"[2]

Thus, a continuing challenge to the territorial integrity of Russia accompanied a sharp decline in Yeltsin's political popularity and credibility. Unable to deliver on many of his other promises, Yeltsin apparently felt the need to demonstrate that, at a minimum, he could defend Russia's statehood. This was the promise – the authority-recouping strategy – implicit in his February and May 1994 speeches. He succeeded with respect to Tatarstan but was not successful with respect to Chechnya. First he tried negotiations; after six months of fruitless effort, they failed. Then, in summer–fall 1994, he tried covert military action. When that failed, he invaded.[3]

The first crucial variable in my reconstruction is authority maintenance: the timing of the invasion was a function of Yeltsin's declining popularity. The second variable is the nature of the issue: a potentially serious challenge to the state's integrity or security. It is this combination that explains the fact and the timing of the invasion.

This squares with the findings of a major study by Richard Ned Lebow of great-power crisis initiation in the nineteenth and twentieth centuries. Lebow found that, when a threat of international reversal coincides with a threat to regime stability or leadership authority, the threshold for risk-taking is lowered dramatically, as is the threshold for wishful thinking. This argument is consistent with considerable theoretical literature on the psychology of risk-taking, which demonstrates that acceptance of risk grows in the face of a threat of loss more than it does in the face of opportunities for gain.[4] Moreover, Lebow's findings suggest an exceptional incentive for risk-taking and wishful thinking: the threat of a *double loss* – the coincidence of an external threat to state interests and an internal threat to regime stability or leadership authority. When we apply this approach to a comparison of Khrushchev,

---

[2] Quoted in Yu. M. Baturin, A. L. Il'in, V. F. Kadatskii, V. V. Kostikov, M. A. Krasnov, A. Ya. Livshits, K. F. Nikiforov, L. G. Pikhoia, and G. A. Satarov, *Epokha Yel'tsina: Ocherki politicheskoi istorii* (Moscow: Vagrius, 2001), p. 457.

[3] By contrast, Peter Reddaway and Dmitri Glinski (*The Tragedy of Russia's Reforms: Market Bolshevism Against Democracy* [Washington, DC: U.S. Institute of Peace, 2001], p. 439) interpret Yeltsin's rhetorical stress on "strengthening the state" as doctrinal cover for strengthening his personal grip on the machinery of the central government.

[4] Yaacov Y. I. Vertzberger, *Risk Taking and Decisionmaking* (Stanford, CA: Stanford University Press, 1998), pp. 36–7.

Brezhnev, Gorbachev, and Yeltsin, we find parallels that help us better to explain the timing of the invasion of Chechnya.

SOVIET AND POST-SOVIET COMPARISONS

If we think of Khrushchev's years in power, the Brezhnev administration, and Gorbachev's time at the helm, we find a pattern that is strikingly similar to that observed under Yeltsin. In all four cases, we witness a similar act of initiating crisis or war at an advanced stage of the leader's years in power: the Cuban Missile Crisis in 1962; the invasion of Afghanistan in December 1979; the assaults on Vilnius and Riga in January 1991;[5] and the invasion of Chechnya in December 1994.

In all four cases, we observe a leader who had built his authority with an ambitious program that promised much more than it could deliver. In all four cases, the act of violence took place shortly after the unworkability of the leader's program had become evident. In all four cases, the initiation of war or crisis took place at a time when the leader was suddenly faced with having to prevent or counter precisely what he had promised he would not let happen: an imminent challenge to fundamental state interests.

In Khrushchev's case, during the twelve months preceding the October 1962 crisis, the United States exposed Soviet strategic inferiority and implied a determination to exploit it. These revelations and U.S. policy undercut Khrushchev's optimistic claims that the correlation of forces was shifting decisively in favor of socialism. In Soviet eyes, the Kennedy administration was claiming a decisive shift in the balance of power. Khrushchev's Cuban adventure was designed to thwart the American challenge.[6]

The second half of 1979 held analogous implications for Soviet interests. The SALT II arms-control treaty was seemingly headed for defeat in the U.S. Congress. The Cuban brigade crisis (August) and American disinterest in according Moscow "most favored nation" status – despite record levels of emigration from the USSR that year – further suggested to Soviet leaders that anti-détente forces had reemerged ascendant in American politics. Worse, all this coincided with a year-long rapprochement between the United States and

---

[5] To this day, Gorbachev denies personal responsibility for this tragedy, while others claim he initiated or allowed the action. I will not enter that debate here but will instead assume the action was not taken against Gorbachev's expressed will.

[6] The best study of the crisis, which accumulates mountains of evidence leading to precisely these conclusions, is Richard Ned Lebow and Janice Stein, *We All Lost the Cold War* (Princeton, NJ: Princeton University Press, 1994).

China, which was rapidly assuming the dimensions of an anti-Soviet military relationship. And only days before the decision to invade Afghanistan was finalized, NATO announced its decision to proceed with the deployment of U.S. Pershing-2 and cruise missiles in response to the Soviet deployment of SS-20s in 1977. The mood within the Soviet political establishment at the time, sensed by Robert Legvold during a visit to Moscow in December 1979, was that it was time to "show the Americans."[7]

In 1990, Gorbachev faced the consequences of his contradictory policies as centrifugal forces within the USSR intensified greatly. Declarations of sovereignty by several republics became harbingers of separatism and secession. The Baltic republics in particular had already insisted upon full independence. Gorbachev's promise to forge a "renewed Union," with strong republics and a strong center, was encountering powerful challenge. The attacks on Vilnius and Riga took place in January 1991.

On this score, the timing of the invasion of Chechnya is analogous. Having proclaimed that 1994 would be a year for strengthening the Russian state, and with the rest of his domestic and foreign policy programs under serious challenge, Yeltsin addressed the threat from Grozny in analogous fashion: with a determination to demonstrate that he could enforce state power on the territory of Russia and thereby at least fulfill the promises associated with his fallback authority-maintenance strategy.

There is still another similarity among the cases. In all four, the leader responded to an authority crisis by narrowing or redefining the circle of his advisers and associates, or by ceding control of policy to hardliners in the leadership. Khrushchev did not consult widely about the necessity or advisability of putting missiles in Cuba. And, as his programs were exposed as failures, he became increasingly arbitrary during 1961–1962 in purging central and local officials, in circumventing the top leadership, in revealing his preferred solutions publicly, and in railroading the Presidium into accepting his schemes.

Brezhnev had neither the health nor the incentive to mimic Khrushchev's political style. But we know that the decision to invade Afghanistan was initiated and pushed by a small subset of the Politburo with very little consultation among the broader political or specialist elites. The decision was largely a product of forceful initiatives by Andropov, Ustinov, and Gromyko – respectively, the heads of the KGB, the armed forces, and the Ministry of Foreign

---

[7] Robert Legvold, "Caging the bear: Containment without confrontation," *Foreign Policy*, no. 40 (Fall 1980), p. 82.

Affairs – with strong support from Suslov (the ideological secretary of the Central Committee) and with Brezhnev's acquiescence or approval.[8]

Gorbachev initiated his famous "shift to the right" precisely four months before the January 1991 events in Vilnius and Riga. He broke with the radical democrats in September 1990 over the "500 days" plan for marketization of the economy, arguing that it would result in the collapse of the USSR. In November 1990, he co-opted hardliners into key leadership positions, fired several liberal advisers, and reorganized institutions to the advantage of the imperial "power ministries."[9] This was the context within which Eduard Shevardnadze angrily announced his resignation as Foreign Minister, only weeks before the crackdown in the Baltics.

Yeltsin's pattern of consultation during 1994 went in a similar direction. His advisors report in their memoirs and newspaper exposés that, during this year, Yeltsin narrowed the circle of his advisers to the hardline group within the Security Council that is generally considered to have been the decision-making body for the Chechnya invasion. He also drastically curtailed his earlier practice of soliciting a wide array of options and viewpoints before making his choice.[10]

The narrowing of consultative patterns, or the ceding of control of policymaking to hardliners, reinforces another attribute of at least three of these cases: wishful thinking about the feasibility or cost of heading off reversal. From all accounts, Khrushchev convinced himself that Kennedy would back down and was genuinely surprised, confounded, and frightened by Kennedy's actual reaction.[11] From all accounts, Brezhnev and his associates

[8] See the revealing newspaper memoir by Oleg Grinevskii, "Kak my 'brali' Afghanistan [How we 'took' Afghanistan]," *Literaturnaia gazeta*, no. 31 (August 2, 1995), p. 14. Grinevskii, who headed the Foreign Ministry's Middle East Department at the time of the invasion, presents minutes of several Politburo meetings, quotations from several participants whom he interviewed, as well as verbatim quotations of statements at the time by Foreign Minister Gromyko. His reconstruction is ambiguous as to the extent of Brezhnev's involvement, but is consistent with a view of Brezhnev as a backstage vetoer or approver of initiatives by associates in the Politburo.

[9] Gorbachev's close aide, Anatolii Chernyaev, reports that this was the point at which Gorbachev stopped soliciting the advice of his liberal advisors, consciously isolating himself from their viewpoints (A. S. Chernyaev, *Shest' let s Gorbachevym* [Moscow: "Progress," 1993], p. 401).

[10] Vyacheslav Kostikov, *Roman s prezidentom* (Moscow: Vagrius, 1997), pp. 284–5, 296–7, 303–7, 325–6; Emil Pain and Arkady Popov in *Izvestiia*, February 7–10, 1995 (article in four installments); Mark Urnov in *Segodnia*, March 22, 1995; Baturin et al., *Epokha*, pp. 598–9, 626, 635; Sergei Filatov, *Sovershenno nesekretno* (Moscow: Vagrius, 2000), pp. 236, 254; Valery Tishkov, *Ethnicity, Nationalism, and Conflict in and after the Soviet Union* (London: Sage, 1997), pp. 212–16. Most of these authors were among those who were marginalized at the time.

[11] Lebow and Stein, *We All Lost the Cold War*, p. 80.

greatly underestimated the risks and costs of sending the Red Army into Afghanistan.[12] Gorbachev's calculations in January 1991, like his decision-making involvement, were less transparent. We know he was frightened by the prospect of an uncontrolled fragmentation of the union and determined, at least in principle, to prevent it – especially in the wake of the collapse of communism in Eastern Europe in late 1989. But we also know that he was opposed to the use of force to achieve his goals. We know less about whether he believed a show of force in Vilnius, Riga, or elsewhere could reverse the centrifugal processes in motion at the time.

Yeltsin expected the invasion of Chechnya to be much smoother and cleaner than it turned out to be, in part because the Chechen opposition had come so close (with covert Russian assistance) to prevailing in November and in part because Defense Minister Grachev promised an easy victory.[13]

It is difficult to measure a subjective phenomenon like wishful thinking. But there does seem to be a pattern in our cases. Leaders on the political defensive initiate or tolerate efforts to reverse a highly adverse trend by means of a dramatic show of force. That creates a politically motivated predisposition to believe that the initiative will succeed.

A POLITICAL–COALITIONAL PERSPECTIVE

My comparison of the four cases has located patterns that transcend the unique features of each leader's personality and that also transcend differences among them in the amount of political power they had accumulated while leading the country. Of the four cases, Khrushchev and Yeltsin garnered more personal power – that is, autonomy to make choices once their authority had begun to decline – than had Brezhnev and Gorbachev. Both Khrushchev and Yeltsin made the key decisions to use force.

By contrast, Brezhnev was ill in March 1979 when Gromyko, Andropov, and Ustinov first tried to push through the Politburo a decision to intervene militarily in Afghanistan. When informed of the decision, Brezhnev vetoed it, arguing that he did not want to spoil his forthcoming summit meeting with President Carter in Vienna (in June) at which he looked forward to signing the SALT II arms-control treaty. Later that year, when prospects for improvement in U.S.–Soviet relations had dimmed, the three Politburo heavyweights

---

[12] Sarah E. Mendelsohn, *Changing Course: Ideas, Politics, and the Soviet Withdrawal from Afghanistan* (Princeton, NJ: Princeton University Press, 1998), pp. 63–4.

[13] Anatol Lieven, *Chechnya: Tombstone of Russian Power* (New Haven & London: Yale University Press, 1998), pp. 89ff.

tried again; this time Brezhnev acquiesced, perceiving little to lose. Thus, Brezhnev played the role first of vetoer and then approver, rather than initiator, of decisive action.[14]

In the case of Gorbachev, who was certainly healthy and involved in high politics, we are still not sure whether he made the final decision to use military force in the Baltics (while retaining "plausible deniability" of responsibility), allowed it to happen while pretending not to know, simply tolerated it, or was surprised by it. Although some scholars believe the answer to be fairly clear and to be consistent with Gorbachev's distaste for the use of force,[15] the record is ambiguous. And well it might be, for Gorbachev frequently dissimulated in front of his colleagues in the leadership in order to maintain plausible deniability of his responsibility if things went wrong (see Chapter 5).

If Khrushchev and Yeltsin clearly initiated action on the decision, but Brezhnev did not and Gorbachev may or may not have, how can we theorize about the nature of Soviet and post-Soviet politics in a way that would explain all four of these choices? Perhaps an authority-maintenance perspective, with its focus on an individual leader making a clear choice with an eye to shoring up his political position, is too restrictive when dealing with specific decisions by leaders who enjoyed varying degrees of personal power and accountability to a collective leadership or competing institutions. However, instead of replacing this perspective with a political–sociological or interest-based approach that denies leadership autonomy and attributes outcomes solely to impersonal institutional forces (the "military–industrial complex," the "Party apparatus," the "party of war," and the like), we can merge an approach based on ideas and choice with a political–coalitional perspective. Such a synthesis highlights both the political constituencies on which leaders base their policies and the relative autonomy of the leader from that political base.

Under Khrushchev, Brezhnev, and Gorbachev, the leader initially consolidated his power and authority by appeasing the interests of the dominant hardline constituents: the Party–ideological apparatus and the military–industrial complex. This was true of Khrushchev in 1953–1954, of Brezhnev in 1965–1968, and of Gorbachev in 1985–1986. Once each was confident of having consolidated his position and having outflanked his rivals within the Politburo, all three men offered comprehensive programs that appealed to a wider range of constituencies than had their earlier programs. But after each of

---

[14] See Grinevskii, "Kak my 'brali' Afghanistan."

[15] Archie Brown, *The Gorbachev Factor* (Oxford & New York: Oxford University Press, 1996), pp. 279ff.

these comprehensive programs failed, each leader again contracted his coalition by selectively playing to hardliners in hopes of maintaining a political base. This is how Khrushchev behaved in domestic (economic and administrative) and foreign policy from mid-1960 through the Cuban Missile Crisis; it describes Brezhnev's realignment on domestic policy during 1973–1975; and it describes Gorbachev's behavior on domestic policy from September 1990 to April 1991. The interventions discussed here all took place during these periods of contracted political coalition and appeasement of hardline forces.

When his comprehensive program lost credibility by early 1994, Yeltsin narrowed his coalition, moving still farther in a hardline direction and relying more on the statists (*gosudarstvenniki*). This period of contraction coincided with his upgrading of state building as a priority task by which his leadership should be judged and also coincided with his redefinition of Chechnya as an urgent matter.

Thus, all four leaders met the challenges to state interests at a time when they had contracted their coalitions and advantaged hardline political constituencies. Of course, they were not simply prisoners of others who were actually in charge. The extent to which each political leader retained freedom to maneuver and relative autonomy from his political constituents varied among the four. But they shared a political field within which hardliners either had seized the initiative or were encouraged or allowed to do so. The mobilized audience for the redefined authority-maintenance strategy was a more hardline constituency than that appealed to during the middle stage of the leader's administration.

From this perspective, Brezhnev's incapacitation and Gorbachev's denial of responsibility do not invalidate my theory. Each of these two interventions was facilitated by the leader's *prior* decision to contract his political coalition and to cede some of the political initiative to hardliners.

IN SEARCH OF COVARIATION

My argument thus far draws upon three sources: (1) comparability to patterns of great-power brinksmanship in the nineteenth and twentieth centuries (as studied by Lebow) and consistency with psychological theories of risk-acceptance; (2) multiple sources of comparability to other cases of the use of force by post-Stalin Soviet leaders during analogous stages of their administrations; and (3) a specific theory of coalition maintenance in Soviet and post-Soviet politics that predicts variations in leaders' reactions to threats to state interests, depending on the fragility of their political authority at the time.

In the social sciences, few tests are definitive and conclusive. We can only add additional tests to see whether our tentative conclusions are reinforced or undermined by those tests. The next step in my analysis of the Chechnya case and its earlier analogs is the most challenging: to explore empirically whether comparable acts occurred during earlier stages of the administrations of these leaders. If such were the case then it would undermine the claim that such acts are products of the political circumstances of the stage of "decline" that follows the discrediting of the leader's program. It would require volumes of research in Soviet archives to document covariation or its absence. Some of that research is currently being conducted (and soon to be published) by scholars such as Mark Kramer, Hope Harrison, and others. For present purposes, I will just discuss some possibilities.

Soviet invasions and crisis initiation certainly had taken place during earlier stages of administrations. The invasions of Hungary (1956) and Czechoslovakia (1968) took place during the stage of political succession struggle. Khrushchev's ultimatum to the West regarding Berlin (November 1958) occurred after he had consolidated his political ascendancy. Thus, political defensiveness per se is not a prerequisite for military intervention or crisis initiation.

This counterargument is challenging. However, one could argue that the interventions in Eastern Europe were fairly predictable – both because political protest in Eastern Europe tended to intensify during periods of Soviet collective leadership and because those collective leaderships (before Gorbachev) were unprepared to "lose" Eastern Europe, defined loss of control by the Communist Party as unacceptable (with factionalization of the Party and the collapse of censorship as key indicators), and had not lost their collective will to use force.[16] Similarly, settlement of the German problem under Khrushchev, by threat and confrontation if necessary, may equally have been a matter of

---

[16] Christopher Jones argued (before Gorbachev came to power) that collapse of the "leading role of the Party" was the trigger for Soviet interventions in Eastern Europe (Christopher D. Jones, *Soviet Influence in Eastern Europe: Political Autonomy and the Warsaw Pact* [New York: Praeger, 1981]). The Soviet archives on the Hungarian and Czech invasions have been available for some years now and demonstrate that the Soviet leadership was hoping to avoid invasion and launched numerous diplomatic initiatives to avert the need. But those archives also show that Soviet leaders were determined to prevent, by one means or another, either factionalization of the Communist Party or renunciation of the Warsaw Pact. They sought to induce local authorities to regain control of the situation, by military means if necessary, and only invaded after they lost hope of such an outcome (personal communications from Professor Andrew Janos of UC Berkeley, Dr. Charles Gati of Johns Hopkins SAIS, and Professor Hope Harrison of George Washington University). In his memoir, former Politburo member Anastas Mikoyan claims that there was no need to invade Hungary in 1956, because he "had already negotiated a peaceful exit from the crisis" (*Tak bylo: Razmyshleniia o minuvshem*

substantial (though not unanimous) consensus – or deference to Khrushchev's optimism – within the leadership.[17] By contrast, military intervention of the sort employed in our four cases was less readily predictable in terms of these usual considerations and involved much less consensus within the leadership. The Cuban Missile Crisis, the invasion of Afghanistan, the assaults on Vilnius and Riga, and the invasion of Chechnya took most outside observers by surprise and were far from consensual decisions of the leadership as a whole.

Another way to look for covariation is to ask whether there were times when similar conditions of political authority existed but the response to threats to state interests was different. Put differently, were there cases during the *late* stages of administrations when such challenges occurred but the response was not to intervene?[18] The two examples that come to mind are Poland in 1980–1981 and Eastern Europe in 1989. The case of Poland hinges on whether the Politburo was willing to invade that country had General Jaruzelski refused to impose martial law. This remains a matter of contention.[19] But even if the Politburo had proved unwilling to invade Poland in 1981, this would

[Moscow: Vagrius, 1999], p. 598; my thanks to Hope Harrison for suggesting this source). See also Sergei N. Khrushchev, *Nikita Khrushchev and the Creation of a Superpower* (University Park: Pennsylvania State University Press, 2000), pp. 195–7. But Mikoyan apparently did not have many (if any) supporters for his position in the Soviet leadership, and there is no way of knowing whether the "peaceful exit" he negotiated would have slowed the revolutionary tide in Hungary. My concern is not whether there was ambivalence, uncertainty, agonizing, an urge to find peaceful exits, or selective political disagreement in the Soviet leadership; the issue is whether the leadership – in the 1950s through the 1970s – ever displayed a collective willingness to tolerate a collapse of the "leading role of the Party" in a Warsaw Pact state. The only exception to this generalization may be the archival evidence presented by Mark Kramer to the effect that, for one day (October 30, 1956), the CPSU Presidium apparently did unanimously decide to let Hungary go and become a noncommunist country. The decision was reversed the following day (Mark Kramer, "The Soviet Union and the 1956 crises in Hungary and Poland: Reassessments and new findings," *Journal of Contemporary History*, vol. 33, no. 2 [April 1998], pp. 163–215) and seems to have reflected confusion rather than loss of commitment.

[17] As claimed by Michael J. Sodaro (*Moscow, Germany and the West from Khrushchev to Gorbachev* [Ithaca, NY: Cornell University Press, 1990]) and Hannes Adomeit (*Soviet Risk-Taking and Crisis Behavior* [London & Boston: Allen & Unwin, 1982]); by contrast, Hope Harrison (personal communication) notes that Mikoyan was also a dissenter on the decision of fall 1958 (see Mikoyan, *Razmyshleniia*, p. 598). Mikoyan's memoir, however, does not indicate that he had allies on this issue.

[18] I exclude from consideration Stalin's failure to invade Yugoslavia in 1948–1949, as my theory extends only to politically competitive regimes.

[19] See Mark Kramer, "Jaruzelski, the Soviet Union, and the imposition of martial law in Poland: New light on the mystery of December 1981," *Cold War International History Project Bulletin*, no. 11 (Winter 1998). Kramer will soon publish a book on the matter, using the fullness of available archival evidence. Kramer shows that the Soviets were telling Jaruzelski that they

not necessarily refute the theory because the Soviet Union was already mired in war in Afghanistan. War on two fronts simultaneously would have been unprecedented for post-Stalinist leaders.

The second example is more challenging. Gorbachev's failure to use military force to prevent the collapse of communism in Eastern Europe and the re-unification of Germany within NATO was certainly inconsistent with past Soviet patterns of behavior. The case would not undermine our theory, however, if one interpreted Gorbachev's comprehensive program of 1987–1989 as already precluding the use of force to retain control of Eastern Europe and interpreted his fallback position of 1990 as retaining the right to use force to prevent the disintegration of the USSR. Moreover, Gorbachev's political authority did not plummet until 1990 – well after the collapse of communism in Eastern Europe – and he was winning accolades abroad for not using military force.[20]

One other case of the use of force contradicts my theory. In November 1991, at an earlier stage of his administration – indeed, at a time when his authority was extremely high – Yeltsin mobilized police (MVD) forces for use against Grozny in the wake of Dudaev's coup d'etat and declaration of Chechnya's independence from (what was then called) the RSFSR. Given that Yeltsin was not then on the political defensive, we have here still another instance of lack of covariation of the first type discussed previously.

Although the case is striking in that it also concerns military intervention by Yeltsin in Chechnya, it does not challenge the theory as much as it would seem to. Yeltsin's level of commitment to this action at the time was quite low, and the action itself barely got off the ground. A fairly small contingent of MVD troops were sent to Grozny in the expectation that their very presence would restore order. The troops did not initiate action; they were unexpectedly fired upon by Chechen troops and did not escalate in response. When his parliament objected to the police action, and in the face of Chechen gunfire, Yeltsin immediately backed off and recalled the contingent – even though he

would not invade. They were telling him to take care of Solidarity on his own and that they would limit themselves to a show of force. However, had Jaruzelski not taken the advice and not cracked down, or had the crackdown gone awry, the Soviet leadership would likely have reconsidered the decision not to invade, assuming there was such a decision and it was not expressed just for its rhetorical impact on the Polish leader. My thanks to Mark Kramer (personal communication) for a synopsis of his book's argument on this point.

[20] On Gorbachev's unwillingness to use force in Eastern Europe and the path through which he came to this sentiment, see Jacques Lévesque, *The Enigma of 1989: The USSR and the Liberation of Eastern Europe* (Berkeley: University of California Press, 1997). However, Gorbachev publicly (in 1990–1991) neither advocated nor ruled out the use of force to prevent disintegration of the USSR.

had the juridical right to follow through (despite parliament's disapproval), even though his troops had been shot at, and even though his vice-president, Aleksandr Rutskoi, strenuously advocated escalation.

It is difficult to imagine Yeltsin behaving the same way once he had committed to action in November–December 1994. His determination to respond in kind to provocation, to follow through with an initiated action, and to ignore parliamentary protests in the later period stood in sharp contrast to the ease and rapidity of decommitment in the earlier period. In the meantime, Yeltsin's perceived political authority and level of political defensiveness had changed markedly.

ALTERNATIVE EXPLANATIONS FOR THE INVASION OF CHECHNYA

Let us now return to an exclusive focus on the invasion of Chechnya and consider several alternative explanations for that specific decision. To the extent that such explanations prove deficient, they increase the persuasiveness of my preferred, political explanation. The scholarly and journalistic treatment of the decision offers a range of interpretations. Some of these treat the outcome as largely inevitable, given Dudaev's unwillingness to compromise on a matter of fundamental Russian interest. Others view the outcome as far from inevitable and as largely a reflection of Yeltsin's combative personality. In between stand those who view the outcome as the product of a process of incremental commitment in which uncertainty and unanticipated consequences accumulated to the point where the leadership unwittingly stumbled into a desperate situation.

Invariant State Interests

One might simply argue that reference to domestic politics is unnecessary, since vital state interests were in question. States do not tolerate secessions, and that is what Dudaev was trying to do. Whatever the condition of Yeltsin's political authority, he would have felt the desire or need to eliminate separatism. The territorial integrity of the state and the territorial reach of state power are "first principles" for decisionmakers, whatever their levels of political legitimacy or defensiveness.

While superficially appealing, this strikes me as an overgeneralization. For one thing, this theoretical perspective is inconsistent with the peaceful dissolution of the USSR in 1991 and of Czechoslovakia in 1993. For another, it cannot explain most of the previous three years of Moscow's relations with

Chechnya before the invasion. Yeltsin's initial response to the Chechen declaration of independence in November 1991 was as this theory would have
predicted: he called on Russian security forces to quell the secession. But his
parliament's response did not conform to such predictions; nor did Yeltsin's
quick reversal of his decision.

Thereafter, Chechnya remained on the back burner for more than two
years. Dudaev continued to proclaim his republic's independence from Russia and Moscow did not press the issue, instead striking deals with other
republics and regions that granted them varying degrees of autonomy short
of secession. Why did Moscow essentially ignore Dudaev for so long? Perhaps because the threat from a Chechen declaration of independence was not
perceived as particularly great. The international community refused to recognize it, and the Chechen authorities could not ally with other states to
affirm their independence from Moscow. Many elites in Moscow considered
the existing level of Chechen defiance to be quite tolerable, while others even
advocated divesting Russia of the burden of holding onto a poor, small, pe-
ripheral, rebellious Muslim region. And why did Chechnya come to the fore
of politics in 1994? Why did Moscow suddenly end its tolerance? Without
factoring in considerations other than invariable, "objective" state interests,
one cannot persuasively answer these questions. Whether the Chechnya situation was tolerable or threatening depended ultimately on subjective considerations: one's vision of Russia and, in the case of the top leaders, the extent
to which one's political authority was hostage to an articulated vision.

Incremental Engagement

From this perspective, the Russian leadership was incrementally "sucked into"
an ever-deepening commitment in Chechnya. Whereas the "invariant state interests" perspective eliminates contingency, the incrementalist raises contingency to a high level.

According to this viewpoint, the following facts are salient. Moscow had
already (at the beginning of 1994) engaged Dudaev in intensive negotiations
as part of a larger effort to develop treaty relations with the most autonomy-
seeking ethnic republics. However, in contrast to the government of Tatarstan, Dudaev was unwilling to accept maximal autonomy within Russia. The
negotiations lasted for about six months, at which time Moscow had the option of dropping the issue or of escalating the pressure. Moscow chose to help
arm and supply the resistance to Dudaev and to engage in covert operations
in an attempt to topple him – but to deny involvement if the covert operations became public. These operations almost succeeded in November 1994

but then suddenly failed at the end of that month. At that point again, Yeltsin could have dropped the issue. But the media in Moscow seized upon the issue and publicized Russian military involvement in the Chechen resistance. This publicity challenged the government to demonstrate that it could finish a job it had started and could avoid defeat at the hands of a secessionist force.

This interpretation cannot explain why, after the failure of negotiations in summer 1994, Moscow decided to escalate. What prevented Moscow from returning the issue to the back burner, where it had stood throughout 1992–1993? Why could Moscow not have continued to live with Dudaev's criminal challenges – as long as he did not engage in frontal assaults against Russian vital interests, such as sabotage of the oil pipeline or pogroms against ethnic Russian citizens of Chechnya? The argument that Chechnya had become the center of a vast criminal underworld – running arms and drugs, hijacking trains, and stealing oil and gas – may have weighed on the minds of Russian decisionmakers, all the more so because the incidence of such crimes had grown during 1991–1994. It is plausible that the growth and spread of Chechnya's intrusion on Russian economic and social interests raised the cost to Russian decisionmakers of temporizing. But it would still need to be demonstrated that the decisionmakers considered it urgent to end those challenges as soon as possible, rather than to live with and contain them or to blunt them by means that stopped short of invasion.

Similarly, after the defeat of covert operations, it is difficult to believe that the media provoked Yeltsin and his associates to do what they were otherwise disinclined to do. They could have disengaged and tried to contain the Chechnya problem; they could have blockaded the region; they could have attempted further covert operations, including perhaps further efforts to assassinate Dudaev; they could have stepped up their efforts to bolster the political opposition in anticipation of Chechen elections scheduled for October 1995. Instead, they chose to invade. Rather than blame publicity, anger, or embarrassment for their decision, I am more inclined to seek an explanation that accounts for the entire, year-long pattern of events. And while the testimony of one decisionmaker cannot necessarily be taken as definitive, it is noteworthy that Deputy Premier Nikolai Yegorov, who was Minister for Nationalities and Regional Affairs and one of the hardliners urging Yeltsin to invade, commented privately that "we now need a small victorious war, as in Haiti. We must raise the president's rating."[21]

---

[21] Valery Tishkov, *Ethnicity, Nationalism, and Conflict*, p. 218. Tishkov, an advisor to Yeltsin on nationalities issues, believes that "[t]he Chechnya crisis could have been resolved without using the army by various means and methods. Such possibilities continued to exist right up

Personality: The Need for Struggle

According to this interpretation, the invasion of Chechnya was simply a re-flection of Yeltsin's personality. From this perspective, Boris Nikolaevich is predisposed to attack problems and conquer them through a titanic struggle. Chechnya was simply one in a series of such campaigns.

Certainly there is truth in the claim that the invasion was consistent with a behavioral tendency that Yeltsin displayed throughout his life. As noted in Chapter 2, his first autobiography reveals a risk-seeker who was inclined to attack problems in traditional Bolshevik fashion. The invasion of Chechnya, by this accounting, was simply Yeltsin's issue of choice in 1994 and reflected his typical way of solving problems. The extreme variant of this explanation would treat Chechnya as Yeltsin's annual dose of intense struggle, which he needed to achieve psychodynamic catharsis; had there been no Chechnya, he would have invented one.

The problem with the interpretation just outlined is that it sells Yeltsin vastly short and ignores the other side of his personality and his record of achievement. He was far more complex than a mere recitation of his most ti-tanic struggles would suggest. His communist upbringing instilled in him a measure of prudence and pragmatism that constituted a competing set of pre-dispositions within his personality. His experience during 1989 interacting with democrats, and with Andrei Sakharov in particular, gave him a clearer sense of what he stood *for* to supplement his sense of what he was struggling *against*.[22] His maturation included growth of tolerance for ambiguity, which often checked or competed with his authoritarian dispositions. Indeed, we have already noted many aspects of Yeltsin's policy record that reflect pru-dence, pragmatism, tolerance of ambiguity, and conscious avoidance of a "struggle" mentality: his efforts at nation building in Russia, his stance toward the Near Abroad, and his attempts to nurture Russian relations with the West.

Moreover, the reality of Yeltsin's personalistic urge, and the memory of his titanic struggles against opponents, should not blind us to his ability to strike a multiplicity of leadership postures depending on the context in which he was operating and the political strength of his opponent or interlocutor. I count at least "six Yeltsins" in evidence since 1987. Three of them are egocentric and inflexible; three, to varying degrees, are accommodative and interactive.

---

until December 1994" (p. 226). Tishkov is also of the opinion that "the President's principal reason [for invading Chechnya] was to bolster his own declining popularity" (p. 218).

22 Timothy J. Colton, "Boris Yeltsin, Russia's all-thumbs democrat," in Timothy J. Colton and Robert C. Tucker (Eds.), *Patterns in Post-Soviet Leadership* (Boulder, CO: Westview, 1995), ch. 3.

In the first grouping is Yeltsin the *awesome antagonist,* who unleashed thunder on Ligachev, Gorbachev, the coup plotters, the Supreme Soviet, and Chechnya when his patience had run out or his relationship with them had reached the point of no return. There is also Yeltsin the *heroic mobilizer of the people,* who won almost 90 percent of the vote in the 1989 elections and who stood on the tank during the August 1991 coup. Then there is Yeltsin the *patriarch,* who treats his political dependents as his extended family – within which he demands obedience and dispenses absolution to those who have "sinned" – and who treats Russia as his patrimony within which he dispenses both sanctions and rewards.

In the second grouping of postures (wherein Yeltsin's autocratic tendencies are restrained or repressed) is Yeltsin the *hard but flexible bargainer,* who alternately implores, cajoles, threatens, and accommodates in order to strike deals, as in his annual struggles with the Duma over the budget. Then there is Yeltsin the *respectful, businesslike interlocutor,* a posture he adopted (when healthy and sober) in his dealings with heads of state of lesser powers over which Russia had little control: China, Eastern Europe, and small or mid-size powers elsewhere.[23] Finally, there is Yeltsin the *chummy pal,* the posture he adopted when dealing with heads of state of the G-7 nations ("my friend" Bill, Helmut, and even Ryu).

Undeniably, Yeltsin's personality played a role in his decisionmaking. Specifically, with respect to 1994, Yeltsin's sensitivity to slight made him less willing to negotiate a compromise with Dudaev. President Shaimiev of Tatarstan related the following to Valery Tishkov:

"While visiting Tatarstan in March 1994, Yeltsin told me that, in spite of not all at the Security Council agreeing with him, he was ready for talks with Dudayev on the Tatarstan model. But then suddenly the press reported (probably it was done deliberately) that Dudayev was speaking negatively of him." Apparently from that moment on, Yeltsin (undoubtedly under the influence of aides and some members of the government who were nursing the presidential ego) crossed Dudayev off the list of those with whom he could somehow communicate.[24]

Nonetheless, negotiation of a compromise is one thing; invasion is another. There were many intermediate alternatives. That Yeltsin chose the most extreme variant in December 1994 cannot be explained with reference to his personality alone.

---

[23] A subcategory of this might be *awed interlocutor,* evident in his earlier behavior when meeting with Patriarch Aleksi; for examples, see Kostikov, *Roman,* pp. 134, 240.

[24] Tishkov, *Ethnicity, Nationalism, and Conflict,* p. 187.

Power versus Authority

Still another alternative to my political interpretation would contest the extent to which Yeltsin felt himself to be politically on the defensive in 1994. We know that relations between parliament and executive during that year were far more stable than they had been during the year preceding adoption of the December 1993 Constitution, which provided for a strong presidency and a weak legislature and which formally shielded the president against easy impeachment. If Yeltsin believed in the reliability and durability of these formal arrangements, then he should not have felt himself exceptionally on the political defensive and could have faced Chechnya with a lower sense of urgency. Presumably, he could have reacted differently to the failure of negotiations with Dudaev and/or the failure of covert operations. He was in an "objectively" strong position.

This argument assumes that politics in weakly institutionalized regimes works in roughly the same way as politics in strongly institutionalized regimes. I would vigorously contest that assumption. Politics in Moscow, both Soviet and post-Soviet, was marked by unusually large measures of uncertainty about the tenure of leaders in office. Leaders constantly worried about how to insure themselves against premature political demise. In contrast to leaders in more strongly institutionalized (or constitutionalized) regimes who may seek only "minimal winning coalitions" on policy, both Soviet and post-Soviet leaders felt the need to substantially *over*insure themselves. This may explain why they all embraced programs that promised a great deal to almost everybody and hence proved impossible to fulfill. In the presence of dashed promises, the insecurity of tenure looms still larger and the leader becomes ever more sensitive to a growingly hostile or skeptical climate of opinion within the political establishment. The leader's time horizons become shorter and his threshold for risk-taking declines. As we have seen in Chapter 8, the memoir evidence supports such an interpretation of Yeltsin's mood in 1994. Even though he (unlike his predecessors) had been elected to a fixed term of office, he, like they, could never take his political security for granted. He feared extraconstitutional acts by elite actors as well as public opinion polls showing his popularity plummeting. Having based his relations with military commanders on personalistic ties, he could not take for granted their loyalty to a procedurally correct, constitutional order. Yeltsin might still have had the power, but he was losing authority – and he knew it.

A political explanation does not deny the role of personality, incremental engagement, and the magnitude of threats to state interests in decisionmakers' choices. Rather, it treats these as insufficient to explain the timing and outcome of this case or to explain variation among analogous cases. It argues that an intervening political variable – the condition of authority maintenance – may make the difference between the choice of militarized versus nonmilitarized responses to threats against state interests. For leaders on the political defensive often overreact to challenges.[25]

---

[25] Boris Yeltsin is not fond of this interpretation. In his latest memoir, he delicately expresses his dissent: "Some have claimed that I aggravated the Chechen situation in order to strengthen my own authority and make the presidential regime more brutal. But that's nonsense, total delirium!" (Boris Yeltsin, *Midnight Diaries* [New York: Public Affairs, 2000], p. 58).

Yeltsin's Many Last Hurrahs

Yeltsin invaded Chechnya in part to recoup political authority. It proved instead to be an unmitigated disaster. One year later, the parliamentary elections of December 1995 yielded a Duma that was even more dominated by radical nationalists and communists than the earlier one had been. Yeltsin's popularity plummeted to unprecedented lows: the percentage of respondents (in a public opinion poll of January 1996) who would have chosen him that day for president was in the low single digits.[1] Presidential elections loomed in June 1996, and it remained unclear whether Yeltsin could recoup his authority with the electorate sufficiently to prevail in that election.

THE PRESIDENTIAL ELECTIONS OF 1996

Yeltsin had to decide what posture to strike in the presidential election campaign. Should he try to co-opt the constituents of his opponents by running on a patriotic, hardline platform? Or should he try to differentiate himself from his opponents by mobilizing moderate and anti-communist constituencies? Initially, Yeltsin was inclined to run on a nationalistic platform as defender of the integrity of the Russian state and nation. In March 1996, however, new advisors persuaded him to switch course. He replaced his old advisory team and decided to present himself as the candidate of peace, order, stability, and progress. He decided to depict his main opponent in the election, Gennadii Ziuganov, as a totalitarian restorationist and himself as the savior of the nation from a return to Stalinism. He had killed communism and now

---

[1] *Vecherniaia Moskva,* January 24, 1996, p. 1, reports the results of a reliable opinion poll that placed Yeltsin in sixth place among prospective candidates, with 4% of respondents.

he would ensure that it stayed dead. He promised to end the war in Chechnya and opened negotiations during the election campaign itself. He used his control of governmental resources, and the support of business tycoons, to dominate the airwaves and smear his opponents. He violated campaign finance laws with impunity. He co-opted the moderate nationalist electorate by drawing General Aleksandr Lebed' into his governmental team before the second-round runoff against Ziuganov. He worked with international organizations on the timing of announcements of economic assistance to Russia. It was a brilliant and successful strategy, albeit one that was riddled with procedural violations of electoral law. As a result, Yeltsin won the election handily.[2]

In 1989–1991, Yeltsin had successfully played a polarizing political game, outbidding Gorbachev at every turn for the energies, votes, and approval of anti-establishment forces. In 1996 he also played a polarizing game, but of a different sort. He successfully defined the campaign as a choice between steady, peaceful "progress" and violent totalitarian restoration. To the extent that media manipulations allowed him to imprint this choice in the mind of the average voter, he was able to appeal to both the radical, anti-communist voters and the moderate, "median" voters who – however much alienated by Yeltsin's policies – feared totalitarian restoration more than they feared a continuation of the status quo. Whereas Yeltsin had helped to bring down communism in 1989–1991 by playing to the most revolutionary forces in society, he defended his position of power in 1996 by dominating the moderate middle of the political spectrum.

Unlike his predecessors, Yeltsin had recouped political authority. He was able to do so only because the electoral system provided a public channel for the revalidation of authority. These channels differed fundamentally from the political structures within which his predecessors had exercised leadership. Gorbachev could have gone this route in 1989 but, by the time he realized how fragile his program had become in the face of centrifugal forces, he lacked the self-confidence to test his authority by organizing a public presidential election.

Having rebuilt his shattered authority, Yeltsin faced a four-year term during which he would be expected to deliver on that promise of a stable and brighter future. In domestic policy, he stood for both stability and marked progress toward a more prosperous future; in foreign affairs, he stood both for the defense of Russia's interests as a "great power" and for cooperation with

---

[2] This summary of the presidential campaign is based on Michael McFaul, *Russia's 1996 Presidential Election: The End of Polarized Politics* (Stanford, CA: Hoover Institution, 1997).

the West. In order to deliver on the mandate of his reelection, Yeltsin had to continue managing the contradictions between his policies and the tensions in the system he had built – and to do so, this time, with better results.

But he had to do so in a much weakened physical condition. In 1995 he suffered a heart attack; several more heart seizures followed in July 1996. In November 1996, he underwent a quintuple bypass operation on his heart, followed by a lengthy bout with pneumonia. He was not able to function consistently again until February 1997. Nor would he ever be consistently healthy again. During the years leading up to his voluntary resignation on December 31, 1999, Yeltsin periodically was hospitalized with bronchitis, pneumonia, or heart troubles. He was never really healthy, but he was periodically functional. And during those periods of functionality he sought to advance the program for which he stood while ensuring that his personal grip on power was firmly maintained.

In retrospect, watching Yeltsin simultaneously pursue his contradictory goals made for high drama – with moments of tragedy, moments of heroism, and many elements of farce. Yeltsin had many "last hurrahs" as well as many embarrassments, but in the end, he had the last laugh.

THE CHANGING MEANING OF "REFORM"

After the "loans for shares" program of 1995, many sectors of the Russian economy were dominated by some 15–20 extraordinarily wealthy men who controlled the largest "financial-industrial groups" and their associated banks.[3] Close ties with high governmental officials allowed these men to siphon off huge sums from the state, including grants and loans from international organizations. Some of the names of these plutocrats are familiar to readers of Western newspapers: Boris Berezovskii, Vladimir Gusinskii, Vladimir Potanin, Pyotr Aven, Mikhail Khodorkovskii, and Rem Vyakhirev, to mention but a few. This new, crony-capitalist economy reflected a symbiosis of state and private interests that effectively re-monopolized key sectors of the economy. Some of these so-called oligarchs, in return for having bankrolled Yeltsin during the presidential election, received cabinet-level positions in Yeltsin's government. A good case has been made that the access some of these men (especially Boris Berezovskii) enjoyed during 1994–1999

---

[3] For a detailed overview, see Juliet Johnson, "Russia's emerging financial–industrial groups," *Post-Soviet Affairs*, vol. 13, no. 4 (October–December 1997).

corrupted Yeltsin's family and left him forced to choose between tolerating the corruption or cracking down on his own family.[4]

Yeltsin's government and circle of influence also included self-proclaimed "reformers" whose stated goals were to fight corruption, bolster tax collection, marketize the economy, restructure industry, and foster competition within re-monopolized sectors.[5] The men associated with this label included Yegor Gaidar, Boris Fyodorov, Anatolii Chubais, Sergei Kirienko, Boris Nemtsov, and others. Prime Minister Viktor Chernomyrdin, until he was fired in 1998, floated between the camps. Yeltsin consciously stood above the two main factions within his presidential and governmental "courts." He shifted back and forth between them and played them off against each other, reserving for himself the role of "ultimate arbiter." Both factions wanted Russia to remain open to the West, not least because the interests of both factions required continuing loans from the IMF and World Bank. Hence, they united in opposition to isolationist and revanchist forces within the parliament. But when these forces were weak or irrelevant to the circumstances of the moment, the "oligarchs" and "reformers" were, more often than not, at each other's throats.[6]

As a result of this new constellation of political forces, "radical reform" came to assume a new meaning. In 1992–1994, during Yeltsin's stage of ascendancy, it stood for a breakthrough into a new system. In 1996–1997, however, Yeltsin redefined his program to emphasize incremental progress within the contours of the new system he had constructed. In this context, "radical reform" meant specific policy measures – legalization of land ownership, improved tax collection, reduced corruption, budgetary restraint, stabilization of the ruble's exchange rate – that seemed to meet the requirements for IMF loans and that sometimes (but not always) ran counter to the entrenched material interests of the oligarchs. Because both the oligarchs and the reformers

---

[4] For the best demonstration of this process of enmeshment, see Peter Reddaway and Dmitri Glinski, *The Tragedy of Russia's Reforms: Market Bolshevism against Democracy* (Washington, DC: U.S. Institute of Peace, 2000), ch. 8.

[5] I place the word "reformers" in quotation marks because some of them allegedly used their power just to feather their own nests at the expense of the plutocrats and were not interested in reducing corruption or de-monopolizing the economy. "Oligarchs" is the term that the "reformers" applied to the plutocrats as a group. For the most forceful statement of this perspective, which targets Anatolii Chubais as the leading wolf in reformer's clothing, see Janine Wedel, *Collision and Collusion: The Strange Case of Western Aid to Eastern Europe* (New York: St. Martin's, 1998).

[6] I am grateful for this insight to Leonid Kil, a doctoral candidate in UC Berkeley's Department of Political Science.

favored IMF subsidies, one observer has even gone so far as to conclude that differences among them were staged in order to manipulate audiences in the international arena.[7]

Given the entrenchment of the oligarchs and their connection both with government officials and with organized criminal elements, reformist measures were much less likely to reshape the economic order than had the macroeconomic stabilization programs of 1992 and the privatization programs of 1992–1995. This led observers to treat Yeltsin's second term in office as principally a farce. Much as Brezhnev during his last six years in power had used progressive rhetoric while presiding over growing stagnation, so Yeltsin has been depicted as cynically mouthing all the right words while doing nothing to try to change the actual situation.[8]

While we cannot know for sure just what was on Yeltsin's mind, it is unlikely that he thought of his actions in this way. As discussed in Chapter 2, Yeltsin had always lived his life on the edge, had always been a risk-*seeker,* possessed a sense of his own predestination to lead his country toward the promised land,[9] detested Brezhnev's period of stagnation, and loathed Gorbachev's "half-measures." He was unlikely to have settled for simply hanging onto power and presiding over systemic stagnation and personal decrepitude. True, he was tired and unhealthy in his last years. But he had also been tired and ill when he decided to run for a second term as president. Nor was he in it for the money; personal material possessions seem never to have motivated this man. In his own mind, and to judge by the rhetoric of his presidential campaign, he still viewed himself as both the guarantor against communist restoration and the guide to a progressive future.[10]

---

[7] See Jerry F. Hough, *The Logic of Economic Reform in Yeltsin's Russia* (Washington, DC: Brookings Institution, 2001).

[8] This too is a theme in Hough, *The Logic of Economic Reform,* as also in Reddaway and Glinski, *The Tragedy of Russia's Reforms.*

[9] Boris Yeltsin, *The Struggle for Russia,* trans. by Catherine A. Fitzpatrick (New York: Random House, 1994), pp. 84, 197; Boris Yeltsin, *Against the Grain: An Autobiography,* trans. by Michael Glenny (New York: Summit, 1990), p. 19. For additional examples by associates and observers, see Valentin Fyodorov, *Bez tsenzury: Yel'tsin* (Moscow: "Golos," 1995), p. 58, and Lev Sukhanov, *Tri goda s Yel'tsinym* (Riga: "Vaga," 1992), p. 225.

[10] For examples, see ITAR-TASS in English, March 6, 1996 (FBIS-SOV-96-045, p. 24); Moscow Russian Television Network, April 6, 1996 (FBIS-SOV-96-068, p. 22, 25, 26); *Rossiiskie vesti,* April 30, 1996 (FBIS-SOV-96-084, p. 26); Moscow Russian Public Television First Channel Network, May 19, 1996 (FBIS-SOV-96-098, p. 5). His self-image as guarantor against communist restoration is a repeated theme also in his last memoir (Boris Yeltsin, *Midnight Diaries* [New York, Public Affairs, 2000], pp. 17, 24, 187, 211–13, 218, 240, 268, 333). These memoirs are largely self-serving and cannot be used to validate claims about what happened and why. But, as with most documents of this sort, they can be useful for what they reveal about

This should not surprise us; leaders tend to develop a self-image and a vision of some sort. Yeltsin once viewed and presented himself as a great revolutionary and then as a great system builder. He was probably not aware of the limits of his ability to change the structure of interests after 1995. But he had campaigned for reelection on a platform of both stability and progress, albeit within the system that he had built. His pattern of observable behavior in 1997–1998 can be viewed as that of a confused but determined leader who was trying to deliver on that promise – but who had only a limited understanding of policy and a narrow repertoire of intuitive responses to frustration.

At the same time, Yeltsin was a political animal operating within a weakly institutionalized system. He could not assume that he was safe from removal from office just because he had revalidated his power in a public election. Nor could he assume that retirement would be a pleasant experience if he could still be prosecuted in court for crimes allegedly committed while president. Hence, during his heart surgery, he relinquished control over the "nuclear button" to Prime Minister Chernomyrdin. But one of his first acts after regaining consciousness was to retake control of that button and to reaffirm that an Acting President was no longer needed; another was to fire Aleksandr Lebed', his national security advisor. In sum, Yeltsin's entire second term was preoccupied both with the management of policy dilemmas and with the protection of his personal political security.

Following his exit from the hospital in early 1997 after a bout with pneumonia, the rest of Yeltsin's second term can be divided into two periods that are separated by the August 1998 financial crash. During the first period, Yeltsin pursued policies that balanced "forward movement" with stability. During the second period (September 1998 through December 1999), he focused principally on maintaining stability, largely conceded his ineffectuality at further reforming the system, and intensified the search for a personal exit strategy. In the wake of the financial crash, threats to his personal security escalated: threats of impeachment, forced retirement, and prosecution of him and his family for corruption. Yeltsin's exit strategy sought to maintain social stability while creating the political conditions that would ensure him a dignified retirement and immunity from prosecution.

underlying assumptions or perspectives of the author and about what he most wants to be remembered for. In addition, they can be taken at face value when they reveal facts that are unflattering to the author, as when Yeltsin revealed that he almost canceled the presidential elections and almost banned the Communist Party in 1996 (ibid., pp. 24–5) or that he became alcohol-dependent in 1994–1995 (ibid., pp. 318–19). Even though Yeltsin did not write this memoir (or earlier ones) himself, we have every reason to believe that his ghost-writer, Valentin Yumashev, was keenly attuned to how Yeltsin wanted himself depicted.

BALANCING STABILITY AND REFORM, FEBRUARY 1997–AUGUST 1998

During fall 1996, Yeltsin's incapacitation led prominent politicians to start positioning themselves for another presidential race. Aleksandr Lebed', Gennadii Ziuganov, and others spoke publicly as if the demise of the president were imminent. The political atmosphere seemed to recapitulate the extremist rhetoric of the first round of the 1996 presidential election. Thus, Lebed and Ziuganov publicly called upon Yeltsin to resign. Both of them spoke in apocalyptic terms about prospective labor unrest, mutiny in the armed forces, confrontation with Ukraine, and U.S. intentions vis-à-vis Russia.[11] Another would-be presidential aspirant, Moscow Mayor Yuri Luzhkov, joined the fray as well, making highly provocative declarations about Russia's rights in Crimea.[12] The cat was away and the mice did play, spurred by a combination of ambition and incentives built into the electoral system: the requirement of a new presidential election within 90 days after the death or incapacitation of the president.

When Yeltsin recovered from heart surgery and pneumonia, he came out swinging. He seemed determined to demonstrate that he was in charge and capable of energizing the system and overcoming sources of stagnation. At his annual State of the Federation speech to parliament on March 6, 1997, the BBC observer noted that "the president looked quite well and his voice was strong. He walked unaided and quite briskly to the lectern and delivered the address standing."[13] The speech was hard-hitting; it conceded a host of problems, declared that the "people's patience is at breaking point," and blamed corrupt, privileged "authorities" and "high-ranking officials" – indeed, everybody but himself – for the crisis. He announced that he was about to replace high-ranking governmental officials with "competent and energetic people." And he proclaimed that he was taking some of these matters under his personal control. Taxes needed to be collected, corruption attacked, privileges rescinded, pensions and wages paid on time, social services improved – a litany of formidable tasks.

---

[11] Moscow television stations NTV and RTR, August 5, 1996; *Izvestiia,* September 7, 1996; ITAR-TASS, September 9, October 1, and October 14, 1996; ORT (television), October 8, 1996; *Vecherniaia Moskva,* September 25, 1996; *Flag Rodiny,* October 5, 1996. Sources were located through a Lexis-Nexis Internet search.

[12] *Izvestiia,* October 3, 1996.

[13] "BBC Summary of World Broadcasts," March 7, 1997; a group of former Yeltsin advisors and governmental officials writes that the president's double recovery – first from heart surgery and then from pneumonia – "gave him an illusion of a return to former form" (Yu. M. Baturin, A. L. Il'in, V. F. Kadatskii, V. V. Kostikov, M. A. Krasnov, A. Ya. Livshits, K. F. Nikiforov, L. G. Pikhoia, and G. A. Satarov, *Epokha Yel'tsina: Ocherki politicheskoi istorii* [Moscow: Vagrius, 2001], p. 732).

As a link to his identity as a system builder, Yeltsin referred to many of these policy changes as "reform": tax reform; reforms to the pension system; reform of housing and municipal services; military reform; reforming the social sphere. But the solutions he proposed were largely within-system policy changes, and they were largely statements of aspiration, not strategies for overcoming the constraints on change presented by the existing configuration of bureaucratic, economic, and political power. The main strategy was to replace slothful officials ("[t]he fundamental causes of our problems lie here") and to "impose order." He ended his speech with the anodyne declaration: "together we shall introduce order – order in Russia, for Russia, for the sake of Russia."[14]

Within days, Yeltsin shook up the highest reaches of his government. He brought back Anatolii Chubais and brought in Boris Nemtsov, a reformist young governor of the Nizhnii Novgorod region; each man was given the title of "first deputy prime minister." He fired the minister of agriculture and the minister of energy, both of whom had been close to Prime Minister Chernoymrdin. He also replaced the minister of defense. Chubais and Nemtsov, in the name of radical "reform," began an assault on some of the oligarchs – though not on the oligarch (Vladimir Potanin) most closely allied with Chubais himself. Prime Minister Chernomyrdin, often viewed as a protector of the oligarchs because of his close ties to the energy–export lobby, was being counterbalanced by a powerful alliance of actors whose main goals did not include protecting Chernomyrdin's favored oligarchs.

The struggle continued throughout 1997 with gains for both sides. Yeltsin stood largely above the fray, allowing the contending forces to battle it out and playing them off against each other. This suited his purposes as ultimate arbiter, and it did not seem to be inhibiting economic progress, for 1997 was marked by a relatively stable economic situation and the first signs of an economic turnaround. Yet by late December, Prime Minister Chernomyrdin had reasserted his power within the government and had re-established himself as the main pacemaker of Russia's economic policy. He convinced Yeltsin to relieve Chubais and Nemtsov of their portfolios as minister of finance and minister of energy and fuel (respectively), even as they remained in the cabinet.

The growth statistics of 1997 were deceptive, however, and signs were accumulating of impending economic and political crises. Even in his unhealthy state, Yeltsin surely was aware that some oligarchs were claiming publicly to be more powerful than the political leadership. Nor could he have been oblivious to the fact that his rhetorical calls for increasing the autonomy of the

---

[14] Yeltsin later wrote of this speech: "It was time to bring order to the government and elsewhere. I would impose it. The government had proven that it was unable to work without being shouted at by the president" (Yeltsin, *Midnight Diaries*, p. 74).

state from the tycoons, to increase tax collection, and to effect a transition from "oligarchic capitalism" to something called "people's capitalism" were having little practical effect.[15] By March 1998, he must have known that the previous year's successes in paying wages had been reversed and that arrears were piling up again. He was certainly informed that worker protests were planned for April 9 and that communist and nationalist parties would try to use that day's events to build momentum toward the parliamentary elections of 1999 and presidential election of the year 2000. In fact, the Duma was planning a vote of "no confidence" in his government. The collapse of oil prices, along with the spread to Russian stock markets of the "Asian flu," only exacerbated economic woes and threatened to reverse progress toward an economic turnaround.

Yeltsin did not need to understand all the complexities; he needed only to sense a trend that held ominous economic and political implications. When younger and healthier, Yeltsin the decisionmaker had combined political intuition with complex calculation. Now that he was older and less healthy, the intuitive sense remained even as the calculative faculties declined. Yeltsin sensed during the first months of 1998 that things were no longer going as he had planned. In his State of the Federation address of February 17, 1998,[16] he acknowledged improvements in the rate of economic growth but reiterated many of the downbeat themes of his 1997 address, demanding that the government "put a stop to the rise in nonpayments" and warning ominously that "[i]f the government is unable to accomplish these strategic tasks, we shall have a different government."

Under analogous circumstances in the past, Yeltsin had typically kept his own counsel and, after a period of either despondency or calculated personal absence, returned with a plan to re-seize the initiative. That is what happened in March 1998. Out of public view for many weeks,[17] he returned with the surprise announcement that he was dismissing the top governmental figures charged with economic administration: Chubais; Anatolii Kulikov, head of the tax police; and, most strikingly, Viktor Chernomyrdin himself, the veteran prime minister. With such an abrupt and complete housecleaning, Yeltsin presumably hoped to demonstrate that he was still in charge and to be feared; presumably he hoped also to build a new team and new policies that were geared toward breaking the stalemate in economic administration and

---

[15] See his speech of September 24, 1997, in which he called for the transfer of state revenues to a soon-to-be-established state bank as a means of reducing the dependence of the state on the tycoons (*Rossiiskie vesti*, September 25, 1997).

[16] BBC Worldwide Monitoring, Former Soviet Union – Political, February 17, 1998, Internet edition, "Yeltsin warns government must reduce public indebtedness or be replaced."

[17] According to *The New York Times*, March 24, 1998.

delivering on his claim of pushing history forward with more vigorous "reformist" policies. Or at least that is the image he tried to project in public.[18]

To replace Chernomyrdin, Yeltsin tapped Sergei Kirienko, the deputy minister of fuel and energy. Kirienko had several traits to recommend him: he was professional, knowledgeable about Russia's macroeconomic situation, forthright, pragmatic, and willing to claim that he knew what was needed to rescue the economy from renewed stagnation.[19] Moreover, Kirienko was young (only 36 years old), had been successful in building his own business (thus he understood both the old and the new systems), and was from the provinces (thus, not yet under the thumb of any of the Moscow-based oligarchs). Kirienko was a protégé of First Deputy Prime Minister Nemtsov but still too young and lacking in stature to threaten the president politically; hence, he was likely to prove both capable and politically deferential. In Kirienko, Yeltsin appeared to have found an intelligent, loyal, energetic, professional technocrat who was willing and ready to play by the political rules set by the president and capable of perhaps attaining positive economic results. He could instill fresh energy into an increasingly stagnant governing regime and possibly prepare it for the major political tests of 1999–2000.[20] And he could do all this without pretending to force the Russian president into early retirement. Thus, Yeltsin made a choice that seemed simultaneously to advance his political power and economic policy goals. The choice certainly appeared to fit with his electoral mandate to combine economic progress with social stability.

Moreover, Yeltsin was prepared to run genuine political risks in order to ensure Kirienko's ratification by the Duma. It took him a full month to prevail – and then only on the third and final vote. Yeltsin alternately threatened, cajoled, sweet-talked, co-opted, and bribed members of the parliament to comply with his choice. After losing on the first two votes, he could have proposed an alternate candidate. But he decided instead to play a game of brinksmanship, daring the Duma to reject his candidate a third time and thereby bring about its dissolution and early parliamentary elections. This was as much a threat to Yeltsin as it was to the Duma, for the Russian president – scorned again in popularity polls – had to fear that new elections would return a parliament still more hostile than the present one. Nonetheless, Yeltsin stuck with Kirienko, made very few policy or personnel concessions to the opposition in the Duma, and ultimately prevailed. Kirienko formed a cabinet of

---

[18] Baturin et al. (*Epokha,* pp. 732, 795) argue that Yeltsin was motivated by a sense of mission, wanting to go down in history as a successful reformer.

[19] On these points, see D. Gornostaev in *Nezavisimaia gazeta,* March 27, 1998, pp. 1–2; see also Yeltsin's discussion of Kirienko in *Midnight Diaries,* pp. 103–14.

[20] For further evidence on these points, see Ye. Grigorieva in *Nezavisimaia gazeta,* April 8, 1998, pp. 1, 3.

economic officials who were primarily young technocrats drawn largely from the provinces. Yeltsin's "coup" of March–April 1998 had been successful. He had reasserted and enhanced his power, re-seized the initiative, and installed a government that held hope of breaking through some of the constraints on economic progress.

Little did Yeltsin know, however, that he had only bought himself a few months' respite.

BALANCING STABILITY AND PERSONAL POWER: AUGUST 1998–DECEMBER 1999

In the first years of his second term as president, Yeltsin sought to combine political stability, personal power, and economic progress. In the last year and a half before his resignation, he tried to ensure stability and personal power while seeking immunity from prosecution after his retirement from office. This search for personal protection dovetailed with Yeltsin's concern for social stability. If a "social explosion" occurred, it might well sweep Yeltsin away. The search for immunity also dovetailed with his self-image as guarantor against communist restoration, for no guarantee of immunity would be worth the paper on which it was written if the communists won the parliamentary and presidential elections of 1999–2000. What Yeltsin dropped from his priorities during this period was the earlier focus on economic progress. This omission was a circumstantial product of the August 1998 financial crash, which displayed the hollowness of the economic system Yeltsin had created and which discredited the "oligarchs" and "radical reformers" alike. Having no idea how to correct the economic situation, Yeltsin concentrated on finding a governmental team that would re-create some modicum of economic and political stability while protecting him from the impeachment threats and charges of corruption that were accumulating around him.[21]

Yeltsin's renewed focus on "stability" led him to fire Kirienko after the August financial crisis and to call back Chernomyrdin.[22] Twice, Yeltsin nominated Chernomyrdin to be prime minister; twice, the Duma rejected the

---

[21] Baturin et al. (*Epokha*, p. 778) argue that, whereas Yeltsin had been driven by a reformist mission before August 1998, thereafter he was dedicated fully to the search for a successor.

[22] In *Midnight Diaries* (pp. 176, 181) Yeltsin claims that he saw in Chernomyrdin a "heavyweight" who could engineer the compromises that would stabilize the situation. Yeltsin had argued that a younger generation was needed to push history forward when he explained his firing of the cabinet in March 1998 and its replacement with a new team of young reformers, led by 36-year-old Sergei Kirienko (*Komsomol'skaia pravda*, April 1, 1998). When this renewed, "breakthrough" strategy led instead to the crash of the ruble in August 1998, Yeltsin tried to go back to an emphasis on social stability. His nomination of Chernomyrdin for this

nomination. Earlier in 1998, when he nominated Kirienko, Yeltsin had been willing to play brinksmanship with the Duma; this time, he lost his nerve. For the third nomination, he begrudgingly proposed Foreign Minister Yevgenii Primakov, whose professionalism gave him an aura of competence to handle the job, whose efforts to assert Russia's "national interests" made him acceptable to the nationalists in the Duma, and whose background in the Communist Party (along with his experience in the security services) made him acceptable to many communist parliamentarians.[23]

Yeltsin's nomination of Primakov – and the Duma's enthusiastic approval – meant that the Russian president had lost the political initiative. But at least Primakov might be able to figure out some way to stabilize the reeling financial system, and he might use his contacts abroad to help Russia secure continuing Western assistance. Equally important, Primakov might prove capable of inducing Yeltsin's antagonists in the Duma to withdraw their impeachment resolutions, end their corruption investigations against Yeltsin's family, and grant the Russian president blanket immunity from prosecution after his retirement.

Primakov labored for more than half a year as prime minister, attempting with some success to stabilize the domestic situation but without much progress toward guaranteeing Yeltsin's political security. The political temperature rose both at home and abroad. NATO bombed Serbia, despite Russia's objections, shortly after NATO had admitted three East European states to membership – also despite Russia's displeasure. Yeltsin's economic program at home was in shambles, his relations with the West were at a low point, and his personal political security was again threatened. How would he deal with the fact that his authority had plummeted ever further and his power was increasingly under threat?

In April 1999, Yeltsin delivered his annual State of the Federation address. This was a short, disjointed, somewhat incoherent, and decidedly defensive statement.[24] He began by denying the importance of the foreign policy setbacks. He attempted to dismiss them in a few sentences, making a virtue of necessity and stressing instead his role as a beacon of stability:

purpose squares with the pattern of discussion in his 1994 memoir (*The Struggle*, pp. 126–7, 155, 168, 169, 200–1, 222–3), where young cadres are praised for their contributions to transformative goals while "experienced" cadres are praised (and recruited) for their contributions to consolidative goals: efficiency and the maintenance of social stability.

[23] One can well understand Primakov's appeal to a wide range of oppositional and establishment forces by reading his memoir (Yevgenii Primakov, *Gody v bol'shoi politike* [Moscow: Sovershenno sekretno, 1999]).

[24] East European Press Service, Russian Political Monitor, April 2, 1999, Internet edition, "Text of Yeltsin's address to the federal assembly."

Russia has made its choice. We will not allow anybody to drag us into an armed conflict. Preventing schisms and discord within the country is our number one task. Of course Russians worry about Yugoslavia, but they worry about their own country even more. Our prestige in the international arena depends on how effectively we solve our own problems.

What really matters, he argued, is the maintenance of order, stability, and security for all, himself included: "order in the corridors of power is needed, as is consent and stability in the economy and the social sphere." But some people were seeking to undermine these conditions: "Some irresponsible and nervous statements are being made. People in the corridors of power are not hiding their irritation with one another."

Yeltsin then tried to diminish the claim that August 1998 had proven the complete bankruptcy of his leadership. But he was clearly on the defensive about this: "August 17 is the only thing that everybody chooses to remember. But there was July before that, wasn't there? A hot month, when the government adopted an anti-crisis program and the International Monetary Fund resolved to give us the first installment of the loan." Then he shifted the blame, suggesting that the August crash might have been averted had the Duma itself acted more responsibly: "The Duma rejected the [anti-crisis] program, and neither Kirienko's government nor I were able to defend it. The Duma sent a bad signal to investors."

Having disclaimed personal responsibility, Yeltsin then shifted to Primakov the responsibility for resolving the current dilemma: "Primakov's government has to take ... decisive steps now." Those steps could not include ceding the initiative to revanchist policymakers. Indeed, Yeltsin resurrected the revanchist spectre with which he had ridden to victory in the 1996 presidential election. He spoke of "enemies of reform" whose "ideas are old," who embrace a "program of revenge," and who "are still calling for directives and plans in the economy, for censorship in media, and for another round of the Cold War and refusal to integrate into the global economy ...." He declared that "another round of centralization would only wreck fragile market institutions." He averred that "[w]e have to prevent the opposition from acting without regard for the law" and from pushing the "swinging pendulum ... into the danger zone."

After resurrecting this binary opposition between the forces of good and evil, Yeltsin declared that he would entertain no amendments to the Constitution before new elections to the Duma were held in December 1999. He thereby undercut a process that Primakov was trying to orchestrate behind the scenes: constitutional amendments to reduce the powers of the presidency in exchange for an end to impeachment proceedings and a grant of immunity to the president. Moreover, Yeltsin ominously proceeded to predict the results of the December parliamentary elections, declaring that a new, younger political elite would assume power to lead the country forward: "the new Duma will consist of decent and uncorrupt people – not professional patriots but patriotic professionals .... Let's give them a chance to decide for themselves whether or not amendments [to the Constitution] are needed." Such a prediction might have been the rhetoric of a democratic politician seeking to create a bandwagon effect. More likely, they were the statements of a leader who was trying to intimidate both the opposition and regional governors by implying that he might rig the elections.

Primakov was on notice: stabilize the economic situation, deliver Western assistance, and get the parliament to rescind its impeachment resolutions. Moreover, he had to do so without promising constitutional amendments to the parliamentary opposition. Primakov was given little time to deliver and probably could not have done so in any case. A familiar pattern therefore repeated itself: very shortly after his March 1997 State of the Federation speech, Yeltsin had reshuffled the government. In the month following his February 1998 speech, he had fired Chernomyrdin. True to form, a month after his April 1999 address, Yeltsin fired Primakov. Whereas he had caved in to parliamentary opposition in September 1998 – when he had accepted Primakov rather than force a third vote on Chernomyrdin – he was now, more characteristically, ready to rumble. He nominated Sergei Stepashin, former head of the Interior Ministry, to replace Primakov. Yeltsin all but dared the Duma to defy him.

The rhetorical heat in Moscow intensified immediately. Outraged parliamentarians expressed their indignation at the firing of Primakov and vowed that Stepashin's nomination would never be ratified. Their rhetoric proved to be a poor predictor of their own behavior. By nominating Stepashin, who symbolized the security agencies, Yeltsin was signaling his possible willingness to resort to force or declare a state of emergency should the nomination fail on all three votes. He was clearly signaling that he would not back down on the third vote, as he had in September 1998. He would dissolve the Duma and force early parliamentary elections, which might or might not change the political balance within the Duma but could certainly deprive many incumbents of their seats and privileges. All this was in the spirit of his speech a month earlier, which must have added credibility to his threats. In the end he prevailed, intimidating the Duma into ratifying his nominee.[25]

[25] Circumstantial support for the proposition that Yeltsin was seeking, after August 1999, primarily to combine economic stabilization with personal political protection can be found in

Stepashin lasted but a few months. He labored valiantly at home and abroad to stabilize the economy and deliver Western economic assistance. But in August 1999, Yeltsin struck again, suddenly replacing Stepashin with an even more shadowy figure, Vladimir Putin, then a 46-year-old former KGB spy who was a seemingly loyal member of the national security establishment within Yeltsin's presidential circle. Yeltsin declared that Putin represented a new generation of leaders and would likely succeed Yeltsin as president when new elections were held in June 2000. A weary Duma narrowly ratified Putin's nomination on the first ballot on August 16, 1999. Why force early elections when the regularly scheduled elections were coming up within four months?

YELTSIN'S VERY LAST HURRAH

During summer 1999, the level of tension in southern Russia escalated rapidly. Armed incursions into neighboring Dagestan by militant Chechen forces threatened to destabilize that multi-ethnic (but largely Islamic) republic of the Russian Federation. Indeed, some Chechen leaders proclaimed their intention to establish an Islamic state within Dagestan. The Russian army, working with local police forces of Dagestan, tried to beat back these incursions. Then apartment buildings began to explode in Moscow, claiming the lives of some 300 Muscovites and terrorizing the city. We do not know who set those explosives. Was it the work of Chechen terrorists, seeking to demoralize the Russian people and to exact revenge for Russia's military reaction to the events in Dagestan? Or was this a provocation by Russia's national-security establishment, intended to create the political pretext for a renewed invasion of Chechnya?

Whatever the case, Yeltsin and Putin cited the explosions as rationales for reinvading Chechnya *en masse.* Perhaps this was a "normal," consensual reaction to provocation or setback in an area of vital interest. More likely, the second war in Chechnya was as "political" as the first. Putin embraced nationalist rhetoric and presented himself as the sponsor of the effort ("we will wipe them out in their outhouses"). A fledgling pro-government political coalition called "Unity" was quickly formed to compete in the parliamentary elections in December. There was little content to the party's program except patriotic (though not ethnically chauvinist) discourse, boilerplate statism, and revenge against the Chechen terrorists. The government unleashed a devastating and

---

Midnight Diaries, where Yeltsin interprets Primakov as in tacit alliance with nefarious forces to gain power and destroy presidential rule (pp. 202–5, 211–13, 218, 268) and where Yeltsin interprets Mayor Luzhkov's actions in analogous fashion (pp. 227, 229–31, 244, 290ff.).

relentless assault on Chechen guerrillas and civilians by Russian airpower, artillery, and ground troops.

The political strategy worked. Through a combination of electoral fraud and genuine appeal to a frustrated electorate that was seeking strong leadership, "Unity" garnered 23.8 percent of the party-list votes for the new Duma, largely at the expense of a coalition led by former prime minister Primakov and Moscow mayor Luzhkov. Yeltsin and Putin were elated. In a televised spot, Yeltsin congratulated Putin and excitedly praised the Russian people for their wisdom.[26]

The vote took place on December 19, 1999. In the days following, Yeltsin pondered the implications and reached the decision to resign. He announced it to a surprised nation in his New Year's Eve address. It was a brilliant stroke. He had been proclaiming for years that he would serve out his full term and be the first freely elected president of his country to turn over power peacefully to his successor. He had been predicting that the communists would not succeed him and that he would retire as the successful guarantor of the country against communist restoration, though he never made clear just how he intended to ensure this. Undoubtedly, Yeltsin's self-image as a state builder inclined him toward realizing this vision; ideally, he would have preferred to serve out his term. But after August 1998, a higher priority arose: that of guaranteeing his personal security – and that of his family – after retirement. The tug between the idealist goals and Yeltsin's personal security was real, but he was not about to sacrifice the latter in pursuit of the former.

The results of the parliamentary elections, together with public opinion polls showing that Putin's popularity was high and rising, shaped the timing of Yeltsin's resignation. By resigning at the end of December, Yeltsin forced new presidential elections within 90 days – a constitutional requirement. Putin's popularity would not likely plummet within three months. By contrast, waiting until June to hold elections might provide time for military setbacks to take place in Chechnya and for the electorate to reconsider its support for Putin. Moreover, Putin was more likely than any of his prime ministerial predecessors to pave the way for Yeltsin to live a secure and comfortable retirement.

Putin did not disappoint him. His first act as Acting President was to grant Boris Yeltsin lifetime immunity from prosecution. The scramble to succeed Yeltsin began, but the outcome looked to be a foregone conclusion. Yeltsin had had the last laugh. As things looked to him on the eve of the new millennium,

---

[26] ORT television carried their joint appearance from the Kremlin on Wednesday, December 22, 1999, three days after the Duma elections (Interfax, December 22, 1999).

he had outmaneuvered his opponents, secured his personal future, prevented communist restoration, built a new system, maintained the territorial unity of Russia, and sustained the vision of integrating Russia into the global capitalist economy. The cost to the country may have been enormous, for which he apologized in his resignation speech.[27] But the alternative, he continued to argue, would have been worse.

CONCLUSION

Yeltsin's second term as Russia's president looks, in retrospect, like a string of initiatives geared toward keeping political opponents and political allies continuously off-balance. This image, in turns, leads one easily to the conclusion that all Yeltsin was interested in was maintaining power. However, as I have argued throughout this book, that is a shortsighted way of thinking about politics, for politicians usually have more on their minds than just power maintenance. The temptation to conclude that power is all that matters is still greater when we observe leaders on the political defensive. They tend to pay more attention to shifting their political alliances or firing would-be rivals during that last stage than during their stage of ascendancy. It is worth recalling, for example, that Khrushchev launched continuous purges of high-level personnel throughout the third stage of his administration. Both Brezhnev and Gorbachev also mimicked this pattern. Yeltsin was no exception. It may be difficult to think back past the image of Yeltsin as a doddering old man engaged in Byzantine political maneuvers. But when we think of the length and breadth of his political strategies from 1985 to the present, we see a man who developed a series of ambitious policy programs on which he staked his political authority – and in which he presumably invested his political identity. By 1996, he was probably a spent force as a transformational leader.[28] Even so, he continued to try (when he had the energy) to combine a larger policy project with a strategy of undercutting actual and potential political rivals. Only after August 1998 did he strike the appearance of a leader whose almost sole concern was for his personal political security.

---

[27] For an English translation of the resignation speech, see Yeltsin, *Midnight Diaries*, pp. 386–7.
[28] For lengthy argumentation of this point, see Reddaway and Glinski, *The Tragedy of Russia's Reforms*, chs. 8–9.

Explaining Leaders' Choices, 1985–1999

The main purpose of this book has been to identify Gorbachev's and Yeltsin's evolving strategies for building, maintaining, and recouping their authority as leaders. In the present chapter, I turn from description and analysis to explanation. Why did Gorbachev and Yeltsin choose these strategies at each stage of their administrations? That these two men occupy center stage in the book should not lead us to assume that their personalities and personal beliefs were always the primary – much less, sole – determinants of their choices. Other factors delimited and shaped their behavior at given points in time: (1) the political organization of the regime and the interests that dominated within it; (2) the regime's ideological traditions and legitimizing credos; (3) the prevailing climate of opinion within the political establishment; (4) the process of political competition for power and authority among elite actors; (5) mobilized social forces within the country; and (6) direct and indirect pressures from abroad.

When Khrushchev and Brezhnev were in power, these factors were relatively limited, stable, and predictable. Politics was a private affair and was dominated by the political and organizational interests of the Party–State apparatus and the budgetary interests of the military–industrial complex. Marxism–Leninism's hostility to liberalism defined the limits of winnable political advocacy. Political competition for power and authority took place within the narrow confines dictated by the political organization and ideological anti-liberalism. Social forces within the country were dominated by the Party–State apparatus; they could affect indirectly the climate of opinion within the political elite but could not mobilize autonomously against that elite. Pressures from abroad could influence individual decisions and the

stability of political coalitions in Moscow.[1] But the influence of foreign governments on Soviet policy choices was limited by Soviet determination to avoid
dependency on global capitalism and to lead an alternative, autonomous
world system: the "socialist international division of labor" and the "world
communist movement."[2] It remains an open historical question as to whether
the trajectory of Soviet policies at home and abroad would have been different
had U.S. policies been different at key turning points in superpower relations.
But it is striking how much greater was the impact of direct and indirect
international pressures on Gorbachev and Yeltsin than on Khrushchev and
Brezhnev.

The influence of many of these factors grew dramatically as Gorbachev's
radical policies took effect. As traditional Soviet organization and ideology
crumbled, the influence of autonomous social forces, direct and indirect international pressures, new rules of political competition, and new political
actors rose sharply. This was a fluid field. The old constraints were not
immediately replaced by new constraints of a different kind. Social and international forces did not immediately rush in to replace Soviet ideology and
organization. Rather, the period from 1987–1993 was one in which many
things were possible. This is the point at which the personalities and beliefs
of Gorbachev and Yeltsin loom large in any explanation of choices – more so
than had been the case with Khrushchev and Brezhnev. For as the structures
of Soviet rule disintegrated, leaders had greater latitude to act as they wished.
Yet these two leaders also played major roles in causing those structures to
crumble in the first place.

Personality and individual beliefs played larger roles at some stages of administration than at others. Soviet organization and ideology, for example,
continued to shape Gorbachev's behavior in the early years of his administration. His personality and personal beliefs played a more decisive role in the
middle stage of his administration. Social forces and direct international pressures played a greater role in the last stage of his administration. Yeltsin exploited, encouraged, and selectively channeled those social forces to assist his
rise to power. Subsequently, Yeltsin's personality and personal beliefs shaped
the choices he made in response to domestic and international pressures

---

[1] See Jack Snyder, "International leverage on Soviet domestic change," *World Politics*, vol. 42,
no. 1 (October 1989), pp. 1–30. For tests of the impact of international events on turning
points in Soviet politics and policy during 1953–1966, see James Richter, *Khrushchev's Double
Bind* (Ithaca, NY: Cornell University Press, 1994).

[2] See Ken Jowitt, *The Leninist Approach to National Dependency* (Berkeley: University of California, Institute of International Studies, 1978).

during the second stage of his administration. By the third stage, however, Yeltsin largely caved in to accumulating interests at home and abroad, interests and pressures that he himself had previously encouraged.

Political competition was a constant during 1985–1999, even as its rules changed several times during those years. Thus, while pressures from domestic social forces and international actors grew as Soviet institutions and ideology crumbled, the impact of those pressures was filtered through a game of politics played by competitors with distinctive personalities and beliefs. In Chapter 9, I attempted to demonstrate how this political game influenced leaders' thresholds for lashing out at threats. In the present chapter, I discuss the extent to which personality, beliefs, politics, social forces, and international pressures may have influenced the *choice of political strategies* at each stage of the Gorbachev and Yeltsin administrations.

Such an exercise is necessarily more speculative than has been the analysis presented in the empirical chapters of this book. Weighing the relative impact of numerous causal influences requires more evidence than I have collected as well as different kinds of tests in order to rule out competing explanations. Absent that research, my judgments must remain far from conclusive. But it makes little sense to avoid making causal claims owing simply to their inconclusiveness. It makes more sense to build upon the evidence presented in this book – including comparisons among our four leaders – to enlarge our supply of credible hypotheses as to why things happened as they did.

GORBACHEV, 1985–1986

Similarities between the behavior of Gorbachev during the first stage of his administration and the behavior of Khrushchev and Brezhnev during their stages of struggle for succession alert us to organizational and ideological constraints on their choices. During the first stage of their administrations, both Khrushchev and Brezhnev built their authority by allying with relatively hardline constituencies (the Party *apparatchiki* and the military–industrial complex), even as they sponsored innovations to lead the country out of the morass into which it had fallen. Both men also worked vigorously to enlarge their political machines and to expand their patronage base within the Party–State apparatus. In all these respects, Gorbachev's strategy resembled the strategies of his major predecessors. Gorbachev deferred to the puritans and technocrats in most realms of domestic policy – and to the hardliners in much of foreign policy – during 1985–1986, even as he built his power base, raised some hard questions about Soviet foreign and defense policy, and began altering the language of politics to legitimize a forthcoming radicalization of policy at home and abroad.

In all three cases, the Party leader managed to occupy a political niche that combined the pursuit of dynamic new goals with the protection of cherished traditional values. Of course, the specific content of those amalgams varied, reflecting both the conditions at the time and the distinctive personalities and beliefs of the leaders in question. But the parallels are striking for what they tell us about the impact of the political and ideological context on choices during this first stage of their administrations. The "private" structure of political organization (which had not yet begun to crumble in 1985–1986), the dominant interests within the political establishment, the process of political competition, the dominant biases of the ideological heritage, and the climate of opinion at the time go farther to explain the political strategies of all three leaders than do their respective personalities or beliefs. At this stage, all three men were deferring to dominant interests and ideals within the establishment at the time. Within this context, Gorbachev (like Khrushchev) fashioned for himself an image as a responsible reformer; Brezhnev projected the image of an enlightened conservative.

GORBACHEV, 1987–1989

Once they had consolidated their power, built their authority, and emerged ascendant within the leadership, all three leaders changed direction – although to greatly varying degrees. All three of them came forth with comprehensive programs for progress at home and abroad, though Brezhnev's definition of "progress" (consistent with the climate of opinion within the Central Committee at the time) was not reformist. The contents of those programs differed greatly, but all were highly ambitious, optimistic, and forward-looking. Khrushchev and Gorbachev promised a "great leap forward" toward a utopian ideal, though they tapped into different strands of the utopian heritage.[3] Brezhnev abandoned both utopianism and reformism, but he did promise significant progress toward the reconciliation of numerous contradictory domestic and foreign policy ambitions. All three programs were touted as consistent with key elements of the Marxist–Leninist tradition.

We do not need to invoke personality to explain the fact that all three programs were ambitious. Rather, this similarity reflected the Soviet regime's

---

[3] On diverse utopian strands within the Marxist and Leninist heritages, see Stephen Hanson, *Time and Revolution* (Chapel Hill: University of North Carolina Press, 1998).

ideological heritage; Soviet political organization facilitated assertive leadership and generated the expectation that a leader, having consolidated power, would outline a program for comprehensive progress at home and abroad. The ideological heritage, in turn, fostered an expectation that the winner would provide dynamic and far-reaching leadership that would propel the country forward through large-scale campaigns. The "leading role of the Party" was enhanced and validated by the conduct of such campaigns. Soviet leadership of the world communist movement, combined with that country's great-power status, further reinforced the expectation of ambitious, demonstrative leadership at home and abroad.

More idiosyncratic factors must be invoked, however, to explain differences in the contents of these comprehensive programs. For example, Gorbachev's program built on the beliefs he had developed as a reform communist in the two decades preceding his selection as general secretary (see Chapter 2). A hypothetical "Ligachev program" would have looked quite different. Khrushchev's program reflected his eagerness to realize many elements of Marx's social vision and of Lenin's political vision (as propounded in Lenin's essay, "State and Revolution"). Brezhnev's program reflected his (and his cohorts') disillusion with Khrushchevian utopianism as well as his political allies' disillusion with reformism.

But there was another difference between Khrushchev's and Brezhnev's stage of ascendancy, on the one hand, and Gorbachev's, on the other. Both Khrushchev and Brezhnev sponsored comprehensive programs that *selectively reincorporated* elements of the programs of their defeated, reformist political rivals. Having denounced Malenkov's emphasis on light industry and chemicals along with Malenkov's sense of urgency about forging a détente relationship with the United States, Khrushchev incorporated both of these goals into his program of 1959–1960 even as he also continued to pursue the goals he had endorsed during the succession struggle. Similarly, having conducted the succession struggle by supporting heavy industry and a militant posture toward the West, Brezhnev incorporated a program for light industry, as well as a major program for détente, into his policy advocacy of 1970–1971 even as he continued to pursue traditional goals.

Selective reincorporation may have been the product of a felt need to expand one's coalition in light of the political insecurity faced even by an ascendant Party leader in a system that promised no fixed term in office and that provided dismal retirement prospects.[4] Whatever the precise motive, it had

---

[4] Parliamentary regimes provide no fixed term of office. But a prime minister can lose a reelection bid and still hope to make a political comeback later on – or pursue a lucrative career

the effect of making the leader's program still more ambitious by promising a great deal to almost all audiences.

Notably, Gorbachev did not engage in selective reincorporation. When faced with the failure of "acceleration" (*uskorenie*) to improve economic performance in 1985–1986 and when faced with continued deadlock in East–West relations, Gorbachev did not propose a comprehensive program based on a mix of "acceleration" and reform, hardline foreign policies and selective concessions. Instead, he abandoned both "acceleration" and traditionalist foreign policies and proposed a comprehensively radicalized program. True, as we saw in Chapters 5 and 6, Gorbachev increasingly tried to hold the line against too rapid or far-reaching a radicalization of domestic policy. But this only means that Gorbachev feared that excessive radicalism could prove counterproductive. It is also true that Gorbachev railed consistently against a vision of the future that was purely market capitalist or *liberal* democratic; but this only means that he was presenting himself throughout his years in office as neither a capitalist nor a liberal democrat. Relative to what he proposed in 1985–1986, Gorbachev's radical programs of 1987–1988, though elaborated with some tactical caution, yielded relatively little to the perspectives of traditionalists within the regime, which is why many conservatives broke with him politically in 1988–1989. He refused to yield to the temptation, in 1987–1988, to seek political security in a compromising, inclusive program. Instead, he yielded to the conclusion that comprehensive progress toward a New Deal at home and abroad was impossible without a transformation of the political system. If one admires Gorbachev's program, one could argue that this was part of his "greatness" as a transformational leader.

The patterns just outlined suggest the following generalizations. The *fact* of Gorbachev's proposing a comprehensive and ambitious program for progress toward an idealized future should not be ascribed principally to his unique personality or beliefs, because the ideology and organization of the regime would have pushed any leader in the direction of an idealized comprehensive program. But the *specific content* of Gorbachev's program, and its comprehensive radicalism at home and abroad, certainly can be ascribed to the man's personality and personal beliefs. Nor do other candidates for causal status make a strong case. Gorbachev's radical policies were not a consensual

---

in the private sector or otherwise maintain his social status. A deposed Soviet leader enjoyed no such opportunities, vanished from top-level political life and publicity, and faced the possibility of criminal prosecution. This was not a "law" of communist regime politics, for some leaders have made comebacks in Eastern Europe and China. But no Soviet Politburo member managed to do so in Soviet times.

response of the Politburo to objective circumstances; in fact, they were highly controversial. Radical social forces were not sufficiently mobilized in 1986–1987, and were too easily cowed, to assign them causal responsibility for the origination of Gorbachev's program.[5] The climate of opinion within the political establishment was impatient for change – and was thus a contributory and permissive factor – but did not specify the scope or content of desirable policy changes. The ideological tradition could have supported diverse approaches to "getting the country moving again."

International influences were both indirect and direct. Indirectly, the attraction of Western prosperity and the magnet of cultural Westernization had grown as Soviet elite self-confidence in the superiority, or even workability, of their system had declined. Directly, governments abroad approved of Gorbachev's political reforms, while U.S. military policy under Ronald Reagan highlighted the inability of an unreformed Soviet Union to continue to compete as a global superpower. Yet none of these influences goes far to explain Gorbachev's domestic political reforms of 1987–1988. Gorbachev's comprehensive program held out the promise of a "socialist" democracy and rejected specific emulation of Western liberal capitalist democracy. Western governments at the time were not pressuring Gorbachev to democratize the Soviet system. Moreover, the conclusion that the Soviet Union needed to reform itself in a more liberal direction in order to compete in the modern world was one that Gorbachev and other "reform communists" had drawn before Ronald Reagan ever came to power.

In short, we could have predicted with confidence that any leader, including Yegor Ligachev, would consolidate power and present a program for comprehensive progress at home and abroad. We could also have predicted that the program would seek to reverse the decline of the Soviet economy. But the way Gorbachev used the power he had accumulated by 1987 can be

---

[5] Note, for example, that as late as spring 1988 – when the Nina Andreeva letter calling for a rollback of *perestroika* was published – the critical intelligentsia of Moscow ducked for cover, expecting a KGB-led crackdown. They only regained courage after Gorbachev and his associates forced through the Politburo a published rebuttal of the Andreeva letter (William & Jane Taubman, *Moscow Spring* [New York: Summit, 1989], pp. 146–86; Michael Urban [with Vyacheslav Igrunov & Sergei Mitrokhin], *The Rebirth of Politics in Russia* [Cambridge University Press, 1997], p. 90). Moreover, Urban and his colleagues, in a thorough study of the emergence of informal organizations and *glasnost'* in 1986–1988, conclude that social forces did not enjoy the political initiative against the authorities until the elections of March 1989: "Until the onset of the electoral process, the informal movement in Russia had remained a marginal phenomenon ... these elections revived the flagging movement" (pp. 121–2); a rally in Moscow on March 22, 1989, "marked the turning point at which political society felt itself sufficiently strong to challenge openly the repressive party–state" (p. 135).

traced to his prior commitments to end the Cold War, to revitalize Soviet society (preferably by nonviolent means), and to build a socialist democracy in the USSR – along with his commitment to do all this by means that salvaged both core "socialist" values and his own political role.[6]

---

[6] The Western literature on Gorbachev's leadership presents diverse explanations for the radicalization of his program. Brown, Hough, Lévesque, and English treat the turn as an expression of Gorbachev's beliefs and as a reflection of his accumulated political power, though they do not distinguish the fact of the program's ambitiousness, comprehensiveness, and utopianism from its specific contents. Hence, they do not search for alternative causal factors to explain the form versus the content of the program. See Archie Brown, *The Gorbachev Factor* (Oxford & New York: Oxford University Press, 1996); Jerry F. Hough, *Democratization and Revolution in the USSR, 1985–1991* (Washington, DC: Brookings Institution, 1997); Jacques Lévesque, *The Enigma of 1989: The USSR and the Liberation of Eastern Europe* (Berkeley: University of California Press, 1997); Robert D. English, *Russia and the Idea of the West: Gorbachev, Intellectuals and the End of the Cold War* (New York: Columbia University Press, 2000). Mikheyev, Volkogonov, and Malia also depict Gorbachev as exceptionally powerful by 1987; they, too, treat the abandonment of "acceleration" as a choice dictated principally by Gorbachev's frustration with the results of that program. But their depiction of Gorbachev's comprehensive program stresses the limits more than the scope of its radicalism. What all these works have in common, however, is a focus on Gorbachev's personality and beliefs as the proximate determinants of the change in course. See Dmitry Mikheyev, *The Rise and Fall of Gorbachev* (Indianapolis, IN: Hudson Institute, 1992); Dmitri Volkogonov, *Autopsy for an Empire: The Seven Leaders Who Built the Soviet Regime* (New York: Free Press, 1998), ch. 7; Martin Malia, *The Soviet Tragedy: A History of Socialism in Russia, 1917–1991* (New York: Free Press, 1994).

By contrast, D'Agostino's ambitious and original study (Anthony D'Agostino, *Gorbachev's Revolution* [New York: NYU Press, 1998]) treats ideas as important in Soviet elite political culture but treats them entirely as instruments of power struggle. They are effective as instruments because they resonate within the political culture, but they are embraced entirely for reasons of political power. D'Agostino therefore views radicalization as part of a historical pattern: Stalin, Khrushchev, and Gorbachev all "escaped forward" when challenged politically. Hence, he views political challenges to Gorbachev in 1987, led by Politburo member Yegor Ligachev, as the impetus for the general secretary to radicalize his program in order to throw his opponents off balance and to prevent their placing limits on his power. Although this bears a resemblance to my framework, which also takes seriously the role of ideas within the political culture and which treats a leader's ability to seize and maintain the political initiative as crucial to authority building and authority maintenance, the resemblance is only superficial. D'Agostino asserts that a Soviet leader must escape the constraints of collective leadership but does not explain *why* he must do so; never does he claim that the alternative is to be overthrown, nor does he explain why Brezhnev accepted a much more constrained position than did Stalin, Khrushchev, or Gorbachev. D'Agostino treats power as primary and "principle" as a disposable instrument in the power struggle. He writes, for example, that neither Gorbachev nor Yeltsin "held any position for which he was willing to suffer the slightest loss of political leverage" (p. 295). Given the massive uncertainty under which the two leaders had to make hard choices (an uncertainty that is conceded when D'Agostino later [pp. 341–3] argues that Gorbachev had no blueprint with which to anticipate the consequences of his choices), and given the political risks each of them accepted at several points in time, this statement about

The radicalization of Gorbachev's foreign policy during this period may also be ascribed to his personality and beliefs. There was no specified political consensus driving the choice of a concessionary foreign policy; nor did social forces, ideology, or the logic of political competition dictate the choice. Westernizers within the intelligentsia supported Gorbachev and urged him on, but they were relatively few in number and did not have the power to sanction him for not following their advice. He chose to heed their advice and to learn from them. The ideological tradition allowed Gorbachev to justify the choice in idealist, even utopian, terms, but that tradition was hardly biased toward abandoning the anti-imperialist struggle. Political competition might have given Gorbachev an incentive to seize the initiative. In the past, however, such competition had led to selective reincorporation and an inclusive program, rather than the far-reaching radicalization that Gorbachev now advocated.

Most Western observers credit Gorbachev with making these choices; some observers, however, qualify the credit by arguing that the strategy of the Reagan administration had left the Soviet leader with little alternative. These people argue that forces *in the international environment* forced Gorbachev to choose between the policies he adopted and intransigent policies that would have been even less in his interest.[7] There is something to be said for this interpretation. Gorbachev unsuccessfully tried to induce President Reagan to accept compromise solutions in 1985–1987. Thereafter, Gorbachev decided that radical concessions were more advantageous than living with the consequences of no agreement. Given his conviction that an end to the Cold War was a necessary precondition for successfully reforming Soviet society,

---

Gorbachev's and Yeltsin's power fixation strikes me as empirically indefensible. Moreover, I see no purpose in trying to assign weights to the causal role of power and principle. I treat politicians as seeking to have it both ways: to find and defend a credible, principled political niche and political identity from which they will build (and try to maintain) their authority and power. D'Agostino writes, for example, that "[r]eform ideas grew more radical in their implications as the struggle with the opposition intensified" (p. 343). I would reverse this equation and argue instead that opposition intensified as reform ideas grew more radical. Part of the difference here is that I, like the other group of scholars, view Gorbachev as a very powerful, ascendant leader by 1987–1988. D'Agostino is able to downgrade the causal role of personality and personal beliefs because (like Mikheyev, Volkogonov, and Malia) he deprecates the radicalism of Gorbachev's program by contrasting it to a liberal democratic, capitalist, and internationally capitulationist ideal. Finally, D'Agostino confuses the reader (or, at least, this reader) by employing a framework that treats ideas as merely instruments of power struggle while at several points characterizing Gorbachev as an idealist (pp. 9, 349).

[7] For this viewpoint, see Beth A. Fischer, *The Reagan Reversal: Foreign Policy and the End of the Cold War* (Columbia: University of Missouri Press, 1997).

he conceded to Reagan's maximalist demands on several fronts. But there was still a major role played here by Gorbachev's personality and beliefs, for many other members of the Soviet leadership were unenthusiastic about Gorbachev's foreign policy decisions. They would not have made the same choices, had they been in control. It follows that Gorbachev had degrees of political freedom to choose otherwise. He could have engaged in "selective reincorporation" in his foreign policy program and yet, as in domestic policy, he chose not to do so.

Thus, whereas political constraints appear to have shaped Gorbachev's choices during 1985–1986, his personality and individual beliefs appear to have been the more decisive determinants of his choices during 1987–1988.[8]

GORBACHEV, 1989–1991

When Gorbachev's programs started to falter in 1989, he might have reacted as Khrushchev and Brezhnev initially had: seeking renewed support from traditionalist constituencies he had appeased during the first stage of his administration. But this was not the way Gorbachev initially reacted to frustration. Instead, while continuing to try to enforce limits on radical change, he pushed forward with radicalization rather than trying to reverse it. He accommodated radical forces by abrogating the "leading role of the Party," conducting republican elections in spring 1990, creating a Soviet presidency independent of the Communist Party, and politically disenfranchising the *nomenklatura*. He further liberalized joint-ventures legislation to open the Soviet economy to the world economy, and he further liberalized policy on emigration, dissent, freedom of association, and freedom of religion. Abroad, he withdrew Soviet forces from Afghanistan and tolerated the collapse of communism in Eastern Europe. There is no reason to ascribe all this to political pressures from within the Party–State establishment; most officials would have counseled holding the line against further radicalization. The KGB remained intact at the time (1989–1990) and could have cracked down if ordered to do so. Soviet tanks

---

[8] Let me here dispose of a straw man. This interpretation does not suggest that Gorbachev's ideas were products of either revelation or omniscience. He was influenced in his thinking by radical reformist advisors and associates both at home and abroad, and he was acting under conditions of uncertainty about what was needed and what would work. But these conditions (influence and uncertainty) are universals of political decisionmaking. Within the context of such universals, some leaders forge ambitious, transformative programs while others yield to constraints and adopt "lowest common denominator" programs. It was Gorbachev's personality and beliefs that led him in the direction of the former rather than the latter.

could have rolled into Eastern Europe; or, at a minimum, Gorbachev could have threatened action. But the Soviet leader chose not to take that route.[9]

Why he chose initially to radicalize rather than to contract his coalition is a different question. An idealist explanation would have it that Gorbachev fervently believed (or had come to believe) in his vision of a demilitarized international order and a consensual polity at home. Hence, he plowed forward despite the risks and uncertainties of doing so. But a purely idealist explanation ignores changes in the social context at home and abroad.[10] An explanation that combines idealism with materialist calculation would argue that, by 1989, active social forces both in Russia and in the other republics of the USSR – along with social forces in Eastern Europe and governmental forces in the West – had so raised the price to be paid for cracking down that Gorbachev perceived the cost of repression to exceed the cost of toleration. He therefore decided to align himself with the less intransigent of those social forces, to make the best of an uncontrolled situation, to make a virtue of necessity, and hopefully to maintain his authority as the "man who changed the world."[11]

---

[9] Mikheyev (*The Rise and Fall*) does not perceive Gorbachev radicalizing in response to the frustrations of 1988–1989. Rather, he views him as shifting to the right (hardline), on domestic issues at least, already in fall 1988 and remaining there. But much of the evidence he brings forth is equally consistent with Gorbachev's efforts to enforce limits to radicalization, which does not distinguish his behavior of 1987–1988 from his behavior of 1989–1991. Similarly, D'Agostino (*Gorbachev's Revolution*) sees Gorbachev "escaping forward" in 1989–1990 by seeking absolute power, purging rivals, and attempting to destroy the capacity of the Party to constrain him. But this undeniable power consolidation strategy is only different in degree from what Gorbachev was doing in 1985–1988; all general secretaries had built a political machine in order to prevail in the succession struggle and sought to expand that machine – and purge rivals – in response to the frustration of their programs. What distinguished Gorbachev was his determination both to consolidate further his personal grip on power and to further radicalize policy through the transfer of power from Party to electorally accountable state institutions.

[10] Brown (*The Gorbachev Factor*) and English (*Russia and the Idea*) offer idealist explanations and approve of Gorbachev's decision; Hough (*Democratization and Revolution*) also focuses on Gorbachev's vision but expresses bafflement that Gorbachev could have been so naïve as to assume that his refusal to use force would not lead to chaos and collapse. None of these authors, however, ignores social and international forces; hence, none could properly be labeled "pure idealists."

[11] I advanced this interpretation in George W. Breslauer, "Evaluating Gorbachev as leader," *Soviet Economy*, vol. 8, no. 4 (October–December 1989), pp. 299–340, which was written in July 1990 (as the journal was behind schedule). The "man who changed the world" phrase, of course, is from Sheehy's volume of that title (Gail Sheehy, *The Man Who Changed the World* [New York: HarperCollins, 1990]). Without explicit endorsement, this explanation of Gorbachev's behavior seems also to inform Lévesque's study (*The Enigma of 1989*).

This combined idealist–materialist explanation gives equal weight to Gorbachev's personality and beliefs, on the one hand, and social forces at home and abroad, on the other. For it was the radicalization of domestic social forces – through self-mobilization and through encouragement by Gorbachev, Yeltsin, and other leading politicians – that raised the cost of repression to such a high level. And it was the deepening Soviet economic crisis that so raised the cost of alienating Western governments, as Gorbachev increasingly counted on those governments to provide material assistance (including arms-reduction treaties) to weather the crisis. But it was Gorbachev's ideals that kept him from attempting a counterrevolutionary restoration to stem the tide. He evidently cared about his image abroad and about the kind of society he was trying to build at home, for he retained in 1989–1990 the institutional capacity to crack down.

As we know, in fall 1990 Gorbachev abandoned further radicalization and allied himself with conservative forces. Events of September 1990 through March 1991 ominously suggested that an effort might be underway to roll back societal radicalization. It is not likely that this shift was forced upon Gorbachev by hardliners in the Central Committee or Supreme Soviet. Only two months earlier, in July 1990, he had purged Ligachev and many other conservatives from the leadership and the Central Committee. Rather, the explanation for this shift is likely to reside in the interaction between Gorbachev's beliefs and the accelerating pace of social mobilization and polarization. An explanation cast entirely in terms of personality would suggest that Gorbachev lost his nerve in the face of cascading failures (at home and abroad) and great uncertainty as to what might stem the tide. An explanation cast at the level of beliefs would point out that social mobilization now clearly threatened to bring down the Soviet Union itself – a value that Gorbachev had never been willing to entertain losing. Hence, when the level of social mobilization threatened disintegration of the USSR, the calculus shifted. The perceived cost of toleration had grown to the point that the cost of repression seemed marginally more acceptable.[12]

And yet this shift to the right lasted only six months, after which Gorbachev shifted back to support for the radicals on the issue of center–periphery relations. Hence, we should not settle too quickly for an explanation of Gorbachev's behavior that is rooted entirely in the interaction between his ultimate beliefs and the level of radicalization of social forces. But nor should

---

[12] By contrast, D'Agostino (*Gorbachev's Revolution,* pp. 280–97) argues that this shift was actually an effort by Gorbachev to bolster his personal power.

we succumb to explanations based purely on power maximization.[13] Gorbachev was indeed determined to protect his power position. He resisted calls by radical associates in 1990 for him to break with the Communist Party and base his power exclusively on the soviets and the presidency. He feared that this would leave powerful institutions in the hands of people who would use those institutions to destroy him and his policies.[14] In addition to maintaining his power and authority, however, Gorbachev was trying to prevent the collapse of the USSR. It was entirely uncertain just how he could do both.

Moreover, when it came to the choice of policies for doing all this, Gorbachev was both internally conflicted and externally cross-pressured. The cost of repression was severe. Internally, he experienced value conflict and ambivalence; externally, he feared the reactions of Western governments if he resorted to repression.

Gorbachev had expressed his distaste for the use of force (*ne streliat'* ["no more shooting"]) as early as 1985. When this conflicted, in 1990–1991, with both the maintenance of his political authority and his ability to contain polarization, Gorbachev was forced to choose between values of importance to him. His ambivalence may have expressed itself in the fact that the Baltic crackdown was limited in both scope and duration. Whether or not Gorbachev gave the order for troops to attack Vilnius and Riga, he *had* created a permissive political context for such a crackdown and yet prevented the repression from escalating to the point that it might have been effective in intimidating secessionist forces.

Gorbachev was also cross-pressured in that the costs of repression would also be felt in foreign relations. A repressive strategy might have led Gorbachev to be censured severely by the governments on which he most counted for economic assistance. He also needed the goodwill of those governments to be able to demonstrate at home that he remained an indispensable link to the international community, which many Soviet citizens hoped would provide material assistance and psychological comfort to their beleaguered country. Repression could also have led to his condemnation by political leaders abroad whom he had come to respect greatly. Indeed, it may not be too strong to say that Gorbachev had developed international referents (George Bush,

---

[13] D'Agostino, for example, writes: "Gorbachev's hard line ... was no longer bolstering his personal power. So he proceeded to discard it like an old coat. Indeed, now he could only save himself by another abrupt turn" (ibid., p. 297).

[14] Brown, *The Gorbachev Factor*, pp. 195–6.

Margaret Thatcher, Felipe Gonzalez, leaders of the Italian Communist Party) whose opinions of him he valued greatly irrespective of their ability to do him harm.

Thus, Gorbachev's shift back to support for the radicals on federal policy in April 1991 appears to have been a reaction to the fact that his support for conservatives had yielded little or nothing – from either an ideal or a material standpoint. The radicals, unlike the conservatives, had social forces mobilized behind them and seemed receptive to the idea of negotiating a treaty that, on paper at least, would retain some sort of unity among the republics of the USSR. The conservatives had only the threat of repression – with all the psychic, political, and material costs this might entail both at home and abroad. It was worth another try to return to negotiations on a treaty.

All of this helps us to understand one of the most extraordinary features of 1991: Gorbachev's acquiescence in the collapse of the state he had served all his life. As we have seen, this was not his preferred outcome. He struggled constantly to prevent it during 1990 and 1991. He was torn between *ratifying and containing* collapse by sponsoring a confederal formula that he feared would not hold and *preventing* collapse by sponsoring a widespread and bloody crackdown against separatist forces. He found himself between a rock and a hard place and responded by sequentially tacking in each direction without going fully to either extreme. Even when he acquiesced in the confederal formula in July 1991, he expressed his ambivalence by dropping hints to associates about the need for emergency rule. He never resolved this ambivalence.

Thus, Gorbachev's zigs and zags during 1990–1991 resulted from a combination of three things: (1) loss of nerve as he witnessed, successively, the potential costs of each policy extreme; (2) confusion as to what would succeed in reconciling his conflicting substantive and political goals; and (3) efforts to reposition himself to maintain credibility and to recoup authority with "healthy forces" of all persuasions. As it turned out, moderates represented a declining percentage of the mobilized and self-confident forces in Soviet politics and society. Gorbachev could no longer position himself as a liaison *between* the forces of the right and the left. The level of polarization had reached the point that Gorbachev's pendular strategy only highlighted to both sides the fact that he had become an eminently dispensable leader. After the failed coup of August 1991, Gorbachev was indeed a spent political force. Had he wished, in fall 1991, to employ force to prevent the juridical dissolution of the Soviet Union, he would have had few takers. All he could do was angrily acquiesce in his forced retirement.

YELTSIN, 1985–1991

Yeltsin comes across as a "larger than life" figure during the Gorbachev years. It is tempting to explain his behavior during 1985–1991 entirely with reference to his personality: his risk-seeking, extraordinary willpower, passion for struggle, and unusual "feel" or intuition for how to relate to the masses when public politics became an option in 1988. Indeed, personality is certainly a large part of the explanation for many of Yeltsin's choices. Absent those personality traits, it is difficult to imagine a regional Party secretary and candidate member of the Politburo reacting to frustrations as Yeltsin did in 1987. It is also difficult to imagine a different personality "crashing" the June 1988 Party Conference and forcing his way to the podium. Personality would also explain the decision to seek a seemingly hard win in Moscow in the March 1989 parliamentary elections rather than the easy win that would have awaited him in Sverdlovsk. Yeltsin's personal attributes were also necessary conditions for sustaining the challenge to Gorbachev during 1989–1991, for attaining the chairmanship of the Russian Supreme Soviet in May 1990, for creating and then winning the Russian presidency in June 1991, for facing down the coup of August 1991, and for dissolving the USSR in December 1991. Moreover, Yeltsin's rhetorical style – and his intuition for finding words, modes of expression, and actions that resonated with mass audiences – well explain his effectiveness in the game of public politics throughout 1988–1991.[15]

Yeltsin's personal beliefs were also sufficiently unusual in the Soviet leadership at this time that, along with his willful personality, they reinforce idiosyncratic explanations of his choices. Many officials combined a "storming" mentality with a predisposition to purge corrupt cadres; each of these traits had deep roots in the Soviet political tradition. Many officials also understood that a "populist" strategy was needed to circumvent bureaucratic constraints on change. Less frequent was the combination of populism and egalitarianism that targeted elite privileges as unjust and an impediment to progress. Khrushchev and Yeltsin were similar in drawing this linkage. Initially, both men defined the problem of bureaucratic corruption in discrete terms, as a "cadres problem": purge the corrupted, replace them with "uninfected" personnel, and the system will work. But as their responsibility for performance grew and their frustrations deepened, each man moved toward a systemic critique. To be sure, both men had the personality traits

[15] Reporters for the *London Times,* after interviewing Yeltsin in 1990, wrote with admiration of "his instinctive grasp of another vital ingredient of politics: 'street credibility'" (quoted in Leon Aron, *Boris Yeltsin: A Revolutionary Life* [London: HarperCollins, 2000], p. 364).

required to move in that perilous direction: impatience for results and political courage.

Once we concede that Yeltsin's personality and beliefs were decisive determinants of his behavior during 1985–1991, is there anything left to say about the contribution of Soviet ideology, the climate of opinion, politics, social forces, and international factors toward an explanation of his choice of political strategy? Yes, to some degree; these factors were contributory and permissive, but not decisive. Let me address them in turn.

Soviet Ideology. The Marxist–Leninist ideological tradition contained an egalitarian vision ("the workers' state"; "to each according to his needs"; "all power to the soviets"; the "classless society") that fueled both Khrushchev's and Yeltsin's sense of self-righteousness as they attacked the privileges of the *nomenklatura.* These features of the tradition allowed Yeltsin in 1985–1987 to present himself as a leader in the struggle for "social justice" and to claim simultaneously that he was acting fully in accord with the Leninist tradition. The multifaceted, internally contradictory ideological tradition thereby contributed to the formulation of Yeltsin's political strategies – and facilitated their implementation, though not their effectiveness – during his 23 months as head of the Moscow Party organization.

After 1988, traditional Soviet ideology became less and less of an influence on Yeltsin's choices, except in the negative sense that it provided a menu of doctrines that Yeltsin was rapidly rejecting. Yeltsin was searching at this time for a counter-ideology to explain his frustrations and to deploy in the public struggle over ideas. He was assisted in his search by liberal democrats like Andrei Sakharov and other radicals within the Congress of People's Deputies. His conversion was hastened by his encounter in September 1989 with the abundance of American capitalism. By 1990, Yeltsin had come to embrace the rhetoric of liberal democratic and then market democratic theory. Soviet ideology played a causal role for Yeltsin after 1988 only in defining the undesirable "other" against which he was helping to mobilize, embolden, or ally with growing numbers of social forces.

Climate of Opinion. The climate of opinion within the Soviet establishment in 1985–1987 also may have influenced certain of Yeltsin's choices in those years. On the one hand, the widespread urge to "get the country moving again" led him to believe that drastic measures would be tolerated (and even welcomed) toward that end.[16] Once he was responsible for delivering results

---

[16] Recall that, at the 27th Party Congress in February 1986 – where Yeltsin delivered a quite radical speech – he explained his failure to deliver as radical a speech five years earlier (under Brezhnev) by saying that he had lacked political courage at the time.

for his leadership in Moscow, his awareness of the climate of opinion lent political reinforcement to his natural impatience. On the other hand, the mixed
and ambiguous content of the prevailing climate – its yearning to find a way
to make the system work without threatening the system's existence – heightened Yeltsin's frustration at the slow pace of change. In such an ambiguous
climate, Gorbachev initially fashioned for himself the image of a responsible
reformer. In the same climate, Yeltsin lost patience with the ambiguities and
found himself being dubbed irresponsible.

Political Organization and Political Competition. Politics also was an independent causal force in several senses. The political organization of the regime
during 1985–1987 was still highly constricted. Yeltsin's frustrations in trying
to "cleanse" Moscow politics during this time were to some extent products
of a system of mutual protection among officials of the central and Moscow
Party apparatus. Yeltsin's decision to offer his resignation was in large measure impelled by a recognition that, in such a regime, he would be made the
scapegoat for his failure to turn Moscow around. His personality and beliefs
might have driven his decision to appeal to the Central Committee in 1987,
but political organization explains both the source of his frustration and the
ease with which he was defeated.

Political organization changed after 1987 as a result of Gorbachev's reforms, which allowed politics to become a still weightier causal force, albeit
in a different way. The definitions of "politics" and of "political organization"
had changed. The fact that political competition was now public increased
the scope for political outbidding by allowing the rate of *societal* political polarization, not just intra-establishment polarization, to determine the niches
that politicians could aspire to occupy. Moreover, by opening new avenues
for political competition, Gorbachev – intentionally or not – allowed his own
stage of ascendancy to become, in effect, a new stage of political succession
struggle. His reforms allowed counter-elites to appeal to newly formed constituencies and thereby to build themselves up into genuine rivals for the votes
of the citizenry. No previous Party leader had used his stage of ascendancy
in this way. Hence, the fact of public political competition, and the polarizing effects of that process in a context of systemic transformation, created
a continuously expanding field of opportunity for Boris Yeltsin and others.
Yeltsin's decisions to exploit the opportunities were products of his personality and beliefs, but the existence of the opportunity was a product of the
changed structure of political competition. Yeltsin's decisions to outbid Gorbachev repeatedly in that context were only in part expressions of his personality; they were also reflections of the logic of public political competition in
a polarizing context. Similarly, Yeltsin's embrace of a liberal democratic and

market democratic counter-ideology was speeded by the intensified struggle over ideas that public political competition encouraged.

Social Forces. Yeltsin's decisions of 1985–1988 were not choices dictated by any effort to keep up with radicalizing social forces; he was ahead of them at the time.[17] During 1989–1991, however, the balance between leadership and autonomous social radicalization shifted greatly. Some of Yeltsin's actions during this period were responses to sudden bursts of social defiance he had not anticipated, such as the miners' strikes of 1989 and the radicalization of demands for autonomy or independence in the Baltic states. But many instances of Yeltsin's public outbidding during 1988–1989 (see Chapter 6) were anticipatory, not reactive, and had the effect of emboldening radical forces to mobilize and express themselves without fear. Yeltsin became a focal point for social activists who viewed his political resurrection as a sure sign that nonviolent revolutionary change was actually possible. Moreover, Yeltsin's response to unanticipated outbursts of social rebellion – in sharp contrast to Gorbachev during 1990–1991 – was typically to accommodate and praise them, thereby encouraging them to continue their defiance of the Kremlin.

Social forces and political competition were permissive factors, not determinants of Yeltsin's behavior. Most other politicians at the time, lacking Yeltsin's personality traits and beliefs, would have behaved quite differently in response to the opportunities.

International Factors. Yeltsin's choices during 1985–1991 were only minimally or indirectly affected by factors in the international environment. He was, of course, influenced indirectly by the decline of the Soviet economy relative to its capitalist competitors. Judging by his autobiographies and his statements at the time, however, Yeltsin was no more focused on the international context than were other regional Party secretaries. Indeed, Gorbachev was more of a reform communist and more attentive to international comparisons than was Yeltsin in 1976–1985. During Yeltsin's tenure as Party first secretary in Moscow (1985–1987), he displayed very little interest in the international context of Soviet policy.

During Yeltsin's political resurrection of 1988–1989, and again during his direct rivalry with Gorbachev of 1990–1991, international comparisons

---

[17] From his first days as first secretary of the Moscow city Party organization, Yeltsin was predicting social and political instability if the authorities did not change their ways and improve the consumer situation. He might genuinely have believed that there would be a reckoning down the road, but he was not (in 1985–1988) responding to concrete manifestations or outbursts of social discontent. If anything, he was trying to encourage people to express their dissatisfactions as a way of pressuring officials or as a justification for purging those officials.

became more salient to Yeltsin. His search for a worldview to substitute for Leninism led him to endorse the alternative – market democracy and liberalism – that had become ideologically hegemonic in the international system during the second half of the 1980s. More concretely, his visit to a Houston supermarket in 1990, he claims, was a traumatic experience; it led him to conclude that socialism was a pipe dream and that capitalism might be the only realistic path to prosperity. Yet there were many other political actors in and around the leadership who had already drawn these conclusions. The hegemony of market democracy internationally, then, was a factor that influenced all those who were rejecting Leninism to consider liberalism as the only feasible alternative. Given his political competition with Gorbachev, however, Yeltsin would have outbid Gorbachev in the anti-system direction whether or not a salient international alternative existed. There is too little reference to international considerations in Yeltsin's public political rhetoric of 1989–1990 to suggest otherwise.

As for direct international pressures, these had even less impact on Yeltsin's political choices. Indeed, it was a source of intense frustration to him in 1989–1990 that Western governments refused to acknowledge him as a legitimate political leader of the USSR. The United States and its West European allies at this time were trying to shore up support for Gorbachev and viewed Yeltsin as an inconvenience, if not a troublemaker. As late as fall 1991, President Bush was trying to forestall the juridical collapse of the Soviet Union. Yeltsin's fundamental political choices during 1989–1991 were largely taken in spite of, not in response to, direct pressures from international actors.

YELTSIN, 1991–1993

The fall of 1991 is generally considered to have been a turning point in Soviet and Russian history. This was Yeltsin's honeymoon period at the beginning of his political ascendancy. His level of charismatic authority had risen to new heights in August 1991, and he seized that moment to begin crafting a comprehensive program for coping with the disintegrating situation he had inherited and for creating the foundations of a new order. The country's spiraling economic crisis, centrifugal forces in the republics, and the further disintegration of state institutions were circumstantial factors that forced Yeltsin's attention, but they did not force him to respond as he did. Moreover, organized social and political forces within Russia proved powerless to compel Yeltsin to respond as they preferred. Actors in the international arena had little direct impact on Yeltsin's *political* choices, but they did influence his decisions on economic reform. In all, Yeltsin was as unconstrained in fall 1991 as he would ever be. He had the opportunity to choose for himself how to respond to the crisis. Accordingly, his personality and beliefs loomed large as determinants of his choices. His decision to seek the right to rule by decree, his resistance to founding a presidential political party, and his decision to distance himself from democratic forces were choices forced on him by no one. They reflected his personal preferences.

Yeltsin's decisions regarding economic reform were shaped by a wider constellation of forces and circumstances. Something had to be done to gain control of the disintegrating economy. Neoliberal advisors (both Russian and foreign) backed by international financial institutions strongly advocated a particular course of action; still other options were being suggested by Russian economists. Yeltsin's receptivity to the neoliberal advice still needs to be explained.

That receptivity reflected his socialization in the Soviet system and a personality that drew him to the role of "stormer" within that system. Given the testimony in his autobiographies, along with the testimony of those who worked for him (see Chapter 7), we can see why "shock therapy" appealed to Yeltsin at the time. He was attracted to a breakthrough strategy for clearing away obstacles to the construction of a new socioeconomic system – a strategy that would contrast with the "half-measures" for which he criticized Gorbachev. Shock therapy, as Yeltsin defined it, resembled a large-scale campaign to transform society, a painful but necessary cure for the lethargy of Russian citizens; it resembled a cultural revolution. It required that all citizens resolve to overcome their slothful ways – or suffer extreme deprivation. It placed its bets on young people.

These preferences were more than just an expression of Yeltsin's personality. They had roots in a Marxist–Leninist tradition that was missionary, progressive, and optimistic. Stalin, Khrushchev, and Gorbachev had all sought to transform society by reshaping (or realizing the potential of) "the human factor" and by explicitly appealing to the younger generation. They, too, had launched nationwide mobilizations to construct an unprecedented social order. Indeed, Yeltsin justifed his economic revolution in terms that were strikingly similar to the justifications of his predecessors. In Hanson's terms, Yeltsin mimicked the Marxist–Leninist search to "transcend historical constraints"[18] – a search that, in this specific and limited sense, did not distinguish him from Stalin, Khrushchev, or Gorbachev. Even though Yeltsin had explicitly rejected Marxism–Leninism, there was something about that tradition's way of thinking that stayed with him. "Building capitalism" under Yeltsin rejected the content of socialism even as it mimicked the approach to "primitive

---

[18] Hanson, *Time and Revolution.*

accumulation" that had marked both early capitalism and the building of socialism in the USSR.

Although organized social and political forces within Russia did not force Yeltsin to adopt this economic strategy, international influences did have an important impact on the choices he made. Indirect international influences included the post–Cold War zeitgeist of the triumph of market democracy and the extraordinary attraction of "Western civilization" as both model and savior. These indirect pressures would have existed whatever the policies of Western governments and international financial institutions at the time, but direct pressures from abroad also played a role. Russia's finances were in dire straits, and Western governments were promising large-scale assistance if Russia adopted the orthodoxy of the International Monetary Fund. Hence, while Yeltsin was predisposed by personality and beliefs to embrace a revolutionary economic strategy, he was also aware that carrots and sticks abroad were pushing him in this direction. He may have felt boxed in by circumstances. But other political actors – including Gorbachev before him – had avoided conceding to Western advice. Rather than viewing Yeltsin as a leader who was forced by the West to do its bidding, we should instead view him as a man whose personality and beliefs predisposed him to accept Western urgings. The "stormer" found "shock therapy" to be the appropriate cure for his country's ills.[19]

Nonetheless, from spring 1992 onward, the "stormer" began to backtrack. The social, economic, psychic, and international costs of his breakthrough strategy had begun to accumulate. Hyperinflation, mass impoverishment, collapse of production at home, and continuing retreat abroad all led to the mobilization of anti-Yeltsin sentiments within the intelligentsia, the managerial corps, and the Congress of People's Deputies. The Russian population largely suffered in silence, but apocalyptic forecasts of how long their patience would last appeared in myriad newspaper articles and public speeches by prominent figures. This was the point at which Yeltsin had to decide whether to persist with the fullness of his program or instead modify and moderate it. He could have persisted – he had the power to do so and Western governments and international organizations promised to reward Russia for doing so – yet he decided to engage in a course correction.

What accounts for this shift? One interpretation would be idiosyncratic: that Yeltsin the Soviet-style "stormer" was also Yeltsin the neo-Leninist who

---

[19] By contrast, Jerry Hough (*The Logic of Economic Reform in Russia* [Washington, DC: Brookings Institution, 2001], p. 129) believes that Yeltsin chose "shock therapy" because it was most consistent with his goal of quickly achieving Russia's independence from the USSR.

understood the need to consolidate gains after an initial thrust. According to this interpretation, Yeltsin was exercising political prudence not because he was forced to do so but rather because he anticipated or feared the consequences of not doing so. The argument would continue as follows.

Having been at the forefront of a revolution that brought down both communism and the USSR, and having advocated immediately thereafter a revolutionary approach to "building capitalism," Yeltsin considered it prudent not to push his luck. He did not know at what point popular patience might snap.[20] He knew how he had come to power, and he knew that he had helped to destroy Gorbachev politically by outbidding him for the allegiance of an aroused populace. He also knew that the forces of restoration were seeking to employ the same strategy against him. He did not want to drive the moderates into the arms of his antagonists within the Supreme Soviet; neither did he want to strengthen the communists' and chauvinists' credibility with the populace. He did not want to remain vulnerable to the charge that he had no strategy for protecting Russia's national interests abroad or for protecting the interests of Russians in the Near Abroad. In short, Yeltsin's behavior was driven by a perception that the accumulating costs of his revolutionary strategy might come back to haunt him unless he engaged in a course correction.[21]

Thus (according to this interpretation), organized political forces within the parliament, the climate of opinion in the country and in the mass media, the pleas of directors of suffering enterprises, and the political insecurity of being president in a weakly institutionalized and highly unruly regime triggered a reaction of prudence by Yeltsin. Prudence, of course, is not the same as capitulation. Yeltsin persisted with the general trajectory of his policies at home and abroad; he simply introduced a course correction.

Another way to interpret this behavior is as an act of political coalition building. It bears resemblance to the kind of selective reincorporation in which Khrushchev and Brezhnev (but not Gorbachev) had engaged at their

---

[20] Recall his anxious promises of November 1991 that things would start to improve in six months (Chapter 7).

[21] A number of observers and associates have noted Yeltsin's political intuition about impending shifts in the mood of the masses (Oleg Poptsov, *Khronika vremyon tsaria Borisa* [Moscow: Sovershenno sekretno, 1996], pp. 55, 107, 167, 384; Fyodor Burlatskii, *Glotok svobody* [Moscow: RIK Kul'tura, 1997], vol. 2, p. 259; Yegor T. Gaidar, *Dni porazhenii i pobed* [Moscow: Vagrius, 1996], pp. 106–7). Whether or not their perceptions were accurate, the observations imply that Yeltsin made these decisions after keeping his own counsel and that he sought to anticipate the reactions of potential antagonists when making his choices. Moreover, in his second memoir (published in early 1994), Yeltsin acknowledges the course correction and justifies it in prudential terms (Boris Yeltsin, *The Struggle for Russia*, trans. by Catherine A. Fitzpatrick [New York: Random House, 1994], pp. 164–7).

stages of ascendancy. This explanation is not antithetical to the one just sketched, but it places somewhat less emphasis on the idiosyncratic and ideological sources of Yeltsin's behavior and more emphasis on politics as a process of political competition. From this perspective, Yeltsin was positioning himself to occupy a political niche in which he would not be isolated at the extreme end of the domestic political spectrum. Instead, he was positioning himself to dominate both the "center" and the "radical wing" of the spectrum. His program remained radical on balance in that it was consistent with maintaining the breakthrough thrust of fall 1991, and it conceded nothing to the unreconstructed communists he had defeated in 1991 or to the Russian chauvinists and imperial restorationists that were growing in strength.[22] One explanation for Khrushchev's and Brezhnev's acts of selective reincorporation was their felt need for outsized coalitions in the face of political insecurity. Yeltsin, in this interpretation, also would have viewed his partial move toward the center as an act of political self-insurance in a highly contentious political context. Even the considerable differences in the structure of politics in the 1990s (as compared to the 1950s–1970s) would not be enough to erase this common response to political insecurity.[23]

Of course, as with both Khrushchev and Brezhnev, selective reincorporation only increased the ambitiousness of the comprehensive program, for it promised to deliver on the new goals with less disruption to traditional concerns and interests than had earlier been anticipated. Nonetheless, Yeltsin's course correction did not have the effect of moderating the rate of political polarization between the legislative and executive branches.

[22] Analogously, Khrushchev and Brezhnev, when fashioning their comprehensive programs, had abandoned the extreme hardline positions once articulated by Molotov and Shelepin. They instead selectively reincorporated reformist positions articulated by Malenkov and Kosygin.

[23] Peter Reddaway and Dmitri Glinski (*The Tragedy of Russia's Reforms: Market Bolshevism against Democracy* [Washington, DC: U.S. Institute of Peace, 2001], pp. 167–72, 234–5), by contrast, argue that Yeltsin "moved to the middle" already in spring 1990, seeking an alliance with the managers of large industrial firms and distancing himself from the extremists of Democratic Russia. The authors then interpret "shock therapy" as based on a coalition of neoliberals and the managerial elite at the expense of the democrats, the communists, and the radical nationalists. This argument would be consistent with a view of Yeltsin as a man who rose to the position of chairman of the Russian Republic Supreme Soviet (May 1990) as an oppositional extremist and then sought to broaden the coalition on which he would base his "rule" in Russia. Reddaway and Glinski offer what amounts to a political interpretation of Yeltsin's behavior at his stage of ascendancy (i.e., a search for political security). Though they do not propose a "stage analysis" of Yeltsin's administration, it is worth noting that their periodization of the stage of political succession and the stage of ascendancy tacitly differs from my periodization. On the other hand, Reddaway and Glinski (p. 288) also argue that Yeltsin moved still further to the middle in mid-1992 and for reasons similar to those I have specified here.

As policy deadlock continued well into 1993, Yeltsin decided to resolve it through confrontation. This was a decision made by Yeltsin himself – encouraged by advisors but mandated by no social forces, international actors, or political imperatives. It was a choice dictated by the combination of his personal threshold for responding to prolonged frustration and by his long-held belief in the higher virtue of personalistic leadership. Therefore, the Constitution that he put to the voters in December 1993 was a close reflection of the super-presidentialist, plebiscitarian, and anti-centrifugal vision of political order he had been touting since fall 1991.

YELTSIN, 1994–1999

As we have seen, Yeltsin was delighted by the passage of his Constitution but shocked by the victory of communists and chauvinists in the parliamentary elections of December 1993. He was disheartened by the decline of his personal popularity and angered by the amnesty accorded (in February 1994) to the leaders of the parliamentary resistance of October 1993. Yeltsin's response to this frustration was to become more reclusive, authoritarian, and patriarchal. If the thrust of his authority-building strategy during 1991–1993 had been transformative, the thrust of his subsequent strategy for maintaining and recouping that authority was consolidative.

Why did he react in this way? Given what we know about Yeltsin's personality, and given the emphasis on personality factors in his aides' memoirs, we might be tempted to ascribe the reaction entirely to idiosyncratic factors. Yeltsin, by this accounting, was predisposed to personalistic leadership and to a patriarchal self-conception. In that respect, he was a product of Soviet socialization, like so many other *apparatchiki* of this type in the post-Stalin era. In the face of frustration, he allowed this orientation to become dominant; he reverted to his roots.

While such an argument has some plausibility, it seems incomplete. Yeltsin's personality, after all, also included a passion for facing challenges and an aversion to stasis. These were also features of a particular type of Soviet *apparatchik*. Furthermore, his self-image – as well as his authority-building strategy – rested on a promise to construct a new political and economic order, which was far from complete in 1994.

An alternative explanation for Yeltsin's reversion to a reclusive political style is political – specifically, political insecurity. Although he had been freely elected as president of Russia and enjoyed enormous charismatic authority after August 1991, these sources of political popularity are wasting assets. During his struggle with the Supreme Soviet in 1992–1993, he could never be certain that he would not be removed from office by force; the abortive coup attempt of 1991 was a very recent memory. Nor, in October 1993, did Yeltsin find it easy to gain military support for assaulting the parliament; many commanders were reluctant to implement his orders. He could never be confident that his administrative staff was devoted to implementing his declared policies; in fact, one memoirist claims that Yeltsin drew the conclusion that parliament had declared amnesty for his political enemies only as a result of the negligence or perfidy of his own staff.[24] Hence, even if he were not already so inclined (which he was), circumstances would have nudged Yeltsin toward suspicion: a heightened insistence on personal loyalty, a growing tendency to test the loyalties of his associates and appointees, a more pronounced urge to show them who was boss, a simultaneous urge to ensure his personal security by developing intimate personal relationships with his defense minister (Pavel Grachev) and his bodyguards, and a decision that divided government just doesn't work.[25]

Thus, political uncertainty was a constant throughout his years as Russian president whereas political self-confidence, authority, and credibility were variables. As Yeltsin's own confidence declined in his ability to solve the country's problems, to mobilize the masses, to control the "force ministries," and to maintain his authority and credibility as an effective leader, his level of reclusive authoritarianism increased. The Constitution might have given the president enormous formal powers, but Russia was a young republic. Yeltsin still had to worry constantly about whether he might become a victim of extra-constitutional acts. Though elected to a five-year term of office in 1991, he could not be confident that – in the face of plummeting popularity among the masses – forces within the political establishment would not seek to remove him from office before the end of his term. And he could not take for granted that the electorate would grant him a second term in the election scheduled for June 1996.

As argued in Chapter 9, Yeltsin's sense of political insecurity in 1994 made a significant contribution to his decision to invade Chechnya at the end of that year. More broadly, however, Yeltsin's reaction to frustration after 1993 was to attempt to consolidate the system he had started to build, rather than to

---

[24] Viacheslav Kostikov, *Roman s prezidentom: zapiski press-sekretaria* (Moscow: Vagrius, 1997), pp. 286–7, 290–3.
[25] On the last point, see Yeltsin, *The Struggle*, p. 238, where (writing in early 1994) he declares his disenchantment with a division of powers among the branches of government.

finish the construction. He touted himself as the man who would never allow the disintegration of Russia. Beyond ensuring territorial integrity, Yeltsin defined his main role as guarantor against communist or revanchist restoration, which led him to marshal a coalition of interests that included moderates and what he called "reformists." He turned a blind eye to the growing corruption within his administration. He endorsed the "loans for shares" privatization scheme of 1995, which created a small class of powerful tycoons who would fight against communist restoration and claim a stake in Yeltsin's reelection. He flirted with the idea of canceling the 1996 presidential election and banning the Communist Party of the Russian Federation. To be sure, he continued attempts to cooperate with the United States and Western Europe, to integrate Russia into Western international institutions, and to secure loans and credits from the West. Increasingly, however, he treated these goals as preconditions for successful consolidation of the new order at home, as guarantees against the instability that could lead to communist restoration, and as markers of his indispensability as a leader who, through his relationships with Western leaders, could bring home the goods.

Yeltsin's choice to react to frustration in this way was not dictated by political "necessity." There was no constellation of political forces after 1993 that was forcing him down this path. Neither the Duma nor social organizations had the power either to compel Yeltsin to adopt a consolidating strategy or to prevent him from adopting a more radical set of policies. The Duma was a more docile organization than the Congress of People's Deputies, in part because of the latter's forced dissolution and in part because of the new rules of the game dictated by the December 1993 Constitution.[26] Social organizations, though numerous, were less powerful than they had been during 1990–1991; this resulted from an ebbing of the revolutionary wave, the reassertion of some political controls, and the impoverishment of much of society owing to shock therapy.[27] Governments abroad were not pushing Yeltsin in this direction, though they did define his continuance in power as an indispensable alternative to communist restoration.

In short, Yeltsin had the option to pursue different policies. He might have pushed forward with radicalization, as Gorbachev and Khrushchev (eventually) had done, but he lacked the inclination, the energy, the health, and the residual political self-confidence to do so. Instead, he tried to manage the

---

[26] See Michael McFaul, *Russia's Troubled Transition from Communism to Democracy: Institutional Change during Revolutionary Transformations* (Ithaca, NY: Cornell University Press, 2001), chs. 6–7.

[27] See Urban et al., *The Rebirth of Politics in Russia,* part IV.

incomplete system he had built, to shore up his grip on power, and to tout himself as the man whose longevity would ensure that the communists could never dismantle the foundations of that system.

Yeltsin was also a victim of constraints he had helped to create; hence, he lacked many of the instruments for completing the edifice on which he had begun construction. Yeltsin was increasingly burdened by decisional overload that often paralyzed policymaking. In this respect, he was partially the victim of his own success in destroying the communist system, for he ruled as president without the benefit of an established apparatus of officials to organize the flow of information to him and the implementation of his requests. Even a healthy leader would have been burdened by this deficiency, but Yeltsin was not a healthy man. He suffered from a weak heart, a painful back injury incurred in Spain in 1990, alcohol dependency, and a regimen of medications that exacerbated his seemingly manic-depressive mood swings. Over time, his press secretary reports, the burden of decisional overload took a further toll, leading Yeltsin to avoid documents, appointments, and (increasingly) decisions.[28] Moreover, given his political insecurity, Yeltsin resisted the obvious conclusion – that he delegate more decisionmaking responsibility to others – perhaps fearing a dilution of his authority or the crystallization of threats to his power.[29]

Yeltsin's emphasis on consolidation rather than continuing transformation (e.g., helping to build a rule of law) was reinforced by his fatalism about the impossibility of reforming the Russian bureaucracy. In his second memoir, which reflected on the lessons of his stage of ascendancy, Yeltsin argued that the Russian bureaucracy was a quagmire out of which little of use could be expected to emerge. He wrote that both the Russian bureaucracy and the Russian people required a "strong hand" to budge them from their inertial and nihilistic behavioral patterns. Unified, strong command was more important than rule of law, for "[e]veryone knows that we Russians do not like

---

[28] Kostikov, *Roman,* pp. 306–7: "Coming into his office, I often found him seated behind an empty table in deep, morose thought. He missed his earlier role of 'Director of all of Russia.' And it seemed that [he] was losing his head in the face of the scale of the deeds he enumerated for himself in his Constitution." Kostikov also reports that, during his entire period as president of Russia, Yeltsin was in physical pain from a variety of ailments, including severe back and leg pain (ibid., p. 196), an observation that is supported by Aleksandr Korzhakov, *Boris Yel'tsin: Ot rassveta do zakata* (Moscow: Izd-vo 'Interbuk,' 1997), p. 202.

[29] Korzhakov (ibid., p. 310) reports that, in the fall of 1993, Prime Minister Chernomyrdin tried to persuade Yeltsin to grant him more responsibilities and duties in order to relieve the presidential workload. Yeltsin, according to Korzhakov, viewed this with deep suspicion, fearing that Chernomyrdin might be seeking more formal power or might be planning to run against him in 1996.

to obey all sorts of rules, laws, instructions, and directives ... rules cut us like a knife."[30] "Somebody had to be the boss," he wrote in his second memoir. "Russia's main paradox was that ... [t]here had not been any real powerful leader in the Republic of Russia." At present, people "are almost incapable of doing anything themselves." Two or three presidencies will have to go by, he claimed, before this situation will change.[31] In this memoir, Yeltsin's very occasional references to rule of law were either ritualistic incantations or were accompanied by a befuddlement about how to make the Russian bureaucracy procedurally accountable: "Unfortunately, the law enforcement agencies are adapting very slowly and poorly to this new crime phenomenon. That's the typical Russian style."[32]

Fatalism about "the system" over which he ruled may also explain the blind eye he increasingly turned to the growing corruption of his government. This is a curious feature of Yeltsin's presidency. Few observers believe that Yeltsin held office largely for his personal material gain. In Sverdlovsk, he was not personally corrupt and he waged campaigns against corruption and privilege. In fact, he was advanced to a position in Moscow precisely because he was "clean" and a proven anti-corruption fighter. When he was first secretary of the Moscow Party committee in 1985–1987, he was famous for his anti-corruption campaigns and for his criticism of the formal privileges of the *nomenklatura*. Yet, despite regular speeches as president about the need to root out corruption, memoirists report a tendency for him increasingly to avoid following up on reports of corruption in his own administration.[33] His attitude of resignation about the unreformability of the Russian bureaucracy and about Russian cultural opposition to rule-driven behavior may also explain his failure to crack down on corruption. Resignation, sheer fatigue, and a lack of ideas about how to reduce corruption without further increasing his political vulnerability may have combined to deter him from tackling the task.

There are other, equally plausible explanations. One would be that Yeltsin cared about corruption only as a means of rising to power and dropped the concern once he became president of Russia. A second interpretation is that Yeltsin actually sought the corruption of all those around him in order to keep them loyal to him and dependent upon him for political protection against

---

[30] Yeltsin, *The Struggle,* pp. 139–40.
[31] Ibid., pp. 6, 7, 18–19.
[32] Ibid., p. 148.
[33] Valerii Streletskii, *Mrakobesie* (Moscow: Detektiv-Press, 1998), pp. 155–6; Kostikov, *Roman,* p. 216.

prosecution.[34] A third interpretation is that Yeltsin could not crack down on corruption without harming his own family – and especially his daughters and their husbands. While the evidence for Yeltsin's personal corruption after 1994 is scant, the evidence for the growing corruption of his children's families from 1994 onward is voluminous.[35] In particular, the business tycoon Boris Berezovskii appears to have enmeshed Yeltsin's family in unearned wealth and illicit associations of which Yeltsin may well have been aware. This raised the personal cost to Yeltsin of cracking down on corruption in his midst.

Whichever interpretation is correct (and they are not all mutually exclusive), the net result was that – for psychological, physical, political, or personal reasons – Yeltsin fought against corruption only rhetorically. This was consistent with his general posture toward transformative change in the period after 1993.

Yet even as he emphasized stability and consolidation during 1994–1999, Yeltsin periodically behaved as if it mattered that he demonstrate his ability to keep pushing history forward toward completion of the capitalist project. Periodically (1995, 1997, 1998), Yeltsin would suddenly emerge from seclusion, fire or demote members of his government, and appoint ministers – such as Boris Nemtsov, Sergei Kirienko, and Sergei Stepashin – who were young, independent of the oligarchs, and inclined to build a market-regulating state. He mandated them to break through constraints on the construction of a capitalist society (see Chapter 10). Whether Yeltsin actually believed what he was saying is impossible to discern. This may have been his way of convincing himself that he had not succumbed to Brezhnev-like stagnation. It may have been his way of trying to convince others, at home and abroad, that he was not a spent political force. It may have been his way of trying to convince the International Monetary Fund that he would not waste its money. Or it may have been a simple strategy of power maintenance: keeping all officials constantly off-balance and bringing in young people who did not have the stature or the connections to threaten his authority. Only when Yeltsin genuinely feared that he or his family could be prosecuted after his retirement from office did he drop the pretense of launching reformist breakthroughs. Even then, in retrospect, he tried to convince readers of his latest memoir that his main purpose in firing ministers during 1998–1999 had not been to protect himself but rather to find the man who would have the ability to prevent the communists from ever coming back to power.[36]

[34] This argument is made in Jerry Hough, *The Logic of Economic Reform.*
[35] See Reddaway and Glinski, *The Tragedy of Russia's Reforms,* ch. 8.
[36] Boris Yeltsin, *Midnight Diaries* (New York: Public Affairs, 2000), ch. 24.

CONCLUSION

In Chapter 1, I argued that structural explanations of leadership behavior in Soviet-type systems take us only so far. Those explanations highlight the constraining effects of political organization and Marxist–Leninist ideology on the scope of discretion available to the would-be authority builder. Within those parameters, however, leaders could fashion diverse authority-building strategies.

Structural explanations of leaders' choices become even less compelling once Gorbachev comes to power and especially after he consolidates power and begins to implement a comprehensive program. After 1986, the personalities and beliefs of individual leaders became ever more determinant of the fundamental choices they made. To be sure, many of their personal beliefs had roots in the Soviet ideological tradition, and their leadership styles mirrored distinctive types of *apparatchik* operating styles within the post-Stalin generations of regional Party officials. Hence, my focus on idiosyncratic factors is not meant to suggest that Gorbachev or Yeltsin were genetic mutations or alien bodies that somehow seized power in the Soviet system. Not at all. In fact, the authority-building and authority-maintenance framework employed in this book focuses our attention on precisely the opposite. It explores the ways in which leaders fashion appeals to political audiences and then use those appeals to build up their credibility and hence their leverage as leaders.

Once we concede that multiple appeals may resonate with the same audiences, and once we acknowledge that authority building is also an act of manipulation of audiences by leaders, then we are back to asking *how much* latitude leaders had to alter the structural constraints (organizational and ideological) of the system. From this perspective, Gorbachev and Yeltsin were less and less constrained as their efforts to transform the Soviet system moved forward in the 1980s. As the organization and ideology of the Soviet system cracked and then crumbled, Gorbachev's and Yeltsin's personalities and mentalities became that much more determinant of the choices they made.

The role of increasingly autonomous social forces also grew steadily during 1987–1993. Gorbachev released those social forces and then relied on them as a base of support for intimidation of the Old Guard within the establishment. By 1989 we can speak of autonomous social forces as being in perpetual interaction with leaders in reshaping the context of Soviet and post-Soviet politics – and in "co-producing" their leadership strategies. Ultimately, Gorbachev would trail in this process. Yeltsin seized the leadership of the process in 1989, but he too would sometimes be surprised by new levels of radical self-assertion by groups in society.

By 1993, radical social mobilization had subsided or had been channeled into legislative arenas. Under those circumstances, Yeltsin opted for an authority-maintenance strategy that appealed to a particular combination of reformist and conservative forces within both the political establishment and the broader society. By 1996, Yeltsin had built the foundations of a new system. To some extent, that system created structural constraints that, during Yeltsin's second term in office, may have limited his discretion to almost the same degree that the established Soviet system had limited the discretion of Brezhnev in his last years in office. President Putin's tortured efforts to fashion a program for significant change appear to be testimony to the resilience of those constraints. But that is a subject for another book.

12

Criteria for the Evaluation of Transformational Leaders

I have devoted most of this book to *analysis* of the political strategies of Gorbachev and Yeltsin. Chapters 9 and 11, however, were devoted to the challenge of *explaining* their choices. There remains an additional exercise of core relevance to the study of leadership: *evaluation*. How should we evaluate Gorbachev and Yeltsin as leaders? This is by far the most difficult task, for it subsumes the other two. We must determine what those men were trying to do and specify how much latitude they had to pursue those goals before we can evaluate the effectiveness of their leadership. And we must employ counterfactual reasoning ("what might have been") to ask whether their actions led to outcomes that would not have happened in the absence of their leadership. The exercise is made even more challenging by the normative component of any evaluation.[1] I begin the exercise with a short chapter that specifies criteria for the evaluation of transformational leaders. I then devote the last two chapters of the book to evaluations of Gorbachev and Yeltsin as transformational leaders.

REQUISITES OF EFFECTIVE TRANSFORMATIONAL LEADERSHIP

Transformational leadership is a process of what Schumpeter called "creative destruction": dismantling of the old system in a way that simultaneously creates the foundations for a new system.[2] This is a tall order for the most talented of leaders. As I argued in Chapter 1, leaders who seek to accomplish creative destruction must:

---

[1] Recall that the root for the word "evaluation" is "value."

[2] Joseph Schumpeter, *Capitalism, Socialism, and Democracy* (New York & London: Harper & Brothers, 1942), pp. 81–6.

- highlight publicly the incompatibility between emerging environmental demands, on the one hand, and current ordering principles and cultural assumptions, on the other;
- outline an alternative vision of political organization and culture that will restore a harmonious relationship between the transformed unit and its environment;
- mobilize constituencies in support of that vision;
- prevent defenders of the existing order from sabotaging transformation; and
- implement specific programs that will result in the replacement of the existing order with one that is better suited to the environmental demands of tomorrow.

When the point of departure is a monopolistic Leninist system, a transformational leader must:

- create and legitimize autonomous public arenas;
- disperse social, economic, political, and informational resources into those arenas;
- construct new institutions for coordination of decentralized social exchange and integration of the new social order; and
- plant the seeds of a new political–economic culture that is consonant with the new social order.

Thus, he must destroy the structures and culture of the old order, put new structures in their place, and help articulate a new culture. That, in any case, is the ideal. Rare is the leader who is able to succeed in both system destruction and system building. Gorbachev and Yeltsin tried to be successful on both counts.

STANDARDS FOR LEADERSHIP EVALUATION

In both journalism and academic scholarship, leadership evaluation takes place all the time – but usually without reflection on the standards being applied. Consequently, different standards may be applied to the same leader by different observers, leading to divergent bottom-line evaluations.

One standard is purely normative, with the norms determined by the observer: Do I agree or disagree with the values and goals being pursued by the leader? If I agree with his values and goals, I call him "great." If I dislike his values and goals then he cannot qualify as "great." A normative approach might also focus on the results of a leader's policies. If I approve of those results, I render a positive evaluation; if I disagree, my judgment will be negative. (As Hoffmann puts it, "a man who is a hero to my neighbor may be a calamity to me."[3]) More often than not, a normative approach to evaluation will conflate intentions and results, treating the latter as a product of the former.

For example, those who disliked what Gorbachev stood for often brought great passion to their negative evaluations, while those who liked what he stood for often displayed "Gorbymania." *Time* magazine might proclaim Gorbachev its "Man of the Decade," but Soviet reactionaries were damning his Westernization of the country while Soviet free-marketeers were damning his stubborn retention of a commitment to the "socialist idea." People at both ends of the Soviet political spectrum expressed dismay that Gorbachev eventually came to be so much admired abroad yet so little admired at home. When the debate over a leader's "performance" hinges largely on acceptance or rejection of the values he pursued or realized, the debate need not detain us long. It is not amenable to resolution through the marshaling of evidence. The debate may take a detour into a philosophical discussion of the relative merits of different values, but that is a different task than evaluating leadership per se.

Although a purely normative approach is too limited, we still need a standard by which to judge a leader's performance. Hence, a second approach to leadership evaluation hinges principally on judgments about *effectiveness*. Since effectiveness can only be determined relative to a set of goals (effective at achieving *what?*), goals and values must be part of the equation. But taking as our standard the *observer's* values does not get us very far if these differ from the values of the leader in question. It makes no sense to evaluate a leader's effectiveness in achieving goals he was not pursuing. Performance evaluation that is based on a standard of effectiveness must take *the leader's* goals and values as the standard and judge his effectiveness in advancing those goals. This is the approach I adopt in the final chapters of this book. How well did Gorbachev and Yeltsin perform as leaders in pursuit of the goals they embraced?

This approach need not entail approval of the leader's goals. An observer who disagrees with the leader's goals may nonetheless begrudgingly concede that he was highly effective in achieving them. Conversely, an observer who agrees with the goals may sadly concede that the leader proved ineffective in achieving them. And to fill out the possibilities: an observer may disagree

[3] Stanley Hoffmann, "Heroic leadership: The case of modern France," in Lewis J. Edinger (Ed.), *Political Leadership in Industrialized Societies* (New York: Wiley, 1967), p. 113.

with the goals and celebrate the leader's ineffectiveness in pursuing them, or the observer may agree with the goals and celebrate the leader's effectiveness in achieving them.

Effectiveness typically comes at a price. Leaders may achieve their goals at high or low cost to other values. Stalin is an obvious case in point. He built up the military and industrial strength of the country at enormous human and economic cost. Leadership evaluation will therefore hinge on the magnitude of the costs associated with goal attainment. Leaders who achieve their goals at low cost to collateral values may be deemed more effective than those who impose a very high price for goal attainment.

It does not follow, however, that observers will dub such leaders "great." Such characterizations hinge more on the observer's values. If we deeply cherish the values sacrificed for the sake of goal attainment – such as the millions of human lives sacrificed by Stalin – then we may concede that Stalin was an effective but dastardly leader who attained his goals at an unacceptable price. Bringing this point closer to the present, one could concede that Boris Yeltsin was effective in sustaining the territorial unity of the Russian Federation yet condemn him for the price he was willing to pay toward this end in waging two wars in Chechnya. Or, with a similar logic, one could give Gorbachev high marks for attaining his goals of liberalization and democratization but condemn him (if one is so inclined) for his willingness to do so at the expense of the disintegration of the Soviet Union.

It is not surprising that those who condemn Yeltsin's leadership most vociferously also view the social and human costs of his policies as huge. They argue as well that those costs (e.g., the decline in the life-span of Russian men and women) were direct products of his policies – that is, costs that would not have been borne in the absence of his policies.[4] Similarly, those who most vociferously condemn Gorbachev's leadership tend to be those who most valued the Soviet system, the USSR, and/or the country's great-power status and who attribute direct causal responsibility to Gorbachev for the loss of those values.[5] Expressed in this way, the cost of goal attainment is acceptable or unacceptable according to the observer's scale of values. This is an appropriate standard for an evaluative exercise, which cannot escape some normative component. But it is not amenable to resolution through the marshaling of

---

[4] Jerry Hough, *The Logic of Economic Reform in Russia* (Washington, DC: Brookings Institution, 2001); Peter Reddaway and Dmitri Glinski, *The Tragedy of Russia's Reforms: Market Bolshevism against Democracy* (Washington, DC: U.S. Institute of Peace, 2000).

[5] This is a rare person in Western scholarship; it is common among Russian journalists of a revanchist persuasion.

evidence. Hence, a social-scientific approach to leadership evaluation will logically veer toward another set of issues: What was the alternative? How effective would alternative strategies have been for attaining the goals at a lower price?

THE INESCAPABILITY OF COUNTERFACTUAL REASONING

Leaders and their supporters often defend themselves against criticism of the costs of their policies by invoking an image of intractable constraints. The implication is that advancement or defense of cherished values could not have been accomplished by other means. That is a counterfactual claim. Thus, Viacheslav Molotov, a leading Politburo member under Stalin, referred to the human and economic cost of Stalinist policies as "regrettable necessities." Unrepentant Stalinists in many countries deflected criticism of the costs of Stalinism by arguing that "you cannot make an omelette without breaking eggs."[6] Gorbachev and his supporters tried to parry criticisms from Party conservatives by arguing that "there is no alternative" and that "there is no other way" (*inogo ne dano*). Defenders of Yeltsin's policies in Chechnya argued that even Abraham Lincoln had to wage a bloody civil war in order to hold the United States together. Defenders of Yeltsin's neoliberal macroeconomic policies frequently argued that alternatives to their preferred policies would not "work."

In all these cases, the counterfactual is usually buttressed by a theoretical claim. Stalin invoked a theory of state building, nation building, and economic development in a hostile international environment that seemed to narrow drastically the set of policies claimed to be effective in such a setting. Gorbachev's defenders suggested that only a policy that shattered the immunity of the Party–State elite could overcome the systemic stagnation that had beset the ancien régime. Yeltsin's defenders claimed that, even in democratic systems, force is required to prevent armed secession. Yeltsin's neoliberal advisers similarly argued that "shock therapy" constituted the only viable strategy for making the transition from a command economy to a market economy.

Both critics and defenders of Gorbachev and Yeltsin often join the argument not on theoretical grounds but on the basis of an empirical estimation of the intellectual availability, political feasibility, and practicability of

---

[6] Prompting Chalmers Johnson to ask: "How many eggs do you have to break to make a one-egg omelette?" (in "Foreword" of Alexander Dallin and George W. Breslauer, *Political Terror in Communist Systems* [Stanford, CA: Stanford University Press, 1970], p. vi).

alternative policies in the given historical context. Thus, when people criticize Gorbachev for not having pushed through a Chinese-style economic
reform and for not having adopted radical price reform early in his tenure,[7]
his defenders claim that he faced great uncertainty about whether the Chinese reforms would work in the Soviet context and about the compatibility
of price liberalization with political stability.[8] When Yeltsin is condemned
for adopting neoliberal policies in January 1992,[9] his defenders argue that, in
the concrete economic circumstances of the time, alternative policies would
have caused a financial and economic collapse with even more dire consequences.[10] And when Yeltsin is criticized for not being more accommodative
of the political opposition in the Supreme Soviet and Duma,[11] his defenders
argue or imply that the opposition was more powerful and more reactionary
in orientation than Yeltsin's critics allow. They argue that the opposition had
both the strength and the inclination to win power and to restore some variant
of the old regime – hence, the alternative (by this observer's scale of values)
would have been worse.[12]

In short, evaluation of a leader's effectiveness in attaining his goals at a pro-
portionate price hinges also on one's image of the strength of the constraints
facing the leader at the time. If the constraints were onerous, we would nor-
mally expect less accomplishment than if the constraints were loose. A leader
who manages to stretch (but not obliterate) the constraints in his environment, and thereby to initiate substantial movement at an acceptable cost, is
typically deemed both effective and impressive. By contrast, a leader who is
defeated by those constraints may be deemed ineffective but doomed to failure
if the constraints are perceived to have been immutable, or he may be judged
ineffective and incompetent if he failed to seize the opportunities available to
him. And if a leader accomplishes much but in a context wherein constraints

[7] Jerry Hough, *Revolution and Democratization in the USSR, 1985–1991* (Washington, DC:
Brookings Institution, 1998).
[8] George W. Breslauer, "Evaluating Gorbachev as leader," *Soviet Economy,* vol. 8, no. 4
(October–December 1989), pp. 299–340.
[9] Reddaway and Glinski, *The Tragedy of Russia's Reforms.*
[10] Anders Åslund, *How Russia Became a Market Economy* (Washington, DC: Brookings Institution, 1995); Andrei Shleifer and Daniel Treisman, *Without a Map: Political Tactics and
Economic Reform in Russia* (Cambridge, MA: MIT Press, 2000).
[11] This is a standard refrain by many scholars contributing to the Internet-based *Johnson's Russia List.*
[12] This is a major theme of Leon Aron, *Boris Yeltsin: A Revolutionary Life* (New York: Harper-
Collins, 2000); contrast this with Hough's depiction of the strength and orientations of the
opposition in *The Logic of Economic Reform.* Intermediate positions are struck by Lilia
Shevtsova, *Yeltsin's Russia: Myths and Realities* (Washington, DC: Carnegie Endowment,
1999) and Reddaway and Glinski, *The Tragedy of Russia's Reforms.*

were few and easily stretched, he may be judged to have been effective but unimpressive ("anybody could have done it").

Thus, leadership cannot be evaluated without some conception of its flip side: opportunity. If the challenge was so great as to be impossible to achieve, then (by definition) no amount of brilliance could have overcome the constraints. Under such circumstances, there was no opportunity to exploit. On the other hand, if the challenge was a simple one, or if existing social and political forces would have pushed through the changes we witnessed in any case, then the leader can hardly be credited with having "made history."

Notice that making these judgments requires us to think in counterfactual terms. We may gather a large amount of evidence regarding the nature of the constraints, the strength of social forces, and the like. But without trying to imagine how these constraints and forces would have evolved _in the absence of the leader in question,_ or in the presence of either a stronger or weaker leader, we cannot estimate either the magnitude of the opportunity or the indispensability of a given leader for exploiting it. Since other leaders were not in power and since other approaches were not attempted, we cannot test with high confidence the size of the opportunity that was available. The difficulty in addressing the "might have beens" of history has led many historians to disparage counterfactual thought experiments as little more than fruitless speculation or parlor games.[13]

But without counterfactual reasoning there can be no evaluation of leadership. Methodologically, a convincing exercise in leadership evaluation must interweave counterfactual reasoning with traditional methods of analysis and explanation. It must combine disciplined speculation about available alternatives with analysis of the strength of constraints and efforts to specify the causes of outcomes. Thus, leadership evaluation must seek to determine how much causal responsibility to assign to the exercise of leadership for the outcomes observed; it must also ask whether hypothetical alternatives were indeed available. It must analyze the magnitude of the task, the magnitude and mutability of the constraints on change, and the magnitude of the divergence from the traditional (and currently available) skills and mentality required to carry out the task in the face of those constraints. Ultimately, it must address such questions as: To what extent was the individual's repertoire of

---

[13] Historians tend to reject counterfactual analysis as a scholarly exercise, whereas social scientists often embrace it. Such historians include E. H. Carr, A. J. P. Taylor, and E. P. Thompson. For a book by social scientists that is devoted to the methodology and application of counterfactual reasoning in the study of international affairs, see Philip Tetlock and Aaron Belkin (Eds.), _Counterfactual Thought Experiments in World Politics_ (Princeton, NJ: Princeton University Press, 1996).

leadership skills, and the leadership strategy he adopted, a necessary (albeit not sufficient) condition for achieving the results observable during his years in power? How different would things have been had he not been in power? Could other individuals who were available at the time have accomplished as much as, or more than, he did? How powerful were the political constraints on his choices? Could he have succeeded in even more than he dared to attempt? Or would he have been forced from power – or at least frustrated – had he tried?

Given all these uncertainties, we might be tempted to abandon the task of leadership evaluation or to consign it to journalistic exercises in special issues of popular magazines.[14] That would be unwise. Historians and social scientists do not abandon their craft because the evidence is inconclusive; they seek to make the best of what they have and then to present their conclusions as always subject to future revision. The same goes for counterfactual speculation, which is not as different from historical explanation, methodologically or epistemologically, as many historians assume.[15] Moreover, no matter how indeterminate the exercise, people will go on evaluating leaders, for better or for worse, and their evaluations of leaders in power will sometimes feed back into the political process. How scholars, politicians, and journalists evaluate current or historical leaders can influence present-day politics. Indeed, with respect to current leaders being evaluated while in office, it can become part of the social constraints they face and can influence the opportunities they enjoy – and thereby affect their prospects of eventually succeeding or failing! Hence, to abandon leadership evaluation because of its inconclusiveness or indeterminacy is to abandon scholarship. And eschewing it because of its normative components and possible political impact is an unnecessary act of scholarly abdication.

Gorbachev and Yeltsin were unmistakably "event-making men."[16] Both of them began as reformers of the system and then sought to transform or replace it, though they chose very different strategies for achieving their goals. Both of them faced huge constraints at home and abroad. Both of them were unique figures within elite circles. It is difficult to imagine other leaders at the time who would have made an analogous degree of difference. In evaluating

---

[14] See, for example, the special issue of *Time* magazine (April 13, 1998) devoted to evaluation of twentieth-century leaders.

[15] See George Breslauer and Richard Ned Lebow, "Gorbachev, Reagan, and the end of the Cold War," in Richard K. Herrmann and Richard Ned Lebow (Eds.), *Learning from the Cold War* (forthcoming).

[16] The concept of "event-making man" is from Sidney Hook, *The Hero in History* (Boston: Beacon, 1943), p. 154.

Gorbachev's and Yeltsin's effectiveness as leaders, then, we must address the extent to which they achieved their stated goals and the price they proved willing to pay toward that end.

AUTHORITY BUILDING AND LEADERSHIP EVALUATION

Transformational leadership is a process, not an event. Such leaders must attend to many issues and dilemmas that unfold unevenly over a period of time. Throughout this process, they must attend as well to the condition of their personal authority. Are they building their authority in ways that will leave them positioned to sponsor a thrust – a breakthrough – that will overcome the constraints on fundamental change? Having accomplished that, they must attend to the challenge of authority maintenance. Have they justified their breakthrough to audiences that may have the capacity to unravel the changes? And, equally important, do they retain the credibility to engage in the follow-up required to elaborate on the changes?

A breakthrough may be required to undo the old structures and delegitimize the old culture. But numerous and repeated follow-up initiatives are required to put new structures in place and to build legitimacy for the new order. A leader's capacity to engage in such follow-up hinges on the condition of his power and authority. Did he squander them in the course of pushing through his breakthrough policies? Or did he position himself to retain the *power* for follow-up and explain himself sufficiently to retain the *authority* for follow-up? As we shall see, both Gorbachev and Yeltsin had mixed records on these scores.

13

Evaluating Gorbachev as Leader

Among observers who shared his goal of transforming the communist system, those who most approve of Gorbachev's record as leader emphasize the extent to which he broke down the ancien régime. Among the same set of observers, those who most disparage Gorbachev's record focus instead on the extent to which he fell short of building the new system he envisaged. Neither of these approaches is wholly satisfying; nor is a combination of the two. They are both linear and rote comparisons of outcomes with baselines. But they are useful starting points toward a more complex analysis.

If the past is our baseline, and if we postpone the problem of determining Gorbachev's distinctive contribution to the outcome, it is easy to sum up what changed under Gorbachev. We witnessed:

- desacralization of the Brezhnevite political–economic order in the eyes of the mass public, including the official principles and mind-set that underpinned it – the leading role of the Party, the "community of peoples," the planned economy, pride in the system's achievements, optimism about state socialism's potential, commitment to "class struggle" abroad, and a national-security phobia that justified a repressive, militarized regime;
- a sharp reduction in the power of constituencies that were pillars of the Brezhnevite political order – in particular, Party officials, ministers, and the military;
- legitimation in principle of movement in the direction of a market-driven economic order, a multiparty system, and the transformation of a unitary state into a democratic federal state;
- changes in politics and structure that (a) greatly decentralized political initiative, (b) created more open and competitive public political arenas –

including parliaments based on competitive, secret-ballot elections, (c) all but disenfranchised the *nomenklatura,* and (d) swept radical majorities into power in the governmental councils of major cities;

- dismantling of much of the command economy and the emergence of a nascent private sector ("cooperatives");
- introduction of civil liberties with respect to dissent, emigration, the media, travel, religion, and association;
- a vast opening of the country to Western political, cultural, and economic influences;
- elimination of Soviet control over Eastern Europe, reduction of Soviet military capabilities, retrenchment in Third World policy, and withdrawal of Soviet troops from Afghanistan; and
- changes in foreign policy that brought an end to the Cold War.

Historically, only revolutions from below have accomplished more in a shorter period of time. And revolutions from below have rarely been marked by the scant violence that Gorbachev's revolution entailed.

Using the same methodology, however, one could specify either how much had *not* changed during the Gorbachev era or had changed for the worse (by a short-term humanitarian standard):

- a doleful consumer situation that, in 1990–1991, was worse than it had been in 1985;
- an economy that was experiencing accelerating negative growth of national income, was ridden by a huge budgetary deficit and monetary overhang, and was suffering from potentially explosive repressed inflation;
- economic disorganization, lack of coordination, and massive corruption resulting from destruction of the institutions of a command economy without the construction of institutions of a market economy;
- widespread intercommunal violence in the southern republics of the USSR;
- disintegration of the unitary state as well as centrifugal pressures that left the country on the verge of separatism by half the republics in the union;
- a sharp increase in the incidence of violent crime throughout the country; and
- failure to induce the rich democracies to underwrite the Soviet economic transition.

Were the changes between 1985 and 1991 on balance positive or negative? This is a normative judgment. The answer depends on the relative weights placed on the values in question. Clearly, one glance at these lists indicates that things worsened with respect to the economic situation and the cohesion of the USSR as an entity; things improved in the areas of political freedom, cultural openness, and East–West relations, where "improvement" is measured according to Gorbachev's professed scale of values.[1]

Another approach would take as its baseline not the past but the vision of a future new order. The easy variant of this approach is simply to measure the shortfall between Soviet reality in mid-1991 and Gorbachev's vision of a stable social(ist)-democratic polity that was integrated into Western institutions and treated internationally as a great power, a tolerable federation or confederation, and a prospectively flourishing mixed economy based on a combination of private, collective, and state ownership.[2] By this standard, Gorbachev surely fell short as a transformational leader. He did not succeed in steering an evolutionary transition from the Soviet system to a system based on these ordering principles. Instead, the house collapsed upon him and he was ousted from office.

GORBACHEV: AN EVENT-MAKING MAN?

If we treat the list of positive changes between 1985 and 1991 as the basis for a positive evaluation of Gorbachev as leader, then we presume that he himself was causally responsible for the changes. That would be too generous a judgment, for we know that many outcomes after 1989 were products of forces over which he had little control. But we can still ask whether, on balance, Gorbachev was an "event-making man" whose uncommon personal traits led to outcomes that would not have taken place in the absence of the leadership he provided. In this exercise, the issue is not normative but causal. It does not matter whether we approve or disapprove of the outcomes, only whether we believe that Gorbachev was responsible for bringing them about. By this standard, Gorbachev was indeed an event-making man.

Changes in social structure during the post-Stalin decades are insufficient to explain the changes that took place during 1985–1989, though a focus on societal initiatives probably does explain much of what happened in 1990–1991. The social forces supportive of *perestroika, glasnost'*, democratization, and "new thinking" in foreign policy encouraged and facilitated Gorbachev's changes. Indeed, they were probably necessary conditions for the changes in

---

[1] Observers who mourn Soviet loss of superpower status and control over Eastern Europe would not place the "end of the Cold War" in the "improvements" category.

[2] For present purposes, I will treat the period of March 1985 to late August 1991 (i.e., through the coup attempt) as the "Gorbachev era." Thereafter, disintegrative trends accelerated sharply and Gorbachev's political authority had all but evaporated.

policy to be enacted, implemented, and sustained. It is difficult, for example, to imagine Gorbachev having accomplished as much as he did had he been leading the Soviet Union in 1955 rather than 1985. But the changes that had taken place in Soviet society, while providing a support base for Gorbachev to activate, were not sufficient to force policymakers to enact the policies Gorbachev sponsored. The relationship between social forces and sociopolitical change was heavily dependent on political leadership.

Gorbachev exercised active, determined leadership in the years following his consolidation of power. He intervened repeatedly to let the *glasnost'* genie out of the bottle, to encourage the public to criticize the bureaucrats, to hold off the forces of backlash, to recall Andrei Sakharov from exile, to release political prisoners, and to force through a democratization program that began the process of transferring power from the Party to the soviets. Gorbachev made the decisions that led to steadily expanding civil liberties of all sorts. Gorbachev made the doctrinal pronouncements that encouraged or tolerated *public* desacralization of the Brezhnevite order. This desacralization induced societal activists to believe that fundamental change was not only desirable and necessary (which many of them probably believed already) but possible as well. And Gorbachev's pronouncements had the simultaneous effect of discouraging recalcitrant bureaucrats from thinking that they could hold back the tide. He did all this at a stage of his administration when predecessors (Khrushchev and Brezhnev) had engaged in selective reincorporation – during their stages of ascendancy (see Chapter 11).

In similar fashion, Gorbachev took the lead on matters of foreign policy, often surprising his domestic political audiences with announcements of Soviet concessions on nuclear and conventional arms control, making the fundamental decision to cut losses in Afghanistan, and pulling the rug from under conservative East European elites by withdrawing the Soviet guarantee of protection against revolutionary forces. Gorbachev articulated a vision of a post–Cold War world, Soviet integration into the European cultural, political, and economic orders, and demilitarization of foreign policy that became the basis for both planning and legitimizing his turnabouts in both domestic and foreign policy. Gorbachev decided to turn on the faucet of emigration once again, allowing Soviet citizens to travel to the West more freely.

To be sure, once sufficiently emboldened and organized, social forces pushed to radicalize Gorbachev's policies more quickly and more fully than he was comfortable with at the time. In the face of this society-driven radicalization, Gorbachev still had a choice: he could have allied with conservatives to "draw the line" and enforce strict limits. Instead – until his course correction of late 1990 and with the exception of his response to intercommunal violence in the south – he typically made a virtue of necessity. He resisted the temptation to use force, often allying with more radical forces, using tactical surprise to further consolidate his power at the top, and purging or holding at bay those who would have preferred to use such radicalization as justification for reversing or halting the reform process. Thus, in 1989–1990, Gorbachev was more reactive than initiatory, but he was still event-making in his ability to prevent the use of state-directed violence against the radicalizing tide. (A tragic exception occurred in Tbilisi in April 1989.[3]) When he lost his nerve in fall 1990, he was no longer event-making at all and had actually though inadvertently created the conditions for both the bloodshed in Vilnius and Riga and the coup of August 1991.

The event-making man not only makes a difference but does so because of his exceptional personal qualities. On this score, the evidence seems to be conclusive. Even those who criticize Gorbachev for the limits of his flexibility in his last years in power acknowledge that he was an unusual member of the Chernenko-led Politburo. No member of that Politburo has been portrayed as capable of seizing the initiative on sociopolitical and international issues the way Gorbachev eventually did. Gorbachev's intellectual capacity and flexibility, his powers of argumentation, his serenity in the midst of social turmoil and faith that turbulence will "smooth out" in the long run,[4] his "sustained, single-minded motivation ... an irrepressible optimism,"[5] his energy, determination, and tactical political skill,[6] and his capacity for learning on the job[7] have been noted by observers and interlocutors alike. By previous Soviet standards, as well as by comparative international standards, he stands

---

[3] A commission of inquiry, which included people closer to Yeltsin than to Gorbachev, exonerated Gorbachev from charges of having ordered the use of force (Archie Brown, *The Gorbachev Factor* [Oxford & New York: Oxford University Press, 1996], pp. 264–7); but it remains the case that he failed to prevent it.

[4] Ronald Tiersky, "Perestroika and beyond," *Problems of Communism*, vol. 39, no. 2 (March–April 1990), p. 114; *Time* magazine, June 4, 1990, pp. 27–34.

[5] Doig and Hargrove find this characteristic to be typical of successful leaders of the public bureaucracies they studied (Jameson W. Doig and Erwin C. Hargrove [Eds.], *Leadership and Innovation* [Baltimore: Johns Hopkins University Press, 1967], p. 19).

[6] See Dusko Doder and Louise Branson, *Gorbachev: Heretic in the Kremlin* (New York: Viking, 1990), pp. 31, 304, and passim.

[7] Ibid., pp. 31, 75, 106, 126–8, 157, 163, 218–19, and 374–6 for examples. See also Brown, *The Gorbachev Factor*, chs. 4 and 7, and Robert D. English, *Russia and the Idea of the West: Gorbachev, Intellectuals and the End of the Cold War* (New York: Columbia University Press, 2000), chs. 5 and 6. Henry Kissinger (*White House Years* [Boston: Little, Brown, 1979], p. 54) has argued that "it is an illusion to believe that leaders gain in profundity while they gain experience .... The convictions that leaders have formed before reaching high office are the intellectual capital they will consume as long as they continue in office." The evolution of Gorbachev's thinking during his first five years in office challenges the applicability to his

out as a man of unusual leadership capacity. Had Gorbachev not been chosen general secretary after Chernenko's death, destruction of the Brezhnevite political order, the creation and nurturing of new democratic institutions and practices, and the radical concessionary turn in Soviet foreign policy would not have taken place as they did – or even at all – in the 1980s.

GORBACHEV'S STRATEGY OF "CULTURE AND POLITICS FIRST"

Gorbachev moved more quickly on political liberalization (*glasnost'*), political democratization, and ending the Cold War than he did on economic reform and federalizing the union. Thus, he treated cultural and political transformation, at home and abroad, as preconditions for sustained improvements in economic performance and inter-ethnic relations. Indeed, Gorbachev was quite explicit about his conclusion that cultural change ("the human factor") was a prerequisite for economic reform: "We have to begin, first of all, with changes in our attitudes and psychology, with the style and method of work," he declared in April 1986. "I have to tell you frankly that, if we do not change ourselves, I am deeply convinced there will be no changes in the economy and our social life."[8] Some of Gorbachev's earliest boosters were quick to notice, and to approve, this theory of transition.[9]

Gorbachev used the resources of his offices to delegitimize the old order – both its institutional framework and the social values it allegedly protected. He simultaneously created new public arenas within which the awakened society could exercise initiative for the political and economic good of the country. He launched *perestroika* by defining the situation of the USSR in the world as one that demanded emergency surgery lest the country descend into second-class status. He reacted to unpleasant surprises (the Chernobyl disaster of April 1986; a young German's landing of a Cessna airplane in Red Square in May 1987) by purging members of the Old Guard and by arguing that those surprises demonstrated the urgent need for cultural and institutional change.

---

leadership of Kissinger's generalization. If that challenge is sustainable, it would strengthen a positive evaluation of Gorbachev's leadership skills. Alternatively, one could argue that Gorbachev's "convictions" were fixed before he came to power and that his learning was largely "tactical" within the bounds of his earlier convictions. Part of the problem in deciding this question is purely definitional. Does "conviction" refer to values alone or also to one's understandings about cause–effect relations within the domestic system, society, and international environment?

[8] Gorbachev speech of April 8, 1986, as quoted in Doder and Branson, *Gorbachev*, p. 137.
[9] Robert C. Tucker, *Political Culture and Leadership in Soviet Russia: From Lenin to Gorbachev* (New York: Norton, 1987), ch. 7; Thomas Naylor, *The Gorbachev Strategy* (Lexington, MA: Lexington, 1988).

He defined a tight connection between his foreign and domestic policies, harnessing forces in the international arena to further the cause of political and cultural change within the Soviet Union. In each case this served organizational and technical ends, but in each case it also served the more important goals of transforming politics, identities, and culture. Gorbachev sought to transform culture by simultaneously altering the ideology and the organization of Soviet politics.

Thus, by opening the Soviet economy to global competition, Gorbachev was trying not only to increase pressure on Soviet managers and draw in foreign capital but also to force elites and masses alike to define progress relative to the achievements of advanced capitalist countries, rather than relative to the Russian or Soviet past. By encouraging McDonald's to open an outlet in Moscow, by televising images of Western living standards, and by encouraging televised discussions of the progress of Chinese economic reforms, he not only whetted consumer appetites but undercut traditional images of "capitalist hell" through which the ruling elite had justified maintenance of a low-opportunity system. By opening the country to cultural Westernization, Gorbachev did more than reduce the political, scientific, and international costs of trying to insulate the country from the information revolution; he also challenged the idea of Russian or Soviet "originality" (*samobytnost'*) that had justified both the Brezhnevite order and the xenophobia of Russian ethno-nationalists. By working to reduce international threats to the USSR, he created preconditions for lowering the defense budget and diluted the national-security phobia that had been used to justify domination of the economy by the military–industrial complex. By repudiating class struggle abroad and by emphasizing the priority of "all-human values," he not only defused regional crises and paved the way for arms control (and other forms of superpower cooperation) but also undermined the rationale for the CPSU's continued monopoly on power and truth. Indeed, the extraordinary importance of ideas and doctrines in Leninist systems made it all the more imperative that transformational leaders in such regimes first delegitimize relevant aspects of traditional elite ideology – and its impact on mass perceptions of what is feasible – as a precondition for creating the political space for new patterns of behavior and organization.

As successful transformational leaders must, Gorbachev recognized that a precondition for fundamental change is the destruction of old identities and tolerance of the social conflict that inevitably accompanies such a passage. He used social and political conflict as occasions for educating citizenry and polity alike to the idea that there is no change without pain and no democracy without conflict. He reacted to unanticipated levels of conflict (except for intercommunal violence and the use of violence against state organs) by claiming them as proof that the old way of doing things was intolerable and, more importantly, was now capable of being changed. He articulated a vision of the USSR as a "normal" modern country on the model of the social democratic European welfare state, even as he fudged the question of whether a market-based pluralist democracy is consistent with "socialism." He spoke the language of evolution, defining change (both at home and abroad) as a long-term process that requires acclimatization to continuous change. Although he did not transform the welfare-state mentality of most of the population, he did foster a widespread belief in (socialist) pluralism and (socialist) markets as the desirable and feasible alternatives to political oppression and economic stagnation.

Gorbachev also tried to legitimize creation of a legal culture that would depersonalize legal institutions of the state and thereby provide a foundation of stable expectations for the protection of person and property. He called for a new legal code, a more independent judiciary, transfer of power from Party organs to soviets at all levels, and transformation of soviets into parliamentary institutions that generate legislation binding on all people. These were some of the components of his professed commitment to a "law-based state" (*pravovoe gosudarstvo*) to replace the previous order's arbitrary rule by Party officials. Of course, building a rule of law and instilling legal consciousness in the citizenry are long-term processes. But Gorbachev started the journey by legitimizing the search for a procedurally predictable alternative to arbitrary, personalistic governance and by disrupting the ability of Party organs to dominate the legal realm.

In like manner, Gorbachev sought to transform the culture of international relations. The targets of his attack were the dominant "realist" paradigm that emphasized the balancing of military power; the "enemy image" that fed worst-case planning and weapons procurement; and the "two camps" mentality that defined superpower competition as a confrontational, zero-sum game. Instead, he justified his concessionary foreign policy by propounding an idealist vision of international politics that sought to transform the image of the USSR into that of a partner in solving all-human problems. His conviction appears to have been that such a transformation in assumptions about the enemy was a prerequisite for ending the Cold War, and that ending the Cold War was a precondition for the kind of international climate needed to support Soviet internal transformation. The "new thinking," then, was aimed at both domestic and foreign audiences. In both cases, the purpose was ideational change; in both cases, the goal was to destroy an old way of thinking and to inculcate a new one.

On his own terms, then, Gorbachev was successful in delegitimizing the inherited approach to political life at home and abroad and its hostility to a democratic political order and a post–Cold War international order. Indeed, such change may be his principal claim to fame as a transformational leader.

Now I turn from Gorbachev's strategy of transformation to the political tactics he employed to make this a *peaceful* and *evolutionary* transformation. One place to look for guidance in this regard is the burgeoning literature on transitions to democracy. The prescriptions in that literature may not be entirely applicable to the case of a Leninist multi-ethnic empire, but they do remain suggestive of tactics for a peaceful political transition. Gorbachev's leadership can then be judged against those standards. If he failed in spite of using such tactics, then this may be more of a reflection on the inapplicability of his overall strategy in the Soviet context than on the appropriateness of his political tactics. Moreover, since Gorbachev's highest-priority domestic task was political reform and transformation, it is appropriate to treat him as a leader who tried to effect a transition to democracy and to judge him against the standards for leadership described in that literature.

GORBACHEV'S TACTICS AND TRANSITIONS TO DEMOCRACY

The Western literature on transitions to democracy has gone through several stages. The first generation of that literature treated democratization as a process that depended for its success on social, cultural, and economic preconditions. Little or no attention was devoted to leadership, which implicitly was treated as a hopeless exercise in the absence of the socioeconomic and cultural prerequisites. The more recent literature, in contrast, is much less deterministic and pessimistic. Its optimism and (some would say excessive) voluntarism are based on a reexamination of the West European historical experience and on observation of the recent successful transitions in Southern Europe, Latin America, and East Asia.[10]

This body of literature takes many confining conditions as mutable and not as decisive obstacles to democratic breakthroughs and democratic consolidation, even though it does acknowledge that some conditions may frustrate even the most skillful leadership strategy. It focuses on coalition-building strategies within the elites and on strategies for creating "political space" for new publics being mobilized into politics by the collapse of authoritarian regimes. Hence, it is primarily interested in leadership as a factor that

---

[10] The most voluntaristic and optimistic of these recent works is Giuseppe di Palma, *To Craft Democracies* (Berkeley: University of California Press, 1991).

not only facilitates the democratic breakthrough and consolidation but also guards against the ever-present threat of military coup and other forms of regression. Since this is precisely what Gorbachev was trying to do – although under socioeconomic and ethnic conditions that were less propitious than those facing traditional authoritarian regimes – a number of prescriptions for successful leadership tactics can be gleaned from this literature and applied as tests to Gorbachev.

Tactic No. 1: *Attempt to discredit alternatives to the democratic path in order to keep them less legitimate in the public and elite consciousness than is the prospective democratic outcome.* As Przeworski puts it: "what matters for the stability of any regime is not the legitimacy of this particular system of domination but the presence or absence of preferable alternatives."[11] From this standpoint, Gorbachev's strategy of initially desacralizing the old order made good sense; his tactic of arguing that "there is no alternative" to continuing along the reformist path likewise constituted good politics. His arguments that Soviet national security and competitiveness in the twenty-first century would be threatened by a failure to join the "modern" world, to become a "normal" country," and to "learn democracy" powerfully advanced the message that hypothetical alternatives to *perestroika* simply were not workable and that they were unpalatable from both liveability and national-security standpoints.

Tactic No. 2: *Mobilize new social forces into politics that will ally with reformist forces within the establishment.* This is precisely what *glasnost'* and democratization accomplished until 1989–1990, when those social forces broke with the establishment. When Gorbachev unveiled his transformational strategy in 1987–1988, he probably did not anticipate how far it would go. But when faced with the consequences in the subsequent two years, he did not lead a backlash. Rather, he accommodated himself to the tide, legitimized its "extremism" (thus making a virtue of necessity), moved himself to the "left" (toward radicalism) on the elite political spectrum, and sought to create new political institutions that would regulate the conflicts now made manifest. This was an important move. It sent out early signals of an attractive democratic game in order to avoid the early disillusion so common during failed transitions.

---

[11] Adam Przeworski, "Some problems in the study of the transition to democracy," in Guillermo O'Donnell, Philippe C. Schmitter, and Laurence Whitehead (Eds.), *Transitions from Authoritarian Rule: Comparative Perspectives* (Baltimore: Johns Hopkins University Press, 1986), pp. 51–2.

From this perspective, it was fortunate that Gorbachev's speech at the January 1987 plenum of the Central Committee called for multicandidate secret elections and general pluralization of the political order. It was also fortunate that the June 1988 Party Conference, and the first meetings of the Congress of People's Deputies and the Supreme Soviet, could be viewed on national television. The combination of pluralization and publicity managed to demystify politics and allowed people to believe that political involvement might be rewarding. Gorbachev was simultaneously mobilizing new social forces, discrediting the old political order, and creating new political institutions to regulate conflict between new social forces and the Old Guard. This also created new political space within which democratic oppositions could develop ties with moderates within the regime.

Tactic No. 3: *Create opportunities for the co-optation of leaders and activists of opposition groups into new political arenas in which they, and reformist members of the establishment, can pursue and learn the pragmatic and accommodative tactics of a democratic process.* In the most general sense, Gorbachev's creation of new political institutions sought to maintain stability by expanding the opportunities for authentic political participation at a rate equal to or exceeding the rate of political mobilization triggered by *glasnost'*.[12] But at the specific level of inter-elite interaction, these institutions proved to be arenas in which general issues of proceduralism, rule of law, parliamentary practice, and the like came to the fore. Although the path was a rocky one and littered with conflict, that is unsurprising in any democratic transition. What is significant is that the slow process of institutionalization got off the ground and gained momentum. Early studies of that process showed that respect for proceduralism had grown not only among reformists but also among fence-sitters and conservatives.[13] As di Palma argued, when moderate conservatives conclude that democratization is the only game in town, they can sometimes become very fast learners.[14]

Tactic No. 4: *Strip the privileged corporate interests of the old regime of their political immunity, but give them enough protection against dispossession that they do not exit en masse and seek allies who would help them to violently reverse the democratization process.* People whose immunity was

---

[12] According to Samuel Huntington (*Political Order in Changing Societies* [New Haven, CT: Yale University Press, 1968]), maintaining a balance between the level of political participation and the level of institutionalization is key to maintaining political stability during times of change.

[13] Victor M. Sergeyev and Nikolai Biryukov, *Russia's Road to Democracy: Parliament, Communism and Traditional Culture* (Aldershot, U.K.: Edward Elgar, 1993).

[14] Giuseppe di Palma, *To Craft Democracies*, ch. IV.

guaranteed under the old regime had to be stripped of that immunity *and* given a sufficient stake in the new order so that they would not resort to "breakdown games."[15] The imperative is to "make institutionalized uncertainty palatable"[16] enough that significant segments of the Old Guard are more willing to play along than to defect. The idea is that they will not only play the game but will also come to learn and (eventually) value the new rules. It is imperative to frighten the conservatives into believing that there is no choice but to join the new democratic game as well as to reassure them that they have a place, protected by the leader, in that game.[17]

From these perspectives, Gorbachev's political tactics look wise. His reforms destroyed the political immunity of the Old Guard and reduced the influence of the military on domestic and foreign policymaking. At the same time, he distanced himself from the radical abolitionist forces and thereby maintained for a time his ties with conservative establishment forces. This strategy manifested itself in: (1) his unwillingness to endorse calls for confiscation of the elite's socioeconomic privileges; (2) his *honorable* retirement of many Politburo and Central Committee members; (3) his willingness to allow many conservative and reactionary forces to speak at televised meetings of the Central Committee and Congress of People's Deputies; (4) his introduction of an electoral system that initially reserved significant proportions of seats to elitist designation by Party, trade union, communist youth league, and Academy of Sciences executive committees; (5) the gap between his proposals at the 19th Party Conference (June 1988) and the proposals offered at that forum by Boris Yeltsin; (6) his approach to economic reform, which allowed many officials to find a stake in the private sector through a process of "spontaneous" or "*nomenklatura*" privatization (which other analysts might refer to as massive insider theft of assets); and (7) his gingerly treatment of the KGB.

To many radicals in the Soviet Union and abroad, these concessions appeared to be unacceptable conservatism and evidence of Gorbachev's upbringing as a believing communist and *apparatchik*. However, from the standpoint of people steeped in the comparative literature on transitions, it made sense.

---

[15] I take this concept from di Palma (ibid., p. 110–11).

[16] Ibid., p. 32.

[17] This power tactic is applicable to pluralist leadership more generally. Thus, writing about presidential power, Richard Neustadt advises the leader "to induce as much uncertainty as possible about the consequences of ignoring what he wants. If he cannot make men think him bound to win, his need is to keep them from thinking they can cross him without risk, or that they can be sure what risks they run. At the same time (no mean feat), he needs to keep them from fearing lest he leave them in the lurch if they support him" (Richard Neustadt, *Presidential Power* [New York: Wiley, 1960], p. 64).

At the same time, Gorbachev's deft use of crises – some manufactured, some not – to purge or marginalize conservatives in the leadership both disarmed forces of backlash and encouraged bandwagoning tendencies among the fence-sitters by maintaining high uncertainty about the chances of success if they bucked him.[18] Instead of being discredited by crises, Gorbachev used them in ways that allowed him to seize the political initiative and further radicalize his programs.

Tactic No. 5: *When stalemates arise, up the ante in order to increase the perceived costs of regression.* This prescription is based on Robert Dahl's famous dictum that democratic breakthroughs hinge on keeping the perceived price of repression higher than the perceived price of toleration.[19] The issue is not whether the current price of toleration is desirable or enjoyable; the issue is whether it is perceived to be more tolerable than the price of a violent backlash.[20]

On this score, Gorbachev pursued a consistently successful strategy during his first five years in power (until mid-1990). He was a "radical centrist," seeking to keep the process moving to the "left" while he himself dominated (but protected) the floating center of the political spectrum. By encouraging the activation of social forces pushing for more radical change, or by joining with those social forces when they surprised him, Gorbachev could more easily argue that the price of restoring the former status quo had become prohibitive. And by encouraging the public expression of popular views that were so impatient for change and so enraged by the privilege and corruption of the old order, Gorbachev could more credibly argue that any effort to restore the former status quo – even if successful in the short run – would only postpone the day of reckoning. At the same time, Gorbachev's selective protection of

---

[18] On the importance of creating incentives for bandwagoning by fence-sitters, see Avery Goldstein, *From Bandwagon to Balance-of-Power Politics: Structural Constraints and Politics in China, 1949–1978* (Stanford, CA: Stanford University Press, 1991); on the importance of using power in ways that simultaneously increase one's legitimacy as leader, see Neustadt, *Presidential Power.*

[19] Robert A. Dahl, *Polyarchy: Participation and Opposition* (New Haven, CT: Yale University Press, 1971), p. 15.

[20] Note here the parallel with Przeworski's ("Some problems in the study ...") theory of relativity regarding legitimacy. In each case – mass legitimacy or elite toleration – the issue is not whether the situation is perceived to be "the best" or even "desirable" but whether it is perceived to be the "least bad" among the alternatives defined at the time to be realistically possible. Note also that, in each case, we are dealing with an assumption of reasonably rational calculation on the part of the actors involved. For a critique that emphasizes the passion and rage in the Soviet Union that made such rational calculation unlikely, see Corbin Lyday, "From coup to constitution: Dilemmas of nation-building in Russia's first republic" (Ph.D. dissertation, Department of Political Science, University of California at Berkeley, 1994).

moderate and conservative interests allowed him to dominate the center of the political spectrum by encouraging the perception of him among middle-of-the-roaders as their protector against radical disenfranchisement.

Finally, by creating avenues of authentic political participation for released social forces, Gorbachev helped to disarm the forces of reactionary backlash during 1985–1990 by robbing them of an excuse to "crush counterrevolution." Rather than allowing the development of a situation in which social forces might have engaged in anomic outbursts or acts of revolutionary violence, Gorbachev pursued policies that at once raised the price of repression *and* lowered the price of toleration. In the process, he dominated the center-left of the political spectrum by increasing the level of felt political dependence upon him by many radical reformers, moderate leftists, and middle-of-the-roaders alike. This accounts for the fact that many reformists criticized Gorbachev's "conservatism" in 1989–1990 yet feared the prospect of his replacement.

Tactic No. 6: *Harness forces in the international environment that will help to maintain the momentum of reform while also helping to raise the costs of retrogression.* This was precisely the aim of Gorbachev's "new political thinking" in foreign policy, his approach to foreign economic relations, and his process of cultural Westernization. By opening the country to Western economic and cultural influences, including travel abroad, he raised dramatically the price in popular tolerance of efforts to reestablish a closed society while raising the actual and prospective benefits of openness. By defusing conflicts with wealthy adversaries, he increased the chances of receiving economic assistance for his program while reducing the prospective burden of defense spending. Furthermore, his concessionary foreign policies sought both to cut losses and to transform the international system so that foreign countries, companies, and publics would develop a perceived interest in adopting policies that favored a continuation of *perestroika*.

By simultaneously adopting radical reform in both domestic and foreign policies, Gorbachev expanded the number of issue areas within which he could seize the initiative, maintain the momentum of his leadership, and keep prospective challengers off balance. By developing such popularity abroad, he was able to build his authority as a statesman and so compensate for lack of economic progress at home. By delivering on his promise to reduce tensions abroad, he carved out a realm in which would-be challengers found it difficult to claim that they could do better than he.[21] Thus, just as his foreign

---

[21] This is how Doder and Branson (*Gorbachev,* p. 210) insightfully interpreted Gorbachev's calculations in convoking a three-day meeting of international intellectual and social elites in Moscow in February 1987: "The occasion, as he fully realized, offered an opportunity to

policies were central to his strategy of domestic cultural and political transformation, so were they crucial to his tactics for simultaneously expanding his political authority and making *perestroika* increasingly difficult to reverse.

In sum, Gorbachev went far to fulfill (whether he knew it or not) many of the prescriptions of those scholars who have examined the lessons of evolutionary strategies for transforming regimes in non-Leninist settings. His strategy and tactics came close to meeting Weiner's pithy summary: "For those who seek democratization, the lessons are these: mobilize large-scale nonviolent opposition to the regime, seek support from the center and, if necessary, from the conservative right, restrain the left ..., woo sections of the military, seek sympathetic coverage from the Western media, and press the United States for support."[22]

MISSED OPPORTUNITIES AND THEORIES OF TRANSITION

Of course, Gorbachev must also take partial responsibility for what was *not* achieved during these years. In particular, the two areas of failure (relative to his goals) were economic transformation and negotiation of a federal or confederal alternative to the Soviet unitary state.[23]

Missed Opportunities on the Economic Front

Because the pace of economic reform lagged far behind the pace of change in other realms of policy, those who evaluate Gorbachev's leadership of the economy tend to arrive at conclusions that are, on balance, negative.[24] The argument is straightforward: If Gorbachev had launched a real and forceful

---

enhance his authority, not just in foreign politics but on the domestic front. His enemies, he knew, were lying in wait, ready to turn on him the moment he blundered on security moves or some other issue. But he was becoming increasingly confident in his diplomatic skills .... He demonstrated to the bureaucracy that he was the day-to-day captain of Soviet foreign policy.... His mastery of detail and the quality of his reflections on display before a glittering audience in the Grand Kremlin Palace proved that the Soviet leader was a forceful figure, commanding the respect of the outside world and thus deserving respect at home."

[22] Myron Weiner, "Empirical democratic theory and the transition from authoritarianism to democracy," *PS*, vol. 10, no. 3 (1987), p. 866.

[23] Brown (*The Gorbachev Factor*) is highly laudatory of Gorbachev's leadership in general. But when discussing the balance of the ledger, he concedes that Gorbachev failed in economic policy and nationalities policy. When set against successes in political reform and foreign relations, however, Brown concludes that, given the circumstances, two out of four is a good batting average.

[24] See, for example, Marshall I. Goldman, *What Went Wrong with Perestroika?* (New York: Norton, 1992).

economic reform in 1985–1986, or if he had chosen to reform agriculture first, or if he had followed the Chinese model of reforming the economy before reforming the political system, then the economy would have been in better shape than it was in 1990–1991.[25] This counterfactual assertion may be correct (though it is not uncontroversial), but linking it to leadership evaluation involves a further logical step: one must argue not only for the practicality and likely effectiveness of alternative strategies in Soviet conditions but also for their intellectual availability and political feasibility at the time they might have been adopted. To what extent were Soviet leaders aware in earlier years of the need for such immediate and radical economic surgery? If they were aware, to what extent did the Party leader have the political capacity in 1985–1987 to force its enactment and implementation?

The evidence is ambiguous, but it suggests that Gorbachev was a convinced radical on matters of economic reform when he came to power even though he was not yet aware of the specifics of a radical program that might work. During 1985, reform economists who were directors of several research institutes – and whom Gorbachev had consulted regularly as secretary of the Central Committee – forwarded to the Politburo programs of radical economic reform. Moreover, the Chinese economic reform was by then seven years old and was showing remarkable results. Hence, even allowing for the inconclusiveness of the historical record, it seems more than likely that radical economic reform of one type or another was intellectually available to the Politburo and Gorbachev already in 1985.

How politically feasible was it at the time – and if it was feasible, at what price? Although Gorbachev consolidated his power faster than any leader in Soviet history, he still had to deal with a challenge that faced any new Soviet leader: to enlarge his political base before radicalizing his program. In the meantime, he had to live with many powerful holdovers from the old regime. Even among the Andropovites who replaced Brezhnevites during 1985–1986, the dominant orientations were more technocratic and anti-corruption than radical reformist. It is entirely conceivable that Gorbachev did not push harder for economic reform in 1985–1986 because he was building his political base.

Yet this would not explain why, even when he began to push for economic reform in 1987, the measures were modest compared to the greater radicalism of proposals advanced by institute directors or compared to the scope of Chinese economic reforms. New laws on joint ventures, cooperatives, "individual labor activity," and the Law on the State Enterprise were radical departures

---

[25] This argument is made forcefully in Jerry F. Hough, *Democratization and Revolution in the USSR, 1985–1991* (Washington, DC: Brookings Institution, 1997), chs. 4 and 11.

compared to the Soviet past, but they constituted a "foot in the door" approach: delegitimizing old values and justifying *in principle* entirely new approaches to economic organization and the world economy. These policies
were revised and (in most cases) made more radical in 1988–1989, but the
crucial issues of price reform, agricultural reform, land reform, privatization
of property ownership, and de-monopolization of the state sector were not
tackled and hence constituted fatal drags on the effectiveness of many of the
measures actually taken. One could argue, therefore, that the economy might
have been more effectively reformed had Gorbachev opted for a much more
radical approach in 1987–1988 – and that he bears responsibility for the failure to do so.

Gorbachev may have feared that urban unrest would result from liberalization of prices; price increases had set off deadly rioting in Novocherkassk
in 1962. He may also have feared that too sudden a transition to the insecurities and risks of a market economy would have been intolerable to a
population that had lived for sixty years without a market economy and for
thirty years with a low-opportunity (but also low-risk) welfare state. He may
have concluded that political reforms – including competitive elections, civil
liberties, and authentic forms of political participation – were a *pre*condition
for economic reform (the reverse of the Chinese model) because they would
provide people with political safety valves for expression of their frustrations
and thereby prevent economic reform from delegitimizing the political system. Of course, a dispassionate assessment of Gorbachev's leadership cannot
take his fears as the measure of reality. He may have been too timid, indeed
wrong, about the likely popular reaction.[26]

Gorbachev also may have been intimidated by the forceful objections to
economic decentralization by some members of the Politburo.[27] Although
Gorbachev had reached his stage of ascendancy within the leadership by
1987–1988, he was not an unconstrained leader. He had more power and authority than he had enjoyed two years earlier, just as Khrushchev and Brezhnev had more latitude for policy initiation and innovation during their stages
of ascendancy. But he still had to live with political constraints. Would the

---

[26] Hough (ibid., pp. 19, 137–8, 345) is incredulous that Gorbachev did not take Ryzhkov's advice on price reform; Brown (*The Gorbachev Factor*, ch. 5) ignores the matter. In his memoirs
(Mikhail Gorbachev, *Zhizn' i reformy*, vol. 1 [Moscow: Novosti, 1996], pp. 361–2), Gorbachev himself admits that his government missed a timely opportunity for necessary price
reform in 1987–1988. He blames journalists and bureaucrats for inciting public opposition
to the prospect, but he does not address any of his own fears at that time of the possible consequences of price liberalization.

[27] Personal communication to the author by former Politburo member Aleksandr Yakovlev.

leadership have tolerated an across-the-board radicalism that encompassed simultaneous transformation in the political, economic, and foreign-policy realms? We know that the leadership was sharply divided at the time on matters of both economic and political reform.[28] It is entirely conceivable that, in exchange for greater radicalism in economic policy, Gorbachev would have had to "trade off" some of his radicalism in foreign policy, defense policy, or policy toward cultural and political reform. This, in turn, could have compromised his efforts to transform the image of the USSR in the eyes of the Western world, which had been the basis of his efforts to undermine xenophobic forces resisting reform at home.

In any case, Gorbachev during 1987–1988 either chose or was forced to go slow on economic reform in exchange for a faster pace in other areas. If he chose to do so and had the power to do otherwise, then one could retrospectively blame him for lacking the vision, understanding, and strategy required by the economic conditions of the time. Alternatively, if one believes that radical economic reform was impractical in the Soviet Union in the absence of prior political, cultural, and international changes, then one could praise Gorbachev for understanding the need for preparatory changes in those realms.

Suppose that Gorbachev had been free to promulgate policy as he wished. Was he privy to a theory of transition that specified the relationship among political, economic, and cultural change in a Soviet-type system? Had there been a consensus within the specialist community as to what would "work," then Gorbachev could be criticized for ignoring it, but such was not the case. No consensus existed among either Soviet or Western specialists on the nature of the relationship between political and economic reform. Analysts and politicians disagreed about the proper sequencing of marketization and democratization. Some specialists argued that the two must proceed simultaneously in order to help break bureaucratic monopolies (thus preventing the development of a racket economy) and to build popular support and consensus during a period of disruption and privation.[29] Others argued that radical economic reform requires an authoritarian regime and that simultaneous political democratization will only undermine economic marketization.[30]

---

[28] On economic reform, see Anders Åslund, *Gorbachev's Struggle for Economic Reform* [updated and expanded edition] (Ithaca, NY: Cornell University Press, 1991); other evidence of discord within the Politburo can be found in previous chapters of the present book, citing memoir sources.

[29] See, for example, Janos Kornai, *The Road to a Free Economy* (New York: Norton, 1990), ch. 3.

[30] See A. Migranian, "Dolgii put' k evropeiskomu domu [The long road to the European home]," *Novii Mir*, no. 7 (1989), pp. 166–84; this was also the perspective that informed the Chinese approach to reform.

Specialists also differed about the workability of the Chinese strategy in Soviet conditions.[31] They disagreed with each other about the workability *and* desirability of varying mixes of equity and efficiency considerations in the setting of economic policy,[32] about the form and degree of political democratization that might best accompany economic reform, and about the forms of economic marketization that might best (i.e., most workably) accompany political democratization.[33] Still others argued that the decisive component of a successful strategy must be international: opening up the economy to world market forces.[34]

None of these theories was correct or incorrect on its face. Each simply pointed to discord among the voices Gorbachev might have heard, directly or indirectly, as he pondered his options. Options that he spurned were indeed intellectually available, but there was no consensus as to their likely consequences. In a confusing and confused intellectual context, Gorbachev made his choices. They did not work.

Lack of theoretical consensus is no excuse for leadership that is ineffective, though it is a mitigating circumstance. But we expect good leaders to have a special ability to sense what will work. Hence, in the realm of economics, Gorbachev's handling of the situation was unimpressive even if we make allowances for the uncertainties and constraints. True, he introduced novel market elements into the economy. However, in this realm he was event-making principally in a negative sense: in his ability to delegitimize values that underpinned the old economic order and to undermine organs of the command economy. Since the rate of disorganization of the (industrial) command economy exceeded by far the rate at which market relations were being introduced, the result was disintegration, not reconstruction. In this realm, it is fair to say that Gorbachev was better at destruction than at creation.

---

[31] The argument against the transferability of the Chinese reform to the Soviet context ran as follows. China's Cultural Revolution (1966–1976) had only recently wreaked havoc on the cohesion of the Communist Party and had greatly weakened local Party control of agriculture. Moreover, in 1978 the Chinese leaders were facing spontaneous decollectivization of agriculture. By contrast, the CPSU and the collective farms were entrenched in the Soviet countryside, and the cadres had not been targets of a campaign of mass terror since the 1930s.

[32] See Ed A. Hewett, *Reforming the Soviet Economy* (Washington, DC: Brookings Institution, 1988).

[33] See Elemer Hankiss, *East European Alternatives* (New York: Oxford University Press, 1990); Alexander Yanov, *Détente after Brezhnev* (Berkeley: Institute of International Studies, University of California at Berkeley, 1977); Boris Kagarlitsky, *The Dialectic of Change* (London: Verso, 1990); Adam Przeworski, *Democracy and the Market* (Cambridge University Press, 1991).

[34] Jerry F. Hough, *Opening Up the Soviet Economy* (Washington, DC: Brookings Institution, 1988); Richard Parker, "Inside the 'collapsing' Soviet economy," *Atlantic Monthly,* no. 4 (June 1990), pp. 68–80.

Missed Opportunities and the Problem of Ethnic Nationalism

Similar counterfactual and theoretical arguments can be made regarding Gorbachev's handling of the ethnic crisis. Gorbachev may have been aware that (what Soviets called) "the nationalities question" was one of the most intractable issues on the agenda of Soviet politics,[35] but he was obviously not aware of the depth of ethno-nationalism, inter-ethnic hatred, and secessionist sentiment lying just below the surface.[36] Nor did he anticipate how quickly or fully his policies of *glasnost'* and democratization would release that potential.[37] Finally, he did not understand that the specific political reforms he chose – making regional Party officials suddenly subject to popular election and having republican parliamentary elections follow (not precede) all-union parliamentary elections – would accelerate the loss of central control.

One could argue that, had Gorbachev called a constitutional convention and offered the opportunity of a democratic federation in 1988, rather than begrudgingly and reactively in 1989–1990, he might have slowed the centrifugal forces and avoided the ultimate collapse of the union. Similarly, had he accepted the secession of the Baltic states in 1989 – assuming he had the power to do so – while defining them as a "special case," then he might have eased the path toward a negotiated federation among the remaining twelve republics. Alternatively, had he used force consistently to police the limits of acceptable protest and defiance of Moscow's writ, then he might by this means have kept the union from fragmenting.[38]

On this score, there was little theory to guide Gorbachev. Some people at home and abroad were urging him at the time to use determined shows of force to rein in centrifugal forces in the republics on the assumption that this would not have had the contrary effect. (State-directed violence sometimes deters escalation, but it sometimes creates rage and heightens defiance.) Other voices at home and abroad urged the negotiation of broader degrees of autonomy for the republics and moves toward a negotiated federation. Gorbachev heeded these voices, but his timing was bad (it proved to be too late) and his offerings tended to be outpaced by rising demands. The critical unknown is whether anything he did, coercive or concessionary, could have averted the centrifugal spiral of 1990–1991.

---

[35] As argued at the time by Jerry F. Hough, "Gorbachev's politics," *Foreign Affairs*, vol. 68, no. 5 (Winter 1989–1990), pp. 26–41.

[36] As argued at the time in Gail W. Lapidus, "Gorbachev and the 'national question': Restructuring the Soviet federation," *Soviet Economy*, vol. 5, no. 3 (July–September, 1989), pp. 201–50.

[37] See Brown, *The Gorbachev Factor*, ch. 8.

[38] As advocated in Hough, *Democratization and Revolution*, chs. 7, 12, 15.

We do not know how the Politburo and Central Committee would have reacted had Gorbachev suggested the nonviolent alternatives.[39] The point may be moot, for both his political strategy and his vision for the USSR left Gorbachev unwilling to consider those alternatives seriously. It is not even clear that, intellectually, he was aware of their availability and practicality. His image of a "third way" between socialism and capitalism was based on a mix of social welfare and democratic politics that had a place in the Marxist heritage, but his thinking shared with that heritage an assumption that economics – not ethnicity – is the primary motivator of human behavior.

To the extent that one views the radicalizing behavior of Boris Yeltsin (and of the government of the RSFSR) as primary causes of the collapse of the Soviet Union, one could argue that one of Gorbachev's key mistakes was allowing Boris Yeltsin back into politics. Gorbachev tried to prevent Yeltsin's victories in the elections of 1989–1991 but to no avail. The more the establishment tried to undercut Yeltsin, the higher his popularity rose in the eyes of the mobilized electorate. Perhaps Gorbachev would have had to bury Yeltsin politically in early 1988, rather than giving him a high position in the Construction Ministry that allowed him to remain involved in the arenas of power. Surely, the fact that he begrudgingly allowed Yeltsin to speak at the June 1988 Party Conference – on national television – gave Yeltsin a platform for mounting a populist comeback.

Perhaps nothing that Gorbachev did, short of aborting his political reforms, could have prevented the disintegration of the USSR. If that is true, then one can still criticize Gorbachev as being quixotic in failing to appreciate the strength of the centrifugal ethnic forces he was facing and unleashing. When we compare the results with his goals, Gorbachev's nationalities policy (like his economic policy) was unimpressive. He did an outstanding job of destroying the Soviet unitary state and of introducing democratic elections in the republics, thereby setting the stage for attempts to negotiate a federal or confederal alternative. But he never succeeded in finalizing those negotiations. Again as in economic policy, he was better at destruction than at creation.

THE BALANCE OF THE LEDGER

Viewed from the perspective of (say) early 1990, the first five years of Gorbachev's time in power looked like a qualified success story. His performance

---

[39] Gorbachev himself has argued (in retrospect, in personal conversation with the former U.S. ambassador) that, had he pushed for a confederation in 1989, the Central Committee would have voted immediately for his ouster as general secretary (Jack Matlock, *Autopsy on an Empire: The American Ambassador's Account of the Collapse of the Soviet Union* [New York: Random House, 1995], p. 659).

in creating a new economic and inter-republican order was unimpressive, but his performance in breaking the hold of the ancien régime in all realms – and in navigating a peaceful transition toward new political and international orders – was path-breaking. In the latter respects, he was an event-making man who exercised unique leadership skills. His policy programs and authority-building strategy were all appropriate to the challenge of forcing an obsolete system onto a new track.

From the perspective of 1990, Gorbachev's political tactics also appeared to be working. By selectively appeasing or allying with conservative forces while simultaneously raising the price of backlash, Gorbachev had been able to maintain the political initiative without inducing a conservative or reactionary coup. By releasing radical social forces but providing them with democratic avenues of political participation, he was able to keep up the momentum of reform while reducing incentives for nihilism on the left and repression on the right. By fashioning a foreign policy that mobilized international forces in support of *perestroika,* he increased the attractiveness of staying the course while raising higher the price to be paid for a backlash.

From the perspective of 1992, however, Gorbachev's leadership strategy appears much less effective. The shortcomings of his ethnic and economic policies came back to haunt him. They interacted with his political reforms such that rising levels of social and political polarization undercut his evolutionary strategy of transformation, destroyed the centrist base required for his political tactics to be effective, and stripped him of both power and authority. Most tragically from the standpoint of Gorbachev's preferences, they led to the dissolution of the country he was trying to transform but certainly not destroy.

Any rendering of Gorbachev's tactical political mistakes in reaction (after 1989) to sliding toward a period of political decline must include two things: (1) the reluctance of his efforts, such as they were, to make political peace with Boris Yeltsin; and (2) his course correction of fall 1990, which included firing several of his most liberal associates and replacing them with men who would eventually lead the coup against him in August 1991. Had Gorbachev had a better sense of the pace of societal polarization and a better appreciation that he could not arrest it without the use of massive force, he would have understood that Yeltsin and the radicals were the wave of the future. He would have kept moving to the "left" (i.e., in a radical direction) to keep pace with those social forces, though without necessarily capitulating to all their policy preferences.[40] Instead, by moving to the right but retaining his commitment not to employ widespread repression, he largely burned his bridges to the

---

[40] This is what I advocated in George W. Breslauer, "Evaluating Gorbachev as leader," *Soviet Economy,* vol. 8, no. 4 (October–December 1989), pp. 333–7. It remains an open question as

radical camp while divesting himself of the tools he would have needed to achieve the right wing's goals. The conservatives and reactionaries understood this better than he; they started preparing seriously for a coup d'etat shortly after Gorbachev rejoined negotiations for a union treaty in April 1991. His seven-month flirtation with conservative forces only increased the level of polarization within society and the political establishment without achieving anything substantive. Moreover, it helped to position the coup plotters for their subsequent adventure, which in turn destroyed all hopes that leaders of the Slavic republics would be willing to sign a new Union Treaty.

Gorbachev lost control of his political reforms and proved unable or unwilling to prevent things that he clearly hoped to avoid: the total collapse of communism in Eastern Europe; reunification of Germany within NATO; collapse of the USSR; and abolition of the Communist Party's right to exist. The balance of the ledger would be that Gorbachev made a great start (1985–1989) but was a poor finisher (1990–1991). This was especially the case in those realms (economics and ethnic policy) in which his performance is generally judged to have been unimpressive, but it was even the case in those realms of policy in which he is generally considered to have been successful. For the outcomes he most wanted to avoid (other than restoration of the ancien régime) were the very outcomes that circumstances forced upon him.

That would be the "harsh" evaluation of Gorbachev as a transformational leader. An alternative might be called the "generous" evaluation. Generous analysts would note that marketizing the economy and federalizing the union were the two most *intractable* problems facing the Soviet regime. The constraints on change and on building viable political coalitions for that purpose were much more formidable than in the areas of political reform and foreign policy. The generous evaluation would concede that perhaps nothing Gorbachev did would have averted the collapse of both the economy and the union – given the forces he had unleashed in 1987–1989, his willingness to allow Boris Yeltsin back into politics, and Yeltsin's political strategy. Moreover, the generous evaluation would emphasize that the realms in which he met with successes have yielded *lasting* change. The democratic political institutions that Gorbachev created (multicandidate secret elections, genuine legislatures, and wide-ranging civil liberties) have lasted beyond his years in power and in that respect qualify as among his greatest achievements as a *creator*. Similarly, even though Gorbachev did not aim for the breakup of the USSR, he did create the conditions that allowed the eventual breakup to be

to whether Yeltsin would have welcomed Gorbachev into the radical camp – or would have upped the ante again in an attempt to outflank Gorbachev. I will say more in Chapter 14 about Yeltsin's role in undermining Gorbachev's chances of success in achieving his goals.

relatively *peaceful* and to remain so in the years thereafter, when Gorbachev was in retirement. Finally, Gorbachev paved the way for a reevaluation of the place of the Soviet Union in the international system and thereby made possible a peaceful and (thus far) enduring end to the Cold War.

Both the harsh and the generous evaluations are based on judgments about Gorbachev's effectiveness in realizing his goals in the near term and long term. They are distinct from evaluations based solely on the observer's ranking of values. One can admire Gorbachev greatly – as I do – for the destruction and the creation he brought about, both intended and unintended (but tolerated); alternatively, one can condemn him for the same destruction and creation. But that is a superficial approach to leadership evaluation. Whether the harsh or the generous evaluation does greater justice to Gorbachev's record is bound to remain a matter of debate. The verdict will hinge principally on answers to the counterfactual question: Could anyone have done better in the circumstances without the benefit of hindsight?

14

Evaluating Yeltsin as Leader

Yeltsin, like Gorbachev, was both a system destroyer and a system builder. During the years that Gorbachev was endeavoring to transform the Marxist–Leninist system into a socialist democracy, Yeltsin evolved into a committed anti-communist revolutionary. His goal became to destroy the communist system along with all those features that Gorbachev hoped to preserve in the name of "socialism" and "Soviet civilization." Then, on the ruins of that system, Yeltsin promised to build on the territory of Russia a new system, which he depicted as a "market democracy." As in the case of Gorbachev, Yeltsin's effectiveness as a system destroyer can be evaluated separately from his effectiveness as a system builder.

YELTSIN AS SYSTEM-DESTROYER

During 1988–1991, Boris Yeltsin evolved into a hero of the anti-communist opposition to Soviet rule. After his overwhelming electoral victories of March 1989 and June 1991, followed by his facing down of the coup plotters in August 1991, his authority at home and abroad had become legendary. He had evolved into a charismatic leader of almost mythic proportions, especially among those who had assumed that the Soviet and communist control structures were unassailable. Thus, as an oppositional leader, Yeltsin is likely to go down in history as a uniquely courageous and effective figure who managed to prevail against seemingly overwhelming odds. His "resurrection" after being purged by the Communist Party apparatus in 1987 was a product of extraordinary political will, intuition, and an uncanny ability to sense and shape the mood of the masses. His success during 1990–1991 in decoupling the concept of "Russian" from that of "Soviet" was both intellectually and politically inspired (given his goals), as was his insistence in March 1991 that Russia choose a president by popular election for the first time in its thousand-year history. Yeltsin was a revolutionary hero who achieved what he did through his extraordinary personal traits. Controversy is likely to be based largely on normative grounds. Those who approve of Yeltsin's role in destroying the communist and Soviet systems will likely acclaim his leadership, and those who disapprove of these ends will censure him accordingly. But neither side would contest the observation, which is value-neutral, that Yeltsin was (in this oppositional leadership role) an "event-making man."

Nothing that has happened since then is likely to alter this evaluation. Yeltsin's oppositional role of the 1980s – like Churchill's wartime leadership of Great Britain – can be judged independently of later events. It is an accomplished feat, capable of being assessed on its own terms.

When Yeltsin came to be president of independent Russia, communist ideology and organization had largely been destroyed. The constraints on progress were no longer products of the entrenchment of formal organizations and doctrines so much as their opposite: the fragmentation of governmental institutions; conflicting political jurisdictions within the inherited polity; disorganization of the economy and impending collapse of government finances; widespread disorientation and anxiety stemming from the collapse of the USSR; and the absence of an accepted world view around which to rally the population, now that Gorbachev's "socialist choice" had been discredited. Yeltsin's agenda therefore had to focus on tasks of *construction:* state building; nation building; building a new economic system and a new political order; forging a new international role for newly independent Russia; and defining an alternative world view to justify the new institutions and policies. The tasks were both ideational and organizational, but in a context quite the opposite of what Gorbachev had faced. Once Yeltsin had finished administering the coup de grace to communist ideology and organization during 1990–1991 – and to the USSR during 1991 – he was faced with the challenge of creating new bases of order to put in their place.

How effective was he in building that alternative? As I did with Gorbachev in Chapter 13, I will first outline the contours of Yeltsin's positive accomplishments. I will then examine the negative – in Yeltsin's case: (1) the rigidity of the systems that Yeltsin built and their lack of adaptability to changing environmental requirements; (2) the exorbitant costs incurred in pursuing his goals; and (3) the counterproductive impact of Yeltsin's operating style on the achievement of his professed goal after 1993, which was to consolidate his gains by "strengthening the Russian state." That said, I will then weigh the balance of the ledger. I will conclude by comparing Gorbachev and Yeltsin with respect to their effectiveness in building and maintaining authority.

YELTSIN AS SYSTEM BUILDER: THE FRUITS OF PERSONALISM

As we have seen in earlier chapters, Yeltsin approached his presidency with a self-conception as a personalistic leader. He was most comfortable exercising leadership that did not have to accommodate multiple institutional constraints. But he also believed that such leadership was necessary to achieve his primary goals.

Yeltsin's personalism need not be treated as a self-evident obstacle to progress. Indeed, given his concern to overturn the formal structures of communist power, to replace them with the formal organizations of a capitalist economy and a liberal democracy – integrated into Western organizations, within the territorial boundaries of the Russian Federation of December 1991, and resistant to both communist restoration and fascist reaction – one could argue that, in the near term, his personalistic approach to leadership went far to achieve those ends. He forced through changes that created the general framework for such a system.

Thus, he and his staff designed and won ratification of the Russian Constitution of 1993, which, however flawed, finally provided a consistent constitutional framework for the nascent Russian state. The parliamentary and presidential elections of 1993, 1995, 1996, and 1999 took place as scheduled and, while procedurally flawed in many respects, their general outcomes were probably not determined by fraud. Yeltsin resisted calls by many of his closest aides to postpone or cancel the gubernatorial elections of 1996–1998, even though these threatened to diminish his political leverage over regional elites. He also resisted the temptation to postpone the presidential election of 1996, even though in January his public approval rating had fallen to single digits and he was strongly tempted to cancel the election, abolish the Duma, and outlaw the Communist Party.[1] Likewise, he resisted calls to postpone or cancel the December 1999 parliamentary elections. Yeltsin also resisted the temptation to roll back the civil rights won by the Russian people under Gorbachev: freedoms to criticize, organize, worship, and travel. Books, newspapers, and television shows regularly roasted or ridiculed the president. They sharply criticized many of his policies, at times to the president's dismay and shock. These institutions survived notwithstanding Yeltsin's presumed distaste for the personal attacks.

Of course, we cannot give Yeltsin credit for declining to roll back progress that had already been made by his predecessor. Nor can we credit such resistance as an act of *creation*. Hence, this is more an indicator of his commitment

---

[1] Boris Yeltsin, *Midnight Diaries* (New York: Public Affairs, 2000), pp. 24–5.

to building a system based on some variant of liberalism than of his "success" as a state builder per se.

With respect to transformation of the economic system, Yeltsin – in the name of creating a class of property holders who would fight to prevent communist restoration – sponsored a program of privatization that allowed the rapid transfer of state property into private hands at a rate (and on a scale) that exceeded anything seen before in world history. Thus, Yeltsin was the "founder" of Russia's oligopolistic and kleptocratic yet nonetheless capitalist economy.

In his policies toward Russia's regions, Yeltsin sponsored a series of ad hoc treaties and agreements between Moscow and individual regions and republics that flexibly defined the respective obligations of the center and the periphery. The Constitution of 1993 tried to rein in centrifugal forces by prescribing a strong role for Moscow, but that document left many areas to joint jurisdiction and was vague on the mechanisms for resolving ambiguities and conflicts. This ambiguity – and the ad hoc treaties and agreements that followed – were consistent with Yeltsin's urge for personal flexibility in striking deals with the heads of different "subjects of the federation."[2] They were also consistent with the prevailing realities: the disparate resource bases of the regions, the varying resolve of their leaders, the lack of consensus among regional governors and republican presidents about constitutional principles, and the center's frequent incapacity to enforce its writ by other means. Only in the case of Chechnya did Yeltsin use the military to enforce the limits of his flexibility.

In the realm of nation building, Yeltsin consistently fought against those who would define the Russian Federation as an exclusionary ethnic-Russian entity. Instead, he sponsored and loudly argued for a civic and tolerant definition of citizenship in Russia, and he prevailed in the definition of policy on these matters.

At the international level, Yeltsin was one of the architects of the Commonwealth of Independent States, established to foster peaceful relations among the successor states to the Soviet Union. While he rhetorically defended the rights of "Russian speakers" resident in the successor states, he also insisted that such issues be resolved peacefully and rejected the arguments of those who would threaten or employ force. He proved to be a generous negotiator – giving far more than he got – with the leaders of Belarus, Ukraine, and Kazakhstan in the interests of maintaining good relations between Russia and those countries.

---

[2] See, for example, Yu. M. Baturin, A. L. Ilin, V. F. Kadatskii, V. V. Kostikov, M. A. Krasnov, A. Ya. Livshits, K. F. Nikiforov, L. G. Pikhoia, and G. A. Satarov, *Epokha Yel'tsina: Ocherki politicheskoi istorii* (Moscow: Vagrius, 2001), p. 397.

In relations with the Far Abroad, Yeltsin protested unsuccessfully against NATO's expansion eastward. But once this expansion became inevitable, he encouraged and monitored the negotiation of a NATO–Russian Charter in order to preserve good relations with Western partners and make NATO expansion tolerable to the Russian political elite. He successfully negotiated the expansion of the G-7 into the G-8. And he proved to be more interested in the "liberal internationalist" than the "statist" component of his policy toward East–West relations.

On the basis of this record, one could arrive at a positive evaluation of Yeltsin's effectiveness in realizing his primary goals: to found a new order, to guarantee that system against restorationist forces, and to integrate Russia into Western institutions. To reach such a positive evaluation, one would have to assume two things, one counterfactual and the other predictive: (1) that, absent Yeltsin as leader of Russia, the forces working for opposing goals would have prevailed in Russian policymaking; and (2) that Yeltsin's achievements have staying power – that they are likely to survive the years following Yeltsin's retirement. Indeed, these facts and assumptions are the bases for positive evaluations that are already in the record.

THE MACROSTRUCTURAL VULNERABILITIES

One could, however, also argue that Yeltsin's urge to found and guarantee a new order of things as quickly as possible – and to do so through personalistic leadership – planted the seeds of crisis that have been growing for several years and that finally came to a head in 1998–1999. In the political realm, Yeltsin's primary macroinstitutional accomplishment (the Constitution of 1993) established a framework that is so executive-heavy and so rigid that it may inhibit the system's adaptation to changing environmental requirements. It established a presidential system under which the powers of the president are enormous and include vast powers of decree, whereas the parliament and the constitutional court enjoy very limited powers. The Constitution was designed to ensure that the president would be (by far) the highest authority in the land, largely unaccountable to institutions and primarily answerable to the electorate at the subsequent presidential election.

Such discretion provides the president with strong incentives to ignore or infantilize the other branches of government. The courts, like parliament, are greatly underfinanced, while the presidency and the executive branch are hugely bloated with redundant personnel. The capacity of the president to bribe or intimidate members of parliament exceeds by far the capacity of parliamentarians to threaten the president. The executive branch serves almost entirely at the pleasure of the president, with little parliamentary control over the composition of the government. Hence, the overwhelming power of the presidency vis-à-vis other central institutions ensures that the general direction of policy is likely to reflect the president's preferences. But this also means that policy development and elaboration will depend largely on the wisdom and foresight emanating from the office of the president.

Yeltsin's "super-presidentialist"[3] constitution also eliminated the office of vice-president, so that no future VP could turn against the president the way Yeltsin's vice-president, Aleksandr Rutskoi, had done during 1992–1993. The lack of a vice-presidency in a system in which the president has such extraordinary powers means that any sign of presidential ill health – or the anticipation of such – sets off a chain of political maneuvering and demagogic rhetoric in anticipation of a new election. The legal ambiguity about the definition of "incapacitation" becomes magnified. Efforts to alter the constitution to establish a vice-presidency, or even to mandate that the prime minister serve out the former president's full term before a new election is held, are impeded by the nearly impossible terms for amendment. Moreover, the constitution provides an incentive for those most hopeful of winning the next election to oppose its amendment. Why reduce the powers of an office that you have reason to believe you can capture?

In the economic realm, Yeltsin's privatization program amounted to the greatest case of insider trading in history. It was consistent with Yeltsin's urge to build an economic elite as quickly as possible that would both support him politically and serve as a powerful bulwark against communist restoration. But the extraordinary concentration of wealth and conspicuous consumption that it allowed – along with the illicit (often criminal) means by which that wealth was acquired, the "crony capitalism" that resulted, and the intertwining of economic and corrupt political power – nurtured a widespread sense of social injustice that could explode in rage or generate anomic social protest at any time. Moreover, the mass impoverishment resulting from the chosen strategy of macroeconomic stabilization adds a powerful economic motivation for protest to the sense of injustice generated by perceived inequality. Even if ideological and organizational obstacles to the mobilization of mass protest prove insurmountable,[4] the situation could still lead to the eventual victory in presidential and parliamentary elections of those who advocate a populist authoritarian alternative.

---

[3] Stephen Holmes, "Superpresidentialism and its problems," *East European Constitutional Review*, vols. 2–3, nos. 4–1 (Fall–Winter 1993–1994), pp. 123–6.
[4] Stephen E. Hanson and Jeffrey S. Kopstein, "The Weimar/Russia comparison," *Post-Soviet Affairs*, vol. 13, no. 3 (July–September 1997), pp. 252–83; Victoria Bonnell and George W. Breslauer, *Russia in the New Century: Stability or Disorder?* (Boulder, CO: Westview, 2000), ch. 1 and passim.

Similarly, Yeltsin's decision to wage war in Chechnya to defend the territorial integrity of the Russian Federation proved disastrous for all concerned. The human toll – among Chechens, Russian civilians in Chechnya, and soldiers of Russia's armed forces – was enormous. Prosecution of the war further shattered the morale and cohesion of the Russian armed forces. And yet, while territorial integrity was temporarily defended, nothing was decided. This led to the decision in fall 1999 to reconquer Chechnya – a war that continues as of this writing. The first war might conceivably have deterred other regional executives from contemplating secession, which would be Yeltsin's sole claim to having played a positive role in preserving Russia's territorial integrity by waging the war. But even he stopped making this claim and admitted the war to have been his biggest mistake. This did not prevent him from launching another war in 1999 whose long-term costs and side effects are yet to be determined.

Then, too, Yeltsin's determination to stand "above political parties" as "director of all of Russia" inhibited the development of political parties, which provide the organizational buttress for a stable representative democracy. In the fall of 1991 and again in the fall of 1993 and 1995, Yeltsin was presented with the opportunity to sponsor presidential parties among reformist forces that might have helped them to build muscular, nationwide Party organizations. These could have expanded the mobilizational capacity of anti-restorationist forces and strengthened the organizational bond between politicians in the center and those in the periphery. The Russian president certainly had control of enormous material resources to invest in such a venture as well as a popular mandate to reshape political organization as he wished. Instead, Yeltsin opted for the ad hoc and personalistic approach to leadership, one that would leave him formally beholden to no particular organization and relatively free to shift support bases as his political instincts dictated. While this was consistent with his self-image as a leader and with his conception of the kind of leadership Russia needed in order to found and guarantee a new order of things, it left the political system demonstrably underdeveloped and fragile.

Yeltsin's strategy of political self-protection also undercut whatever contribution he might have made to cultural transformation in Russia. He made an excellent start in 1990–1991 with his secular and tolerant rhetoric of Russian nationhood and statehood. But throughout 1989–1991, the absolutist rhetoric of anti-communism, based on binary oppositions, was the dominant and most salient feature of his rhetoric. The two rhetorics coexisted thereafter, and it was to Yeltsin's credit that he did not sacrifice the tolerant to the intolerant. Nonetheless, continuation of the absolutist rhetoric after the collapse of communism polluted political language and led to popular cynicism about the politics and policies of the Russian government. Thus, just as he had defined either the Communist Party or the Soviet center as the enemy in 1989–1991, so he continued with "us versus them" rhetoric after 1991. Those who supported Yeltsin's policies were deemed "reformers," "democrats," and "marketizers," even when his policies were authoritarian, corrupt, or plutocratic. All those who opposed his policies were dubbed conservatives, reactionaries, or "neo-Bolsheviks."[5] These were not the rhetorical conditions under which the Russian citizenry was likely to learn to appreciate either markets or democracy. For the negative side effects of Yeltsin's policies – including the sustained failure to pay wage arrears and pensions – fostered cynicism about both capitalism and democracy in the minds of many Russians.

Yeltsin had the opportunity in 1991 to play the role of "father of the nation," embodying its dignity. Indeed, after the coup attempt of August 1991, this was both his self-image and his image in the eyes of anti-communist publics in Russia. Yet he managed, during his years as president of independent Russia, to squander the good will he had accumulated. It is extraordinary to note the contrast between Yeltsin's popularity ratings and public demeanor in 1991 and the same indicators in 1994. In contrast to de Gaulle, who managed to mobilize French patriotism in support of his policies and leadership, Yeltsin could only neutralize or deter neo-imperial chauvinism. He proved incapable of articulating and broadcasting a positive, patriotic message to mobilize support for the kinds of popular sacrifices his policies demanded.

Yeltsin did a brilliant job of exploiting the public arenas created during Gorbachev's efforts to transform the Soviet system. During his stage of ascendancy, Yeltsin tried to use the public arena to maintain and enhance his stature as father of the nation and hero of the people. However, he found himself in a situation of "dual power." The parliament of 1992–1993 was an arena for competitive politics that played to sentiments among the voting publics. The prolonged confrontation with this parliament – and Yeltsin's military suppression of that body – left Yeltsin soured on the idea that public politics should be based on divided government. The parliamentary elections of December 1993 left him painfully aware that the populace no longer viewed him as a hero. The result was that, just as an autonomous public arena had been

---

[5] Jerry F. Hough, *The Logic of Economic Reform in Russia* (Washington, DC: Brookings Institution, 2001). Yeltsin's rhetoric thus reinforced the mentality of "binary oppositions" that Michael Urban ("The politics of identity in Russia's postcommunist transition: The Nation against itself," *Slavic Review*, vol. 53, no. 3 [Fall 1994], pp. 733–7) claims to be a key feature of Russian political culture.

Yeltsin's ticket to power during the Gorbachev years, that same public arena had become the source of political frustration during his stage of ascendancy. He reacted to the double disillusionment by drawing inward and allowing re-privatization of the state. He allowed electoral machinations to corrupt some of the legitimacy of democratic elections, grossly violated campaign finance laws, and restricted his opponents' access to the televised airwaves during election campaigns. It is one indicator of Yeltsin's shortcomings as a transformational leader that he failed to institutionalize a genuinely competitive public arena.

The net result of all these shortcomings is that the cultural and organizational infrastructures of the Russian system are extremely weak: like a skeleton without ligaments, they are prone to collapse of their own weight or when they meet countervailing force – such as the international economic downturn it met in August 1998. Transformational leaders and the systems they build are frequently able to weather such times if they have created sufficient popular consensus and good will. But Yeltsin managed to squander his charisma and good will and later to discredit political and economic liberalism in the popular mind. Having discredited socialism in his role as an oppositional revolutionary and liberalism more recently, Yeltsin opened the door to the one ideology that had not yet been discredited: Russian nationalism. Perhaps radical nationalism will not emerge ascendant owing to its weak resonance among the Russian people and to the widespread awareness among elites of the country's real weakness. If radical nationalism does seize the initiative, however, it could destroy Yeltsin's greatest ideational accomplishment – acceptance of a secular and tolerant definition of citizenship – along with the fragile organizational system he set up.[6]

MISSED OPPORTUNITIES AND EXORBITANT COSTS PAID

The collapse of the Russian financial system in August–September 1998 and the subsequent withdrawal of IMF assistance served to highlight the fragility of the political and economic systems created during Yeltsin's presidency. Some observers took the opportunity to argue that this financial collapse

---

[6] For a comprehensive study of Russian nationalism before the collapse of the USSR, see Yitzhak M. Brudny, *Reinventing Russia: Russian Nationalism and the Soviet State, 1953–1991* (Cambridge, MA: Harvard University Press, 1998); for a study of the evolution of Russian chauvinist ideologies and organizations since 1991, see Veljko Vujacic, "Serving Mother Russia: The communist left and nationalist right in the struggle for power, 1991–1998," in Bonnell and Breslauer, *Russia in the New Century*, pp. 290–325.

revealed Yeltsin's leadership of independent Russia to have been an unmitigated disaster.[7] Other observers instead debated more broadly on how it had come to this.

Some analysts argued that a collapse was all but inevitable, regardless of what Yeltsin had done during his years as Russia's president. Hence, they are less inclined to blame him personally for the collapse. There are four explanations that run along these lines, though they are not mutually exclusive. One is cultural, arguing that Russian culture had never developed orientations compatible with impersonal markets, rule of law, or representative democracy. A second is institutional, claiming that the administrative fragmentation, tacit privatization, and widespread criminalization of the Soviet state during the late-Gorbachev era – or, in some versions of the argument, already under Brezhnev – constituted a legacy that the Yeltsin regime could not possibly overcome in so short a period of time. A third argument for inevitability is circumstantial: that Gorbachev had made a mess of the Soviet economy, the Soviet Union, and Soviet foreign economic relations by 1991. The result was a rupturing of economic relationships and dire economic straits that the Yeltsin regime, again, could not have overcome. The fourth is international: the circumstances of international dependency in which Russia found itself at the time placed it at the mercy of demands by governments of the rich democracies for certain types of policies – policies that ultimately led to the ruin of Russia's economy. If we combine these explanations and treat them as mutually reinforcing features of the domestic and international legacies bequeathed to Yeltsin, then the image of futility and inevitability becomes that much more credible.

An alternative approach (which I endorse) to the question of historical causality treats the current situation as a product of contingent policy choices made by Boris Yeltsin and his governments during 1991–1998. Without denying that the foregoing constraints were real, this argument claims that the constraints were not determinant of the fullness of the outcomes. That is, opportunities were missed to relieve these constraints; to build a new system more democratic, humane, productive, and resilient than the one that Yeltsin built; and to do so at a much lower cost than was paid by the regime in power.

Thus, a corrupt and "weak" state might have been difficult to avoid, given the initial conditions. But the scope and depth of political corruption, the administrative fragmentation and criminalization, and the "virtual economy"

---

[7] See Stephen F. Cohen, "Russian studies without Russia," *Post-Soviet Affairs,* vol. 15, no. 1 (January–March 1999), pp. 37–55; Stephen F. Cohen, *Failed Crusade: America and the Tragedy of Post-Communist Russia* (New York: Norton, 2000).

of 1998[8] were products of policy choices made in 1992–1995. Those choices included the particular approach to macroeconomic stabilization adopted in January 1992; the "loans for shares" program of 1995; and the growing encouragement or toleration over time of large-scale embezzlement of state assets.

Similarly, the fragility of democratic institutions might have been a product of the "dual power" built into the constitution in force in 1991, and that fragility might have been exacerbated by the widespread disorientation and political conflict caused by Russia's loss of its empire and global role. Nonetheless, the ongoing gridlock in executive–legislative relations, the declining influence of democratic forces, and the entrenchment of an overbearing presidency were products of choices about party building and state building made in fall 1991 (and again in fall 1995) and choices about constitutional design made in 1993–1994.

Limited adherence to "rule of law" and spotty protection of the population from physical insecurity might have been inherent in the early stages of any transition following the collapse of a state, especially in a society in which both the supply and the demand for rule of law were so low.[9] But the minuscule progress in building legal and judicial institutions and the extent of police withdrawal from law enforcement were products of decisions made in 1992 and of a continuous lack of priority given to the development of legal institutions.

Persistent defiance of central authority by the government of Chechnya might have been the bane of any Kremlin leader. Even so, the costs and consequences of the war against Chechen secession were products of policy choices made by the Yeltsin leadership in 1994–1995 and again in fall 1999.

Dependence on international assistance would have been a condition faced by any Russian government. But willingness to accept the prescriptions of the International Monetary Fund was a decision made by Yeltsin and his cabinet, and the corrupt use of those funds was a product of internal circumstances over which they had some control. Given the fears in Western capitals of "losing Russia," it is implausible to claim that the rich democracies would have abandoned Russia to her fate had Moscow adopted a different strategy of economic stabilization, marketization, and privatization.

In all, given its bequeathed legacy, Russia probably would have been in difficult circumstances regardless of the policies chosen during 1992–1998. With

---

[8] Clifford G. Gaddy and Barry W. Ickes, "Russia's virtual economy," *Foreign Affairs*, vol. 77, no. 5 (September/October 1998), pp. 53–67.

[9] On the supply and demand for law in post-Soviet Russia, see Kathryn Hendley, *Trying to Make Law Matter* (Ann Arbor: University of Michigan Press, 1995).

different policies, however, Russia would not have been in such dire straits, and prospects for a sustainable recovery would have been stronger.[10]

Had Yeltsin done things differently in many realms of policy, we would have been better positioned to assess the resilience or malleability of cultural, institutional, circumstantial, and international constraints on change. But Yeltsin's initiatives instead typically acquiesced in or exacerbated the legacy he inherited. Hence, we cannot say with confidence just *how much* would have been different had Yeltsin acted differently. It does seem safe to argue that many of his general goals could have been advanced at a lower cost – in some cases, perhaps a much lower cost. Put differently, Yeltsin was not simply a victim of circumstances; he had opportunities to do things differently, but he missed them.[11]

Indeed, it was Yeltsin himself who rendered precisely this verdict on his leadership of Russia. Announcing his resignation on December 31, 1999, he averred:

I want to ask you for forgiveness, because many of our hopes have not come true, because what we thought would be easy turned out to be painfully difficult. I ask you to forgive me for not fulfilling some hopes of those people who believed that we would be able to jump from the grey, stagnating, totalitarian past into a bright, rich and civilised future in one go.

I myself believed in this. But it could not be done in one fell swoop. In some respects I was too naive. Some of the problems were too complex. We struggled on through mistakes and failures.

The man who had helped to destroy Gorbachev politically by accusing him of "half-measures" and of trying to "leap across a chasm in two steps" left office admitting that one could not bridge that chasm "in one fell swoop" after all.

PERSONALISM AND ADMINISTRATIVE RATIONALIZATION, 1994–1999

During 1994–1999, Yeltsin claimed that his goals had evolved and that his main goal was now to "strengthen the Russian state" in order to deliver peace, order,

---

[10] The economic recovery of year 2000 was based on windfall oil prices and the near-term impact of ruble devaluation following the 1998 crash. Neither condition can be counted upon to last, and accumulated debt payments will soon come due. Hence, the present-day recovery may well prove to be a temporary boom. For an analysis of what needs to be done to sustain the recent rebound, see Jacques Sapir, "The Russian economy: From rebound to rebuilding," *Post-Soviet Affairs,* vol. 17, no. 1 (January–March 2001), pp. 1–22.

[11] For the argument that Yeltsin missed even more opportunities than the ones I have enumerated, see Peter Reddaway and Dmitri Glinski, *The Tragedy of Russia's Reforms: Market Bolshevism against Democracy* (Washington, DC: U.S. Institute of Peace, 2000), pp. 636–41.

and prosperity to the Russian people. We may therefore evaluate his effectiveness as a leader in those years relative to the advancement of these goals. The verdict is a negative one. Even if he was sincere about his promises, the tactics Yeltsin employed for maintaining his power and authority actually impeded realization of those goals. Instead, Yeltsin's operating style undermined administrative efficiency throughout his years in office. His organization of the presidential apparatus and manipulation of the executive branch went far to strengthen his grip on the formal reins of power and perhaps to make possible the defense of his system *building* goals, but they simultaneously strengthened the corrupt bureaucracy's capacity to avoid rationalization and thereby undermined the consolidation and sustainability of Yeltsin's achievements.

Consider his approach to both the organization of advice within the presidency and the articulation of interests within government. On both scores, Yeltsin's preferred approach was individualized, anti-procedural, and anti-institutional. Within his personal staff and advisory corps, Yeltsin resisted the crystallization of even informal constraints on his power over the "children." He did not treat the political organization of his staff as a rational distribution of formal powers (*polnomochia*). Rather, he wanted to maintain fluidity and redundancy of jurisdictions in order to maximize his capacity to play subordinates off against each other and to maximize their sense of dependence on him for protection against the others. According to a former high-level staff member,[12] Yeltsin wished to get advice from staff members on an individual, not a collective, basis. He did not want his staff to get together, work out a common viewpoint on an issue, and present it to him as a collective judgment. Nor did he care to meet with them as a collective. Instead, he wanted each of them to come to him individually with their ideas. When they defied this preference, he could be strict.

Yeltsin's approach to interest articulation and aggregation was also suffused by personalism. He was highly responsive to particularistic pleading for tax exemptions, licenses, and subsidies. He preferred to deal with governors, military commanders, and ministers on an ad hoc, individual basis rather than through their organizations. While there may have been a *political* rationality to some of these preferences, the effect was to undermine the development of organized collectivities on which modern public administration is based. As Huskey aptly observes, it was "a style of rule associated more with traditional monarchs than modern chief executives."[13]

---

[12] Interview, Moscow, June 1998. Published support for this characterization can also be found in Aleksandr Korzhakov, *Boris Yel'tsin: Ot rassveta do zakata* (Moscow: Izd-vo "Interbuk," 1997), p. 221, and Baturin et al., *Epokha*, p. 212.

[13] Eugene Huskey, *Presidential Power in Russia* (Armonk, NY: M.E. Sharpe, 1999), p. 50.

It is true that, in all public administration, there is an inherent tension between the requirements of political control and those of administrative efficiency. What distinguishes administrative leaders, however, is how they deal with this tension and whether their solutions strike a balance that is consistent with the realization *and consolidation* of their general policy goals. Leaders like Charles de Gaulle, Franklin Roosevelt, and Kemal Ataturk understood this. In Yeltsin's case, the sacrifice of administrative rationality to the requisites of political control was such as to threaten the sustainability of his program. Bureaucratic fragmentation, corruption, and unaccountability worsened as a result of his approach to administrative control.

Yeltsin's approach to administrative organization of the presidential and executive branches was reminiscent of Khrushchev's approach in the early 1960s during the analogous (third) stage of Khrushchev's administration: constant reorganization, high turnover of personnel, and the regular creation of new units with jurisdictions that duplicated those of existing units.[14] The presidential administration evolved into a huge bureaucracy – larger in size than the CPSU's Central Committee apparatus and with at least as many departments. But there was scant rationalization of jurisdictions within the apparatus and between the apparatus and the ministries. Officials of the apparatus were left with neither stable expectations nor the requisite information to perform their jobs.

In theory, one could view the blurring of jurisdictions and the inhibition of stable expectations as a sensible way to organize a presidential administration. Organization theorists have long known that formal organization charts are a poor guide to how organizations actually run – or ought to run. Franklin Roosevelt found it useful to establish redundant jurisdictions to ensure that he received multiple sources of information and a variety of viewpoints on a given situation.

This was not the way in which Yeltsin ran his presidential administration and cabinet. Instability of expectations concerned not so much the sequencing of tasks as the continued existence of the agency and thus the maintenance of perquisites and privileges that accompany employment in the president's administration. Blurring of jurisdictions was not so much a functional means of ensuring diverse viewpoints as a proliferation of redundancies that left units unclear as to who actually was responsible for task fulfillment. Instead of fostering healthy coverage on all issues, the exponential increase in the size

---

[14] Huskey refers to the last of these tendencies as "the politics of redundancy"; see Eugene Huskey, "The state–legal administration and the politics of redundancy," *Post-Soviet Affairs*, vol. 11, no. 2 (April–June 1995), pp. 115–43.

of the presidential administration fostered duplication of the governmental–ministerial structure, duplication of jurisidictions between the executive and presidential branches, and proliferation of decisional arenas to which bureaucrats and others could turn in order to subvert the implementation of presidential decrees or parliamentary legislation. The frequent creation and abolition of agencies left officials little time for programmatic thinking and focused their attention largely on personal political survival.

More generally, Yeltsin preferred to manipulate diversity in ways that played factions off against each other and thereby maintained or enhanced his leverage as the "ultimate arbiter." Within the presidential administration, Yeltsin included representatives of all political orientations save intransigent communists and radical nationalists. This is certainly a rational strategy for power maintenance. It can also be a rational strategy for eliciting a diversity of inputs and for building one's authority with a multitude of constituencies. But it works this way only if officeholders and advisors feel reasonably secure in their jobs. If, instead, the "ultimate arbiter" frequently shifts back and forth between preferred factions and then forces the losers to pay with their jobs, the result is more likely to be sycophancy, individualized efforts to curry favor with the president, or collective efforts to destroy the credibility and favor of the competing factions ("backstabbing"). Yeltsin's modus operandi was to fire leading officials and their deputies with great frequency and sometimes to "balance off" a dismissal with the arbitrary dismissal of an equivalent figure in the opposing faction.[15]

One result of such an operating style was that ideological or professional factions crystallized within the presidential administration for mutual protection against the insecurities of working under an unpredictable commander. Another result of the general atmosphere of profound uncertainty and insecurity was widespread and deep-seated corruption within the presidential administration and portions of the executive branch. Many officials simply found it too tempting to resist feathering their nests while the opportunity was there. And why not? They lived with persistent uncertainty as to what actions were likely to fulfill the tasks assigned to them. They were equally uncertain as to how long they would keep their jobs regardless of their performance. They

---

[15] According to Kostikov, when Yeltsin formally fired his vice-president, Aleksandr Rutskoi, he also fired cabinet member Shumeiko. The latter had done nothing wrong, but Yeltsin told Kostikov that Shumeiko had to be "sacrificed" in order to "balance off" the firing of Rutskoi (Viacheslav Kostikov, *Roman s prezidentom: zapiski press-sekretaria* [Moscow: Vagrius, 1997], p. 210); conversely, Baturin et al. (*Epokha,* p. 209) claim that Yeltsin appointed the "democrat" Sergei Filatov to head the presidential administration in order to balance out the recent appointment of Viktor Chernomyrdin as prime minister.

found themselves in a privileged position that afforded many opportunities for using public office for private material gain, and knew that they might not be able to gather such resources – or avoid criminal prosecution – outside of government. In sum, rather than engendering a healthy dose of competition and uncertainty, Yeltsin's approach to administration of the presidential and executive branches did a good job of protecting his personal power against challenge and a poor job of creating the institutional and political support for rational decisionmaking.[16]

Apparently, Yeltsin did not understand the contradictions between his operating style and the requirements of administrative reliability. Put differently, he did not understand that his personalism actually increased the opportunities for midlevel officials to undermine his policies. Vague presidential decrees that either circumvented parliament or violated the Constitution had the dual effect of leaving interpretation up to the bureaucrats and of undermining the credibility of parliament as a force for oversight or discipline of the bureaucracy. The result was that the bureaucrats had both the intellectual and political space to ignore or reinterpret decrees to their own benefit.[17]

Yeltsin understood the general direction in which he wanted to push the country. But when it came to elaborating complex programs that would consolidate his gains by strengthening the state, Yeltsin fell short. Some memoirists criticize Yeltsin for allegedly lacking a political strategy or philosophy of transformation, as does one of his foreign advisors;[18] some point to his personality as a source of regular depressions or ambivalence that caused him to

---

[16] Viktor Baranets argues that the bloated and impenetrable mechanism of Russian political decisionmaking allowed Yeltsin to exercise ultimate control over his bureaucracy, including military officialdom. Every minor decision had to be processed by a multitude of organizations and administrative departments and only then submitted to the president for final approval. When Yeltsin was incapacitated, the situation became even worse. Many of the most pressing problems of either strategic or tactical importance never got solved and kept accumulating; V. N. Baranets, *Yel'tsin i ego generaly: zapiski polkovnika genshtaba* (Moscow: "Sovershenno Sekretno," 1998), p. 50. See also Anatol Lieven, *Chechnya: Tombstone of Russian Power* (New Haven & London: Yale University Press, 1998), pp. 294–9, for a case study of the impact of this operating style on military reform in Russia.

[17] This point is made and documented in Victor M. Sergeyev, *The Wild East: Crime and Lawlessness in Post-Communist Russia* (Armonk, NY: M.E. Sharpe, 1998) pp. 84ff., and in Nikolai Biryukov and Victor M. Sergeyev, *Russian Politics in Transition* (Brookfield, VT: Aldershot, 1997), pp. 260–9. Alternatively, Yeltsin may have understood very well what he was doing (i.e., maintaining his political control) and did not regret the side effects; this is the view propounded in Hough, *The Logic of Economic Reform*.

[18] O. Poptsov, *Khronika vremyon "Tsaria Borisa"* (Moscow: "Sovershenno sekretno," 1997), p. 431; Kostikov, *Roman*, pp. 300–1, 323–4; Anders Åslund, *How Russia Became a Market Economy* (Washington, DC: Brookings Institution, 1995), p. 91.

squander his political assets.[19] Whatever the source of his policy choices, the implications for realization of his consolidative goals were negative ones.

THE BALANCE OF THE LEDGER: PLUSES, MINUSES, AND MITIGATING FACTORS

Yeltsin was most successful in combining creativity with destruction, in balancing transformation with identity and stability, and in neutralizing the forces of reaction in three realms: East–West relations, relations with the Near Abroad, and Russian nation building. In a difficult international context, he managed to defend a combination of liberal internationalism and *realpolitik* that flexed Russia's muscles while acknowledging its weakness and seeking new associations abroad to offset that weakness. In a difficult internal political context, Yeltsin advocated a combination of patriotism, ethnic pride, and liberal nationalism that rejected the extreme alternatives being offered by the "red-brown" coalition. In all these realms, he also helped to create institutions that could sustain a liberal orientation over the longer term. Thus, his successes were both organizational and cultural – and held promise of sustainability.

With respect to state building and economic transformation, however, Yeltsin was much less effective. In these realms Yeltsin proved least able: (1) to engage in *creative* destruction by initiating construction of the regulatory infrastructure of a market economy and representative democracy; (2) to transform cultural and political attitudes toward belief in the new order; and (3) to create a climate and processes for sustaining the transformation in the long term. Instead, by tolerating the de facto creation of a corrupt state and re-monopolized market that bore much resemblance to the Soviet system they had replaced, Yeltsin put at risk his entire transformative project. By the time of his retirement, the market democratic project was treated skeptically, if not with hostility, by the majority of the population, and nationalistic attitudes were on the rise that could lead eventually to a reversal of the liberal successes in nation building, relations with the Near Abroad, and East–West international relations.

In evaluating leaders, it is insufficient to point to their successes and failures. One must also consider the magnitude of the constraints and obstacles they faced in each realm. Easy successes, or failures in "no-win" situations, are not appropriate indicators of an individual's leadership capacity.

---

[19] Yegor T. Gaidar, *Dni porazhenii i pobed* (Moscow: Vagrius, 1996), pp. 106–7, 310–14; Kostikov, *Roman*, pp. 141–2, 168–9, 174; Korzhakov, *Boris Yel'tsin*, p. 315.

Evaluation of Yeltsin's failures in the areas of economic transformation and state building must consider important mitigating factors. Scholars dispute the alternatives available to Yeltsin in 1991–1993; we cannot resolve those disputes with the evidence drawn in this book. Yet if one believes that few alternative strategies were practical in late 1991, then one would credit Yeltsin with making the best of an unraveling economic situation at that time.[20] Similarly, if one believes that the only politically feasible alternatives in 1993 were reaction or gridlock, then one would credit Yeltsin with sustaining democratic processes and instituting a new constitutional framework through the sheer force of his will.[21] Moreover, Yeltsin's failure to construct a robust organizational infrastructure happened to concern the most difficult problems for a president to overcome in a short period of time. Some presidents – notably, FDR and Charles de Gaulle – were up to the challenge, building organizations that would ultimately become the sinews of the U.S. and French regulatory states. Yeltsin was not up to this challenge, but he was also starting (his mandate notwithstanding) from a considerably more dire set of circumstances than either Roosevelt or de Gaulle faced.

The challenges of state building and economic transformation also required Yeltsin to overcome obstacles and constraints that were far more resilient than those he dealt with in the realms of foreign policy and nation building. It is much easier to strike a deal with a foreign leader than to effect

[20] Yeltsin has been roundly condemned for his "shock therapy" approach to economic reform in 1992. But little attention has been given to the counterfactual: what would have been the consequences of an alternative strategy for dealing with the dire economic circumstances – both macroeconomic and microeconomic – at the time? Critics speak vaguely of "gradualism" or an "evolutionary" approach without specifying how such a "policy" would have checked the economic crisis of late 1991. Strategies recommended by reformist Soviet economists for the stable conditions of 1986–1987 were not necessarily workable in the conditions of 1992. Hence, it is far from clear whether credible, alternative strategies were intellectually available and practicable when Yeltsin made his choice on behalf of shock therapy. Indeed, comparative analyses of post-communist economic reform suggest that Yeltsin's mistake may have been the opposite: to back off from shock therapy after April 1992 in favor of a broader coalition among economic elites, thus miring Russia in a condition of partial reform that encouraged massive corruption. See Joel Hellman, "Winners take all: The politics of partial reform in postcommunist transitions," *World Politics,* vol. 50, no. 2 (January 1998). Recently, some severe critics of Yeltsin's economic policies have proposed alternatives that might have been appropriate to the circumstances of 1992; see Reddaway and Glinski, *The Tragedy of Russia's Reforms,* pp. 252–5, 286–8, and Hough, *The Logic of Economic Reform in Russia,* pp. 127–9. See especially the impressive discussions of alternatives in Lawrence R. Klein and Marshall Pomer (Eds.), *The New Russia: Transition Gone Awry* (Stanford, CA: Stanford University Press, 1991).

[21] The link between this counterfactual conclusion and a positive evaluation of Yeltsin's leadership is exemplified by Leon Aron, *Boris Yeltsin: A Revolutionary Life* (New York: Harper-Collins, 2000), pp. 540ff.

a durable change in the culture and process of public administration. It is easier to speak publicly about the need for tolerance in inter-ethnic relations than to deliver material satisfaction to the populace. It is also easier to withdraw troops from the Baltic States than to design and build the operating institutions of a regulatory state. Proper functioning of the "rule of law" requires organizational and cultural change, both of which require a good deal of time and effort. Moreover, in these domestic realms, Yeltsin faced more political and administrative constraints than in foreign policy. Unlike Gorbachev, he did not have a large apparatus of officials to process information and to whom he could delegate subtasks. He had to construct a "presidential administration" on the fly in 1991–1992 and was rapidly overloaded with decisionmaking responsibility. Given the constitutional ambiguities he inherited, the opposition he faced from the Supreme Soviet in 1992–1993 would have impeded ambitious efforts to construct a rule of law in Russia regardless of who was in power. In short, any leader put in Yeltsin's situation at the end of 1991 would have faced a daunting array of constraints on implementing a coherent, effective, and far-reaching strategy of state building and economic transformation. Yeltsin's successes were easier to attain than his failures were to avoid.

Comparison with Gorbachev helps to avoid double standards in evaluations of their leadership. Like Yeltsin, Gorbachev's greatest successes lay in destroying the old system and in preventing its restoration. Thereafter, like Yeltsin, Gorbachev was most successful in two realms of policy: Gorbachev in foreign policy and political democratization; Yeltsin in foreign policy and in constructing a new political and national order. Like Gorbachev's, Yeltsin's leadership was singularly unimpressive in two realms: consolidation of the new state and construction of a market economy. And like Yeltsin, given the constraints he faced, Gorbachev's successes were probably easier to attain (though not "easy" in an absolute sense) than his failures were to avoid.

These observations could be the basis for an evaluation of the two leaders that treats their accomplishments as essentially equivalent. The argument would go as follows. Both men were hugely successful in bringing down the political order they sought to supersede or destroy. Both men receive mixed grades for effectiveness in their system-building efforts. The areas in which they experienced success and failure were analogous, suggesting that they were frustrated by analogous constraints and helped by analogous opportunities.

Hence (the argument would continue), if we credit Gorbachev for "successfully" following a concessionary foreign policy, then we should credit Yeltsin for having done much the same vis-à-vis both the rich democracies and many states in the Near Abroad at a time of rising *realpolitik* sentiment within the

Russian elite. Similarly, if we praise Gorbachev for breaking the political and psychological bonds of Leninist doctrine, then we should praise Yeltsin for defending a secular and tolerant definition of Russian citizenship and nationhood at a time of rising revanchist sentiment among parliamentarians. If we laud Gorbachev for liberalizing and democratizing the system at the risk of bringing down both communist rule and the Soviet Union itself, then we may praise Yeltsin for tackling the issue of economic reform in 1992 – something Gorbachev never managed to do and that was becoming a dire necessity by the end of 1991 – even at the risk of impoverishing large numbers of citizens. If we praise Gorbachev for trying to negotiate democratic federalism as an alternative to the Soviet unitary state, then we may credit Yeltsin for negotiating treaties with the major regions of Russia as an alternative to the regional fragmentation and feudalization that was rampant at the time. If we praise Gorbachev for resisting the temptation to "restore order" in the face of political challenges, then we should give Yeltsin some credit for retaining the civil liberties enacted under Gorbachev and for resisting the temptation to impose the kind of one-man dictatorship found in so many successor states of the former Soviet Union.

Gorbachev looks better than Yeltsin, however, when we consider the *magnitude* and not just the nature of the constraints they faced. The domestic opposition to "new thinking" in foreign relations in 1986–1989 was much stronger than the domestic opposition to continuing an essentially pro-Western tilt after 1991. Support for a solidary conception of "the Soviet people" was stronger within the political establishment under Gorbachev than was support for Russian chauvinism and imperial revanchism under Yeltsin. Gorbachev's democratization program entailed the risky *diffusion* of power to unpredictable social actors, whereas Yeltsin's economic and political programs of 1992–1993 entailed the *reconcentration* of power after a subsiding revolutionary wave. Gorbachev's agonies of 1990–1991 were products of trying simultaneously to resist accelerating disintegration, to avoid a reactionary crackdown, and to negotiate an intermediate federal equilibrium. By contrast, Yeltsin's "asymmetrical federalism" came after the reconcentration of power and resulted in separate deals that avoided the challenge of institutionalizing either a federal or a unitary order. In this realm, Gorbachev was seeking to institutionalize a long-term solution; Yeltsin was seeking only to cope with near-term threats and pressures. Gorbachev plowed forward with his program in 1987 and 1989, resisting the political temptation to compromise his basic goals, whereas Yeltsin sought a centrist compromise at his stages of ascendancy and decline.

Then, too, Yeltsin and Gorbachev were interdependent political actors in ways that must be factored into an evaluation of their records. That is, Yeltsin himself was a conscious and powerful impediment to Gorbachev's success in negotiating an equilibrium to slow the disintegration of the political system. Put differently: Gorbachev's policies initiated a process of disintegration and political polarization, but Yeltsin served as a focal point for social forces seeking to accelerate the rate of both; absent Yeltsin, Gorbachev might have been more successful in renegotiating an equilibrium. In a similar vein, the magnitude of the constraints facing Yeltsin in 1991–1992 was in part a product of his own actions in 1989–1991. By consciously accelerating the polarization and disintegration, he ensured that, if he emerged ascendant, he would face a situation of collapse that might leave him few options. To the extent that a positive evaluation of Yeltsin's leadership hinges on the claim that he was forced to cope with dire circumstances in 1991–1992, such an evaluation must also attend to the fact that Yeltsin helped to create those very circumstances.

Furthermore, Yeltsin's strategies for founding and guaranteeing a new order of things were – more so than Gorbachev's – insensitive to the human costs of those strategies. If we take both men at their word (based on their public rhetoric), Gorbachev was committed to a peaceful management of the transformation process at home and abroad. He remained true to that goal, even at the cost of failure to prevent the collapse of communism in Eastern Europe and of the USSR itself. Gorbachev also rejected both "unbridled" capitalism and abolition of the Communist Party; even at the expense of his political power, he fought to the end to avoid these costs. Yeltsin built his authority championing greater equality, opposing privilege and corruption, opposing the use of military force against secessionist forces, and calling for the creation of a market democracy. What he tolerated when in charge, however, looked quite different: the creation and indulgence of a plutocratic elite; growing corruption within the political elite; inattention to widespread social misery; infantilizaton of political parties, judicial institutions, and parliament; and the wanton use of violence in Chechnya.

Only if one argues that Gorbachev missed many opportunities to do better – and that Yeltsin enjoyed many *fewer* opportunities to do better – can one make the case that Yeltsin was the more impressive transformational leader. Similarly, one can reach that conclusion only if one argues that Yeltsin faced constraints that were significantly more formidable than those facing Gorbachev. I find it hard to make that case.

AUTHORITY BUILDING AND AUTHORITY MAINTENANCE

Still another way to evaluate leaders is to ask: How good were they at exercising power in ways that built and maintained their credibility, stature, and legitimacy as leaders? It is noteworthy that Khrushchev, Brezhnev, Gorbachev, and Yeltsin all proved adept at building their authority initially, when they fashioned images for themselves that facilitated seizing the initiative and out-flanking political rivals. Subsequently, they all "rode high" with comprehensive programs that appealed to a range of political audiences. Were we to conduct leadership evaluations after the first 4–5 years of each man's rise, we would arrive at strikingly similar conclusions: all four leaders did excellent jobs of building their power and authority among relevant audiences and of achieving a position of political ascendancy within the establishment.[22]

Yet it is equally noteworthy that all four leaders ended their political lives on notes of failure or repudiation. Khrushchev and Gorbachev were forced from office. Brezhnev died in office with his domestic and foreign policy programs in shambles. Yeltsin ended his presidency with approval ratings in single digits and with many of his programs discredited.

What went wrong in the relatively short period between the successful consolidation of power and the radical decline of these leaders' authority and effectiveness? Answering this question requires a broad perspective on both leadership in general and leadership in the Soviet and post-Soviet systems. Globally, it is often the case that leaders who are successful at one stage of their political careers, or in grappling with one historical challenge, prove unsuccessful at later stages of their careers or in grappling with other historical challenges. Hence, the experiences of these four leaders are hardly exceptional; rather, they are indicative of the intrinsic difficulties of sustaining good performance and maintaining the authority one has built. Authority cannot be hoarded; one must use it or lose it. But frequently, in the process of using accumulated authority, one encounters obstacles that are more difficult to overcome than those met earlier. Or one proves to have a repertoire of skills that are better suited to resolving some problems than others, or one runs out of gas and makes mistakes that squander accumulated authority. Once one's reputation for success is damaged, those on whom one relied for political support begin to hedge their bets.[23] The result can be a cascading loss of authority.

Similarly, the process of initially building one's authority often takes place in a context in which competitors make promises but are not yet required to take responsibility for delivering the goods. Sometimes, one can accumulate

---

[22] Of course, they do not deserve equal praise for this achievement, since they each faced different degrees of challenge in accomplishing the feat. Brezhnev's challenge was clearly the easiest. Gorbachev's and Yeltsin's challenges were the hardest.

[23] This last observation was a theme of Neustadt's (Richard E. Neustadt, *Presidential Power: The Politics of Leadership* [New York: Wiley, 1960], ch. 4), though he generalized it only to the American presidency in normal (i.e., noncrisis) times.

authority simply by criticizing the proposals or past performance of political rivals in lieu of presenting a platform of one's own. To the extent that leaders succeed in building authority by these means, they are bound to experience a deflation. For once they emerge ascendant, they are expected to sponsor a comprehensive program for progress in many realms of policy. That is their function as leader. Once they do so, however, they are bound to experience some diminution of their authority as they take responsibility for policy performance, as results prove to be a mix of successes and failures, and as the costs of their comprehensive programs are felt.

These are universals of competitive politics in modern times. But the Soviet and post-Soviet contexts accelerated the transition from political ascendancy to political decline. In retrospect, we can see that Soviet and post-Soviet leaders could not avoid being dogged by manifold contradictions as they sought to deliver the goods. They could not avoid the basic contradiction between ideological aspirations and systemic capacity. Those contradictions ensured that leaders who had built their authority by promising to cure many of the country's ills would face mounting frustrations and that their authority would decline as a result.

Ironically, operating in a post-Soviet context, Yeltsin inherited some features of the Soviet mind-set that perpetuated this problem. He – like Khrushchev, Brezhnev, and Gorbachev – promised far more than he could possibly deliver. Yeltsin, like his predecessors in the Kremlin, embraced a campaignist approach to solving problems. He, like the others, believed that answers to contradictions lay in some combination of popular mobilization, cadre selection and motivation, money, and technology. He, like the others, failed to understand or appreciate the *institutional* requirements for coordination of economic exchange within a decentralized system. And some of the political constituencies on which he relied shared with him many of these features of the Soviet-era mind-set.

Some people argue that the Soviet system was doomed to collapse at some point, given its leaders' incapacity to conceive and "sell" programs that could transform it peacefully into a marketized and democratized system or (in Yeltsin's case) that could build such a system in Russia on the ruins of communism. If one believes that fragmentation and collapse of the Soviet system were inevitable and that Russia would follow a similar path because of the cultural and institutional legacy of communism, then all four leaders would come across as historically tragic, quixotic, or myopic figures.

I noted in Chapter 13 that Gorbachev got off to a great start but proved a disappointing finisher on many counts. The same can be said for Yeltsin; on their own terms, it can also be said of Khrushchev and Brezhnev. Perhaps that common outcome was less a product of their personal failings than of the intrinsic dilemmas they faced in the Soviet and post-Soviet contexts.

Such a conclusion lends broader perspective to the task of evaluating these leaders by expanding our appreciation of the constraints facing Soviet and Russian leaders during the past fifty years. But it is not entirely satisfying. It is difficult to believe that nothing they did could have averted the deflation of authority they all experienced. One can, of course, avoid a complex evaluation of leaders' performance in office by embracing a philosophy of history that leads to the deterministic conclusion. But if one rejects such an approach without going to the opposite extreme of assuming that "anything was possible," then one is back in the game of evaluating leaders on their own terms and of asking whether they could have done a better job in light of the constraints and opportunities they faced.

For example, had Gorbachev subjected himself to a competitive election for president of the USSR in 1989 – which he stood an excellent chance of winning – then he might have revalidated his popular authority and increased his leverage within the political arena, thereby heading off (or at least postponing) the radical deflation of authority he experienced in 1990–1991. At a minimum, it would have advantaged him in the political competition with Boris Yeltsin. Maximally, it might have positioned him better to propose a real federation or confederation without having to worry about his being deposed by the Central Committee. To take another example: had he not given Yeltsin a high position in the government after purging him from the Party apparatus, Gorbachev might have avoided the public political competition with Yeltsin that went so far to destroy Gorbachev's political base.

As for Yeltsin, he did an impressive job of building his authority in 1989–1991. Thereafter, he was successful in some policy areas and unsuccessful in others. He squandered his accumulated authority but proved to be exceptionally skilled at keeping would-be opponents off-balance and at maintaining his grip on power. If things improve in Russia, he may yet be credited with greater accomplishment than he currently is. If things go haywire, he is likely to be condemned for having created a fragile and unsustainable system at exorbitant cost. Either way, future archival research may permit a deeper understanding of the magnitude of the constraints he faced. As Dean Acheson put it: "Sometimes it is only in retrospect and in the light of how things work out that you can distinguish stubbornness from determination."[24]

---

[24] As quoted in Marshall D. Shulman in *The New York Review of Books* (June 17, 1990), p. 5.

Index